# The new journalism

D1500208

Tom Wolfe's other books are: *The Kandy-Kolored Tangerine-Flake Streamline Baby* (1965), *The Pump House* (1968), *The Electric Kool-Aid Acid Test* (1968), *Radical Chic & Mau-Mauing the Flak Catchers* (1970), *The Painted Word* (1975), *Mauve Gloves & Madmen, Clutter & Vine* (1976), *The Right Stuff* (1979), *In Our Time* (1980), *From Bauhaus to Our House* (1981), *The Purple Decades* (1983), *The Bonfire of the Vanities* (1987) and *A Man in Full* (1998).

E. W. Johnson is the author of *The Winner* (a novel), *Courting the Mad* (poems), and editor of *Short Stories International* and *Contemporary American Thought*.

Tom Wolfe
# The new journalism
with an anthology edited by
Tom Wolfe and E. W. Johnson

PICADOR

First published in Great Britain 1975 by Picador

This edition published 1996 by Picador
an imprint of Pan Macmillan Ltd
Pan Macmillan, 20 New Wharf Road, London N1 9RR
Basingstoke and Oxford
Associated companies throughout the world
www.panmacmillan.com

ISBN 978-0-330-24315-5

19 18 17 16 15 14 13

A CIP catalogue record for this book is available from
the British Library.

Printed and bound in the UK by
CPI Mackays, Chatham ME5 8TD

Visit **www.picador.com** to read more about all our books and to buy
them. You will also find features, author interviews and news of any author
events, and you can sign up for e-newsletters so that you're always first to hear
about our new releases.

# Contents

Preface 11

Part One:
The new journalism
by Tom Wolfe
1 The feature game 15
2 Like a novel 23
3 Seizing the power 37
   Appendix 52

Part Two:
The new journalism: an anthology 69
edited by Tom Wolfe and E. W. Johnson
Preface to the selections

Rex Reed
from Do you sleep in the nude? 72

Gay Talese
from The overreachers 81

Richard Goldstein
Gear 96

Michael Herr
Khesanh 101

Truman Capote
from In cold blood 135

Joe Eszterhas
Charlie Simpson's apocalypse 147

Terry Southern
from Red dirt marijuana and other tastes 184

Hunter S. Thompson
The Kentucky Derby is decadent and depraved 195

Norman Mailer
from The armies of the night 212

Nicholas Tomalin
The general goes zapping Charlie Cong 221

Tom Wolfe
from The electric kool-aid acid test  228

Barbara L. Goldsmith
La dolce viva  244

Joe McGinniss
from The selling of the president 1968  253

George Plimpton
from Paper lion  266

James Mills
The detective  286

John Gregory Dunne
from The studio  309

John Sack
from M  321

Joan Didion
from Slouching towards Bethlehem  334

'Adam Smith'
from The money game  351

Robert Christgau
Beth Ann and macrobioticism  363

Hunter S. Thompson
from The hell's angels, a strange and terrible saga  373

Garry Wills
Martin Luther King is still on the case  390

Tom Wolfe
from Radical chic & mau-mauing the flak catchers  412

# Acknowledgements

Grateful acknowledgement is made for permission to reprint the following:

'The Feature Game' and 'Like a Novel' by Tom Wolfe. Copyright © 1972 by the NYM Corp., under the titles 'The Birth of "The New Journalism"': An Eyewitness Report' and 'The New Journalism: A la Recherche des Whichy Thickets'. Reprinted with the permission of *New York* magazine.

'Seizing the Power' and 'Appendix' by Tom Wolfe were first published in *Esquire* magazine under the title 'Why They Aren't Writing the Great American Novel Anymore'.

'Khesanh', by Michael Herr. Copyright © 1969 by Michael Herr. Originally appeared in *Esquire* magazine, September 1969. Reprinted by permission of Robert Lantz-Candida Donadio Literary Agency, Inc.

'The Soft Psyche of Joshua Logan', from *The Overreachers* by Gay Talese. Copyright © 1961 by Gay Talese. Reprinted by permission of Candida Donadio & Associates Inc.

Excerpt from *In Cold Blood*, by Truman Capote. Copyright © 1965 Truman Capote (Hamish Hamilton London). Originally appeared in *The New Yorker* in slightly different form.

'Charlie Simpson's Apocalypse', by Joe Eszterhas. Copyright © 1972 by Joe Eszterhas. First appeared in *Rolling Stone* magazine, 6 July 1972. Reprinted by permission of International Famous Agency and Joe Eszterhas.

'Twirling at Ole Miss' from *Red Dirt Marijuana and Other Tastes* by Terry Southern. Copyright © 1955, 1956, 1957, 1959, 1960, 1962, 1963, 1964, 1967 by Terry Southern. Reprinted by permission of A. D. Peters and Company.

'The Kentucky Derby is Decadent and Depraved', by Hunter S. Thompson. Copyright © 1970 by Hunter S. Thompson. First appeared in *Scanlan's Monthly*, June 1970. Reprinted by permission of International Famous Agency and Hunter S. Thompson.

Excerpt from *Armies of the Night* by Norman Mailer. Reprinted by permission of the Scott Meredith Literary Agency, Inc.

'The General Goes Zapping Charlie Cong', by Nicholas Tomalin, appeared originally in *The Times*, 5 June 1966. Reprinted by permission of *The Times*.

Excerpt from *M* by John Sack. Copyright © 1966, 1967 by John Sack. Reprinted by permission of A. M. Heath and Company Ltd.

Excerpt from *The Electric Kool-Aid Acid Test* by Tom Wolfe. Copyright © 1968 by Tom Wolfe. Reprinted by permission of Farrar, Straus & Giroux, Inc.

'In a time when so much of narrative art has yielded itself to reportage, you have sustained a vital tradition of ...'

First twenty-one words of
honorary doctor of letters citation for Saul Bellow
at Yale commencement ceremonies,
June, 1972

# Preface

When E. W. Johnson first came to me with the idea of putting to-gether an anthology of New Journalism, the fantasy was that we were simply going to assemble twenty or so examples of the genre and write a five- or six-page introduction, and that would be it. We assumed it might be useful as a textbook. So I sat down one night to write the five or six pages – but I soon ran into a question that I could tell was going to take me on a much longer trip.

Namely, what is it precisely – in terms of technique – that has made the New Journalism as 'absorbing' and 'gripping' as the novel and the short story, and often more so? This led, eventually, to two discoveries that I think are crucial for anyone interested in writing. One: There are four specific devices, all of them realistic, that underlie the emo-tionally involving quality of the most powerful prose, whether fiction or non-fiction. Two: Realism is not merely another literary approach or attitude. The introduction of detailed realism into English literature in the eighteenth century was like the introduction of electricity into machine technology. It raised the state of the art to an entirely new magnitude. And for anyone, in fiction or nonfiction, to try to improve literary technique by abandoning social realism would be like an engineer trying to improve upon machine technology by abandoning electricity. The analogy happens to work because each gets down to an elemental principle in its field.

I don't really expect any of the current set of fiction writers to take serious note of what I've said. In a way, I suppose, I'm even banking on their obtuseness. Fiction writers, currently, are busy running back-ward, skipping and screaming, into a begonia patch that I call Neo-Fabulism. I analyze it in some detail in an appendix. I must confess that the retrograde state of contemporary fiction has made it far easier to make the main point of this book: that the most important literature being written in America today is in nonfiction, in the form that has been tagged, however ungracefully, the New Journalism.

# Part one
# The new journalism

## Tom Wolfe

# 1 The feature game

I doubt if many of the aces I will be extolling in this story went into journalism with the faintest notion of creating a 'new' journalism, a 'higher' journalism, or even a mildly improved variety. I know they never dreamed that anything they were going to write for newspapers or magazines would wreak such evil havoc in the literary world ... causing a panic, dethroning the novel as the number one literary genre, starting the first new direction in American literature in half a century ... Nevertheless, that is what has happened. Bellow, Barth, Updike – even the best of the lot, Philip Roth – the novelists are all out there right now ransacking the literary histories and sweating it out, wondering where they stand. Damn it all, Saul, the *Huns* have arrived ...

God knows I didn't have anything new in mind, much less anything literary, when I took my first newspaper job. I had a fierce and unnatural craving for something else entirely. Chicago, 1928, that was the general idea ... Drunken reporters out on the ledge of the *News* peeing into the Chicago River at dawn ... Nights down at the saloon listening to 'Back of the Yards' being sung by a baritone who was only a lonely blind bulldyke with lumps of milk glass for eyes ... Nights down at the detective bureau – it was always nighttime in my daydreams of the newspaper life. Reporters didn't work during the day. I wanted the whole movie, nothing left out ....

I was aware of what had reduced me to this Student Prince Maudlin state of mind. All the same, I couldn't help it. I had just spent five years in graduate school, a statement that may mean nothing to people who never served such a stretch; it is the explanation, nonetheless. I'm not sure I can give you the remotest idea of what graduate school is like. Nobody ever has. Millions of Americans now go to graduate schools, but just say the phrase – 'graduate school' – and what picture leaps into the brain? No picture, not even a blur. Half the people I knew in graduate school were going to write a novel about it. I thought about it myself. No one ever wrote such a book, as far as I know. Everyone used to sniff the air. How morbid! How poisonous! Nothing else like it in the world! But the subject always defeated them. It defied literary exploitation. Such a novel would be a study of frustration, but a form of frustration so exquisite, so ineffable, nobody could describe it. Try to imagine the worst part of the worst Antonioni movie you ever saw, or reading *Mr Sammler's Planet* at one sitting, or just reading it, or being locked inside a Seaboard Railroad roomette, sixteen miles from Gainesville, Florida, heading north on the Miami-to-New York run, with no water and the radiator turning red in an amok psychotic over-boil, and George McGovern sitting beside you telling you his philosophy of government. That will give you the general atmosphere.

In any case, by the time I received my doctorate in American studies in 1957 I was in the twisted grip of a disease of our times in which the sufferer experiences an overwhelming urge to join the 'real world.' So I started working for newspapers. In 1962, after a cup of coffee here and there, I arrived at the *New York Herald Tribune* ... This must be the place! ... I looked out across the city room of the *Herald Tribune*, 100 moldering yards south of Times Square, with a feeling of amazed bohemian bliss ... Either this is the real world, Tom, or there is no real world ... The place looked like the receiving bin at the Good Will ... a promiscuous heap of junk ... Wreckage and exhaustion everywhere ... If somebody such as the city editor had a swivel chair, the universal joint would be broken, so that every time he got up, the seat would keel over as if stricken by a lateral stroke. All the intestines of the building were left showing in diverticulitic loops and lines — electrical conduits, water pipes, steam pipes, effluvium ducts, sprinkler systems, all of it dangling and grunting from the ceiling, the walls, the columns. The whole mess, from top to bottom, was painted over in an industrial sludge, Lead Gray, Subway Green, or that unbelievable dead red, that grim distemper of pigment and filth, that they paint the floor with in the tool and die works. On the ceiling were scalding banks of fluorescent lights, turning the atmosphere radium blue and burning bald spots in the crowns of the copy readers, who never moved. It was one big pie factory ... A Landlord's Dream ... There were no interior walls. The corporate hierarchy was not marked off into office spaces. The managing editor worked in a space that was as miserable and scabid as the lowest reporter's. Most newspapers were like that. This setup was instituted decades ago for practical reasons. But it was kept alive by a curious fact. On newspapers very few editorial employees at the bottom — namely, the reporters — had any ambition whatsoever to move up, to become city editors, managing editors, editors-in-chief, or any of the rest of it. Editors felt no threat from below. They needed no walls. Reporters didn't want much ... merely to be *stars*! and of such minute wattage at that!

That was one thing they never wrote about in books on journalism or those comradely blind-bulldagger boots-upon-the-brass-rail swill-boar speakeasy memoirs about newspaper days and children of the century ... namely, the little curlicues of newspaper status competition... For example, at the desk behind mine in the *Herald Tribune* city room sat Charles Portis. Portis was the original laconic cutup. At one point he was asked onto a kind of *Meet the Press* show with Malcolm X, and Malcolm X made the mistake of giving the reporters a little lecture before they went on about how he didn't want to hear anybody calling him 'Malcolm,' because he was not a dining-car waiter – his name happened to be 'Malcolm X.' By the end of the show Malcolm X was furious. He was climbing the goddamned acoustical tiles. The original laconic cutup, Portis, had invariably and continually addressed him as 'Mr. X' ... 'Now, Mr. X, let me ask you this...' Anyway, Portis had the desk behind mine. Down in a bullpen at the far end of the room was Jimmy Breslin. Over to one side sat Dick Schaap. We were all engaged in a form of newspaper competition that I have never known anybody to even talk about in public. Yet Schaap had quit as city editor of the *New York Herald Tribune*, which was one of the legendary jobs in journalism – moved *down* the organizational chart, in other words – just to get in this secret game.

Everybody knows about one form of competition among newspaper reporters, the so-called *scoop* competition. Scoop reporters competed with their counterparts on other newspapers, or wire services, to see who could get a story first and write it fastest; the bigger the story – i.e., the more it had to do with the matters of power or catastrophe – the better. In short, they were concerned with the main business of the newspaper. But there was this other lot of reporters as well... They tended to be what is known as 'feature writers.' What they had in common was that they all regarded the newspaper as a motel you checked into overnight on the road to the final triumph. The idea was to get a job on a newspaper, keep body and soul together, pay the rent, get to know 'the world,' accumulate 'experience,' perhaps work some of the fat off your style – then, at some point, quit cold, say goodbye to journalism, move into a shack somewhere, work night and day for six months, and light up the sky with the final triumph. The final triumph was known as The Novel.

That was Someday, you understand... Meanwhile, these dreamboaters were in there banging away, in every place in America that had a newspaper, competing for a tiny crown the rest of the world wasn't even aware of: Best Feature Writer in Town. The 'feature' was the newspaper term for a story that fell outside the category of hard news. It included everything from 'brights,' chuckly little items, often from the police beat... There was this out-of-towner who checked into a hotel in San Francisco last night, bent upon suicide, and he threw himself out of his fifth-story window — and fell nine feet and sprained his ankle. What he didn't know was — the hotel was on a steep hill! ... to 'human interest stories,' long and often hideously sentimental accounts of hitherto unknown souls beset by tragedy or unusual hobbies within the sheet's circulation area... In any case, feature stories gave a man a certain amount of room in which to write.

Unlike the scoop reporters, the feature writers did not openly acknowledge the existence of their competition, not even to one another. Nor was there any sort of scorecard. And yet everyone in the game knew precisely what was going on and went through the most mortifying sieges of envy, even resentment, or else surges of euphoria, depending on how the game was going. No one would ever admit to such a thing, and yet all felt it, almost daily. The feature writers' arena differed from the school reporters' in another way. Your competition was not necessarily working for another publication. You were just as likely to be competing with people on your own paper, which meant you were even less likely to talk about it.

So here was half the feature competition in New York, right in the same city room with me, because the Herald Tribune was like the main Tijuana bullring for feature writers ... Portis, Breslin, Schaap ... Schaap and Breslin had columns, which gave them more freedom, but I figured I could take the both of them. You had to be brave. Over at the Times there was Gay Talese and Robert Lipsyte. At the Daily News there was Michael Mok. (There were other contenders, too, on all the newspapers, including the Herald Tribune. I am only mentioning those I remember most clearly.) Mok I had been up against before, when I worked on the Washington Post and he worked on the Washington Star. Mok was tough competition, because, for one thing, he was willing to risk his hide on a feature story with the same wild courage he later showed in covering Vietnam and the Arab–Israel war for Life.

Mok would do . . . eerie things. For example, the *News* sends Mok and a photographer out to do a feature on a fat man who is trying to lose weight by marooning himself on a sailboat anchored out in Long Island Sound ('I'm one of those guys, I walk past a delicatessen and breathe deep, and I gain ten pounds'). The motorboat they hire conks out about a mile from the fat man's sloop, with only four or five minutes to go before the deadline. This is March, but Mok dives in and starts swimming. The water is about 42 degrees. He swims until he's half dead, and the fat man has to fish him out with an oar. So Mok gets the story. He makes the deadline. There are pictures in the *News* of Mok swimming furiously through Long Island Sound in order to retrieve this great blob's diet saga for two million readers. If, instead, he had drowned, if he had ended up down with the oysters in the hepatitic muck of the Sound, nobody would have put up a plaque for him. Editors save their tears for war correspondents. As for feature writers — the less said, the better. (Just the other day I saw one of the *New York Times*'s grand panjandrums react with amazement to superlative praise for one of his paper's most popular writers, Israel Shenker, as follows: 'But he's a *feature* writer!') No, if Mok had bought the oyster farm that afternoon, he wouldn't even have rated the quietest award in journalism, which is 30 seconds of silence at the Overseas Press Club dinner. Nevertheless, he dove into Long Island Sound in March! Such was the raging competition within our odd and tiny grotto!

At the same time everybody in the game had terrible dark moments during which he lost heart and told himself: 'You're only kidding yourself, boy. This is just one more of your devious ways of postponing the decision to put it *all* on the line . . . and go into the shack . . . and write your novel.' Your Novel! At this late date — partly due to the New Journalism itself — it's hard to explain what an American dream the idea of writing a novel was in the 1940s, the 1950s, and right into the early 1960s. The Novel was no mere literary form. It was a psychological phenomenon. It was a cortical fever. It belonged in the glossary to *A General Introduction to Psychoanalysis*, somewhere between Narcissism and Obsessional Neuroses. In 1969 Seymour Krim wrote a strange confession for *Playboy* that began: 'I was literally made, shaped, whetted and given a world with a purpose by the American realistic novel of the mid- to late-1930s. From the age of fourteen to seventeen, I gorged myself with the works of Thomas Wolfe (beginning with *Of Time and the River*, catching up with *Angel* and then keeping pace till Big Tom's stunning end), Ernest Hemingway, William Faulkner,

James T. Farrell, John Steinbeck, John O'Hara, James Cain, Richard Wright, John Dos Passos, Erskine Caldwell, Jerome Weidman, and William Saroyan, and knew in my pumping heart that I wanted to be a novelist.' The piece turned into a confession because first Krim admitted that the idea of being a novelist had been the overwhelming passion of his life, his spiritual calling, in fact, the Pacemaker that kept his ego ticking through all the miserable humiliations of his young manhood – then he faced up to the fact that he was now in his forties and had never written a novel and more than likely never would. Personally I was fascinated by the article, but why *Playboy* was running it, I didn't know, unless it was the magazine's monthly 10 cc. of literary penicillin ... to hold down the gonococci and the spirochetes ... I couldn't imagine anyone other than writers being interested in Krim's Complex. That, however, was where I was wrong.

After thinking it over, I realized that writers comprise but a fraction of the Americans who have experienced Krim's peculiar obsession. Not so long ago, I am willing to wager, half the people who went to work for publishing houses did so with the belief that their real destiny was to be novelists. Among people on what they call the creative side of advertising, those who actually dream up the ads, the percentage must have reached 90 per cent. In 1955, in *The Exurbanites*, the late A. C. Spectorsky depicted the well-paid Madison Avenue advertising genius as being a man who wouldn't read a novel without checking out the dust jacket blurb and the picture of the author on the back ... and if that ego-flushed little bastard with the unbuttoned shirt and the wind rushing through his locks was younger than he was, he couldn't bear to open the goddamn book. Such was the grip of the damnable Novel. Likewise among people in television, public relations, the movies, on the English faculties of colleges and high schools, among framing shop clerks, convicts, unmarried sons living with Mom ... a whole swarm of fantasizers out there steaming and proliferating in the ego mulches of America ...

The Novel seemed like one of the last of those superstrokes, like finding gold or striking oil, through which an American could, overnight, in a flash, utterly transform his destiny. There were plenty of examples to feed the fantasy. In the 1930s all the novelists had seemed to be people who came blazing up into stardom from out of total obscurity. That seemed to be the nature of the beast. The biographical notes on the dust jackets of the novels were terrific. The author, you would be assured, was previously employed as a hod carrier (Stein-

beck), a truck dispatcher (Cain), a bellboy (Wright), a Western Union
boy (Saroyan), a dishwasher in a Greek restaurant in New York (Faulkner), a truck driver, logger, berry picker, spindle cleaner, crop duster
pilot ... There was no end to it ... Some novelists had whole strings of
these credentials ... That way you knew you were getting the real
goods...

By the 1950s The Novel had become a nationwide tournament.
There was a magical assumption that the end of World War II in 1945
was the dawn of a new golden age of the American Novel, like the
Hemingway–Dos Passos–Fitzgerald era after World War I. There was
even a kind of Olympian club where the new golden boys met face-to-
face every Sunday afternoon in New York, namely, the White Horse
Tavern on Hudson Street ... Ah! There's Jones! There's Mailer!
There's Styron! There's Baldwin! There's Willingham! In the flesh –
right here in this room! The scene was strictly for novelists, people
who were writing novels, and people who were paying court to The
Novel. There was no room for a journalist unless he was there in the
role of would-be novelist or simple courtier of the great. There was no
such thing as a *literary* journalist working for popular magazines or
newspapers. If a journalist aspired to literary status – then he had
better have the sense and the courage to quit the popular press and try
to get into the big league.

As for the little league of feature writers – two of the contestants,
Portis and Breslin, actually went on to live out the fantasy. They wrote
their novels. Portis did it in a way that was so much like the way it
happens in the dream, it was unbelievable. One day he suddenly quit as
London correspondent for the *Herald Tribune*. That was generally regarded as a very choice job in the newspaper business. Portis quit cold
one day; just like that, without a warning. He returned to the United
States and moved into a fishing shack in Arkansas. In six months he
wrote a beautiful little novel called *Norwood*. Then he wrote *True Grit*,
which was a best seller. The reviews were terrific ... He sold both
books to the movies ... He made a fortune ... A *fishing* shack! In
*Arkansas*! It was too goddamned perfect to be true, and yet there it
was. Which is to say that the old dream, The Novel, has never died.

And yet in the early 1960s a curious new notion, just hot enough to
inflame the ego, had begun to intrude into the tiny confines of the
feature statusphere. It was in the nature of a discovery. This discovery,
modest at first, humble, in fact, deferential, you might say, was that it
just might be possible to write journalism that would ... read like a

novel. *Like* a novel, if you get the picture. This was the sincerest form of homage to The Novel and to those greats, the novelists, of course. Not even the journalists who pioneered in this direction doubted for a moment that the novelist was the reigning literary artist, now and forever. All they were asking for was the privilege of dressing up like him ... until the day when they themselves would work up their nerve and go into the shack and try it for real ... They were dreamers, all right, but one thing they never dreamed of. They never dreamed of the approaching irony. They never guessed for a minute that the work they would do over the next ten years, as journalists, would wipe out the novel as literature's main event.

# 2 Like a novel

*What inna namea christ is this* – in the fall of 1962 I happened to pick
up a copy of *Esquire* and read a story called 'Joe Louis: the King as a
Middle-aged Man.' The piece didn't open like an ordinary magazine
article at all. It opened with the tone and mood of a short story, with a
rather intimate scene; or intimate by the standards of magazine journalism in 1962, in any case:

' "Hi, sweetheart!" Joe Louis called to his wife, spotting her waiting
for him at the Los Angeles airport.

'She smiled, walked toward him, and was about to stretch up on her
toes to kiss him – but suddenly stopped.

' "Joe," she said, "where's your tie?"

' "Aw, sweetie," he said, shrugging, "I stayed out all night in New
York and didn't have time—"

' "All *night!*" she cut in. "When you're out here all you do is sleep,
sleep, sleep."

' "Sweetie," Joe Louis said, with a tired grin, "I'm an ole man."

' "Yes," she agreed, "but when you go to New York you try to be
young again." '

The story featured several scenes like that, showing the private life
of a sports hero growing older, balder, sadder. It wound up with a
scene in the home of Louis's second wife, Rose Morgan. In this scene
Rose Morgan is showing a film of the first Joe Louis–Billy Conn fight
to a roomful of people, including her present husband.

'Rose seemed excited at seeing Joe at the top of his form, and every
time a Louis punch would jolt Conn, she'd go, "Mummm" (sock).
"Mummm" (sock). "Mummm."

'Billy Conn was impressive through the middle rounds, but as the
screen flashed Round 13, somebody said, "Here's where Conn's gonna
make his mistake; he's gonna try to slug it out with Joe Louis." Rose's
husband remained silent, sipping his Scotch.

'When the Louis combinations began to land, Rose went "Mummmm, mummmmm," and then the pale body of Conn began to collapse against the canvas.

'Billy Conn slowly began to rise. The referee counted over him. Conn had one leg up, then two, then he was standing – but the referee forced him back. It was too late.'

– and then, for the first time, from the back of the room, from out of the downy billows of the sofa, comes the voice of the present husband – *this Joe Louis crap again*—

' "I thought Conn got up in time," he said, "but that referee wouldn't let him go on."'

'Rose Morgan said nothing – just swallowed the rest of her drink.'

*What the hell is going on?* With a little reworking the whole article could have read like a short story. The passages in between the scenes, the expository passages, were conventional 1950s-style magazine journalism, but they could have been easily recast. The piece could have been turned into a non-fiction short story with very little effort. The really unique thing about it, however, was the reporting. This I frankly couldn't comprehend at first. I really didn't understand how anyone could manage to do reporting on things like the personal by-play between a man and his fourth wife at an airport and then follow it up with that amazing cakewalk down Memory Lane in his second wife's living room. My instinctive, defensive reaction was that the man had piped it, as the saying went ... winged it, made up the dialogue ... Christ, maybe he made up whole scenes, the unscrupulous geek ... The funny thing was, that was precisely the reaction that countless journalists and literary intellectuals would have over the next nine years as the New Journalism picked up momentum. *The bastards are making it up!* (I'm telling you, Ump, that's a *spitball* he's throwing...) Really stylish reporting was something no one knew how to deal with, since no one was used to thinking of reporting as having an esthetic dimension.

At the time I hardly ever read magazines like *Esquire*. I wouldn't have read the Joe Louis piece except that it was by Gay Talese. After all, Talese was a reporter for the *Times*. He was a player in my own feature game. What he had written for *Esquire* was so much better than what he was doing (or was allowed to do) for the *Times*, I had to check out what was going on.

Not long after that Jimmy Breslin started writing an extraordinary local column for my own paper, the *Herald Tribune*. Breslin came to the *Herald Tribune* in 1963 from out of nowhere, which is to say he had written a hundred or so articles for magazines like *True*, *Life*, and *Sports Illustrated*. Naturally he was virtually unknown. At that time knocking your brains out as a free-lance writer for popular magazines was a guaranteed way to stay anonymous. Breslin caught the attention of the *Herald Tribune*'s publisher, Jock Whitney, through his book about the New York Mets called *Can't Anybody Here Play This Game?* The *Herald Tribune* hired Breslin to do a 'bright' local column to help offset some of the heavy lumber on the editorial page, paralyzing snoremongers like Walter Lippmann and Joseph Alsop. Newspaper columns had become a classic illustration of the theory that organizations tend to promote people up to their levels of incompetence. The usual practice was to give a man a column as a reward for outstanding service as reporter. That way they could lose a good reporter and gain a bad writer. The archetypical newspaper columnist was Lippmann. For 35 years Lippmann seemed to do nothing more than ingest the *Times* every morning, turn it over in his ponderous cud for a few days, and then methodically egest it in the form of a drop of mush on the foreheads of several hundred thousand readers of other newspapers in the days thereafter. The only form of reporting that I remember Lippmann going for was the occasional red-carpet visit to a head of state, during which he had the opportunity of sitting on braided chairs in wainscotted offices and swallowing the exalted one's official lies in person instead of reading them in the *Times*. I don't mean to single out Lippmann, however. He was only doing what was expected of him ...

In any case, Breslin made a revolutionary discovery. He made the discovery that it was feasible for a columnist to actually leave the building, go outside and do reporting on his own, genuine legwork. Breslin would go up to the city editor and ask what stories and assignments were coming up, choose one, go out, leave the building, cover the story as a reporter, and write about it in his column. If the story were big enough, his column would start on page one instead of inside. As obvious as this system may sound, it was unheard of among newspaper columnists, whether local or national. If possible, local columnists are even more pathetic. They usually start out full of juice, sounding like terrific boulevardiers and raconteurs, retailing in print all the marvellous *mots* and anecdotes they have been dribbling away over lunch for the past few years. After eight or ten weeks, however, they start to dry up. You can see the poor bastards floundering and gasping. They're dying of thirst. They're out of material. They start writing about funny things that happened around the house the other day, homey one-liners that the Better Half or the Avon lady got off, or some fascinating book or article that started them thinking, or else something they saw on the TV. Thank God for the TV! Without television shows to cannibalize, half of these people would be lost, utterly catatonic. Pretty soon you can almost see it, the tubercular blue of the 23-inch screen, radiating from their prose. Anytime you see a columnist trying to ·squeeze material out of his house, articles, books, or the television set, you've got a starving soul on your hands ... You should send him a basket ...

But Breslin worked like a Turk. He would be out all day covering a story, come back in at 4 p.m. or so and sit down at a desk in the middle of the city room. It was quite a show. He was a good-looking Irishman with a lot of black hair and a great wrestler's gut. When he sat down at his typewriter he hunched himself over into a shape like a bowling ball. He would start drinking coffee and smoking cigarettes until vapor started drifting off his body. He looked like a bowling ball fueled with liquid oxygen. Thus fired up, he would start typing. I've never seen a man who could write so well against a daily deadline. I particularly remember one story he wrote about the sentencing, on a charge of extortion, of a Teamster boss named Anthony Provenzano. Early in the story Breslin set up the image of the sun coming through the moldering old windows of the Federal courthouse and exploding off Provenzano's diamond pinky ring:

'It did not seem like a bad morning at all. The boss, Tony Provenzano, who is one of the biggest men in the Teamsters Union, walked up and down the corridor outside of this Federal courtroom in Newark and he had a little smile on his face and he kept flicking a white cigarette holder around.

'"Today is the kind of a day for fishing," Tony was saying. "We ought to go out and get some fluke."

'Then he spread his legs a little and went at this big guy named Jack, who had on a gray suit. Tony stuck out his left hand so he could throw a hook at this guy Jack. The big diamond ring on Tony's pinky flashed in the light coming through the tall windows of the corridor. Then Tony shifted and hit Jack with a right hand on the shoulder.

'"Always the shoulder," one of the guys in the corridor laughed. "Tony is always banging Jack on the shoulder." '

The story went on in that vein with Provenzano's Jersey courtiers circling around him and fawning, while the sun explodes off his pinky ring. Inside the courtroom itself, however, Provenzano starts getting his. The judge starts lecturing him, and the sweat starts breaking out on Provenzano's upper lip. Then the judge sentences him to seven years, and Provenzano starts twisting his pinky ring finger with his right hand. Then Breslin wraps it up with a scene in a cafeteria where the young prosecutor who worked the case is eating fried scallops and fruit salad off a tray.

'Nothing on his hand flashed. The guy who sunk Tony Pro doesn't even have a diamond ring on his pinky.'

Well – all right! Say what you will! There it was, a short story, complete with symbolism, in fact, and yet true-life, as they say, about something that happened today, and you could pick it up on the newsstand by 11 tonight for a dime ...

Breslin's work stirred up a certain vague resentment among both journalists and literati during the first year or two of his column – vague, because they never fully understood what he was doing ... only that in some vile Low Rent way the man's output was *literary*. Among literary intellectuals you would hear Breslin referred to as 'a cop who writes' or 'Runyon on welfare.' These weren't even intelligent insults, however, because they dealt with Breslin's attitude, which seemed to be that of the cabdriver with his cap tilted over one eye. A crucial part of Breslin's work they didn't seem to be conscious of at all: namely, the reporting he did. Breslin made it a practice to arrive on the scene long before the main event in order to gather the off-camera material, the by-play in the make-up room, that would enable him to create character. It was part of his *modus operandi* to gather 'novelistic' details, the rings, the perspiration, the jabs on the shoulder, and he did it more skillfully than most novelists.

Literary people were oblivious to this side of the New Journalism, because it is one of the unconscious assumptions of modern criticism that the raw material is simply 'there.' It is the 'given.' The idea is: Given such-and-such a body of material, what has the artist done with it? The crucial part that reporting plays in all story-telling, whether in novels, films, or non-fiction, is something that is not so much ignored as simply not comprehended. The modern notion of art is an essentially religious or magical one in which the artist is viewed as a holy beast who in some way, big or small, receives flashes from the godhead, which is known as creativity. The material is merely his clay, his palette ... Even the obvious relationship between reporting and the major novels – one has only to think of Balzac, Dickens, Gogol, Tolstoy, Dostoyevsky, and, in fact, Joyce – is something that literary his-

al with only in a biographical sense. It took the New Journalism to ....ing this strange matter of reporting into the foreground.

But these were all matters that came up later. I don't remember a soul
talking about them at the time. I certainly didn't. In the spring of 1963
I made my own entry into this new arena, although without meaning to. I have already described (in the introduction to *The Kandy-
Kolored Tangerine-Flake Streamline Baby*) the odd circumstances
under which I happened to write my first magazine article — 'There
Goes (Varoom! Varoom!) That Kandy-Kolored (Thphhhhhh!) Tangerine-Flake Streamline Baby (Rahghhh!) Around the Bend (Brummm-
mmmmmmmmmmmmmm)....' — in the form of what I thought was
merely a memorandum to the managing editor of *Esquire*. This article
was by no means like a short story, despite the use of scenes and
dialogue. I wasn't thinking about that at all. It is hard to say what it
was like. It was a garage sale, that piece ... vignettes, odds and ends of
scholarship, bits of memoir, short bursts of sociology, apostrophes,
epithets, moans, cackles, anything that came into my head, much of it
thrown together in a rough and awkward way. That was its virtue. It
showed me the possibility of there being something 'new' in journalism. What interested me was not simply the discovery that it was
possible to write accurate non-fiction with techniques usually associated with novels and short stories. It was that — plus. It was the
discovery that it was possible in non-fiction, in journalism, to use any
literary device, from the traditional dialogisms of the essay to stream-
of-consciousness, and to use many different kinds simultaneously, or
within a relatively short space ... to excite the reader both intellectually and emotionally. I am not laying all those gladiolas on that rather
curious first article of mine, you understand. I'm only talking about
what it suggested to me.

I soon had the chance to explore every possibility I could think of.
The *Herald Tribune* assigned me split duties, like a utility infielder's.
Two days a week I was supposed to work for the city desk as a general
assignment reporter, as usual. The other three days I was supposed to
turn out a weekly piece of about 1,500 words for the *Herald Tribune*'s
new Sunday supplement, which was called *New York*. At the same time,
following the success of 'There Goes (Varoom! Varoom!) That Kandy-
Kolored (Thphhhhhh!) Tangerine-Flake Streamline Baby (Rahghhh!)
Around the Bend (Brummmmmmmmmmmmmm)....' — I was also
cranking out stories for *Esquire*. This setup was crazy enough to begin

with. I can remember flying to Las Vegas on my two regular days off from the *Herald Tribune* to do a story for *Esquire* — 'Las Vegas!!!!' — and winding up sitting on the edge of a white satin bed in a Hog-Stomping Baroque suite in a hotel on the Strip — in the decor known as Hog-Stomping Baroque there are 400-pound cut-glass chandeliers in the bathrooms — and picking up the phone and dictating to the stenographic battery of the *Trib* city desk the last third of a story on demolition derbies in Long Island for *New York* — 'Clean Fun at Riverhead' — hoping to finish in time to meet a psychiatrist in a black silk mohair suit with brass buttons and a shawl collar, no lapels, one of the only two psychiatrists in Las Vegas County at that time, to take me to see the casualties of the Strip in the state mental ward out Charleston Boulevard. What made it crazier was that the piece about the demolition derbies was the last one I wrote that came anywhere close to being 1,500 words. After that they started climbing to 3,000, 4,000 5,000, 6,000 words. Like Pascal, I was sorry, but I didn't have time to write short ones. In nine months in the latter part of 1963 and first half of 1964 I wrote three more long pieces for *Esquire* and twenty for *New York*. All of this was in addition to what I was writing as a reporter for the *Herald Tribune* city desk two days a week. The idea of a day off lost all meaning. I can remember being furious on Monday, November 25, 1963, because there were people I desperately needed to talk to, for some story or other, and I couldn't reach them because all the offices in New York seemed to be closed, every one. It was the day of President Kennedy's funeral. I remember staring at the television set ... morosely, but for all the wrong reasons.

Yet in terms of experimenting in non-fiction, the way I worked at that point couldn't have been more ideal. I was writing mostly for *New York*, which, as I say, was a Sunday supplement. At that time, 1963 and 1964, Sunday supplements were close to being the lowest form of periodical. Their status was well below that of the ordinary daily newspaper, and only slightly above that of the morbidity press, sheets like the *National Enquirer* in its 'I Left My Babies in the Deep Freeze' period. As a result, Sunday supplements had no traditions, no pretensions, no promises to live up to, not even any rules to speak of. They were brain candy, that was all. Readers felt no guilt whatsoever about laying them aside, throwing them away or not looking at them at all. I never felt the slightest hesitation about trying any device that might conceivably grab the reader a few seconds longer. I tried to yell right in his ear: *Stick around!* ... Sunday supplements were no place for diffi-dent souls. That was how I started playing around with the device of point-of-view.

For example, I once did a story about the girls in jail at the Women's House of Detention in Greenwich Village at Greenwich Avenue and the Avenue of the Americas, an intersection known as Nut Heaven. The girls used to yell down to boys on the street, to all the nice free funky Village groovies they saw walking around down there. They would yell every male first name they could think of — 'Bob!' 'Bill!' 'Joe!' 'Jack!' 'Jimmy!' 'Willie!' 'Benny!' — until they hit the right name, and some poor fool would stop and look up and answer. Then they would suggest a lot of quaint anatomical impossibilities for the kid to perform on himself and start laughing like maniacs. I was there one night when they caught a boy who looked about twenty-one named Harry. So I started the story with the girls yelling at him:

' "Hai-ai-ai-ai-ai-ai-ai-ai-ai-ai-ai-ai-ai-ai-ai-ai-ai-ai-ai-ai-ai-ai-ai-ai-ai -ai-ai-ai-ai-ai-ai-ai-ai-ai-ai-ai-ai-ai-ai-ai-aireeeeeeeeeeeeeeeeeeee!" '

I looked at that. I liked it. I decided I would enjoy yelling at the little bastard myself. So I started lambasting him, too, in the next sentence:

'O, dear Sweet Harry, with your French gangster-movie bangs, your Ski Shop turtleneck sweater and your Army–Navy Store blue denim shirt over it, with your Bloomsbury corduroy pants you saw in the *Manchester Guardian* airmail edition and sent away for and your sly intellectual pigeon-toed libido roaming in Greenwich Village — that siren call really for you?'

Then I let the girls have another go at it:

' "Hai-ai-ai-ai-ai-ai-ai-ai-ai-ai-ai-ai-ai-aireeeeeeeeee!" '

Then I started in again, and so on. There was nothing subtle about such a device, which might be called the Hectoring Narrator. Quite the opposite. That was precisely why I liked it. I liked the idea of starting off a story by letting the reader, via the narrator, talk to the characters, hector them, insult them, prod them with irony or condescension, or whatever. Why should the reader be expected to just lie flat and let these people come tromping through as if his mind were a subway turnstile? But I was democratic about it, I was. Sometimes I would put myself into the story and make sport of me. I would be 'the man in the brown Borsalino hat,' a large fuzzy Italian fedora I wore at the time, or 'the man in the Big Lunch tie.' I would write about myself in the third person, usually as a puzzled onlooker or someone who was in the way, which was often the case. Once I even began a story about a vice I was also prone to, tailor-made clothes, as if someone else were the hectoring narrator ... treating *me* in a flippant manner: 'Real buttonholes. That's it! A man can take his thumb and forefinger and unbutton his sleeve at the wrist because this kind of suit has real buttonholes there. Tom, boy, it's terrible. Once you know about it, you start seeing it. All the time!' ... and so on ... anything to avoid coming on like the usual non-fiction narrator, with a hush in my voice, like a radio announcer at a tennis match.

The voice of the narrator, in fact, was one of the great problems in non-fiction writing. Most non-fiction writers, without knowing it, wrote in a century-old British tradition in which it was understood that the narrator shall assume a calm, cultivated and, in fact, genteel voice. The idea was that the narrator's own voice should be like the off-white or putty-colored walls that Syrie Maugham popularized in interior decoration ... a 'neutral background' against which bits of color would stand out. *Understatement* was the thing. You can't imagine what a positive word 'understatement' was among both journalists and literati ten years ago. There is something to be said for the notion, of course, but the trouble was that by the early 1960s understatement had become an absolute pall. Readers were bored to tears without understanding why. When they came upon that pale beige tone, it began to signal to them, unconsciously, that a well-known bore was here again, 'the journalist,' a pedestrian mind, a phlegmatic spirit, a faded personality, and there was no way to get rid of the pallid little troll, short of ceasing to read. This had nothing to do with objectivity and subjectivity or taking a stand or 'commitment' — it was a matter of personality, energy, drive, bravura ... style, in a word ... The standard non-fiction writer's voice was like the standard announcer's voice ... a drag, a droning ...

To avoid this I would try anything. For example, I wrote a story about Junior Johnson, a stock car racer from Ingle Hollow, North Carolina, who had learned to drive by running moonshine whiskey to Charlotte and other distribution points. 'There ain't no harder work in the world than making whiskey,' Junior would say. 'I don't know of any other business that compels you to get up at all times of night and go outdoors in the snow and everything else and work. H'it's the hardest way in the world to make a living, and I don't think anybody'd do it unless they had to.' Now, as long as Junior Johnson was explaining the corn liquor industry, there was no problem, because (a) dialogue tends to be naturally attractive, or involving, to the reader; and (b) Johnson's

Ingle Hollow lingo was unusual. But then I had to take over the explanation myself, in order to compress into a few paragraphs information that had come from several interviews. So ... I decided I would rather talk in Ingle Hollow accents myself, since that seemed to go over all right. There is no law that says the narrator has to speak in beige or even New York journalese. So I picked up the explanation myself, as follows: 'Working mash wouldn't wait for a man. It started coming to a head when it got ready to and a man had to be there to take it off, out there in the woods, in the brush, in the brambles, in the muck, in the snow. Wouldn't it have been something if you could have just set it all up inside a good old shed with a corrugated metal roof and order those parts like you want them and not have to smuggle all that copper and all that sugar and all that everything out here in the woods and be a coppersmith and a plumber and a cooper and a carpenter and a pack horse and every other goddamned thing God ever saw in the world, all at once.

'And live decent hours — Junior and his brothers, about two o'clock in the morning they'd head out to the stash, the place where the liquor was hidden after it was made ...'

I was feigning the tones of an Ingle Hollow moonshiner, in order to create the illusion of seeing the action through the eyes of someone who was actually on the scene and involved in it, rather than a beige narrator. I began to think of this device as the *downstage voice*, as if characters downstage from the protagonist himself were talking.

I would do the same thing with descriptions. Rather than just come on as the broadcaster describing the big parade, I would shift as quickly as possible into the eye sockets, as it were, of the people in the story. Often I would shift the point of view in the middle of a paragraph or even a sentence. I began a story on Baby Jane Holzer, entitled 'The Girl of the Year,' as follows:

'Bangs manes bouffant beehives Beatle caps butter faces brush-on lashes decal eyes puffy sweaters French thrust bras flailing leather blue jeans stretch pants stretch jeans honeydew bottoms eclair shanks elf boots ballerinas Knight slippers, hundreds of them, these flaming little buds, bobbing and screaming, rocketing around inside the Academy of Music Theater underneath that vast old moldering cherub dome up there — aren't they super-marvelous!

'"Aren't they super-marvelous!" says Baby Jane, and then: "Hi, Isabel! Isabel! You want to sit backstage — with the Stones!"

'The show hasn't even started yet. The Rolling Stones aren't even on the stage, the place is full of a great shabby moldering dimness, and these flaming little buds.

'Girls are reeling this way and that way in the aisle and through their huge black decal eyes, sagging with Tiger Tongue Lick Me brush-on eyelashes and black appliqués, sagging like display-window Christmas trees, they keep staring at – her – Baby Jane – on the aisle.'

The opening paragraph is a rush of Groovy clothes ending with the phrase '– aren't they super-marvelous!' With this phrase the point-of-view shifts to Baby Jane, and one is looking through her eyes at the young girls, 'the flaming little buds,' who are running around the theater. The description continues through Jane's eyes until the phrase 'they keep staring at – her – Baby Jane,' whereupon the point-of-view shifts to the young girls, and the reader is suddenly looking through *their* eyes at Baby Jane: 'What the hell is this? She is gorgeous in the most outrageous way. Her hair rises up from her head in a huge hairy corona, a huge tan mane around a narrow face and two eyes opened – swock! – like umbrellas, with all that hair flowing down over a coat made of ... zebra! Those motherless stripes! Oh, damn! Here she is with her friends, looking like some kind of queen bee for all flaming little buds everywhere.'

In fact, three points-of-view are used in that rather short passage, the point-of-view of the subject (Baby Jane), the point-of-view of the people watching her (the 'flaming little buds'), and my own. I switched back and forth between points-of-view continually, and often abruptly, in many articles I wrote in 1963, 1964, and 1965. Eventually a reviewer called me a 'chameleon' who instantly took on the coloration of whomever he was writing about. He meant it negatively. I took it as a compliment. A chameleon ... but exactly!

Sometimes I used point-of-view in the Jamesian sense in which fiction writers understand it, entering directly into the mind of a character, experiencing the world through his central nervous system throughout a given scene. Writing about Phil Spector ('the First Tycoon of Teen'), I began the article not only inside his mind but with a virtual stream of consciousness. One of the news magazines apparently regarded my Spector story as an improbable feat, because they interviewed him and asked him if he didn't think this passage was merely a fiction that appropriated his name. Spector said that, in fact, he found it quite accurate. This should have come as no surprise, since every detail in the passage was taken from a long interview with Spector about exactly how he had felt at the time:

'All these raindrops are *high* or something. They don't roll down the window, they come straight back, toward the tail, wobbling, like all those Mr. Cool snowheads walking on mattresses. The plane is taxiing out toward the runway to take off, and this stupid infarcted water wobbles, sideways, across the window. Phil Spector, 23 years old, the rock and roll magnate, producer of Philles Records, America's first teenage tycoon, watches ... this watery pathology ... it is *sick, fatal.* He tightens his seat belt over his bowels ... A hum rises inside the plane, a shot of air comes shooting through the vent over somebody's seat, some ass turns on a cone of light, there is a sign stuck out by the runway, a mad, cryptic, insane instruction to the pilot — Runway 4, Are Cylinder Laps Mainside DOWN? — and beyond, disoriented crop rows of sulphur blue lights, like the lights on top of a New Jersey toothpaste factory, only spreading on and on in sulphur blue rows over Los Angeles County. It is ... disoriented. Schizoid raindrops. The plane breaks in two on takeoff and everybody in the front half comes rushing toward Phil Spector in a gush of bodies in a thick orange — *napalm!* No, it happens aloft; there is a long rip in the side of the plane, it just rips, he can see the top ripping, folding back in sick curds, like a sick Dali egg, and Phil Spector goes sailing through the rip, dark, freezing. And the engine, it is *reedy*—

' "Miss!"

'A stewardess is walking to the back to buckle herself in for the takeoff. The plane is moving, the jets are revving. Under a Lifebuoy blue skirt, her fireproof legs are clicking out of her Pinki-Kinki-Panti Fantasy—'

I had the feeling, rightly or wrongly, that I was doing things no one had ever done before in journalism. I used to try to imagine the feeling readers must have had upon finding all this carrying on and cutting up in a Sunday supplement. I liked that idea. I had no sense of being a part of any normal journalistic or literary environment. Later I read the English critic John Bayley's yearnings for an age when writers had Pushkin's sense of 'looking at all things afresh,' as if for the first time, without the constant intimidation of being aware of what other writers have already done. In the mid-1960s that was exactly the feeling I had.

I'm sure that others who were experimenting with magazine articles, such as Talese, began to feel the same way. They were moving beyond the conventional limits of journalism, but not merely in terms of technique. The kind of reporting they were doing struck them as far more

ambitious, too. It was more intense, more detailed, and
time-consuming than anything that newspaper or maga
including investigative reporters, were accustomed to. Th           veloped
the habit of staying with the people they were writing about for days at
a time, weeks in some cases. They had to gather all the material the
conventional journalist was after – and then keep going. It seemed all-
important to *be there* when dramatic scenes took place, to get the
dialogue, the gestures, the facial expressions, the details of the environment. The idea was to give the full objective description, plus
something that readers had always had to go to novels and short
stories for: namely, the subjective or emotional life of the characters.
That was why it was so ironic when both the journalistic and literary
old guards began to attack this new journalism as 'impressionistic.'
The most important things one attempted in terms of technique depended upon a depth of information that had never been demanded in
newspaper work. Only through the most searching forms of reporting
was it possible, in non-fiction, to use whole scenes, extended dialogue, point-of-view, and interior monologue. Eventually I, and others,
would be accused of 'entering people's minds' ... But exactly! I figured
that was one more doorbell a reporter had to push.

Most of the people who eventually wrote about my style, however,
tended to concentrate on certain mannerisms, the lavish use of dots,
dashes, exclamation points, italics, and occasionally punctuation that
never existed before : : : : : : : : : and of interjections, shouts,
nonsense words, onomatopoeia, mimesis, pleonasms, the continual use
of the historical present, and so on. This was natural enough, because
many of these devices stood out even before one had read a word. The
typography actually *looked* different. Referring to my use of italics and
exclamation points, one critic observed, with scorn, that my work
looked like something out of Queen Victoria's childhood diary. Queen
Victoria's childhood diaries are, in fact, quite readable; even charming.
One has only to compare them with the miles of official prose she laid
on Palmerston, Wellington, Gladstone in letters and communiqués
and on the English people in her proclamations to see the point I'm
making. I found a great many pieces of punctuation and typography
lying around dormant when I came along – and I must say I had a good
time using them. I figured it was time someone violated what Orwell
called 'the Geneva conventions of the mind' ... a protocol that had
kept journalism and non-fiction generally (and novels) in such a tedious

bind for so long. I found that things like exclamation points, italics, and abrupt shifts (dashes) and syncopations (dots) helped to give the illusion not only of a person talking but of a person thinking. I used to enjoy using dots where they would be least expected, not at the end of a sentence but in the middle, creating the effect ... of a skipped beat. It seemed to me the mind reacted – *first!* ... in dots, dashes, and exclamation points, then rationalized, drew up a brief, with periods.

I soon found that people loved to parody my style. By 1966 the parodies began to come in a rush. I must say I read them all. I suppose it's because at the heart of every parody there is a little gold ball of tribute. Even hostile parodies admit from the start that the target has a distinct voice.

It is not very often that one comes across a new style, period. And if a new style were created not via the novel, or the short story, or poetry, but via journalism – I suppose that would seem extraordinary. It was probably that idea – more than any specific devices, such as using scenes and dialogue in a 'novelistic' fashion – that began to give me very grand ideas about a new journalism. As I saw it, if a new literary style could originate in journalism, then it stood to reason that journalism could aspire to more than mere emulation of those aging giants, the novelists.

# 3 Seizing the power

I have no idea who coined the term 'the New Journalism' or even when
it was coined. Seymour Krim tells me that he first heard it used in 1965
when he was editor of *Nugget* and Pete Hamill called him and said he
wanted to write an article called 'The New Journalism' about people
like Jimmy Breslin and Gay Talese. It was late in 1966 when you first
started hearing people talk about 'the New Journalism' in conversation,
as best I can remember. I don't know for sure.... To tell the truth, I've
never even liked the term. Any movement, group, party, program,
philosophy or theory that goes under a name with 'New' in it is
just begging for trouble. The garbage barge of history is already full of
them: the New Humanism, the New Poetry, the New Criticism, the New
Conservativism, the New Frontier, il Stilo Novo ... The World Tomorrow.... Nevertheless, the New Journalism was the term that
caught on eventually. It was no 'movement.' There were no manifestos,
clubs, salons, cliques; not even a saloon where the faithful gathered,
since there was no faith and no creed. At the time, the mid-Sixties, one
was aware only that all of a sudden there was some sort of artistic
excitement in journalism, and that was a new thing in itself.

I don't know what history, if any, lay behind it. I wasn't interested in
the long view just then. All I knew was what certain writers were doing
at *Esquire*, Thomas B. Morgan, Brock Brower, Terry Southern and,
above all, Gay Talese ... even a couple of novelists were in on it,
Norman Mailer and James Baldwin, writing nonfiction for *Esquire* ...
and, of course, the writers for my own Sunday supplement, *New York*,
chiefly Breslin, but also Robert Christgau, Doon Arbus, Gail Sheehy,
Tom Gallagher, Robert Benton and David Newman. I was turning out
articles as fast as I could write and checking out all these people to see
what new spins they had come up with. I was completely wrapped up
in this new excitement that was in the air. It was a regular little league
they had going.

As a result I never had the slightest idea that any of it might have an
impact on the literary world or, for that matter, any sphere outside the

small world of feature journalism. I should have known better, however. By 1966 the New Journalism had already been paid literary tribute in its cash forms: namely, bitterness, envy and resentment.

This had come bursting forth during a curious episode known as *The New Yorker* affair. In April of 1965, in the New York *Herald Tribune*'s Sunday magazine, *New York*, I had made what I fancied was some lighthearted fun of *The New Yorker* magazine with a two-part article entitled 'Tiny Mummies! The True Story of the Ruler of 43rd Street's Land of The Walking Dead!' A very droll *sportif* performance, you understand. Without going into the whole beanball contest I can tell you that there were many good souls who did not consider this article either lighthearted or *sportif*. In fact, it caused a hulking furor. In the midst of it the kentucky colonels of both Journalism and Literature launched their first attack on this accursed Low Rent rabble at the door, these magazine writers working in the damnable new form....

The longest attacks came in two fairly new but highly conservative periodicals. One was mounted by what had already become the major organ of traditional newspaper journalism in the United States, the *Columbia Journalism Review*, and the other by the major organ of America's older literary essayists and 'men of letters,' *The New York Review of Books*. They presented lists of 'errors' in my piece about *The New Yorker*, marvelous lists[1] as arcane and mystifying as a bill from the body shop — whereupon they concluded that *there* you had the damnable new genre, this 'bastard form,' this 'Parajournalism,' a tag they awarded not only to me and to my magazine *New York* and all its works but also to Breslin, Talese, Dick Schaap and, as long as they were up, *Esquire*.[2] Whether or not one accepted the lists, the strategy itself was revealing. My article on *The New Yorker* had not even been an example of the new genre; it used neither the reporting techniques nor the literary techniques; underneath a bit of red-flock *Police Gazette* rhetoric, it was a traditional critique, a needle, an attack, an 'essay' of the old school. It had little or nothing to do with anything I

1. Prepared, in both instances, by *New Yorker* staff members, if one need edit.
2. The first of two *New York Review of Books* articles on 'Parajournalism' (August, 1965) said: 'The genre originated in *Esquire* but it now appears more flamboyantly in the New York *Herald Tribune*' . . . 'Dick Schaap is one of the *Trib*'s parajournalists' . . . 'Another is Jimmy Breslin . . . the tough-guy-with-the-heart-of-schmaltz bard of the little man and the big celeb'. . . . Later the piece spoke of 'Gay Talese, an *Esquire* alumnus who now parajournalizes mostly in *The Times*, in a more dignified way, of course'. . . . 'But the king of the cats is, of course, Tom Wolfe, an *Esquire* alumnus who writes mostly for the *Trib*'s Sunday magazine, *New York*, which is edited by a former *Esquire* editor, Clay Felker. . . .'

had written before. It certainly had nothing to do with any other writer's work. And yet I think the journalists and literati who were so furious were sincere. I think they looked at the work a dozen or so writers, Breslin, Talese and myself among them, were doing for *New York* and *Esquire*, and they were baffled, dazzled.... This *can't* be right.... These people must be piping it, winging it, making up the dialogue.... Christ, maybe they're making up whole scenes, the unscrupulous geeks (I'm telling you, Ump, those are *spit*balls they're throwing). They needed to believe, in short, that the new form was illegitimate ... a 'bastard form.'

Why newspaper people were upset was no mystery. They were better than railroad men at resisting anything labeled new. The average newspaper editor's idea of a major innovation was the Cashword Puzzle. The literary opposition was more complex, however. Looking back on it one can see that what had happened was this: the sudden arrival of this new style of journalism, from out of nowhere, had caused a status panic in the literary community. Throughout the twentieth century literary people had grown used to a very stable and apparently eternal status structure. It was somewhat like a class structure on the eighteenth-century model in that there was a chance for you to compete but only with people of your own class. The literary upper class were the novelists; the occasional playwright or poet might be up there, too, but mainly it was the novelists. They were regarded as the only 'creative' writers, the only literary artists. They had exclusive entry to the soul of man, the profound emotions, the eternal mysteries, and so forth and so on.... The middle class were the 'men of letters,' the literary essayists, the more authoritative critics; the occasional biographer, historian or cosmically inclined scientist also, but mainly the men of letters. Their province was analysis, 'insights,' the play of intellect. They were not in the same class with the novelists, as they well knew, but they *were* the reigning practitioners of nonfiction.... The lower class were the journalists, and they were so low down in the structure that they were barely noticed at all. They were regarded chiefly as day laborers who dug up slags of raw information for writers of higher 'sensibility' to make better use of. As for people who wrote for popular ('slick') magazines and Sunday supplements, your so-called free-lance writers – except for a few people on *The New Yorker*, they weren't even in the game. They were the lumpenproles.

And so all of a sudden, in the mid-Sixties, here comes a bunch of these lumpenproles, no less, a bunch of slick-magazine and Sunday-supplement writers with no literary credentials whatsoever in most cases — only they're using all the techniques of the novelists, even the most sophisticated ones — and on top of that they're helping themselves to the insights of the men of letters while they're at it — and at the same time they're still doing their low-life legwork, their 'digging,' their hustling, their damnable Locker Room Genre reporting — they're taking of *all* of these roles at the same time — in other words, they're ignoring literary class lines that have been almost a century in the making.

The panic hit the men of letters first. If the lumpenproles won their point, if their new form achieved any sort of literary respectability, if it were somehow accepted as 'creative,' the men of letters stood to lose even their positions as the reigning practitioners of nonfiction. They would get bumped down to Lower Middle Class. (Appendix 4.) This was already beginning to happen. The first indication I had came in an article in the June, 1966, *Atlantic* by Dan Wakefield, entitled 'The Personal Voice and the Impersonal Eye.' The gist of the piece was that this was the first period in anybody's memory when people in the literary world were beginning to talk about nonfiction as a serious artistic form. Norman Podhoretz had written a piece in *Harper's* in 1958 claiming a similar status for the 'discursive prose' of the late Fifties, essays by people like James Baldwin and Isaac Rosenfeld. But the excitement Wakefield was talking about had nothing to do with essays or any other traditional nonfiction. Quite the contrary; Wakefield attributed the new prestige of nonfiction to two books of an entirely different sort: *In Cold Blood*, by Truman Capote, and a collection of magazine articles with a title in alliterative trochaic pentameter that I am sure would come to me if I dwelled upon it.

Capote's story of the life and death of two drifters who blew the heads off a wealthy farm family in Kansas ran as a serial in *The New Yorker* in the Fall of 1965 and came out in book form in February of 1966. It was a sensation — and a terrible jolt to all who expected the accursed New Journalism or Parajournalism to spin itself out like a fad. Here, after all, was not some obscure journalist, some free-lance writer, but a novelist of long standing ... whose career had been in the doldrums ... and who suddenly, with this one stroke, with this turn to the damnable new form of journalism, not only resuscitated his reputation but elevated it higher than ever before ... and became a celebrity of the most amazing magnitude in the bargain. People of all sorts read

*In Cold Blood*, people at every level of taste. Everybody was absorbed in it. Capote himself didn't call it journalism; far from it; he said he had invented a new literary genre, 'the nonfiction novel.' Nevertheless, his success gave the New Journalism, as it would soon be called, an overwhelming momentum.

Capote had spent five years researching his story and interviewing the killers in prison, and so on, a very meticulous and impressive job. But in 1966 you started seeing feats of reporting that were extraordinary, spectacular. (Appendix 6.) Here came a breed of journalists who somehow had the moxie to talk their way inside of any milieu, even closed societies, and hang on for dear life. A marvelous maniac named John Sack talked the Army into letting him join an infantry company at Fort Dix, M Company, 1st Advanced Infantry Training Brigade – not as a recruit but as a reporter – and go through training with them and then to Vietnam and into battle. The result was a book called *M* (appearing first in *Esquire*), a nonfiction *Catch-22* and, for my money, still the finest book in any genre published about the war. George Plimpton went into training with a professional football team, the Detroit Lions, in the role of reporter playing rookie quarterback, rooming with the players, going through their workouts and finally playing quarterback for them in a preseason game – in order to write *Paper Lion*. Like Capote's book, *Paper Lion* was read by people at every level of taste and had perhaps the greatest literary impact of any writing about sports since Ring Lardner's short stories. But the all-time free-lance writer's Brass Stud Award went that year to an obscure California journalist named Hunter Thompson who 'ran' with the Hell's Angels for eighteen months – as a reporter and not a member, which might have been safer – in order to write *Hell's Angels: The Strange and Terrible Saga of the Outlaw Motorcycle Gang*. The Angels wrote his last chapter for him by stomping him half to death in a roadhouse fifty miles from Santa Rosa. All through the book Thompson had been searching for the single psychological or sociological insight that would sum up all he had seen, the single golden *aperçu*; and as he lay sprawled there on the floor coughing up blood and teeth, the line he had been looking for came to him in a brilliant flash from out of the heart of darkness: 'Exterminate all the brutes!'

At about the same time, 1966 and 1967, Joan Didion was writing those strange Gothic articles of hers about California that were eventually collected in *Slouching Towards Bethlehem*. Rex Reed was writing his celebrity interviews – this was an old journalistic exercise, of course, but no one had ever quite so diligently addressed himself to the question of, 'What is So-and-so *really* like?' (Simone Signoret, as I recall, turned out to have the neck, shoulders and upper back of a middle linebacker.) James Mills was pulling off some amazing reporting feats of his own for *Life* in pieces such as 'The Panic in Needle Park,' 'The Detective,' and 'The Prosecutor.' The writer–reporter team of Garry Wills and Ovid Demaris was doing a series of brilliant pieces for *Esquire*, culminating in 'You All Know me – I'm Jack Ruby!'

And then, early in 1968, another novelist turned to nonfiction, and with a success that in its own way was as spectacular as Capote's two years before. This was Norman Mailer writing a memoir about an anti-war demonstration he had become involved in, 'The Steps of the Pentagon.' The memoir, or autobiography (Appendix 3), is an old genre of nonfiction, of course, but this piece was written soon enough after the event to have a journalistic impact. It took up an entire issue of *Harper's Magazine* and came out a few months later under the title of *The Armies of the Night*. Unlike Capote's book, Mailer's was not a popular success; but within the literary community and among intellectuals generally it couldn't have been a more tremendous *succès d'estime*. At the time Mailer's reputation had been deteriorating in the wake of two inept novels called *An American Dream* (1965) and *Why Are We In Vietnam?* (1967). He was being categorized somewhat condescendingly as a journalist, because his nonfiction, chiefly in *Esquire*, was obviously his better work. *The Armies of the Night* changed all that in a flash. Like Capote, Mailer had a dread of the tag that had been put on him – 'journalist' – and had subtitled his book 'The Novel as History; History as the Novel.' But the lesson was one that nobody in the literary world could miss. Here was another novelist who had turned to some form of accursed journalism, no matter what name you gave it, and had not only revived his reputation but raised it to a point higher than it had ever been in his life.

By 1969 no one in the literary world could simply dismiss this new journalism as an inferior genre. The situation was somewhat similar to the situation of the novel in England in the 1850's. It was yet to be canonized, sanctified and given a theology, but writers themselves could already feel the new Power flowing.

The similarity between the early days of the novel and the early days of the New Journalism is not merely coincidental. (Appendix 1.) In both cases we are watching the same process. We are watching a group of writers coming along, working in a genre regarded as Lower Class (the novel before the 1850's, slick-magazine journalism before the 1960's), who discover the joys of detailed realism and its strange powers. Many of them seem to be in love with realism for its own sake; and never mind the 'sacred callings' of li erature. They seem to be saying: 'Hey! Come here! This is the way people are living now — just the way I'm going to show you! It may astound you, disgust you, delight you or arouse your contempt or make you laugh. . . . Nevertheless, this is what it's like! It's *all* right here! You won't be bored! Take a look!'

As I hardly have to tell you, that is not exactly the way serious novelists regard the task of the novel today. In this decade, the Seventies, The Novel will be celebrating the one-hundredth anniversary of its canonization as *the* spiritual genre. Novelists today keep using words like 'myth,' 'fable' and 'magic.' (Appendix 2.) That state of mind known as 'the sacred office of the novelist' had originated in Europe in the 1870's and didn't take hold in the American literary world until after the Second World War. But it soon made up for lost time. What kind of novel should a sacred officer write? In 1948 Lionel Trilling presented the theory that the novel of social realism (which had flourished in America throughout the 1930's) was finished because the freight train of history had passed it by. The argument was that such novels were a product of the rise of the bourgeoisie in the nineteenth century at the height of capitalism. But now bourgeois society was breaking up, fragmenting. A novelist could no longer portray a part of that society and hope to capture the Zeitgeist; all he would be left with was one of the broken pieces. The only hope was a new kind of novel (his candidate was the novel of ideas). This theory caught on among young novelists with an astonishing grip. Whole careers were altered. All those writers hanging out in the literary pubs in New York such as the White Horse Tavern rushed off to write every kind of novel you could imagine, so long as it wasn't the so-called 'big novel' of manners and society. The next thing one knew, they were into novels of ideas, Freudian novels, surrealistic novels ('black comedy'), Kafkaesque novels and, more recently, the catatonic novel or novel of immobility, the sort that begins: 'In order to get started, he went to live alone on an island and shot himself.' (Opening line of a Robert Coover short story.)

As a result, by the Sixties, about the time I came to New York, the most serious, ambitious and, presumably, talented novelists had abandoned the richest terrain of the novel: namely, society, the social tableau, manners and morals, the whole business of 'the way we live now,' in Trollope's phrase. (Appendix 2.) There is no novelist who will be remembered as the novelist who captured the Sixties in America, or even in New York, in the sense that Thackeray was the chronicler of London in the 1840's and Balzac was the chronicler of Paris and all of France after the fall of the Empire. Balzac prided himself on being 'the secretary of French society.' Most serious American novelists would rather cut their wrists than be known as 'the secretary of American society,' and not merely because of ideological considerations. With fable, myth and the sacred office to think about – who wants such a menial role?

That was marvelous for journalists – I can tell you that. The Sixties was one of the most extraordinary decades in American history in terms of manners and morals. Manners and morals *were* the history of the Sixties. A hundred years from now when historians write about the 1960's in America (always assuming, to paraphrase Céline, that the Chinese will still give a damn about American history), they won't write about it as the decade of war in Vietnam or of space exploration or of political assassination . . . but as the decade when manners and morals, styles of living, attitudes towards the world changed the country more crucially than any political events . . . all the changes that were labeled, however clumsily, with such tags as 'the generation gap,' 'the counter culture,' 'black consciousness,' 'sexual permissiveness,' 'the death of God,' . . . the abandonment of proprieties, pieties, decorums connoted by 'go-go funds,' 'fast money,' swinger groovy hippie drop-out pop Beatles Andy Baby Jane Bernie Huey Eldridge LSD marathon encounter stone underground rip-off. . . . This whole side of American life that gushed forth when postwar American affluence finally blew the lid off – all this novelists simply turned away from, gave up by default. That left a huge gap in American letters, a gap big enough to drive an ungainly Reo rig like the New Journalism through.

When I reached New York in the early Sixties, I couldn't believe the scene I saw spread out before me. New York was pandemonium with a big grin on. Among people with money – and they seemed to be multiplying like shad – it was the wildest, looniest time since the 1920's . . . a universe of creamy forty-five-year-old fashionable fatties with walnut-shell eyes out on the giblet slab wearing the hip-huggers and the minis and the Little Egypt eyes and the sideburns and the boots and the bells and the love beads, doing the Watusi and the Funky Broadway and jiggling and grinning and sweating and sweating and grinning and jiggling until the onset of dawn or saline depletion, whichever came first.... It was a hulking carnival. But what really amazed me was that as a writer I had it practically all to myself. As fast as I could possibly do it, I was turning out articles on this amazing spectacle that I saw bubbling and screaming right there in front of my wondering eyes — New York! — and all the while I just knew that some enterprising novelist was going to come along and *do* this whole marvelous scene with one gigantic daring bold stroke. It was so ready, so *ripe* — beckoning ... but it never happened. To my great amazement New York simply remained the journalist's bonanza. For that matter, novelists seemed to shy away from the life of the great cities altogether. The thought of tackling such a subject seemed to terrify them, confuse them, make them doubt their own powers. And besides, it would have meant tackling social realism as well.

To my even greater amazement I had the same experience when I came upon 1960's California. This was the very incubator of new styles of living, and these styles were right there for all to see, ricocheting off every eyeball — and again a few amazed journalists working in the new form had it all to themselves, even the psychedelic movement, whose waves are still felt in every part of the country, in every grammar school even, like the intergalactic pulse. I wrote *The Electric Kool-Aid Acid Test* and then waited for the novels that I was sure would come pouring out of the psychedelic experience ... but they never came forth, either. I learned later that publishers had been waiting, too. They had been practically crying for novels by the new writers who must be out there somewhere, the new writers who would do the big novels of the hippie life or campus life or radical movements or the war in Vietnam or dope or sex or black militancy or encounter groups or the whole whirlpool all at once. They waited, and all they got was the Prince of Alienation ... sailing off to Lonesome Island on his Tarot boat with his back turned and his Timeless cape on, reeking of camphor balls.

Amazing, as I say. If nothing else had done it, that would have. The — New Journalists — Parajournalists — had the whole crazed obscene uproarious Mammon-faced drug-soaked mau-mau lust-oozing Sixties in America all to themselves.

So the novelists had been kind enough to leave behind for our boys quite a nice little body of material: the whole of American society, in effect. It only remained to be seen if magazine writers could master the techniques, in nonfiction, that had given the novel of social realism

such power. And here we come to a fine piece of irony. In abandoning
social realism novelists also abandoned certain vital matters of technique. As a result, by 1969 it was obvious that these magazine writers
— the very lumpenproles themselves! — had also gained a technical
edge on novelists. It was marvelous. For journalists to take Technique
away from the novelists — somehow it reminded me of Edmund Wilson's old exhortation in the early 1930's: Let's take communism away
from the Communists.

If you follow the progress of the New Journalism closely through the
1960's, you see an interesting thing happening. You see journalists
learning the techniques of realism — particularly of the sort found in
Fielding, Smollett, Balzac, Dickens and Gogol — from scratch. By trial
and error, by 'instinct' rather than theory, journalists began to discover
the devices that gave the realistic novel its unique power, variously
known as its 'immediacy,' its 'concrete reality,' its 'emotional involvement,' its 'gripping' or 'absorbing' quality.

This extraordinary power was derived mainly from just four devices,
they discovered. The basic one was scene-by-scene construction, telling
the story by moving from scene to scene and resorting as little as
possible to sheer historical narrative. Hence the sometimes extraordinary feats of reporting that the new journalists undertook: so that
they could actually witness the scenes in other people's lives as they
took place — and record the dialogue in full, which was device No. 2.
Magazine writers, like the early novelists, learned by trial and error
something that has since been demonstrated in academic studies:
namely, that realistic dialogue involves the reader more completely
than any other single device. It also establishes and defines character
more quickly and effectively than any other single device. (Dickens has
a way of fixing a character in your mind so that you have the feeling he
has described every inch of his appearance — only to go back and
discover that he actually took care of the physical description in two or
three sentences; the rest he has accomplished with dialogue.) Journalists were working on dialogue of the fullest, most completely revealing
sort in the very moment when novelists were cutting back, using dialogue in more and more cryptic, fey and curiously abstract ways.

The third device was the so-called 'third-person point of view,' the
technique of presenting every scene to the reader through the eyes of a
particular character, giving the reader the feeling of being inside the
character's mind and experiencing the emotional reality of the scene as
he experiences it. Journalists had often used the first-person point of

view – 'I was there' – just as autobiographers, memoirists and novelists had. (Appendix3.) This is very limiting for the journalist, however, since he can bring the reader inside the mind of only one character – himself – a point of view that often proves irrelevant to the story and irritating to the reader. Yet how could a journalist, writing nonfiction, accurately penetrate the thoughts of another person?

The answer proved to be marvelously simple: interview him about his thoughts and emotions, along with everything else. This was what I had done in *The Electric Kool-Aid Acid Test*, what John Sack did in *M* and what Gay Talese did in *Honor Thy Father*.

The fourth device has always been the least understood. This is the recording of everyday gestures, habits, manners, customs, styles of furniture, clothing, decoration, styles of traveling, eating, keeping house, modes of behaving toward children, servants, superiors, inferiors, peers, plus the various looks, glances, poses, styles of walking and other symbolic details that might exist within a scene. Symbolic of what? Symbolic, generally, of people's *status life*, using that term in the broad sense of the entire pattern of behaviour and possessions through which people express their position in the world or what they think it is or what they hope it to be. The recording of such details is not mere embroidery in prose. It lies as close to the center of the power of realism as any other device in literature. It is the very essence of the 'absorbing' power of Balzac, for example. Balzac barely used point of view at all in the refined sense that Henry James used it later on. And yet the reader comes away feeling that he has been even more completely 'inside' Balzac's characters than James's. Why? Here is the sort of thing Balzac does over and over. Before introducing you to Monsieur and Madame Marneffe personally (in *Cousine Bette*) he brings you into their drawing room and conducts a social autopsy: 'The furniture covered in faded cotton velvet, the plaster statuettes masquerading as Florentine bronzes, the clumsily carved painted chandelier with its candle rings of molded glass, the carpet, a bargain whose low price was explained too late by the quantity of cotton in it, which was now visible to the naked eye – everything in the room, to the very curtains (which would have taught you that the handsome appearance of wool damask lasts for only three years)' – everything in the room begins to absorb one into the lives of a pair of down-at-the-heel social climbers, Monsieur and Madame Marneffe. Balzac piles up these details so relentlessly and at the same time so meticulously – there is scarcely a detail in the later Balzac that does not illuminate some points of status – that he triggers the reader's memories of his own status life, his own ambitions, insecurities, delights, disasters, plus the thousand and one small humiliations and the status coups of everyday life, and triggers them over and over until he creates an atmosphere as rich and involving as the Joycean use of point of view.

I am fascinated by the fact that experiments in the physiology of the brain, still the great terra incognita of the sciences, seem to be heading toward the theory that the human mind or psyche does not have a discrete, internal existence. It is not a possession locked inside one's skull. During every moment of consciousness it is linked directly to external clues as to one's status in a social and not merely a physical sense and cannot develop or survive without them. If this turns out to be so, it could explain how novelists such as Balzac, Gogol, Dickens and Dostoevsky were able to be so 'involving' without using point of view with the sophistication of Flaubert or James or Joyce. (Appendix 5.)

I have never heard a journalist talk about the recording of status life in any way that showed he even thought of it as a separate device. It is simply something that journalists in the new form have gravitated toward. That rather elementary and joyous ambition to show the reader *real life* — 'Come here! Look! This is the way people live these days! These are the things they do!' — leads to it naturally. In any case, the result is the same. While so many novelists abandon the task altogether — and at the same time give up two thirds of the power of dialogue — journalists continue to experiment with all the devices of realism, revving them up, trying to use them in a bigger way, with the full passion of innocents and discoverers.

Their innocence has kept them free. Even novelists who try the new form . . . suddenly relax and treat themselves to forbidden sweets. If they want to indulge a craving for Victorian rhetoric or for a Humphrey Clinkerism such as, 'At this point the attentive reader may wonder how our hero could possibly . . .' — they go ahead and do it, as Mailer does in *The Armies Of The Night* with considerable charm. In this new journalism there are no sacerdotal rules; not yet in any case. . . . If the journalist wants to shift from third-person point of view to first-person point of view in the same scene, or in and out of different characters' points of view, or even from the narrator's omniscient voice to someone else's stream of consciousness — as occurs in *The Electric Kool-Aid Acid Test* — he does it. For the gluttonous Goths there is still only the outlaw's rule regarding technique: take, use, improvise. The result is a form that is not merely *like a novel*. It consumes devices that happen to have originated with the novel and mixes them with every other device known to prose. And all the while, quite beyond matters of technique, it enjoys an advantage so obvious, so built-in, one almost forgets what a power it has: the simple fact that the reader knows *all this actually happened*. The disclaimers have been erased. The screen is gone. The writer is one step closer to the absolute involvement of the reader that Henry James and James Joyce dreamed of and never achieved.

At this point, as I have already discovered, the student of literature tends to say: Even if I grant you that, what about the *higher* accomplishments of the great fiction writers? You haven't even mentioned the creation of character, much less such matters as psychological depth, a sense of history, the struggle of ideas, the moral consciousness of man, the great *themes* of EngLit, in short. To which I would say: I am talking about technique; as for the rest, from character to moral consciousness (whatever that may be), it depends upon the writer's experience and intellect, his insights, the quality of his emotions, his ability to see into others, his 'genius,' to use the customary word — and this remains so whether he is working in fiction or in journalism. My argument is that the genius of any writer — again, in fiction or in nonfiction — will be severely handicapped if he cannot master, or if he abandons, the techniques of realism. The psychological, moral, philosophical, emotional, poetic, visionary (one may supply the adjective as needed) power of Dickens, Dostoyevsky, Joyce, Mann, Faulkner, is made possible only by the fact that they first wired their work into the main circuit, which is realism.

Novelists have made a disastrous miscalculation over the past twenty years about the nature of realism. Their view of the matter is pretty well summed up by the editor of the *Partisan Review*, William Phillips: 'In fact, realism is just another formal device, not a permanent method for dealing with experience.' I suspect that precisely the opposite is true. If our friends the cognitive psychologists ever reach the point of knowing for sure, I think they will tell us something on this order: the introduction of realism into literature by people like Richardson, Fielding and Smollett was like the introduction of electricity into machine technology. It was *not* just another device. It raised the state of the art to a new magnitude. The effect of realism on the emotions was something that had never been conceived of before. No one was ever moved to tears by reading about the unhappy fates of heroes and heroines in

Homer, Sophocles, Molière, Racine, Sydney, Spenser or Shakespeare. But even the impeccable Lord Jeffrey, editor of the *Edinburgh Review*, had cried – actually blubbered, boohooed, snuffled and sighed – over the death of Dickens' Little Nell in *The Old Curiosity Shop*.

One doesn't have to admire Dickens or any of the other writers who first demonstrated this power in order to appreciate the point. For writers to give up this unique power in the quest for a more sophisticated kind of fiction – it is as if an engineer were to set out to develop a more sophisticated machine technology by first of all discarding the principle of electricity. In any case, journalists now enjoy a tremendous technical advantage. They have all the juice. This is not to say they have made maximum use of it. The work done in journalism over the past ten years easily outdazzles the work done in fiction, but that is saying very little. All that one can say is that the material and the techniques are now available, and the time is right.

The status crisis that first hit literature's middle class, the essayists or 'men of letters,' has now hit the novelists themselves. Some have turned directly to nonfiction. Some, such as Gore Vidal, Herbert Gold, William Styron and Ronald Sukenick, have tried forms that land on a curious ground in between, part fiction and part nonfiction. Still others have begun to pay homage to the power of the New Journalism by putting real people, with their real names, into fictional situations.... They're all sweating bullets.... Actually I wouldn't say the novel is dead. It's the kind of comment that doesn't mean much in any case. It is only the prevailing fashions among novelists that are washed up. I think there is a tremendous future for a sort of novel that will be called the journalistic novel or perhaps documentary novel, novels of intense social realism based upon the same painstaking reporting that goes into the New Journalism. I see no reason why novelists who look down on Arthur Hailey's work couldn't do the same sort of reporting and research he does – and write it better, if they're able. There are certain areas of life that journalism still cannot move into easily, particularly for reasons of invasion of privacy, and it is in this margin that the novel will be able to grow in the future.

When we talk about the 'rise' or 'death' of literary genres, we are talking about status, mainly. The novel no longer has the supreme status it enjoyed for ninety years (1875–1965), but neither has the New Journalism won it for itself. The status of the New Journalism is not secured by any means. In some quarters the contempt for it is boundless ... even breathtaking.... With any luck at all the new genre will never be sanctified, never be exalted, never given a theology. I probably shouldn't even go around talking it up the way I have in this piece. All I meant to say when I started out was that the New Journalism can no longer be ignored in an artistic sense. The rest I take back.... The hell with it.... Let chaos reign ... louder music, more wine.... The hell with the standings.... The top rung is up for grabs. All the old traditions are exhausted, and no new one is yet established. All bets are off! the odds are cancelled! it's anybody's ball game! ... the horses are all drugged! the track is glass! ... and out of such glorious chaos may come, from the most unexpected source, in the most unexpected form, some nice new fat Star Streamer Rockets that will light up the sky.

# Appendix

## 1 The early status of the novel

When Truman Capote insisted that *In Cold Blood* was not journalism but a new literary genre he had invented, 'the nonfiction novel,' a flash went through my mind. It was the familiar 'Aha!' flash. In this case: 'Aha! the ever-clever Fielding dodge!' When Henry Fielding published his first novel, *Joseph Andrews*, in 1742, he kept protesting that his book was not a novel — it was a new literary genre he had invented, 'the comic epic poem in prose.' He made the same claim for *Tom Jones*. He compared his books to the *Margites*, which was believed to be a lost comic epic of ancient Greece (by Homer, some said). What he was doing, of course — and what Capote would be doing 223 years later — was trying to give his work the cachet of the reigning literary genre of his time, so that literary people would take it seriously. The reigning genre in Fielding's time was epic poetry and verse-drama of the classical sort. The status of the novel was so low — well, it was as low as the status of magazine journalism in 1965 when Capote started publishing *In Cold Blood* in *The New Yorker*.

Thanks to this initial 'Aha!' flash, I began to notice a curious thing. The early days of this new journalism were beginning to look like an absolute rerun of the early days of the realistic novel in England. A slice of literary history was repeating itself. I don't mean repetition in the vague sense of 'there's nothing new under the sun.' I mean exact repetition, *déjà vu*, finicky details. . . . The very same objections that greeted the novel in the eighteenth and nineteenth centuries were starting to greet the New Journalism. In each case the new form is seen as 'superficial,' 'ephemeral,' 'mere entertainment,' 'morally irresponsible.' Some of the arguments were so similar it was uncanny. For example, one day I'm on a panel with a critic, Pauline Kael, and she says that one of the worst defects of the New Journalism is that it's 'noncritical.' She explains that it merely gets people 'excited,' and 'you are left not knowing how to feel about it except to be excited about it,' which she considers morally enervating for young people, 'because the same way they go for movies that have intensity and excitement, they like writing that has intensity and excitement. But it leaves them no basis at all for evaluating the material, and ultimately it simply means that the writing has to go from one charge to the next.' I listen to that and ... all at once I can hear a critic from more than a century before, John Ruskin himself, and he is objecting that *novels* are morally enervating, especially for young people, because of the mindless 'excitement': 'It is not the badness of a novel that we should dread,' he is saying, 'but its overwrought interest ... its excitement,' which simply 'increases the morbid thirst' for more and more excitement.

Underlying such an attitude is the assumption that it is the duty of serious literature to give moral instruction. The notion had flowered in the seventeenth century, when literature was regarded not merely as an art form but as a branch of religion or ethical philosophy, the branch that taught by examples instead of precepts. Literature should 'require the exertion of thought,' as Coleridge put it later in objecting to the novel. It should be deep, morally serious, cosmic, and not too easy to read. It should deal with eternal truths and characters of grandeur and stature whose lives brought one closer to serious issues, the soul of man and the inner meaning of life. Like the New Journalism today, novels – and especially the realistic novels of men like Fielding, Sterne and Smollett (and, later, Dickens and Balzac) – seemed to fail all the vital tests. They had low aims ('mere entertainment'). They dwelt on manners ('superficial') rather than the verities and the soul. And they were so damnably Low Rent ... all this morbid curiosity about the lives of footmen, farm wenches, innkeepers, degenerate clergymen, valets, blacksmiths, clerks, petty thieves, music-hall conductors, philanderers and mistresses and other people who had neither stature nor grandeur. Dr. Johnson dismissed Fielding's novels by saying his characters were so 'low life,' you would think that Fielding himself must be an 'ostler.' Ostlers were the people who cleaned out the stables, the lowest of the Low Rent.

I couldn't help but think of that quaint complaint from two centuries before as I started hearing the New Journalism dismissed as 'zoot-suited prose' (John Leonard, editor of *The New York Times Book Review*) and 'zippy prose about inconsequential people' (Renata Adler), people such as petty bureaucrats, Mafiosi, line soldiers in Vietnam, pimps, hustlers, doormen, socialites, shyster lawyers, surfers, bikers, hippies and other accursed Youth, evangelists, athletes, 'arriviste Jews'

(Renata Adler again), people, in other words, who have neither stature nor grandeur.

I don't object to the style of the New Journalism being called 'zippy' or 'zoot-suited.' If these seem like negative qualities, one need only try to imagine their opposites. But I don't think anyone cán support the charge that the New Journalism has shirked the task of 'evaluating the material.' All the New Journalists I have mentioned in this piece customarily go to great lengths (even overboard in some cases) to analyze and evaluate their material, although seldom in a moralistic fashion. None of them simply provides 'documentaries.' Nor can it be claimed that they have written only about 'inconsequential' people or subjects. The charge is meaningless, in any case; but to meet it on its own grounds, one need only mention Talese's book on *The New York Times* (*The Kingdom and the Power*), Mailer's books on political conventions and the moon shot, Joe McGinniss' book on Nixon's 1968 campaign (*The Selling of the President*), 'Adam Smith''s book on Wall Street (*The Money Game*), Sack's, Breslin's and Michael Herr's (*Khesanh*) writing about the war in Vietnam, Gail Sheehy's book on the Black Panthers (*Panthermania*), a book on black–white confrontations called *Radical Chic & Mau-Mauing the Flak Catchers*, Garry Wills on the Southern Christian Leadership Conference ... in fact, I can't think of a 'consequential' subject or issue (except possibly in the sciences) that has not been dealt with in the new genre.

## 2 Myth vs. realism in the novel

The idea that the novel has a spiritual function of providing a mythic conscjousness for the people is as popular within the literary community today as the same idea was with regard to poetry in the seventeenth and eighteenth centuries in England. In 1972 the novelist Chandler Brossard writes that 'true and original fiction is vision, and fiction writers are visionaries. It is myth and magic, and the writers of it are magicians and shamans, mythmakers and mythologists.' Mark J. Mirsky writes a manifesto for a new periodical called *Fiction*, devoted to reviving the art in the 1970's, and he says: 'We simply cannot believe that people have tired of stories, that the ear of America has atrophied permanently and is now deaf to myth, fable, puzzle, paradox.' 'In the mythos,' he says, quoting Thoreau, 'a superhuman intelligence uses the unconscious thoughts of men as its hieroglyphics to address men unborn.'

Nothing could have been further from the minds of the realists who

established the novel as the reigning genre over a hundred years ago.
As a matter of fact, they were turning their backs, with a kind of
mucker's euphoria, on the idea of myth and fable, which had been the
revered tradition of classical verse and French- and Italian-style court
literature. It is hard to realize today just how drenched in realism the
novel was at the outset – *réalisme pour le réalisme!* – *all this is true to
life!* Defoe presents *Robinson Crusoe* as the actual memoir of a ship-
wrecked sailor. Richardson presents *Pamela* as the actual correspondence of a young lady in the clutches of a man who wants to make her
his mistress instead of his wife. In the town of Slough the villagers
gather around the blacksmith as he reads the episodes of *Pamela* aloud
– and on the day he reaches the part where she finally wins her battle
and maneuvers her pursuer into marrying her, they run off cheering
and ringing church bells. In the mid-nineteenth century critics routinely
checked out novels for literal accuracy, as if it were understood that
this was one of the product's advertising promises and the novelist had
better make good on it. It was very much like the way moviegoers used
to (and perhaps still do) monitor movies for anachronisms and write
the studios letters saying, 'If this movie is supposed to be about gang-
sters in the Thirties, then how come in the scene where the man's head
is shot off with a deer rifle outside the Nightfish Aquarium there is a
1941 Plymouth parked along the curb, which you can tell by the butter-
fly shape of the grille and—' Novelists routinely accepted the unpleasant task of doing reporting, legwork, 'digging,' in order to *get it just
right*. That was part of the process of writing novels. Dickens travels to
three towns in Yorkshire using a false name and pretending to be looking for a school for the son of a widowed friend – in order to get inside
the notorious Yorkshire boarding schools to gather material for *Nicholas Nickleby*.

Social realists like Dickens and Balzac seemed so often to delight in
realism pure and simple that it was held against them throughout their
careers. Neither was regarded as a literary *artist* in his own lifetime
(Balzac was not even invited into the French Academy). From the
1860's on, literary people – novelists as well as critics, I should add –
began to develop the following theory: Realism is a powerful device
but is of trivial interest unless it is used to illumine a higher reality . . .
the cosmic dimension . . . eternal values . . . the moral consciousness
. . . a road that led them right back to the classical tradition by and by,
to the idea that literature has a spiritual mission, that it 'speaks to
men unborn,' that it is magic, fable, myth, the mythos. By the 1920's,

in both France and England, the novel of social realism already seemed gauche.

Thanks in part to the Depression, which stimulated *the* great phase of social realism in the American novel, the European 'mythic' vogue did not come into American literature until after the second World War. By now, however, it is going strong. Almost all 'serious' American novelists today come out of the universities, and there they usually learn to look to such models as Beckett, Pinter, Kafka, Hesse, Borges, and, more recently, Zamyatin (or the Zamyatin of *We*, in any case). The upshot has been a puzzling sort of fiction — puzzling to those outside the fraternity — in which the characters have no background, no personal history, are identified with no social class, ethnic group or even nationality, and act out their fates in a locale that has no place name, often some timeless and elemental terrain such as forest, swamp, desert, mountain or sea. They often speak, if they speak at all, in short and rather mechanical sentences that, again, betray no specific background, or else they use inexplicably archaic diction. They respond to inexplicable forces, are obsessed with inexplicable dreads, and often perform fantastical physical feats. What are such narrative devices typical of? Why ... myth, fable, parable, legend.

I think that unconsciously the strategy of these Neo-Fabulists has run as follows: 'Realism has been taken over by the new journalists, with whom I am powerless to compete. Besides, realism is old hat. So what is left for me to do? Why, to return to those most elemental and pure forms of story-telling, the forms from which literature itself has sprung; namely, myth, fable, parable, and legend!'

Some of the Neo-Fabulists get right down to it. They write directly in the form and rhythms of the fable, the fairy tale and the old epic histories: John Barth ('Dunyazadiad'), Borges, John Gardner, James Purdy, James Reinbold ('Family Portrait'), Alan V. Hewat, and Gabriel García Márquez. The rest pay homage to Neo-Fabulism, if only by observing such conventions as No Background, No Place Name, No Dialogue and the Inexplicables.

There have been certain peculiarly modern problems with the neo-fable, however. For one thing, at its best the fable is not a printed story but one told out loud. The fable is 'primordial' only in the sense that it predates print. The fable was never able to compete with the power of the realistic printed story and can't now. By giving up the devices of realism — such as realistic dialogue, status detail and point of view – the Neo-Fabulist becomes like the engineer who decides to give up electricity because it has 'been done.'

While myth, fable, etc., may have come first, they never stood a chance, once more sophisticated techniques were discovered as a printed literature developed.

## 3 Is the New Journalism really new?

This is usually only a rhetorical question that says: Of course it isn't. I have never seen anyone stick around for an answer. Nevertheless, I will try to provide one:

The question is very much like the question scholars once debated as to whether or not the realistic novel may be said to originate in the eighteenth century with Richardson and Fielding (or Defoe, Richardson and Fielding). There have been some convincing demonstrations of their indebtedness to Cervantes, Rabelais, the French *roman*, Thomas Nashe's *The Unfortunate Traveller*, and even to a line of little-known novelists such as Thomas Deloney, Francis Kirkman, Mary de la Rivière Manley and Eliza Haywood. And yet if one actually reads these earlier novelists, one sees that they simply have not done what Richardson and Fielding did. They have not rendered character, language, milieu and manners with a detailed and 'everyday' realism.

Likewise in the case of the New Journalism. The person who asks if the New Journalism is really new often supplies names of writers who he believes did it all years ago, decades ago, even centuries ago. Upon inspection one finds that these writers usually fall into one of four categories: (1) they weren't writing nonfiction at all – as in the case of Defoe; and Addison and Steele in the 'Sir Roger de Coverley Papers'; (2) they were traditional essayists, doing very little reporting and using few if any of the techniques of the New Journalism – such as Murray Kempton, I. F. Stone, and Baldwin, in the often cited case of *The Fire Next Time;* (3) autobiographers; (4) Literary Gentlemen with a Seat in the Grandstand. The last two categories deserve some amplification:

AUTOBIOGRAPHY. The word autobiography dates back to the late eighteenth century. It is the one form of nonfiction that has always had most of the powers of the novel. The technical problem of point of view is solved from the outset, because the autobiographer presents every scene from the same point of view, i.e., his own. In the best autobiographies this works perfectly, because the protagonist – the author himself – was at the center of the action. He has not been a reporter; he has simply lived his story and presumably knows it in detail; the autobiographer, by convention, is allowed to present dialogue from the past in extended detail on the grounds that he was there and can recall it. The line runs from De Quincey's *Confessions of an English Opium-Eater* to Mark Twain's *Life on the Mississippi* to Orwell's *Homage to Catalonia* to Claude Brown's *Manchild in the Promised Land* and is as powerful a form today as it ever was.

Many reporters attempting to write the New Journalism use an autobiographical format — 'I was there and this is how it affected me' — precisely because this does seem to solve so many technical problems. The New Journalism has often been characterized as 'subjective' journalism for that very reason; e.g., Richard Schickel, in *Commentary*, defined it as 'a form in which it is understood that the writer keeps himself in the foreground at all times.' In fact, most of the best work in the form has been done in third-person narration with the writer keeping himself absolutely invisible, such as the work of Capote, Talese, the early Breslin, Sack, John Gregory Dunne, Joe McGinniss.

In the late 1960's the notion of 'subjectivity' came up in quite another way. The term New Journalism began to be confused with 'advocacy journalism.' With the rise of the New Left you began to see more and more journalists of the technically most old-fashioned sort, such as Jack Newfield of *The Village Voice*, calling themselves New Journalists. I think the attraction was the word *new*. 'If I am a journalist of the New Left — then I must be a New Journalist.' Fortunately this phase seems about over; even Newfield has abandoned the position. But I think it really came to an end about the third time Newfield grouped himself with Jimmy Breslin as Us Two New Journalists. This must have made Breslin's flesh crawl.

THE LITERARY GENTLEMAN WITH A SEAT IN THE GRANDSTAND. This is an ancient and honorable type of essayist whose work differs from the New Journalism in the crucial matter of reporting. He has usually not done nearly enough reporting, nor the right type of reporting, to use the devices the new genre depends on.

William Hazlitt is often mentioned as 'someone who was doing your "new" journalism 150 years ago,' and Exhibit A is his famous essay 'The Fight,' concerning a bareknuckle prizefight between Bill Neate and the Gas-man. What one finds in this piece is some vivid writing about the blows that were struck, the grimaces on the fighters' faces, and so on — and that is it. There is nothing that could not have been as easily observed (if perhaps not as well described) by any other Gentleman in the Grandstand, or in the crowd at ringside in this case. I am sure that Hazlitt would have been too much of a gentleman, or too diffident, to do the sort of reporting that would have enabled him to bring the reader not merely inside the ring but inside the point of view of the fighters themselves, which is to say inside their lives — by following them through their training, going to their homes, talking to their children, their wives, their friends, as, for example, Gay Talese did in a story on Floyd Patterson.

Some enterprising scholar could write quite a nice monograph on the subject of 'The Seventeenth-Century Code of the Gentleman as Preserved Within the Literary Worlds of England and the United States.' The hypothesis would be that the experience of the literary man as (quite literally) the houseguest of the aristocracy in the seventeenth century created certain *social* attitudes concerning literary behavior and that these attitudes have persisted to this day, have been preserved through revolutions, war, depressions, bohemias, bell-bottoms and tank tops and convulsions of every sort, so that a certain *social* protocol is still in effect.

The genteel tradition in nonfiction is summed up in the phrase 'the polite essay.' Legwork, 'digging,' reporting, especially reporting of the Locker Room Genre, is ... well, beneath one's dignity. It puts the writer in such an awkward position. He not only has to enter the bailiwick of the people he is writing about, he also becomes a slave to their schedules. Reporting can be tedious, messy, physically dirty, boring, dangerous even. But worst of all, from the genteel point of view, is the continual posture of humiliation. The reporter starts out by presuming upon someone's privacy, asking questions he has no right to expect an answer to — and no sooner has he lowered himself that far than already he has become a supplicant with his cup out, waiting for information or for something to happen, hoping to be tolerated long enough to get what he needs, adapting his personality to the situation, being ingratiating, obliging, charming, whatever seems to be called for, enduring taunts, abuse, even the occasional roughing up in the eternal eagerness for 'the story' — behavior that comes close to being servile or even beggarly.

The Literary Gentleman in the Grandstand neither presumes nor begs; nor, in many cases, does he even take out the beggar's cup, which is the notebook. He maintains a gentlemanly posture in the grandstand — like most of the novelists who wrote 'socially conscious'

nonfiction in the 1930's (e.g., John Dos Passos' 'The Anacostia Flats').
They seldom used point-of-view or dialogue except in the most per-
functory way. They supply mainly 'vivid description' plus sentiment. D.
H. Lawrence's description of a Hopi snake dance in New Mexico is
little more than that, despite the initiative he showed in getting there
in the first place. He obviously regarded what he was doing as a secondary form of literature and employed none of the sophisticated devices he would have used in a scene in a short story.

After all the enthusiasm I had seen critics generate over James
Agee's *Let Us Now Praise Famous Men* — a book about poor folks in
the Appalachians during the Depression — reading it was a great disappointment. He showed enterprise enough, going to the mountains
and moving in briefly with a mountain family. Reading between the
lines I would say his problem was extreme personal diffidence. His
account abounds in 'poetic' descriptions and is very short on dialogue.
It uses no point of view other than his own. Reading between the lines
you get a picture of a well-educated and extremely shy man ... too
polite, too diffident to ask personal questions of these humble folk or
even draw them out. Even Mailer's work shows the same odd defect,
the same reluctance to take out the notebook and cross the genteel line
and head through the doors marked Keep Out. There is very little in
either *Miami and the Siege of Chicago* or *Of a Fire on the Moon* that
could not have been observed by any other Literary Gentleman in the
Grandstand. Perhaps the most diffident soul of all has been Murray
Kempton. Kempton has never been able to bring himself down from the
grandstand. He is up there to this day, crocheting his weird imitation
British Essays full of elegant and stupefying tautologies such as: 'Mrs.
Jessie McNab Dennis, an assistant curator for Western European arts,
had attended the hearing as an observer, since not only her sentiments
about the project but her expression of them were not of an order of
docility her Director would find serviceable in a witness.'

NOT HALF-BAD CANDIDATES. Nevertheless, one can go back into literary
history and find examples of nonfiction written by reporters, and not
autobiographers or literary gentlemen in the grandstand, showing
many of the characteristics of the New Journalism. For a start, Boswell. One thing I like about Boswell is the way he would actually try to
thrust Johnson into situations so that he could report on them, get the
dialogue, dote on the manners; such as the time he tricked Johnson
into going to dinner at the house of his literary enemy, John Wilkes.

... Dickens' *Sketches by Boz;* descriptions of the everyday rounds of typical London figures, duns, beadles, coachmen, etc., written for the *Morning Chronicle* and other sheets, a form used fairly often by New Journalists today.... Henry Mayhew's *London Labour and the London Poor,* remarkable chiefly for the fact that Mayhew was willing to search out the very lowest classes of people in the East End of London and for the skill with which he caught their language.... Mark Twain's *Innocents Abroad;* unlike the autobiographical *Life on the Mississippi,* this was a case in which Twain set out as a reporter with the idea of recording scenes and dialogue.... Chekhov's curious book *A Journey to Sakhalin;* the great dramatist and short-story writer sets out, at the height of his fame, to a penal colony off Russia's Pacific coast in order to expose conditions thereon; uneven, didactic, full of essays and statistics, but it includes some notable scenes (especially 'The Pigs')....
Stephen Crane's vignettes of the Bowery for the New York *Press;* mostly 'vivid description,' however, and very little penetration of the lives of their characters; just warm-ups for novels.... John Reed's *Ten Days That Shook the World;* parts of it anyway, especially the scene where the proles challenge the authority of the naval officer...; Orwell's *Down and Out in Paris and London,* a case in which, if I am not mistaken, Orwell went through the experience in order to write about it (i.e., he approached it as a reporter).... The 'reportage' school of the 1930's, which was centered about the magazine *New Masses;* theoreticians such as Joseph North had in mind a new journalism as full-bodied as anything I've been talking about, but most of the work degenerated into propaganda of a not very complex sort; it amuses me that North complained that literary people were calling his boys' new journalism 'a bastard form.' ... Some (but not much) of Hemingway's 'reportage' from the same period.... Several of John Hersey's articles in the early 1940's, such as a sketch called 'Joe Is Home Now.' (*Life,* July 3, 1944); here we start getting into the direct ancestry of the present-day New Journalism.... Hersey's *Hiroshima;* very novelistic, takes up a whole issue of *The New Yorker* in 1946, has great influence on other *New Yorker* writers, such as Truman Capote and Lillian Ross.... Capote's profile of Marlon Brando and his account of an American cultural-exchange troupe's trip to Russia; A. J. Liebling's profile of an old *National Enquirer* columnist called 'Colonel Stingo'; Lillian Ross's famous evisceration of Ernest Hemingway ('How Do You Like It Now, Gentlemen?').... Various writers for *True,* notably Al Stump, author of an extraordinary chronicle of the last days of Ty Cobb....

(And, as John F. Szwed and Carol Anne Parssinen of the University of Pennsylvania have pointed out to me, some of Lafcadio Hearn's pieces for Cincinnati newspapers in the 1870's; e.g., 'Slow Starvation,' Cincinnati *Enquirer*, February 15, 1874.)

A new journalism was in the works during the 1950's, and it might have grown out of the work at *The New Yorker* or *True* or both, except for one thing: during the 1950's the novel was burning its last bright flame as the holy of holies. The worship of the novel as a sacred form reaches a peak in that decade, then suddenly begins to tail off as it becomes apparent that there is to be no golden 'Postwar Period' in the novel. By the early 1960's a more spectacular form of new journalism — more spectacular in terms of style — has begun in *Esquire* and, shortly thereafter, *New York*. But if anyone wants to maintain that the current tradition starts with *The New Yorker* and *True*, I will not contest the point. There were also a few free-lance writers such as the late Richard Gehman who at one time or another in the 1950's used most of the techniques I have talked about.

## 4 The man of letters

Many American men of letters actually had hopes in the mid-1960's of ascending to the upper class of literature, on at least a par with the novelists, a notion that probably would have puzzled even the sophisticated reading public at the time. Its appreciation of the phrase 'man of letters' was probably closer to that of T. S. Eliot who once called them 'minds of the second order' (and made it worse by saying we *need* minds of the second order, to do the bookkeeping and help circulate the ideas of others) or that of Balzac, who once said that 'the designation "man of letters" is the cruelest insult one can offer to an author' (since it indicates his status is derived more from his literary associations than his talent as a writer). The man of letters is often a critic, sometimes a literary historian or theoretician, and invariably a homeopathic idea doctor who uses his literary essays as an occasion to comment on morals and society. Nevertheless, the man of letters had once, for about twenty years, been the reigning literary figure.

This was in the period 1820–1840 in England following the decline of poetry, a decline in status quite similar to the current 'death of the novel.' This occurred in the very moment when the great British reviews were on the rise, starting with the *Edinburgh Review* in 1802. The reviews established many literary conventions that persist unchanged to this day, such as the role of the literary man as a dissenter and opponent of entrenched power and the use of the form known as the 'review-article,' in which the literary man uses the book under review as a stepping-off point for a nature walk through a more general subject. The reviews had considerable political influence, and their editors were celebrities. In 1831 Thomas Carlyle said that the reigning poet of the period, Byron, had told him that the poet was no longer the undisputed king of literature; he now had to share the throne with the man of letters. By 1840 Carlyle believed that the man of letters now had it all to himself. He delivered a famous series of lectures on the Hero; lecture No. 5 was on 'our most important person,' the Hero as Man of Letters. Ironically, it was in that very decade, 1840–1850, that a band of literary Visigoths emerged from out of nowhere and dethroned the man of letters as quickly as he had risen: viz., the realistic novelists.

In New York in the early 1960's, what with all the talk of 'the death of the novel,' the man of letters seemed to be on the rise again. There was considerable talk of creating a 'cultural elite,' based on what the local literati believed existed in London. Such hopes were dashed, of course, by the sudden emergence of yet another horde of Visigoths, the New Journalists.

## 5 The physiology of realism (A prediction)

This note is not concerned with history but the near future. I have already referred to current studies in the physiology of the brain. Over the next several decades experimenters in this area will begin focusing on the as-yet-mysterious process that serves as a God principle for most writers and other artists: creativity. Part of what they will discover about the powers of the written word (I predict) will be this:

Print (as opposed to film or theater) is an indirect medium that does not so much 'create' images or emotions as jog the reader's memories. For example, writers describing drunk scenes seldom try to describe the state of drunkenness itself. They count on the reader having been drunk at some time in his life. They as much as say, 'So-and-so was drunk – and, well, you know what that's like.' (With regard to more arcane highs, such as LSD or methedrine, the writer can make no such assumption – and this has stymied many writers.) For that matter, writers have a hard time even creating a picture of a human face. Detailed descriptions tend to defeat their own purpose, because they break up the face rather than create an image. Writers are much more likely to provide no more than a cartoon outline. In *One Day in the Life of Ivan Denisovich* Aleksandr Solzhenitsyn will speak of 'Big Ivan, a tall, scrawny sergeant with black eyes. The first time you saw him he scared the pants off you....' Or: 'There was a blank look on the Tartar's hairless, crumpled face' ... and that is the extent of facial description. The reader's memory (if any) of such individuals is invited to fill in the rest.

Yet this basic operation – jogging the reader's memory – has some unique and rather marvelous advantages. If students of the brain are correct so far, human memory seems to be made up of sets of meaningful data – as opposed to what the older mechanistic theory presumed: viz., that it is made up of random bits of meaningless or haphazard data that are then combined and given meaning by the mind. These memory sets often combine a complete image and an emotion. The power of a single image in a story or song to evoke a complex feeling is well known. I have always enjoyed the opening lines of a country and western song by Roger Miller called 'King of the Road.' 'Trailers for Sale or Rent,' it begins, 'Room to Let Fifty Cents.' It is not the part about the trailers that I enjoy so much as the 'Room to Let.' This is the sort of archaic wording that, in my experience, is found only in windows or in door frames in the oldest and most run-down section of a city. It immediately triggers in my memory a particular view of a particular street near Worcester Square in New Haven, Connecticut. The emotion it calls up is one of loneliness and deprivation but of a rather romantic sort (bohemia). One's memory is apparently made up of millions of such sets, which work together on the Identikit principle. The most gifted writers are those who manipulate the memory sets of the reader in such a rich fashion that they create within the mind of the reader an entire world that resonates with the reader's own real emotions. The events are merely taking place on the page, in print, but the emotions are real. Hence the unique feeling when one is 'absorbed' in a certain book, 'lost' in it.

Only certain specific devices can jog or trigger the memory in such a rich fashion however; the same four devices I have already mentioned: scene-by-scene construction, dialogue, point of view and the detailing of status life. Two of these devices, scenes and dialogue, can be handled better on film than in print. But the other two, point of view and the detailing of status life, work far better in print than on film. No film maker has ever successfully brought the audience inside the mind or central nervous system of a character – something that even bad novelists are able to accomplish as a matter of routine. Film makers

have tried everything. They have tried voice-over narration. They have
tried making the camera the 'eyes' of the protagonist, so that the only
time you see him is when he stands in front of a mirror. The current
fashion is 'memory flashes,' quick cuts, sometimes in filtered tones, to
memories of the past. None of it successfully puts you inside the skull
of a character on film. (What came closest, for me, was the use of
asides into the camera by Michael Caine in *Alfie;* they started out as
comic bits, à la the movie *Tom Jones*, but ended up as rather moving
moments, far more effective, strangely, than asides in a stage play.)
Certain realistic novels are successful because they dwell so realisti-
cally, so effectively, on the mental life and emotional atmosphere of a
particular character. These stories are almost always disasters when
put on screen; e.g., *Tropic of Cancer* and *Portnoy's Complaint*. The
makers of such movies usually run up the flag of defeat by finally
having someone, via voice-over or on screen, recite great chunks of the
novel itself, as if in the hope that *this* will recapture the power of the
goddamned book. The power, unfortunately for them, is completely
wrapped up in the unique physiological relationship between written
language and the memory.

The movies are almost as bad at dealing with status life. In print a
writer can present a status detail and then nudge the reader to make
sure he knows its significance, and it all seems very natural. In the
opening scene of *Madame Bovary* Flaubert introduces Charles Bovary
as a boy of fifteen on his first day at boarding school. 'He wore his hair
cut straight across the forehead, *like a cantor in a village church....*'
My italics; here and throughout the passage Flaubert keeps nudging
the reader to make sure the picture he is describing adds up to a
country boy, a *rustaud*, who looks ridiculous to his schoolmates. The
movies, of course, can present the same details but cannot point out
the significance except through dialogue, which soon becomes very
labored. As a result the movie rendition of status life is the broad
stroke ... the mansion, the servants, the Rolls, the bum, the switch-
board operator with the 'Bronx' accent.... Since the movie maker cannot nudge the viewer, he often ends up making his status points over-
obvious visually ... the mansion that is *too* big, the servants who are
*too* formal....

The first movie maker to deal successfully with point of view and
status life will be the first giant in that field. Sad to say, the students of
cognition may discover that technically and physiologically it is an
impossible problem for film.

## 6 Reporting

There is no history of reporting, so far as I know. I doubt that it ever occurred to anyone, even in the journalism schools, that the subject might have historical phases. The sort of reporting that one now finds in the New Journalism probably begins with the travel literature of the late eighteenth and early nineteenth centuries (and, as I say, with the singular figure of Boswell). Many of the travel writers seem to have been inspired by the success of autobiographies. Their idea was to create some autobiography for themselves by heading off to foreign places in search of color and adventure. Melville, for example, began his career in the travel and adventure vein with *Omoo* and *Typee*.

Historically the interesting thing is how seldom it occurred to writers of nonfiction that they could do this sort of reporting in anything other than autobiography. I am talking about the kind of comprehensive reporting that enables one to portray scenes, extensive dialogue, status life and emotional life, in addition to the usual data of the essay-narrative. In the nineteenth century novelists did much more of this sort of reporting than journalists. I have already cited the examples of Balzac and Dickens. The sort of research that Dostoevsky did for *The Possessed* is another example. One reason that nonfiction writers were slow to see the possibilities of this approach was that nonfiction, except for the autobiography, was seen as a didactic genre, at least in its highest expression. A writer seeking to teach a lesson usually was after no more content that it took to make his case appear solid. In *A Journey to Sakhalin* one can see Chekhov struggling against this convention and breaking free of it only in spots.

One of the greatest changes brought about by the new breed of journalists has been a reversal of this attitude – so that the proof of one's technical mastery as a writer becomes paramount and the demonstration of moral points becomes secondary. This passion for technical brilliance has lent them a strange sort of objectivity, an egotistical objectivity but an objectivity of sorts in any case.

When one moves from newspaper reporting to this new form of journalism, as I and many others did, one discovers that the basic reporting unit is no longer the datum, the piece of information, but the scene, since most of the sophisticated strategies of prose depend upon scenes. Therefore, your main problem as a reporter is, simply, managing to stay with whomever you are writing about long enough for the scenes to take place before your own eyes. There are no rules or craft secrets of reporting that will help a man pull this off; it is completely a test of his personality. Reporting never becomes any easier simply because you have done it many times. The initial problem is always to approach total strangers, move in on their lives in some fashion, ask questions you have no natural right to expect answers to, ask to see things you weren't meant to see, and so on. Many journalists find it so ungentlemanly, so embarrassing, so terrifying even, that they are never able to master this essential first move. Murray Kempton and Jack Newfield are examples of two reporters hobbled by this fear. The only strangers Newfield apparently feels comfortable about approaching are people like this month's revolutionary macho of the century who has been previously assured that the reporter is friendly.

Reporters themselves tend to grossly overestimate the difficulty of getting close to the people they want to write about and staying with them. The sociologist Ned Polsky used to complain that criminologists studied criminals only in jail – where they lied their heads off in hopes of parole – on the assumption that of course they could never approach the criminal in his own habitat. Polsky contended, and proved in his own work, that criminals do not look upon themselves as criminals but merely as people hustling to make their way in the world and can be fairly easily approached as such. Furthermore, they often feel that their exploits deserve being preserved in literature. Gay Talese proved this theory to a great extent by penetrating a Mafia family and writing *Honor Thy Father* (although he steered clear of one key area, their criminal activities themselves).

Most good journalists who hope to get inside someone else's world and stay there awhile come on very softly and do not bombard their subjects with questions. In his extraordinary reporting feats with the sports world George Plimpton adopted the strategy of hanging back in the shadows with such diffidence and humility that *they* would finally ask him to f'r chrissake come on out and play. But, again, it is mainly a matter of one's own personality. If a reporter stays with a person or group long enough, they – reporter and subject – will develop a personal relationship of some sort, even if it is hostility. More often it will be friendship of some sort. For many reporters this presents a more formidable problem than penetrating the particular scene in the first place. They become stricken with a sense of guilt, responsibility, obligation. 'I hold this man's reputation, his future, in my hands' – that becomes the frame of mind. They may begin to feel like voyeurs – 'I have preyed upon this man's life, devoured it with my eyes, made no commitment myself, etc.' People who become overly sensitive on this score should never take up the new style of journalism. They inevitably turn out second-rate work, biased in such banal ways that they embarrass even the subjects they think they are 'protecting.' A writer needs at least enough ego to believe that what he is doing as a writer is as important as what anyone he is writing about is doing and that therefore he shouldn't compromise his own work. If he doesn't believe that his own writing is one of the most important activities going on in contemporary civilization, then he ought to move on to something else he thinks is ... become a welfare eligibility worker or a clean-investment counselor for the Unitarian Church or a noise abatement surveyor....

Assuming that this side of it isn't too overwhelming, Saturation Reporting, as I think of it, can be one of the most exhilarating trips, as they say, in the world. Often you feel as if you've put your whole central nervous system on red alert and turned it into a receiving set with your head panning the molten tableau like a radar dish, with you saying, 'Come in, world,' since you only want ... all of it.... Some of the nicest times are when Pesky Danger rises, and the adrenalin flows, and the whole riot is on, and the shitfire rains from on high – and you discover that your set it still on! you're still combing the chaos for the details! the creamy stuff you can use! ... Why, that horrible fiend who just threw the sapper bomb in the ballet master's lap – was that a mishar or a bandana he had around his neck? And where is that little ace who was right up there next to him, the one with no chin – I can probably get the filthy Tartar's name from him – and ... 'Get whitey! Get whitey! Get whitey!' – they've started that crap again and they're heading straight this way – but did you ever notice that Mongol women are louder than the men, and bigger? – huge, fat and horrible, like the Green Bay Packers, the filthy rhinos ... and that one that's heading straight for me – Get whitey! – bleeding shitfire from her eyeballs – a 200-pound mongoloid porkchop Tartar – what the fuck is that she has stuck in her hair – why, it's a goddamned angel's food cake cutter ... and as it all comes down, as the world comes to an end, with an angel's food cake cutter slicing through the temporal fossa of my very melon – the wires have gotten crossed ... but in what a delicious way ... one coming straight from the Terror Panic terminal but the other carrying the message to a panting world: Friends! Citizens! Magazine readers! What a *scene* this is going to make! So help me, this is the way people live now! This is the – (gork)))))))))

# Part two
# The new journalism:
# An anthology

edited by Tom Wolfe
and E W Johnson

## Preface to the selections

E. W. Johnson and I chose these twenty-three pieces mainly with an eye toward illustrating the techniques writers have used in the New Journalism. It was only afterward that we saw that they also happen to cover a wide range of subjects, race, youth, war, politics, the money market, crime, the arts, show business, sports, and, in many different ways, the changes in styles of living in America over the past decade. They also range from pieces written in the early phases of the New Journalism (Gay Talese's and Terry Southern's) to Joe Eszterhas's 'Charlie Simpson's Apocalypse,' which was published only several weeks before this book was completed.

A number of these pieces are rough in spots, and here and there you will see writers giving in to old and rather banal conventions of magazine journalism, but that does not bother me. As yet the New Journalism has no canon of its own, and that may help to explain its vitality.

One more thing occurs to me as I glance over these pieces: not only is the New Journalism the first new direction in American literature in the last fifty years, but it was started mainly by writers in their thirties. A few were in their twenties when they wrote the pieces that appear here (Christgau, Goldstein, Eszterhas and Thompson), but the great majority were in their thirties (and two, Capote and Mailer, were in their forties). In most cases the New Journalism has been something that the writer has arrived at after spending years at another form of writing. Only now are large numbers of young writers beginning to aim straight toward the New Journalism from the outset. – T.W.

# Rex Reed from
# Do you sleep in the nude?

*Rex Reed, as I say, raised the celebrity interview to a new level through his frankness and his eye for social detail. He has also been a master at capturing a story line in the interview situation itself – in this case by picturing Ava Gardner as the aging star demanding star treatment. Reed occasionally uses the first person but never obtrusively; more on the order of Nick Carraway in The Great Gatsby, even when, as in this case, the interviewer – himself – becomes a factor in the story. Reed is excellent at recording and using dialogue. T.W.*

### Ava: Life in the afternoon

She stands there, without benefit of a filter lens against a room melting under the heat of lemony sofas and lavender walls and cream-and-peppermint-striped movie-star chairs, lost in the middle of that gilt-edge birthday-cake hotel of cupids and cupolas called the Regency. There is no script. No Minnelli to adjust the CinemaScope lens. Ice-blue rain beats against the windows and peppers Park Avenue below as Ava Gardner stalks her pink malted-milk cage like an elegant chee-tah. She wears a baby-blue cashmere turtleneck sweater pushed up to her Ava elbows and a little plaid mini-skirt and enormous black horn-rimmed glasses and she is gloriously, divinely barefoot.

Elbowing his way through the mob of autograph hunters and thrill seekers clustered in the lobby, all the way up in the gilt-encrusted elevator, the press agent Twentieth Century-Fox has sent along mur-murs, 'She doesn't see *anybody*, you know,' and 'You're very lucky, you're the only one she asked for.' Remembering, perhaps, the last time she had come to New York from her hideout in Spain to ballyhoo *The Night of the Iguana* and got so mad at the press she chucked the party and ended up at Birdland. And nervously, shifting feet under my Brooks Brothers polo coat, I remember too all the photographers at whom she allegedly threw champagne glasses (there is even a rumor that she shoved one Fourth Estater off a balcony!), and – who could forget, Charlie? – the holocaust she caused the time Joe Hyams showed up with a tape recorder hidden in his sleeve.

Now, inside the cheetah cage without a whip and trembling like a nervous bird, the press agent says something in Spanish to the Spanish maid. 'Hell, I've been there ten years and I still can't speak the goddamn language,' says Ava, dismissing him with a wave of the long porcelain Ava arms. 'Out! I don't need press agents.' The eyebrows angle under the glasses into two dazzling, sequined question marks. 'Can I trust him?' she asks, grinning that smashing Ava grin, and pointing at me. The press agent nods, on his way to the door: 'Is there anything else we can do for you while you're in town?'

'Just get me *out* of town, baby. Just get me *outta* here.'

The press agent leaves softly, walking across the carpet as if treading on rose glass with tap shoes. The Spanish maid (Ava insists she is royalty, 'She follows me around because she digs me') closes the door and shuffles off into another room.

'You *do* drink – right, baby? The last bugger who came to see me had the gout and wouldn't touch a drop.' She roars a cheetah roar that sounds suspiciously like Geraldine Page playing Alexandra Del Lago and mixes drinks from her portable bar: Scotch and soda for me, and for herself a champagne glass full of cognac with another champagne glass full of Dom Perignon, which she drinks successively, refills, and sips slowly like syrup through a straw. The Ava legs dangle limply from the arm of a lavender chair while the Ava neck, pale and tall as a milkwood vase, rises above the room like a Southern landowner inspecting a cotton field. At forty-four, she is still one of the most beautiful women in the world.

'Don't look at me. I was up until four A.M. at that goddam premiere of *The Bible*. Premieres! I will personally kill that John Huston if he ever drags me into another mess like that. There must have been ten thousand people clawing at me. I get claustrophobia in crowds and I couldn't breathe. Christ, they started off by shoving a TV camera at me and yelling, "Talk, Ava!" At intermission I got lost and couldn't find my goddam seat after the lights went out and I kept telling those little girls with the bubble hairdos and the flashlights, "I'm with John Huston," and they kept saying, "We don't know no Mr. Huston, is he from Fox?" There I was fumbling around the aisles in the dark and when I finally found my seat somebody was sitting in it and there was a big scene getting this guy to give me my seat back. Let me tell you, baby, Metro used to throw much better circuses than that. On top of it all, I lost my goddam mantilla in the limousine. Hell, it was no souvenir, that mantilla. I'll never find another one like it. Then Johnny Huston takes me to this party where we had to stand around and smile at Artie Shaw, who I was married to, baby, for Chrissake, and his wife, Evelyn Keyes, who Johnny Huston was once married to, for Chrissake. And after it's all over, what have you got? The biggest headache in town. Nobody cares who the hell was there. Do you think for one minute the fact that Ava Gardner showed up at that circus will sell that picture? Christ, did you *see* it? I went through all that hell just so this morning Bosley Crowther could write I looked like I was posing for a monument. All the way through it I kept punching Johnny on the arm and saying, "Christ, how could you let me do it?" Anyway, nobody cares what I wore or what I said. All they want to know anyway is was she drunk and did she stand up straight. This is the last circus. I am not a bitch! I am not temperamental! I am scared, baby. *Scared.* Can you possibly understand what it's like to feel scared?'

She rolls her sleeves higher than the elbows and pours two more champagne glasses full. There is nothing about the way she looks, up close, to suggest the life she has led: press conferences accompanied by dim lights and an orchestra; bullfighters writing poems about her in the press; rubbing Vaseline between her bosoms to emphasize the cleavage; roaming restlessly around Europe like a woman without a country, a Pandora with her suitcases full of cognac and Hershey bars ('for quick energy'). None of the ravaged, ruinous grape-colored lines to suggest the affairs or the brawls that bring the police in the middle of the night or the dancing on tabletops in Madrid cellars till dawn.

The doorbell rings and a pimply faced boy with a Beatle hairdo delivers one dozen Nathan's hot dogs, rushed from Coney Island in a limousine. 'Eat,' says Ava, sitting cross-legged on the floor, biting into a raw onion.

'You're looking at me again!' she says shyly, pulling short girlish wisps of hair behind the lobes of her Ava ears. I mention the fact that she looks like a Vassar co-ed in her mini-skirt. 'Vassar?' she asks suspiciously. 'Aren't they the ones who get in all the trouble?'

'That's Radcliffe.'

She roars. Alexandra Del Lago again. 'I took one look at myself in *The Bible* and went out this morning and got all my hair cut off. This is the way I used to wear it at MGM. It takes years off. What's *that*?' Eyes narrow, axing her guest in half, burning holes in my notebook. 'Don't tell me you're one of those people who always go around scribbling everything on little pieces of paper. Get rid of that. Don't take notes. Don't ask questions either because I probably won't answer any of them anyway. Just let Mama do all the talking. Mama knows best. You want to ask something, I can tell. Ask.'

I ask if she hates all her films as much as *The Bible*.

'Christ, what did I ever do worth talking about? Every time I tried to act, they stepped on me. That's why it's such a goddam shame, I've been a movie star for twenty-five years and I've got nothing, *nothing* to show for it. All I've got is three lousy ex-husbands, which reminds me, I've got to call Artie and ask him what his birthday is. I can't remember my own family's birthdays. Only reason I know my own is because I was born the same day as Christ. Well, almost. Christmas Eve, 1922. That's Capricorn, which means a lifetime of *hell*, baby. Anyway, I need Artie's birthday because I'm trying to get a new passport. I tramp around Europe, but I'm not giving up my citizenship, baby, for *anybody*. Did you ever try living in Europe and renewing your passport? They treat you like you're a goddam Communist or something. Hell, that's why I'm getting the hell out of Spain, because I hate Franco and I hate Communists. So now they want a list of all my divorces so I told them hell, call *The New York Times* — they know more about me than I do!'

But hadn't all those years at MGM been any fun at all? 'Christ, after seventeen years of slavery, you can ask that question? I hated it, honey. I mean, I'm not exactly stupid or without feeling, and they tried to sell me like a prize hog. They also tried to make me into something I was not then and never could be. They used to write in my studio bios that I was the daughter of a cotton farmer in Grabtown. How's that grab ya? Grabtown, North Carolina. And it looks exactly the way it sounds. I should have stayed there. The ones who never left home don't have a pot to pee in but they're happy. Me, look at me. What did it bring me?' She finishes off another round of cognac and pours a fresh one. 'The only time I'm happy is when I'm doing absolutely nothing. When I work I vomit all the time. I know nothing about acting so I have one rule — trust the director and give him heart and soul. And nothing else.' (Another cheetah roar.) 'I get a lot of money so I can afford to loaf a lot. I don't trust many people, so I only work with Huston now. I used to trust Joe Mankiewicz, but one day on the set of *The Barefoot Contessa* he did the unforgivable thing. He insulted me. He said, "You're the sittin'est goddam actress," and I never liked him after that. What I really want to do is get married again. Go ahead and laugh, everybody laughs, but how great it must be to tromp around barefoot and cook for some great goddam son of a bitch who loves you the rest of your life. I've never had a good man.'

What about Mickey Rooney? (A glorious shriek.) 'Love comes to Andy Hardy.'

Sinatra? 'No comment,' she says to her glass.

A slow count to ten, while she sips her drink. Then, 'And Mia Farrow?' The Ava eyes brighten to a soft clubhouse green. The answer comes like so many cats lapping so many saucers of cream. 'Hah! I always knew Frank would end up in bed with a boy.'

Like a phonograph dropping a new LP, she changes the subject. 'I only want to do the things that don't make me suffer. My friends are more important to me than anything. I know all kinds of people — bums, hangers-on, intellectuals, a few phonies. I'm going to see a college boy at Princeton tomorrow and we're going to a ballgame. Writers. I love writers. Henry Miller sends me books to improve my mind. Hell, did you read *Plexus?* I couldn't get through it. I'm not an intellectual, although when I was married to Artie Shaw I took a lot of courses at U.C.L.A. and got A's and B's in psychology and literature. I have a mind, but I never got a chance to use it doing every goddam lousy part in every goddam lousy picture Metro turned out. I *feel* a lot, though. God, I'm sorry I wasted those twenty-five years. My sister Dee Dee can't understand why after all these years I can't bear to face a camera. But I never brought anything to this business and I have no respect for acting. Maybe if I had learned something it would be different. But I never did anything to be proud of. Out of all those movies, what can I claim to have done?'

'*Mogambo, The Hucksters*—'

'Hell, baby, after twenty-five years in this business, if all you've got to show for it is *Mogambo* and *The Hucksters* you might as well give up. Name me one actress who survived all that crap at MGM. Maybe Lana Turner. Certainly Liz Taylor. But they all hate acting as much as I do. All except for Elizabeth. She used to come up to me on the set and say, "If only I could learn to be good," and by God, she made it. I haven't seen *Virginia Woolf* — hell, I *never* go to the movies — but I hear she is good. I never cared much about myself. I didn't have the emotional makeup for acting and I hate exhibitionists anyway. And who the hell was there to help me or teach me acting was anything else? I really tried in *Show Boat* but that was MGM crap. Typical of what they did to me there. I wanted to sing those songs — hell, I've still got a Southern accent — and I really thought Julie should sound a little like a

Negro since she's supposed to have Negro blood. Christ, those songs like "Bill" shouldn't sound like an opera. So, what did they say? "Ava, baby, you can't sing, you'll hit the wrong keys, you're up against real pros in this film, so don't make a fool of yourself." *Pros!* Howard Keel? And Kathryn Grayson, who had the biggest boobs in Hollywood? I mean I like Graysie, she's a sweet girl, but with her they didn't even need 3-D! Lena Horne told me to go to Phil Moore, who was her pianist and had coached Dorothy Dandridge, and he'd teach me. I made a damn good track of the songs and they said, "Ava, are you outta your head?" Then they got Eileen Wilson, this gal who used to do a lot of my singing on screen, and *she* recorded a track with the same background arrangement taken off *my* track. They substituted her voice for mine, and now in the movie my Southern twang stops talking and her soprano starts singing — hell what a mess. They wasted God knows how many thousands of dollars and ended up with crap. I still get royalties on the goddam records I did.'

. The doorbell rings and in bounces a little man named Larry. Larry has silver hair, silver eyebrows, and smiles a lot. He works for a New York camera shop. 'Larry used to be married to my sister Bea. If you think I'm something you ought to see Bea. When I was eighteen I came to New York to visit them and Larry took that picture of me that started this whole megilah. He's a sonuvabitch, but I love him.'

'Ava, I sure loved you last night in *The Bible*. You were really terrific, darlin'.'

'Crap!' Ava pours another cognac. 'I don't want to hear another word about that goddam *Bible*. I didn't believe it and I didn't believe that Sarah bit I played for a minute. How could anybody stay married for a hundred years to *Abraham*, who was one of the biggest bastards who ever lived?'

'Oh, darlin', she was a wonderful woman, that Sarah.'

'She was a jerk!'

'Oh, darlin', ya shouldn't talk like that. God will hear ya. Don'tcha believe in God?' Larry joins us on the floor and bites into a hot dog, spilling mustard on his tie.

'Hell, no.' The Ava eyes flash.

'I pray to him every night, darlin'. Sometimes he answers, too.'

'He never answered me, baby. He was never around when I needed him. He did nothing but screw up my whole life since the day I was born. Don't tell *me* about *God!* I know all about that bugger!'

The doorbell again. This time a cloak-and-dagger type comes in;

he's wearing an ironed raincoat, has seventeen pounds of hair, and looks like he has been living on plastic vegetables. He says he is a student at New York University Law School. He also says he is twenty-six years old. 'What?' Ava takes off her glasses for a closer look. 'Your father told me you were twenty-seven. Somebody's lying!' The Ava eyes narrow and the palms of her hands are wet.

'Let's get some air, fellas.' Ava leaps into the bedroom and comes out wearing a Navy pea jacket with a Woolworth scarf around her head. Vassar again.

'I thought you were gonna cook tonight, darlin',' says Larry, throwing his fist into a coat sleeve.

'I want spaghetti. Let's go to the Supreme Macaroni Company. They let me in the back door there and nobody ever recognizes anybody there. Spaghetti, baby. I'm starved.'

Ava slams the door shut, leaving all the lights on. 'Fox is paying, baby.' We all link arms and follow the leader. Ava skips ahead of us like Dorothy on her way to Oz. Lions and tigers and bears, oh my! Moving like a tiger through Regency halls, melting with hot pink, like the inside of a womb.

'Are those creeps still downstairs?' she asked. 'Follow me.'

She knows all the exits. We go down on the service elevator. About twenty autograph hunters crowd the lobby. Celia, queen of the autograph bums, who leaves her post on the door at Sardi's only on special occasions, has deserted her station for this. Ava's in town this week. She sits behind a potted palm wearing a purple coat and green beret, arms full of self-addressed postcards.

Cool.

Ava gags, pushes the horn-rims flat against her nose, and pulls us through the lobby. Nobody recognizes her. 'Drink time, baby!' she whispers, shoving me toward a side stairway that leads down to the Regency bar.

'Do you know who that was?' asks an Iris Adrian type with a mink-dyed fox on her arm as Ava heads for the bar. We check coats and umbrellas and suddenly we hear the soundtrack voice, hitting E-flat.

'You sonuvabitch! I could buy and sell you. How dare you insult my friends? Get me the manager!'

Larry is at her side. Two waiters are shushing Ava and leading us all to a corner booth. Hidden. Darker than the Polo Lounge. Hide the star. This is New York, not Beverly Hills.

'It's that turtleneck sweater you're wearing,' whispers Larry to me as the waiter seats me with my back to the room.

'They don't like me here, the bastards. I never stay in this hotel, but Fox is paying, so what the hell? I wouldn't come otherwise. They don't even have a jukebox, for Chrissake.' Ava flashes a smile in Metrocolor and orders a large ice-tea glass filled with straight tequila. 'No salt on the side. Don't need it.'

'Sorry about the sweater—' I begin.

'You're beautiful. Gr-r-r!' She laughs her Ava laugh and the head rolls back and the little blue vein bulges on her neck like a delicate pencil mark.

Two tequilas later ('I *said* no salt!') she is nodding grandly, surveying the bar like the Dowager Empress in the Recognition Scene. Talk buzzes around her like hummingbird wings and she hears nothing. Larry is telling about the time he got arrested in Madrid and Ava had to get him out of jail and the student is telling me about N.Y.U. Law School and Ava is telling *him* she doesn't believe he's only twenty-six years old and can he prove it, and suddenly he looks at his watch and says Sandy Koufax is playing in St. Louis.

'You're kidding!' Ava's eyes light up like cherries on a cake. 'Let's go! Goddamit we're going to St. Louis!'

'Ava, darlin', I gotta go to work tomòrrow.' Larry takes a heavy sip of his Grasshopper.

'Shut up, you bugger. If I pay for us all to go to St. Louis we go to St. Louis! Can I get a phone brought to this table? Someone call Kennedy airport and find out what time the next plane leaves. I *love* Sandy Koufax! I *love* Jews! God, sometimes I think I'm Jewish myself. A Spanish Jew from North Carolina. *Waiter!*'

The student convinces her that by the time we got to St. Louis they'd be halfway through the seventh inning. Ava's face falls and she goes back to her straight tequila.

'Look at 'em, Larry,' she says. 'They're such babies. Please don't go to Vietnam.' Her face turns ashen. Julie leaving the showboat with William Warfield singing 'Ol' Man River' in the fog on the levee. 'We gotta do it. . . .'

'What are you talkin' about, darlin'?' Larry shoots a look at the law student who assures Ava he has no intention of going to Vietnam.

'. . . didn't ask for this world, the buggers made us do it. . . .' A tiny bubble bath of sweat breaks out on her forehead and she leaps up from the table. 'My God, I'm suffocating! Gotta get some air!' She turns over the glass of tequila and three waiters are flying at us like bats, dabbing and patting and making great breathing noises.

*Action!*

The N.Y.U. student, playing Chance Wayne to her Alexandra Del Lago, is all over the place like a trained nurse. Coats fly out of the checkroom. Bills and quarters roll across the wet tablecloth. Ava is on the other side of the bar and out the door. On cue, the other customers, who have been making elaborate excuses for passing our table on their way to the bathroom, suddenly give great breathy choruses of 'Ava' and we are through the side door and out in the rain.

Then as quickly as it started it's over. Ava is in the middle of Park Avenue, the scarf falling around her neck and her hair blowing wildly around the Ava eyes. Lady Brett in the traffic, with a downtown bus as the bull. Three cars stop on a green light and every taxi driver on Park Avenue begins to honk. The autograph hunters leap through the polished doors of the Regency and begin to scream. Inside, still waiting coolly behind the potted palm, is Celia, oblivious to the noise, facing the elevators, firmly clutching her postcards. No need to risk missing Ava because of a minor commotion on the street. Probably Jack E. Leonard or Edie Adams. Catch them next week at Danny's.

Outside, Ava is inside the taxi flanked by the N.Y.U. student and Larry, blowing kisses to the new chum, who will never grow to be an old one. They are already turning the corner into Fifty-seventh Street, fading into the kind of night, the color of tomato juice in the headlights, that only exists in New York when it rains.

'Who was it?' asks a woman walking a poodle.

'Jackie Kennedy,' answers a man from his bus window.

# Gay Talese from
# The overreachers

*This was the first story that Gay Talese wrote completely within a short-story format. Talese had been a great fan of the short stories of Irwin Shaw and John O'Hara and had been interested to see if he could adapt their techniques to nonfiction. He used to block out his stories scene by scene on a large wallboard to see if he could bring out every point he wanted to make via a scene rather than historical narration. Talese almost always kept the narrator — i.e., the reporter himself — invisible, as O'Hara and Shaw tended to do. Talese did not start using full-blown point of view, however, until the late 1960s. The device would have strengthened a story such as this one; but the technical polish is still impressive. T.W.*

### The soft psyche of Joshua Logan

The theatre lights dimmed, and the jewels in the audience sparkled like a city seen at night from an airplane; then the music began, the curtain went up, and row upon row of bow ties settled, like a flutter of black butterflies, into their seats. It was the premier performance of *Mr. President* and, though the road reviews were disastrous and the show was unimproved at this Broadway opening, the audience rushed backstage at the final curtain with their furs and first-night faces to greet the director, Joshua Logan, with 'Dah-ling, it was mahvelous!' ... 'Joshua, congratulations!' ... 'Wonderful, Josh, wonderful!'

He knew they did not mean it, and they knew they did not mean it, but very little truth is exchanged backstage on opening nights; the newspaper critics panned the show, with one, John McClain of the *Journal-American*, asking: 'Whatever became of the unerring hand of Mr. Logan?'

The unerring hand, Mr. Logan would have liked to have replied, had been tied behind his back by his associates during rehearsals, but such a disclosure would be to no avail and hardly gracious; and so here he was, in the Fall of 1962, stung successively by three critical flops (the two others being *All American* and *There Was a Little Girl*), knowing that his next Broadway play, opening in eight weeks, had better be good. Already there was talk around Sardi's that his directorial taste was lost in vulgarity, and some of his friends noticed with concern the increasing pressure he was subjecting himself to with *Tiger Tiger Burning Bright*. In 1941 and 1953, he had spent time in mental institutions.

From the very first week of *Tiger*'s rehearsals, at the Booth Theatre on Forty-fifth Street, there was tension, strange reactions and uncertainty, and the actors – all but one of them Negroes – seemed suspicious of Logan and envious of each other's roles. Claudia McNeil, the star of *Tiger*, an enormous woman, very dark, glared silently each day at Logan, measuring him, seeming to possess in her attitude the secret of his weakness and the power to destroy him; and Joshua Logan, at fifty-four, white-haired, white-mustached, big and broadshouldered but somehow soft and very pale, stood in front of the Negro cast of this play about a mother who dominates her children in a dream world she has created in Louisiana – a play that gradually, as rehearsals progressed, churned up more and more memories for Logan, haunting memories of his days in Mansfield, Louisiana, on his grandfather's cotton plantation, where, in his boyhood dreams, he often saw himself as a strong man riding through the streets of Mansfield standing on a horse, arms folded high across his chest. In real life, young Joshua Logan had recognized in himself not the slightest resemblance to his imaginary masculine hero.

He saw himself as a flabby and effete boy who, since his father's early death, was reared on his maternal grandfather's plantation under the almost claustrophobic attention of females. There was his sister, Mary Lee, endlessly worrying about him; his Negro nurse, Amy Lane, often mad at him but always watching him through the kitchen window and saying, 'Mah, he walkin' jes like ole Judge Logan!'; and there was his mother, Susan, who dressed him prettily, read him poetry, and tried to divert him from all that was crude or vulgar. One afternoon in the middle of a Biblical movie, just before Judith of Bethulia sliced off the head of Holofernes, Susan Logan, not wanting Joshua to see it, blocked his view by pushing him under the seat; then she whispered, sharply, 'Think of a field of yellow daisies ... think of a field of yellow daisies!'

Susan Logan was an elegant, genteel lady of the Old South whose family, like that of her late first husband's (he was also named Joshua Lockwood Logan), had originally settled in South Carolina. The first

Joshua Lockwood had come to America from County Kent, England, and died sixteen miles outside of Charleston in the middle 1700's. While carrying his remains for burial to Charleston, the cortege was attacked by a pack of wolves and was compelled to bury his bones by the roadside nine miles from Charleston, and the widow was so shocked that she quickly returned to England. But some years later one of her sons, also named Joshua, returned to Charleston, and here his family later enjoyed a congeniality with two other Charleston families, the Logans and the Lees, and subsequently there was intermarriage; so today, Susan, descendant from the Lees, is not only the mother of the Broadway director, she is also his cousin.

By the 1830's some branches of the Lockwoods, Lees and Logans had moved from South Carolina down into Alabama, and a generation later others moved into northwest Louisiana, where Susan's father settled on a cotton plantation, into which she moved upon the death of her husband with her three-year-old son, Joshua, her infant daughter, Mary Lee, and that ruler of the rear of the house, Amy Lane.

Susan despised Mansfield; it was an uncultured, wide-open pioneer town of feuds and barroom brawls, having none of the tradition of the Old South, the Charleston of her dreams, but reeking instead of the Wild West, with its heavy accent on bad manners and maleness. Susan tried, as best she could, to see that none of the crudity of this town infected Joshua, and she succeeded even though one day, perhaps when a circus was moving into town, there suddenly registered in Joshua the image of the man riding through Mansfield standing up on a horse – a marvelous man, perfectly balanced; a free man, ignoring the reins.

As Joshua Lockwood Logan approached his teens, his grandfather began to complain that Susan was making the boy into a sissy. Joshua adored his grandfather ('I put Tabasco in my milk to please him') and soon became a superb swimmer, a subscriber to the Charles Atlas bodybuilding course, and, at Culver Military Academy in Indiana – which Joshua attended because of his mother's remarriage in 1917 to Colonel Howard F. Noble, an administrator there – he also became trained as a boxer. Encouraged by Colonel Noble, to whom Joshua later dedicated his play, *The Wisteria Trees*, he trained hard in the ring, eventually winning the boxing title of the platoon, the company, the battalion, and finally the regiment. But every time he won, and had his hand held high in victory, Joshua would moan to himself, 'Oh, God!' – the triumph meaning he had to fight somebody else, and he hated it.

After Culver there was Princeton, a school selected by Joshua's mother because it was 'nice' and 'there would be less drinking there'; and after Princeton, where he became president of the Triangle Club, and after a trip to Moscow where he studied for six months under Stanislavski, Joshua Logan settled in New York and embarked on a career as a theatrical director. When Colonel Noble died, Joshua's mother drove up to New York and moved in with him; and later, when he was directing two shows at once – one in New Jersey by night, the other in New York by day – his mother would greet him at Pennsylvania Station each morning with a pint of fruit juice. 'The only way Josh could get away from his mother,' said a friend who knew him very well, 'was through the door of an insane asylum – a door that locked.'

After his first mental breakdown in 1941, from sheer exhaustion and dejection over his work, he recovered in a Philadelphia sanitarium and, by 1942, was back on Broadway directing a successful show, *By Jupiter*. In 1953, while rehearsing *Kind Sir* and battling simultaneously with agents and lawyers over the film rights to Michener's novel, *Sayonara*, Logan had another breakdown; a year later, he had recovered and had another hit, *Fanny*.

Now, almost nine years later, in these daily rehearsals of *Tiger Tiger Burning Bright*, adapted for the stage by Peter S. Feibleman from his novel, *A Place Without Twilight*, Joshua Logan discovered that he was becoming so emotionally involved with the script, and identifying so strongly with its characters – and at the same time becoming intimidated by the actors, especially by Claudia McNeil, who he felt was acting like Amy Lane – that it seemed he might be involved once again with Mansfield, the source of his old wounds and boyhood complexities; a trip, one might assume, that he could ill afford to make. He needed the success of this play, and he had many obligations, both mundane and financial; he and his wife, Nedda, had two adopted children in private school; there was the upkeep on his fabulous apartment on the East River, and his directorial staff, and his film company, his chauffeur, his cook, his psychiatrist that he visits five mornings a week, his big Connecticut home with its sprawling grounds and magnificently manicured gardens. Though Logan earns in the neighborhood of $500,000 a year, it somehow seems barely enough and one evening after a hard day's rehearsal of *Tiger*, Logan left the theatre and said, wearily, 'I work for gardens and psychiatrists.'

He went easy on the actors. When they fumbled their lines, he remained patient. He gave them the benefit of his knowledge of 'South-western' diction — 'down there they pronounce it "LOU-iz-iana," not "Lou-e-ZEE-ana"' — and he would relieve the tension (or, at least, try) by telling anecdotes about past Broadway shows he directed, about Mary Martin in *South Pacific*, and about *Mister Roberts*, all the while speaking with warmth, and admitting that he did not yet know all the answers about how to stage *Tiger*, and welcoming any actor's suggestions at any time. 'I'm not a puppeteer,' he would tell them. 'I am simply an editor, a sort of audience, and a friend, a sort of encourager that nobody should be scared of — or *angry* at.'

Then, in the second week of rehearsals, things got worse. Parts of the first act were rewritten, the actors had to learn new lines and forget old ones, and they were disappointed that the role of the male lead, the prowling son who is to symbolize the tiger cat, went to Alvin Ailey, a dancer. Even some of Logan's associates, who sat in the dark theatre each day watching, were becoming uneasy.

'Goddamit, Josh, that Alvin just doesn't move like a tiger!'

'No,' Logan admitted, 'he's Nijinsky.'

'For that part you need a black Brando.'

'Yes,' said Logan.

'We open in three weeks.'

'Christ!' said Feibleman.

'Oh, don't worry,' said Oliver Smith, the co-producer.

'I *am* worried,' said Logan.

The next day, after Ailey had played a sultry scene with the curvaceous, hip-swinging Diana Sands, he suddenly flew across the stage and buried his face in a corner behind the curtain. There was silence for a second. Then, slowly, the theatre began to echo with what sounded like high, howling laughter; then, more quickly, the laughter dissolved into uncontrollable, almost hysterical sobbings. Everybody was stunned; nobody moved — neither on the stage nor in the orchestra.

Finally, Peter Feibleman, who had been sitting near the back of the theatre, came rushing down the aisle to Logan, sitting in the seventh row.

'Josh,' Feibleman whispered, 'you better do something.'

'What can *I* do?' Logan said, running his hand through his long white hair. 'He'll just have to get it out of him.'

'I want the Miltown concession on this play,' said Joe Curtis, one of Logan's assistants, sitting across the aisle.

'Trouble is,' Logan said, 'I'll take it all.' Then, shaking his head as Ailey's sobbing continued, with Claudia McNeil now comforting him,

Logan said to Curtis, 'You know, I'm getting a real vicarious pleasure out of this. Alvin's doing just what I want to do — just lie down and cry!'

Still Logan, Feibleman and Oliver Smith all thought Ailey could do the part; he certainly *looked* the part, they agreed, possessing a muscular body that seemed more powerful than Sonny Liston's; and besides, it was a little late to be shopping around for a new tiger. Logan felt that, if the book were stronger, the actors would feel more secure; so for the next three days Logan disappeared with Feibleman in a little room offstage and reworked the book — removing some of Feibleman's literary flavor in the spots where Logan felt the audience would want action.

'Where the hell *is* Logan?' Claudia McNeil grumbled, on the third morning of rehearsing lines under the production stage manager, David Gray, Jr. Claudia was still furious at Logan for having left the theatre at midafternoon earlier in the week without having 'the courtesy, the respect' to let her know he'd not return that day; now, with Logan working elsewhere on the script and ignoring the acting completely, Claudia was smoldering. With the other actors gathered around her offstage, as in a family scene in the play itself, she roared: 'Logan should be here! We ain't gettin' no direction.'

'And our reputations are at stake,' Diana Sands said.

'His is, too!' Claudia snapped. 'He doesn't realize it, but if he thinks he's going to blame this one on me if it's a flop, well, he ain't: I'll just get on that phone and call Sally Hammond over at the *Post*, or that guy at the *Tribune* — what'shisname? one that married that actress? Morgenstern, that's it — and I'll tell 'em the whole story, about how we have to come here and listen to nine of his jokes, and all about LOU-iziana, and then he don't show up for three days!'

The others nodded, and she went on, 'All this rewriting should be done at night! What the hell does he do at night? *Sheet!* People gonna look at me and think I shot my bolt in *Raisin in the Sun* and have nothing new to offer; well, that ain't fair.... I got enough trouble, working with a lot of kids in this show, and carrying the responsibility for my whole race, being in the theatre thirty years, and this man Logan don't even show up! *Sheet!*'

A few minutes later, the door swung open, and in walked Logan, followed by Peter Feibleman, who was carrying fresh, revised pages of Act I. As Logan waved and walked down the side steps off the stage toward the orchestra, Claudia watched him go up the aisle toward the back of the theatre, and she waited; within ten minutes, she saw her chance.

In the middle of one of her monologues. Claudia caught a glimpse of Logan whispering to Feibleman. It was as if she were Amy Lane catching Joshua's little hand in the cookie jar. Flaring up, Claudia bellowed to Oliver Smith, the co-producer, sitting alone about nine rows back, 'Mr. Logan is talking! And I can't go on!'

'I am *not* talking,' Logan yelled from the back, his voice tense and angry.

'You *were* talking,' Claudia said. 'I could hear what you were saying!'

'I was *not* talking,' he insisted. 'Somebody else was talking. It was *not* me!'

'YOU were talking!' she shouted, hunching her big shoulders and blazing her big eyes at him. 'And you spoiled the meter of my speech!'

'Look,' Logan said, stomping down the aisle toward where Oliver Smith sat, 'I do not want any more rages from *you!*'

'You're in a rage, not me!' she said.

'Well, I'm not going to stand for this!'

'You want me to leave?' she asked, challengingly.

'Look,' he said, more softly, 'everybody here is trying to get this play. I cannot s-t-a-n-d these outrages. What do you want us to do, close the show?'

Claudia now turned, hunched her shoulders again, and paced back and forth.

'Now,' Logan said, trying to get things moving again, noticing that the rest of the cast was standing in almost fixed, dumb-struck poses on the stage. 'Now, why don't you go back further and begin again?'

'I *can't* begin,' she said, casually. 'You spoiled my meter.'

'O-h-h-h, Oliver,' Logan groaned, his hand on his forehead, 'I can't stand these rages!'

'Well,' she shot in, 'that's *your* problem.'

'*You're my problem!*' Logan screamed.

Now, everybody in the theatre was squirming. Fortunately, Claudia did not answer him; she just shuffled around a bit, like a sumo wrestler waiting for the decision; in the prolonged silence, things calmed a bit, and Claudia did her monologue and David Gray yelled 'Curtain,' and everybody sighed. There was a break.

Standing outside the Booth Theatre, his hands in his pockets and the cold breezes of autumn whistling through his long white hair, Joshua Logan said, 'Right now I'm allowing Claudia McNeil to do a lot of things just because I trust her, and admire her creative talent, and do not want to freeze that talent, and yet I know I have a block with her.

'You see,' he said, 'Amy Lane, every once in a while, would get mad and her face would turn grey. When Amy Lane was happy her face was brown, sometimes purple; but she used to scare me when she was mad; and when she was happy she used to help me, dress me, tie up my shoelaces and do my buttonholes; and now I've got this show, and a sort of Amy Lane that every once in a while turns grey. And I want to help her — I've got to help her — figure out the creative shoelaces and buttonholes. And sometimes I wonder if I'm strong enough to do that.'

He walked around a bit more, inhaling deeply along Shubert Alley next to the theatre. 'It's funny,' he finally said, 'but somehow I'm actually happy doing this play. Maybe it's the Negroes. Somehow, in a small way, I'm making up for ... for how they have been made to feel. I don't know. But *something* must be making me happy. I remember, as a child, wanting to *be* a Negro; I remember their sweetness, their gentle voices, and mostly their freedom — they were free to run and run without shoes, without clothes, they didn't have to be clean, didn't have to go to church three times a week. They did not have, in the modern term, to conform. In a sense,' he said, slowly, 'they ruled *us* — kind of kept us in our place; they were more powerful, the power of the weak; only they weren't weak, they had the power of servility.'

Now he was back in the dark theatre, the lights of the stage beaming on the actors going through a scene in the garden of their Louisiana shack; Claudia McNeil's voice was now softer because she had had a touch of laryngitis a few days before. But at the end of the scene, she raised her voice to its full power, and Logan, in a pleasant tone, said, 'Don't strain your voice, Claudia.'

She did not respond, only whispered to another actor on stage.

'Don't raise your voice, Claudia,' Logan repeated.

She again ignored him.

'CLAUDIA!' Logan yelled, 'don't you give me that actor's vengeance, Claudia!'

'Yes, Mr. Logan,' she said with a soft, sarcastic edge.

'I've had enough of this today, Claudia.'

'Yes, Mr. Logan.'

'And stop Yes-Mr.-Logan-ing me.'

'Yes, Mr. Logan.'

'You're a shockingly rude woman!'

'Yes, Mr. Logan.'

'You're being a beast.'

'Yes, Mr. Logan.'

'Yes, Miss Beast.'

'Yes, Mr. Logan.'

*'Yes, Miss Beast!'*

Suddenly, Claudia McNeil stopped. It dawned on her that he was calling her a beast; now her face was grey and her eyes were cold, and her voice almost solemn as she said, 'You ... called ... me ... out ... of ... my ... name!'

'Oh, God!' Logan smacked his forehead with his hand.

'You ... called ... me ... out ... of ... my ... name!'

She stood there, rocklike, big and angry, waiting for him to do something.

'Oliver!' Logan said, turning toward the co-producer, who had lowered his wiry, long body into his chair as if he were in a foxhole. He did not want to be cornered into saying something that might offend Logan, his old friend, but neither did he want Claudia McNeil to come barreling down the aisle and possibly snap his thin frame in half.

'Oliver,' Logan went on, 'I just don't know what to do with her. She's like some queen up there, or something. ...'

'You're the queen!' she bolted back.

'All right, all right, I'm the queen,' Logan said, too weary to argue about it. 'What do we do now?'

'Get yourself another actress,' she said.

'All right, fine,' Logan said. 'Fine,' he repeated. 'We can close the show, and, we can. ...' Now he was walking up the aisle, and it seemed that he might be leaving the theatre.

'Look,' Claudia quickly said. He stopped.

'Look,' she began again, realizing that if this show closed *she* would be the reason for all the other actors' unemployment, 'I ... I gotta man at home I can get mad at ... and I been in the theatre thirty years ... and nobody is ever going to point a finger at me that I walked off a show ... and. ...'

She went on like this, and Logan knew he had her; he could have played with her a while, letting her sweat it out, but he didn't. Instead he walked toward the stage, climbed it, and then, faster now, he moved toward Claudia and, arms outstretched, moved into her, his white mustache pressing against her cheek — and then, dramatically, her big, black arms lashed around the back of his white shirt and pulled him close.

They were almost tearful in their reunion, these two big, soft figures under the lights; they suddenly were spent, and the cast gathered around and whistled, hollered and clapped.

Then, cheerfully, Claudia pulled back and, grinning as she shook her fist, said, 'But when this show is over, I'm gonna hit you in the mouth so-o-o hard!'

'When this show is over,' he laughed back, 'you won't be able to catch me!'

'I'll catch you,' she promised.

'You'll need a long reach,' he said, 'because I'll be gone!'

After this scene, the show improved tremendously in the final two weeks. Nobody was saying it was going to be a hit; but they were saying it would at least open. Claudia was not sure if Logan would condone another shooting match, so she calmed down. Logan, of course, did not look for trouble. If, while Claudia was rehearsing on stage, he wished to get some fresh air, he did not leave by way of the stage door (where she might see him) but would often slip through the darkness near the back of the theatre — an operation that meant he had to unhinge four latches and a lock and move quietly, in the manner he might have sneaked out of the house in Mansfield, hoping Amy Lane would not hear. On returning, he would be just as quiet; Claudia would be onstage but would not hear him: he was safe.

In addition to the improved relations between Logan and Claudia, the script was much better and Alvin Ailey had mastered the difficult tiger role, because he got control of himself, partly through Logan's help. Al Freeman, Jr.'s portrayal of Ailey's weak brother produced some fine comic acting, and the play was also strengthened by two late additions — Roscoe Lee Browne, who played the sinister clergyman who blackmails Ailey, and Paul Barry, the only white actor in the show, who won the part of a seedy Louisiana redneck over five other actors, one of them an old acquaintance of Joshua Logan's from Mister Roberts. Logan greeted his Roberts friend warmly, but soon realized that the actor was portraying a redneck as if he were a Naval officer, and so Logan shook his hand — 'Thanks, Bob, but I think, chemically, and from the point of view of age, you're not right for the part' — and then he said to Feibleman, 'You can't go back, can you, Peter?'

'You sure can't, Josh,' Feibleman said, quietly.

●    ●    ●

But if Logan were able to go back, there is no doubt it would be to the days of *Mister Roberts*, which he described as those 'high, happy times' with that tragic young novelist, Thomas Heggen. They got along famously as co-authors of the play, Logan said, because 'I was a corpulent manic depressive and Heggen was a thin manic depressive.' Sprawled out one night on a red, yellow and blue rug that Nedda had bought at a Bridgeport junk shop, Logan and Heggen dashed off the whole second act in one hilarious session. The show ran on Broadway for 1,157 performances.

These were the days when Howard Lindsay declared that Logan was a 'genius' and when the late Oscar Hammerstein II said Logan was blessed with everything a great director should have — a good eye for pictorial composition and movement, an ear for dialogue and diction, a charm that keeps a big company working happily together, a talent for analyzing a script and improving it by criticism and revision. Playwright Paul Osborn then said that Logan could not 'walk along a street and watch a kid pick a cigarette butt up out of the gutter without wanting to grab the kid and tell him to pick it up better.'

Then, in May, 1949, Heggen, who was unable to get his own writing going again, drowned in his bathtub. He was twenty-nine years old. But Logan has still tried to hold onto the memory of the glorious days of *Mister Roberts*. He named his son Thomas Heggen Logan, and he still keeps the old red, yellow and blue rug from the junk shop in an honored place within his Connecticut home.

Logan has had many triumphs since then — *South Pacific*, *The Wisteria Trees*, *Picnic* — but he still looks back on *Mister Roberts* as the high point, and still says, slowly and rather sadly, 'That was the happiest time of my life.'

In 1953 Logan was back in Louisiana to open *Kind Sir* in New Orleans, and was battling at the same time to get the screen rights to *Sayonara*, and then, almost too suddenly to know how it all happened, he found himself one day back in Mansfield. He wandered about the old plantation. He looked at the wisteria tree that his grandfather had been unable to chop down. Then, not quite realizing what he was doing, Joshua Logan crawled back into 'Jolly Den,' the playhouse that his grandfather had built long ago for Joshua and Mary Lee. Then Logan drove back to New Orleans. He committed himself to De Paul Hospital.

'You ask if I shall finally be able to stop going to the psychiatrist,' he said, walking across Third Avenue toward his apartment one evening a week before the opening of *Tiger Tiger Burning Bright.* 'Well, I don't really know. You ask what's the matter with me, what it is that keeps me from being satisfied or completely happy, or smug, or completely serene about my life, and I think it is something that happened to me when I was a young boy and set a standard for myself that I could never live up to. I could never be as good as I wanted to be – would never ride through Mansfield standing on a horse with my arms folded high in front of me.'

This does not mean that Logan has failed to make *some* peace with himself in his later years; for one thing, he said, almost proudly, 'I have finally stopped being a shit-kicker. Know what a shit-kicker is, don't you? That's one of those modest bastards, those falsely modest, aw-shucks guys' – and he demonstrated by walking, hands in pockets, head down, with feet dragging. No, he is by no means modest, he said, even though his mother is a bit disappointed in him, and once, after he had reminded her that he was a Pulitzer Prize winner (for *South Pacific*) she reminded him that *that* was for a collaboration – letting him know she knew the difference between a man who could win such a prize, and a man who could ride the horse *alone.*

'Anyway,' Logan went on, 'I know what I can do. I know I have the ability to organize accident. I know I can pump people full of confidence. I can reassure a person who is in doubt. I know that every artist is in despair, and to allow them more despair would kill hope, and so I try to bring hope and banish despair. When I feel it coming on, I will it away, when I can – I not always can – but I know if I should panic in the midst of a big production, then the production would fall apart. I have directed people who, they say, couldn't be directed, such as Marilyn Monroe, and I knew she needed affection, respect, love and care, and so that's what I did, and no matter how her panic showed, I never let it make me angry or impatient.

'But,' he continued, now more slowly, thinking more deeply, 'I think if I were free of whatever it is – if I were free-r – I think I could write ... write more than Marcel Proust ... couldn't *stop* writing. But it is as though it were all dammed up to here,' he said, gripping his throat with his left hand, 'and I have a theory – *just* a theory – that if I wrote, it would please my mother *too much.* It would be what she wanted. And maybe ... maybe *then* I'd become like my father. And I would die.'

Now Logan was silent the rest of the way home. Then, on the fourteenth floor, the locale of his grand apartment overlooking the East River, he was greeted at the door by the butler and, in the next room, by Nedda, an erect, smiling, lovely woman who was his leading lady in one of his first big Broadway hits, *Charley's Aunt*, and who has remained constant through all his good and bad days. While Logan went into the other room for a moment, Nedda talked about their seventeen years of marriage that began, on December 8, 1945, with a civil ceremony in Greenwich, Connecticut; then they drove back to New York to inform Susan, who said, according to Nedda, 'Well, isn't that lovely. Let us have a little glass of sherry.'

In those days Nedda had been living at the Hotel Lombardy, at 111 East 56th Street, while Joshua's mother was at 102 East 56th Street; now, Nedda said, with her address being 435 East 52nd, Joshua's mother was at 424 East 52nd. 'I am exactly the same distance from Mrs. Noble now as I was then,' Nedda said, smiling as only a good actress can.

When Joshua returned to the room, and realized the conversation had gotten back to his mother, he joined Nedda in telling their favorite Susan Noble stories. Joshua recalled that once he received a letter from her telling him that one of his relatives had just been drafted, and was being sent to Fort Bragg, North Carolina, and how nice it was for the drafted relation to be in North Carolina 'at rhododendron time.'

And Nedda recalled a family trip they all made a few years ago to Charleston, during which a visit was made to the cemeteries where the earlier Lockwoods, Lees and Logans were buried. Upon seeing these familiar names on the gravestones, these names she had so long worshiped, Susan suddenly was as graceful as a young ballerina, picking her way delicately and joyously and whirling around; finally, seeing Nedda with a camera, Susan pulled Josh toward her and asked Nedda to shoot a picture of the two of them standing next to the tomb of a very special ancestor. 'Stand *here*, Josh ... over *here*,' Susan snapped, because Josh was too far from the gravestone, '*here* next to Dorothea ... she's the important one; *she*'s the one that makes us cousins!'

They told other stories about Susan, too, and Josh concluded, 'Oh, she'll fascinate you!'

'She's seventy-six,' said Nedda, 'and she'll outlive us all.'

'You *should* meet her,' Logan said.

A few days later, on one of New York's most unseasonably warm autumn days, Susan Noble opened the door of her apartment. Behind her, under the mantel, a big fire was blazing. 'Good moan-nin.' She smiled. 'I hope you don't mind the fa'ar.'

She was a remarkable-looking woman, not seeming much older than fifty, with grey-blue eyes, a trim figure, and hair that was still black streaked with grey, and pulled back from her face, which was soft, gentle and vivacious. In the vestibule hung a portrait of Colonel Noble, straight-spined in military splendor; on another wall, a print by William Blake, and, in the living room, there was furniture from the South – from the plantation, some of it in the family for several generations. After pouring coffee and serving cookies, she displayed, on request, that which she treasures, the family album, and in no time at all her alert eyes were sparkling, her hand was moving softly over the pages, and her voice was dramatically rich.

'Look,' she said, smiling at the little figure of Joshua in a colonial outfit, 'pink satin. See! I did the coat.... And *here* is little May-rey.... And this was my mother's voice teacher. Wasn't she pretty? ... And this, now *this* was my great-aunt.... And look at that dapper! Oh, I just adore that man, one of my cousins, Henry Lee! ... And now this, this is Grandfather Lee, John Bachman Lee, named after old Dr. John Bachman, you know, a friend of Audubon, with many birds named Bachman.... And this, sitting next to John McHenry Nabors, is Nimrod, the dog named for that great hunter in the Bible...' – and then, at the mention of her father, she paused. 'He thought I was pulling Josh too hard, but Josh grew up loving beauty. My father felt I was making Josh into a sissy, but that was not true. He was a *man* – a *man* from the time he was a child. And I did all I could to make him a man. That's all I *could* do! I couldn't play baseball. But,' she said, 'I also felt that a man has a right to that which is beautiful in life.'

Then she glanced down at the book again. 'Look,' she said, her eyes once more sparkling, 'there's Caroline Dorothy Logan, Josh's great-great-grandmother.... And here, here's Josh again! ... And here, I believe, is Nedda....'

On Saturday night, December 22, outside the Booth Theatre, all dressed up – as in a picture album – they came to see *Tiger Tiger Burning Bright.* There was Susan Noble arriving early ... and next Nedda, in a fur cape and red satin dress ... and Logan's assistant, Joe Curtis ... and Oliver Smith ... and Peter Feibleman, a white carnation in his trimly tailored tuxedo ... and there was Richard Rodgers and Carson McCullers and Geoffrey Holder and Santha Rama Rau....

'Where's Josh?' Roger Stevens, the co-producer, asked Nedda.

'102 degrees,' she said.

He was in bed in his apartment, alone except for the children; he was, for the first time he could remember, sick on opening night. He was very pale and very quiet, and he spoke about a trip to Acapulco that he, Nedda and the two children would take after Christmas. After that, he was not sure what he wanted to do. There were movies. There were other shows. But he did not know. It had been a tough year. He went on like this, talking softly, until eleven, when the telephone rang.

'Darling,' said Nedda, her voice coming through over the clinking of glasses from Sardi's, 'darling, Dick Rodgers wants to speak with you.'

'Hello, Josh?'

'Hello, Dick!'

'Now, listen, Josh, this thing you got here tonight, no crap, Josh, it was marvelous!'

Logan seemed unable to speak.

'Really!' Rodgers went on, 'I think it's the best job you've done in many years, Josh. It was brilliant! Can't tell you how much I enjoyed it!'

'Oh, Dick.' Logan seemed almost happy enough for tears. 'Thank you, Dick ... thank you....'

Then Nedda was back on the phone, then Feibleman, then Oliver Smith, and then others – all saying that the premier of *Tiger* was a thing of beauty which the audience loved.

Since there was a New York newspaper strike then, Logan got the reviews over television while sitting in bed: Walter Kerr of the *Herald-Tribune* liked some parts, not others; Howard Taubman of the *Times* was ecstatic, giving it possibly his warmest review of the year; the other reviews varied, but one television announcer summed them up as 'respectful.'

This is all Logan had hoped for. Something respectful. He did not need the big, box-office smash; he'd had plenty of those. And what he *did* want, he suspected he might never get.

Well, at least he had stopped being a shit-kicker; and – who knows? Soon some new young genius might come up with another *Mister Roberts*. So Logan settled back in the big bed waiting for Nedda. Three days later he, Nedda and the children left for Acapulco.

And after thirty-three performances, the play closed.

# Richard Goldstein
# Gear

*'Gear' was one of a series of pieces in the* Village Voice *that made a name for Richard Goldstein shortly after his graduation from the Columbia School of Journalism in 1966. The form, which attracted many journalists during the 1960s, is the 'sketch.' Dickens* (Sketches by Boz), *Thackeray* (The Yellowplush Papers, A Book of Snobs), *Stephen Crane and many other nineteenth-century novelists wrote journalistic sketches that are generally viewed as warm-ups for their novels. In fact, there is little to distinguish a sketch from a short story except for the writer's primarily journalistic intention of presenting a realistic picture of a current character-type rather than telling a story. The tone is usually light, and the strength of the sketch is usually in the details of status life and a single, central insight into the type. The sketch is a special case and qualifies as journalism only because it aspires to nothing more than to give an accurate picture of a type of person rather than a specific individual. If pushed much beyond that it can hardly be characterized as journalism. T.W.*

Too early to get up, especially on Saturday. The sun peeks over his windowsill. Isolated footsteps from the street. Guys who have to work on Saturday. Boy! That's what they'll call you all your life if you don't stay in school. Forty-five definitions, two chapters in *Silas Marner*, and three chem labs. On Sunday night, he will sit in his room with the radio on, bobbing back and forth on his bed, opening the window wide and then closing it, taking a break to eat, to comb his hair, to dance, to hear the Stones – anything. Finally, cursing wildly and making ugly faces at himself in the mirror, he will throw *Silas Marner* under the bed and spend an hour watching his tortoise eat lettuce.

In the bathroom he breaks three screaming pimples. With a tooth-pick he removes four specks of food from his braces, skirting barbed wires and week-old rubber bands. Brooklyn Bridge, railroad tracks, they call him. Metal mouth. They said he smiled like someone was forcing him to. Bent fingers with filthy nails. Caved-in chest with eight dangling hairs. A face that looks like the end of a watermelon, and curly hair – not like the Stones, not at all like Brian Jones – but muddy curls running down his forehead and over his ears. A bump. Smashed by a bat thrown wildly. When he was eight. Hunchback Quasimodo – Igor – Rodan on his head. A bump. Nobody hip has a bump or braces. Or hair like a fucking Frankenstein movie. He licks his braces clean and practices smiling.

Hair straight and heavy. Nose full. Lips bulging like boiling frank-furters. Hung. Bell bottoms and boss black boots. He practices his Brian Jones expressions. Fist held close to the jaw. Ready to spring, ready to spit. Evil. His upper brace catches on a lip.

He walks past his parents' room, where his mother sleeps in a gauzy hairnet, the covers pulled over her chin, her baby feet swathed in yellow calluses. Her hand reaches over to the night table where her eyedrops and glasses lie. He mutters silently at her. The night before there had been a fight – the usual fight, with Mommy shouting 'I'll give you money! Sure, you rotten kid! I'll give you clothing so you can throw it all over the floor – that's blood money in those pants of yours!' And him answering the usual 'geh-awf-mah-bak' and her: 'Don't you yell at me, don't you – did you hear that (to no one). Did you hear how that kid...?' and him slamming the door – the gray barrier – and above the muffled '...disrespects his mother ... He treats me like dirt under his feet! ... and he wants me to buy him ... he'll spit on my grave' ... and finally dad's groaning shuffle and a murmured 'Ronnie, you better shut your mouth to your mother,' and him whispering silently, the climatic, the utter: 'Fucking bitch. Cunt. Cunt.'

Now she smiles. So do crocodiles. He loves her. He doesn't know why he cursed, except that she hates it. It was easy to make her cry and though he shivers at the thought of her lying across the bed sob-bing into a pillow, her housedress pulled slightly over a varicose thigh, he had to admit doing it was easy.

On the table he sees the pants she bought him yesterday. Her money lining his pocket, he had taken the bus to Fordham Road and in Alex-ander's he had cased out the Mod rack. Hands shaking, dying for a cigarette, he found the pants – a size small but still a fit. He bought them, carried them home clutched in his armpit, and deposited them before her during prime 'Star Trek' TV time.

'Get away. I can't see. Whatsamaddah, your father a glazier or

something?' and when he unveiled the pants and asked for the usual
cuff-making ritual (when he would stand on the ladder and she, holding
a barrage of pins in her mouth, would run the tailor's chalk along his
shoeline and make him drag out the old black sewing machine), the
fight began — and ended within the hour. The pants, hemmed during
'The Merv Griffin Show' as the last labor of the night, now lay exposed
and sunlit on the table. $8.95 pants.

 - They shimmer. The houndstooth design glows against the formica.
Brown and green squares are suddenly visible within the gray design.
He brushes the fabric carefully so the wool bristles. He tries them on,
zipping up the two-inch fly, thinking at first that he has broken the
zipper until he realizes that hip-huggers have no fly to speak of. They
buckle tightly around his hips, hug his thighs, and flare suddenly at his
knees. He races to the mirror and grins.

His hips are suddenly tight and muscular. His waist is sleek and his
ass round and bulging. Most important, the pants make him look hung.
Like the kids in the park. The odor of stale cigarettes over their clothing, medallions dangling out of their shirts. Their belt buckles ajar.
They are hip. They say 'Check out that bike.' Get bent on Gypsy. Write
the numbers of cruising police cars all over the walls. ROT, they call
themselves. Reign of Terror. In the park they buzz out on glue, filling
papers bags and breathing deeply, then sitting on the grass slopes,
watching the cars. Giggling. Grooving. High.

Sometimes they let him keep the models that come with the glue. Or
he grubs around their spot until, among the torn bags and oozing
tubes, he finds a Messerschmitt or Convair spread across the grass
ruins as though it had crashed there.

He unzips his pants and lets them hang on the door where he can
watch them from the living room. He takes a box of Oreos from the
kitchen, stacking the cookies in loose columns on the rug. He pours a
cup of milk and turns on the TV. Farmer Gray runs nervously up and
down the screen while a pig squats at ease by his side. His pants are
filled with hornets. He runs in a cloud of dust toward a pond which
appears and disappears teasingly, leaving Farmer Gray grubbing in the
sand. Outasight!

He fills his mouth with three Oreos and wraps his feet around the
screen so he can watch Farmer Gray between his legs. Baby habit.
Eating cookies on the floor and watching cartoons on Saturday morning. Like thumbsucking. They teased him about it until he threw imaginary furniture into their faces. A soft bulge on his left thumb from

years of sucking – cost them a fortune in braces. Always busting his hump.

He kills the TV picture and puts the radio on softly, because he doesn't want to wake Daddy who is asleep on his cot in the middle of the living room, bunched up around the blanket, his face creased in a dream, hands gripping his stomach in mock tension. Daddy snores in soft growls.

He brushes a flock of Oreo crumbs under the TV and rubs a milk stain into the rug. Thrown out of your own bed for snoring. You feel cheap, like Little Bo Peep; beep beep beep beep.

There is nothing to stop him from going downstairs. The guys are out already, slung over cars and around lampposts. The girls are trickling out of the project. It's cloudy, but until it actually rains he knows they will be around the lamppost, spitting out into the street, horsing around, grubbing for hooks, singing. He finishes four more cookies and stuffs half an apple onto his chocolate-lined tongue.

Marie Giovanni put him down bad for his braces. When she laughs her tits shake. Her face is pink; her hair rises in a billowing bouffant. In the hallway, she let Tony get his fingers wet. Yesterday she cut on him; called him metal mouth.

He flicks the radio off, grabs the pants from the hanger, and slides into them. He digs out a brown turtleneck from under a rubble of twisted clothing (they dress him like a ragpicker) and shines his boots with spit. They are chipping and the heels are worn on one side, but they make him look an inch taller, so he wears them whenever he can.

He combs his hair in the mirror. Back on the sides, over the ears, so the curl doesn't show. Over the eyes in the front to cover up his bump. Straight down the back of his neck, so it rests on his collar. He checks his bald spot for progress and counts the hairs that come out in his brush. In two years he knows he will be bald in front and his bump will look like a boulder on his forehead.

He sits on his bed and turns the radio on. From under the phonograph he lifts a worn fan magazine – *Pop* in bright fuchsia lettering – with Zal Yanovsky hunched over one P, Paul McCartney contorted over the other, and Nancy Sinatra touching her toes around the O. He turns to the spread on the Stones and flips the pages until he sees The Picture. Mick Jagger and Marianne Faithfull. Mick scowling, waving his fingers in the air. Marianne watching the camera. Marianne, waiting for the photographer to shoot. Marianne. Marianne, eyes fading brown circles, lips slightly parted in flashbulb surprise, miniskirt spread apart, tits like two perfect cones under her sweater. He had to stop looking at Marianne Faithfull a week ago.

He turns the page and glances at the shots of Brian Jones and then his eyes open wide because a picture in the corner shows Brian in Ronnie's pants. The same check. The same rise and flare. Brian leaning against a wall, his hands on the top of his magic hiphuggers. Wick-ked!

He flips the magazine away and stands in a curved profile against the mirror. He watches the pants move as he does. From a nearby flower-pot he gathers a fingerful of dirt and rubs it over his upper lip. He checks hair, nose, braces, nails, and pants. He likes the pants. They make him look hung. He reaches into his top drawer and pulls out a white handkerchief. He opens his fly and inserts the rolled cloth, pat-ting it in place, and closing the zipper over it. He looks boss. Un-fuckinbelievable.

In the elevator Ronnie takes a cigarette from his three-day-old pack and keeps it unlit in his mouth. Marie Giovanni will look at his pants and giggle. Tony will bellow 'Check out them pants,' and everyone will groove on them. In the afternoon, they will take him down to the park and turn him on, and he will feel the buzz they are always talking about and the cars will speed by like sparks.

Brian Jones thoughts in his head. Tuff thoughts. He will slouch low over the car and smoke with his thumb over the cigarette – the hip way. And when he comes back upstairs they will finally get off his back. Even on Fordham Road, where the Irish kids crack up when he walks by, even in chemistry and gym, they will know who he is and nod a soft 'hey' when he comes by. He'll get laid.

Because clothing IS important. Especially if you've got braces and bony fingers and a bump the size of a goddam coconut on your head.

And especially if you're fourteen. Because – ask anyone. Fourteen is shit.

# Michael Herr
# Khesanh

*Michael Herr was an obscure young movie reviewer for the* New Leader *when he wangled a vague assignment from* Esquire *in 1967 to go to Vietnam to do a column on the Americanization of Saigon. The approach, presumably, was going to be somewhat light and cynical. As far as Herr was concerned the Tet offensive of early 1968 had put an end to any such approach to the war. He wound up going to Khesanh during the famous siege. It looked like the final showdown between the armies of the United States and North Vietnam.*

*The first plane Herr was to have taken to Khesanh was blown to pieces. He had gotten off in Hué at the last moment. He revved his nerve back up and went to Khesanh three times at the height of the siege, for three days, then four days, then five days. Reporters, like everyone else at Khesanh, could survive only by staying in the slit trenches. 'You lost your noncombatant status very quickly,' Herr told me, 'because nobody thought they were going to get out alive. At first I didn't feel like I was covering anything. I just felt very lost.'*

*In terms of technique, then, one of the interesting things about* 'Khesanh' *is that Herr did not give in to the temptation to make the story autobiographical . . . Little Me 'n' No Man's Land. . . . Instead he attempted the far more difficult feat of penetrating the psyches, the points of view, of the line troops themselves, using the third as well as the first person. I don't think anyone has yet equaled Herr in capturing the peculiar terrors of the war in Vietnam. Certainly no novelists have. So far all the best writing about the war has been in the New Journalism or autobiography (such as Colonel Jack Broughton's* Thud Ridge). *T.W.*

During the bad maximum incoming days of the late Winter of 1968 there was a young Marine at Khesanh whose Vietnam tour had run out. Nearly five of his thirteen months in-country had been spent there at the Khesanh Combat Base with the 26th Marines, who had been slowly building to full and then reinforced regimental strength since the previous spring. He could remember a time, not long before, when the 26th considered themselves lucky to be there, when the guys talked of it as though it were a reward for whatever their particular outfits had been through. As far as this Marine was concerned, the reward was for an ambush that autumn on the Cam Lo-Conthien road, when his unit had taken forty percent casualties, when he himself had taken shrapnel in the chest and arms. (Oh, he'd tell you, but he had seen some shit in this war.) That was when Conthien was the name everyone knew, long before Khesanh had taken on the proportions of a siege camp and lodged itself as an obsession in the heart of the Command, long before a single round had ever fallen inside the perimeter to take off his friends and make his sleep something indistinguishable from waking. He remembered when there was time to play in the streams below the plateau of the base, when all anybody ever talked about were the six shades of green that touched the surrounding hills, when he and his friends had lived like human beings, aboveground, in the light, instead of like animals who were so spaced out that they began taking pills called Diarrhea-Aid to keep their walks to exposed latrines at a minimum. And on this last morning of his tour, he might have told you that he'd been through it all and hacked it pretty well.

He was a tall blond from Michigan, probably about twenty, though it was never easy to guess the ages of Marines at Khesanh since nothing like youth ever lasted in their faces for very long. It was the eyes: Because they were always either strained or blazed-out or simply blank, they never had anything to do with what the rest of the faces were doing, and it gave everybody the look of extreme fatigue or even a glancing madness. (And age. If you take one of those platoon photographs from the Civil War and cover everything but the eyes, there is no difference between a man of fifty and a boy of thirteen.) This Marine, for example, was always smiling. It was the kind of smile that verged on the high giggles, but his eyes showed neither amusement nor embarrassment nor nervousness. It was a little insane, but it was mostly esoteric in the way that so many Marines under twenty-five became esoterics after a few months in I Corps. On that young, nondescript face, the smile seemed to come out of some old knowledge, and it said, 'I'll tell you why I'm smiling, but it will make you crazy.'

He had the name Marlene tattooed on his upper arm, and up on his helmet there was the name Judy, and he said, 'Yeah, well, Judy knows all about Marlene. That's cool, there's no sweat there.' On the back of his flak jacket he had once written, 'Yea, though I walk through the

Valley of the shadow of Death I shall fear no Evil, because I'm the meanest Motherfucker in the Valley,' but he had tried later, without much success, to scrub it off because, he explained, every damn dude in the D.M.Z. had that written on their flak jackets. And he'd smile.

He was smiling on this last morning of his tour. His gear was straight, his papers in order, his duffel packed, and he was getting through all of the last-minute business of going home, the backslapping and goosing; the joshing with the Old Man ('Come on, you know you're gonna miss this place.' 'Yes sir. Oh wow!'); the exchanging of addresses; the odd, fragmented reminiscences blurted out of awkward silences. He had a few joints left, wrapped up in a plastic bag (he hadn't smoked them because, like most Marines at Khesanh, he expected a ground attack, and he didn't want to be stoned when it came), and he gave these to his best friend, or rather, his best surviving friend. His oldest friend had been blown away in January, on the same day that the ammo dump had been hit. He had always wondered whether Gunny, the company gunnery sergeant, had known about all the smoking. After three wars, Gunny probably didn't care much; besides, they all knew that Gunny was into some pretty cool shit himself. When he dropped by the bunker they said good-bye, and then there wasn't anything to do with the morning but to run in and out of the bunker for a look at the sky, coming back in every time to say that it really ought to clear enough by ten for the planes to get in. By noon, when the good-bye's and take-care's and get-a-little-for-me's had gone on for too long by hours, the sun started to show through the mist. He picked up his duffel and small A.W.O.L. bag and started for the airstrip and the small, deep slit trench on the edge of the strip.

Khesanh was a very bad place then, but the airstrip there was the worst place in the world. It was what Kehsanh had instead of a V-ring, the exact, predictable object of the mortars and rockets hidden in the surrounding hills, the sure target of the big Russian and Chinese guns lodged in the side of CoRoc Ridge, eleven kilometers away across the Laotian border. There was nothing random about the shelling there, and no one wanted anything to do with it. If the wind was right, you could hear the N.V.A. .50 calibers starting far up the valley whenever a plane made its approach to the strip, and the first incoming artillery would precede the landings by seconds. If you were waiting there to be taken out, there was nothing you could do but curl up in the trench and try to make yourself small, and if you were coming in on the plane, there was nothing you could do, nothing at all.

There was always the debris of one kind of aircraft or another piled up on or near the strip, and sometimes the damage would cause the strip to be closed off for hours while the Seabees or the 11th Engineers did the clearing. It was so bad, so predictably bad, that the Air Force stopped flying in their star transport, the C-130, and kept to the smaller, more maneuverable C-123. Whenever possible, loads were parachuted in on pallet drops from 1500 feet, pretty blue and yellow chutes, a show, dropping down around the perimeter. But obviously passengers had to be flown in or picked up on the ground. These were mostly replacements, guys going to or returning from R and R's, specialists of one kind or another, infrequent brass (most Staff from Division and higher made their own travel arrangements for Khesanh) and a lot of correspondents. While a planeload of passengers tensed and sweated and made the run for the trench over and over in their heads, waiting for the cargo hatch to drop, ten to fifty Marines and correspondents huddled down in the trench, worked their lips futilely to ease the dryness and then, at the exact same instant, they would all race, collide, stampede, exchanging places. If the barrage was a particularly heavy one, the faces would all distort in the most simple kind of panic, the eyes going wider than the eyes of horses caught in a fire. What you saw was a lucid blur, sensible only at the immediate center, like a swirly-chic photograph of Carnival, and you'd glimpse a face, a shell fragment cased in white sparks, a piece of gear somehow suspended in air, a drift of smoke, and you'd move around the flight crews working the heavy cargo strapping, over scout dogs, over the casually arranged body bags that always lay not far from the strip, covered with flies. And men would still be struggling on or off as the aircraft turned slowly to begin the taxi before the most accelerated takeoff the machine had it in it to make. If you were on board, that first movement was an ecstasy. You'd all sit there with empty, exhausted grins, covered with the impossible red dust that laterite breaks down to, dust like scales, feeling the delicious after-chill of the fear, that one quick convulsion of safety. There was no feeling in the world as good as being airborne out of Khesanh.

On this last morning, the young Marine caught a ride from his company position that dropped him off fifty meters from the strip. As he moved on foot he heard the distant sound of the C-123 coming in, and that was all he heard. There was hardly more than a hundred-foot ceiling, scary, bearing down on him. Except for the approaching engines, everything was still. If there had been something more, just one incoming round, he might have been all right, but in that silence the sound of his own feet moving over the dirt was terrifying to him. He later said that this is what made him stop. He dropped his duffel and looked round. He watched the plane, his plane, as it touched down, and then he ran leaping over some discarded sandbags by the road. He lay out flat and listened as the plane switched loads and took off, listened until there was nothing left to listen to. Not a single round had come in.

Back at the bunker there was some surprise at his return, but no one said anything. Anyone can miss a plane. Gunny slapped him on the back and wished him a better trip the next time out. That afternoon he rode in a jeep that took him all the way to Charlie Med, the medical detachment for Khesanh that had been set up insanely close to the strip, but he never got himself past the sandbagging outside of the triage room.

'Oh no, you raggedy-assed bastard,' Gunny said when he got back to the outfit. But he looked at him for a long while this time.

'Well,' the kid said. 'Well. . . .'

The next morning, two of his friends went with him to the edge of the strip and saw him into the trench. ('Good-bye,' Gunny said. 'And that's an order.') They came back to say that he'd gotten out for sure this time. An hour later, he came up the road again, smiling. He was still there the first time I left Khesanh, and while he probably made it out eventually, you can't be sure.

Such odd things happen when tours are almost over. It's the Short-Timer Syndrome. In the heads of the men who are really in the war for a year, all tours end early. No one expects much from a man when he is down to one or two weeks. He becomes a luck freak, an evil-omen collector, a diviner of every bad sign. If he has the imagination, or the experience of war, he will precognize his own death a thousand times a day, but he will always have enough left to do the one big thing, to Get Out.

Something more was working on the young Marine, and the Gunny knew what it was. In this war they called it 'acute environmental reaction,' but Vietnam has spawned a jargon of such delicate locutions that it's often impossible to know even remotely the thing being described. Most Americans would rather be told that their son is undergoing acute environmental reaction than to hear that he is suffering from shell shock, because they could no more deal with the fact of shell shock than they could with the reality of what had happened to this boy during his five months at Khesanh.

Say that his legs just weren't working. It was clearly a medical matter, and the sergeant was going to have to see that something was done about it. But when I left, the kid was still there, sitting relaxed on his duffel and smiling, saying, 'Man, when I get home, I'll have it knocked.'

## 2

The terrain above II Corps, where it runs along the Laotian border and into the D.M.Z., is seldom referred to as the Highlands by Americans. It has been a matter of military expediency to impose a new set of references over Vietnam's older, truer being, an imposition that began most simply with the division of one country into two and continued — it has its logic — with the further divisions of South Vietnam into four clearly defined tactical corps. It has been one of the exigencies of the war, and if it has effectively obliterated even some of the most obvious geographical distinctions, it has made for clear communication, at least among members of the Mission and many components of the Military Assistance Command, Vietnam, the fabulous M.A.C.V. In point of geographical fact, for example, the delta of Vietnam comprehends the Plain of Reeds and frames the Saigon River, but on all the charts and deep in all the sharp heads, it ends at the map line dividing III and IV Corps. Referentially, the Highlands are confined to II Corps, ending abruptly at the line which got drawn just below the coastal city of Quang Ngai. Everything between that and the D.M.Z. is just I Corps. All in-country briefings, at whatever level, come to sound like a Naming-of-the-Parts, and the language is used as a cosmetic, but one that diminishes beauty. Since most of the journalism from the war is framed in that language or proceeds from the view of the war which those terms imply, it would be as impossible to know what Vietnam looks like from reading most newspaper stories as it would be to know about how it smells. Those Highlands don't simply vanish at the Corps border, but go all the way up in a section of North Vietnam that Navy fliers call the Armpit, running in a chain with the wonderful name of the Annamese Cordillera that spans more than seventeen hundred miles from the Armpit to a point just below Pleiku, cutting through much of the north, through the D.M.Z., through the valley fastness (Theirs) of the A Shau, and through the piedmont that was once the Marine Combat Base of Khesanh. And since the country it traverses is very special, with its special evocations, my insistence on placing Khesanh there is much more than some recondite footnote to a history of that sad place and the particular ways in which so many Americans suffered their part of the war there.

Because the Highlands of Vietnam are spooky, unbearably spooky, spooky beyond belief. They are a run of erratic mountain ranges, gnarled valleys, jungled ravines and abrupt plains where Montagnard villages cluster, thin, and disappear as the terrain steepens. The Montagnards, in all of their tribal components, make up the most primitive and mysterious portion of the Vietnamese population, a population that has always confused Americans even in its most Westernized segments. Strictly speaking, the Montagnards are not really Vietnamese at all, certainly not *South* Vietnamese, but a kind of upgraded, demi-enlightened Annamese aborigine, often living in nakedness and brooding silence in their villages. Most Vietnamese and most Montagnards consider each other inferior, and while many Montagnards hire out as mercenaries to the American Special Forces, that older, racially based enmity has often slowed down the Allied effort. Many Americans consider them to be nomadic, but the war has had more to do with that than anything in their temperament. We napalm off their crops and flatten their villages, and then admire that restlessness in their spirit. Their nakedness, their painted bodies their recalcitrance, their silent composure before strangers, their benign savagery and the sheer, awesome ugliness of them combine to make most Americans who are forced to associate with them a little uncomfortable over the long run. It would seem fitting, ordained, that they should live in the Highlands, among triple canopies, where sudden, contrary mists offer sinister bafflement, where the daily heat and the nighttime cold keep you perpetually, increasingly on edge, where the silences are interrupted only by the sighing of cattle or the rotor thud of a helicopter, the one sound I know that is both sharp and dull at the same time. The Puritan belief that Satan dwelled in Nature could have been born here, where even on the coldest, freshest mountaintops you could smell jungle and that tension between rot and genesis that all jungles give off. It is a ghost-story country, and for Americans it has been the scene of some of the war's vilest surprises. The Ia Drang battles of late 1965 constituted the first and worst of these surprises. It was the first wholesale appearance of North Vietnamese regulars in the South, and no one who was around then can ever forget the horror of it nor, to this day, get over the confidence and sophistication with which entire battalions came to engage Americans in a war. A few correspondents, a few soldiers back for second and third tours still shudder uncontrollably at what they remember: Impromptu positions held to the last man and then overrun; Americans and North Vietnamese stiff in one another's death embrace, their eyes wide open, their teeth bared or sunk deep into enemy flesh; the number of helicopters shot down (relief missions after relief missions after relief missions . . .); the N.V.A. equipment hauls which included the first AK-47 assault rifles, the first RPG-7 rockets, the hundreds of aluminum grave markers. No, a lot of the ones who saw that, the toughest of them, don't even like to talk about it today. The very best of our divisions, the First Air Cavalry, was blooded in the Ia Drang that autumn, and while the official number of dead was released at around three hundred, I never met anyone who had been there, including officers of the Cav, who would settle for less than three or even four times that figure.

There is a point of view which says that the United States got involved in the Vietnam war, commitments and interests aside, simply because we thought it would be easy. But after the Ia Drang, that first arrogance sat less and less well about the shoulders of the Command; it never vanished. There was never again a real guerrilla war after Ia Drang, except in the Delta, and the old Giap stratagem of interdicting the South through the Highlands, cutting the country in two, came to be taken seriously, even obsessively by many influential Americans.

Oh, that terrain! The bloody, maddening uncanniness of it! When the hideous Battle of Dakto ended at the top of Hill 875, we announced that 4000 of them had been killed; it had been the purest slaughter, our losses were bad, but clearly it was another American victory. But when the top of the hill was reached, the number of N.V.A. found was four. Four. Of course more died, hundreds more, but the corpses kicked and counted and photographed and buried numbered four. Where, colonel? And how, and why? Spooky. Everything up there is spooky, and it would be that way even if there were no war. You are there in a place where you don't belong, where things are glimpsed for which you will have to pay and where things go unglimpsed for which you will also have to pay, a place where they don't play with the mystery but kill you straight off for trespassing. The towns have names that lay a quick, chilly touch on your bones: Kontum, Dak Mot Lop, Dak Roman Peng, Polei Kleng, Buon Blech, Pleiku, Plei Me, Plea Vi Drin. Just moving through those towns or being based somewhere above them spaces you out, and every time I'd have that vision of myself lying dead somewhere, it was always up there, in the Highlands.

It was enough to make an American commander sink to his knees and plead, 'Oh God! Just *once*, let it be our way. We have the strength, give us the terms!' Not even the Cav, with their style and courage and mobility, were able to penetrate that abiding Highland face. They killed a lot of Communists, but that was all they did, because the number of Communist dead meant nothing, changed nothing.

Sean Flynn, photographer and connoisseur of the Vietnam war, told me that he once stood on the vantage of a fire base up there with a battalion commander. It was at dusk, those ghastly mists were fuming out of the valley floor, ingesting light. The colonel squinted at the distance for a long time. Then he swept his hand very slowly along the line of jungle across the hills and ridges running into Cambodia (the Sanctuary!). 'Flynn,' he said, 'somewhere out there ... is the *entire First N.V.A. Division*.'

Oh dear God, just once!

## 3

Somewhere Out There, within artillery range of the Khesanh Combat Base, within a twenty-kilometer radius, a day's march, assuming the 'attack posture,' concealed and silent and ominous, lay five full divisions of North Vietnamese Regulars. This was the situation during the closing weeks of 1967:

Somewhere to the southwest was the 304th N.V.A. Division. Due east (somewhere) was the 320th. The 325C was deployed in an unknown fashion to the northwest, and the 324B (a cause for real alarm among enemy-division buffs) was somewhere to the northeast. There was also an unidentified division just the other side of the Laotian border, where their big artillery had been dug so deeply into the mountainsides that not even our B-52's could harm them. All of that terrain, all of that cover, ridge after ridge, murderous slides and gorges, all cloaked by triple canopy and thick monsoon mists. And whole divisions were out there in that.

Marine Intelligence (While I see many hoof-marks going in, I see none coming out), backed by the findings of increasing Air Force reconnaissance missions, had been watching and evaluating the buildup with alarm since spring. Khesanh had always been in the vicinity of major infiltration routes, 'sat astride' them, as the Mission put it. That slight but definite plateau, rising abruptly from the foothills bridging Laos and Vietnam, had been of value for as long as the Vietnamese had been at war. The routes now used by the N.V.A. had been used twenty years earlier by the Vietminh. Khesanh's original value to the Americans might be gauged by the fact that in spite of the known infiltration all around it, we held it for years with nothing more than a Special Forces A Team; less than a dozen Americans and around four hundred indigenous troops, Vietnamese and Montagnard. When the Special Forces first moved in there in 1962, they built their teamhouse, outbuildings, club and defenses over bunkers that had been left by the French. Infiltrating columns simply diverted their routes a kilometer or so away from the central Khesanh position. The Green Berets ran out regular, extremely cautious patrols. Since they were almost always surrounded by the infiltrators, Khesanh was not the most comfortable duty in Vietnam, but there was seldom anything more than the random ambush or the occasional mortaring that was standard for A Teams anywhere in-country. If the N.V.A. had considered Khesanh tactically crucial or even important, they could have taken it at any time. And if we had thought of it as anything more than a token outpost – you can't have infiltrators running around without putting someone in there for a look – we could have created it as a major base. No one builds bases like Americans.

In the course of routine patrols during the early Spring of 1966, Special Forces reported what appeared to be a significant increase in the number of enemy troops in the immediate Khesanh area, and a battalion of Marines was sent to reinforce the patrols. A year later, in April and May of 1967, during large but routine Search-and-Destroy operations, the Marines found and engaged battalion-strength units of North Vietnamese holding the tops of Hills 881 North and South, and a lot of people were killed on both sides. The battles grew into the bloodiest of the spring. The hills were taken and, weeks later, abandoned. The Marines that might have maintained the hills (where better to observe infiltration than from a vantage of 881 meters?) were sent instead to Khesanh, where the First and Third Battalions of the 26th Marine Regiment rotated, increasing their harassment of the N.V.A., hoping, if not to drive them out of the sector, to at least force their movements into predictable patterns. The 26th, a hybrid regiment, was formed out of the T.A.O.R. of the 5th Marine Division, a numerical designation which remained on paper even after the actual command of the regiment became the responsibility of the Third Marine Division, headquartered at Dong Ha, nearby in the D.M.Z.

By summer, it became obvious that the battles for 881 North and South had engaged a relatively small number of the enemy thought to be in the area. Patrols were stepped up (they were now thought to be among the most dangerous in I Corps), and additional elements of the 26th Marines were airlifted into what was now being called the Khesanh Combat Base. The Seabees laid down a 600-meter tarmac airstrip, a beer hall and an air-conditioned officers' club were built, and the Regimental Command set up its Tactical Operations Center in the largest of the deserted French bunkers. Yet Khesanh continued to be only a moderate, private concern of the Marine Corps. A few old hands in the press corps knew vaguely about the base and about the small *ville* of about a thousand Montagnards which lay four kilometers to the south. It was not until November, when the regiment had grown to full and then reinforced strength (6000 Marines, not including units added from the 9th Marine Regiment), with six hundred Vietnamese Rangers, two detachments of Seabees, a helicopter squadron and a small Special Forces Compound, that the Marines began 'leaking' the rather remarkable claim that by building up the base, we had lured an unbelievable number of enemy to the area. It was at about this time that copies of the little red British paperback edition of Jules Roy's *The Battle of Dienbienphu* began appearing wherever members of the Vietnam press corps gathered. You'd spot them around the terrace bar of the Continental Hotel, in L'Amiral Restaurant and Aterbea, at the 8th Aerial Port of Tan Son Nhut, in the Marine-operated Danang Press Center and in the big briefing room of JUSPAO in Saigon, where every afternoon at four-forty-five, spokesmen conducted the daily war briefing which was colloquially referred to as the Five O'Clock Follies, an Orwellian grope through the day's events as seen by the Mission. (It was very hard-line.) Those who could find copies were reading Bernard Fall's Dienbienphu book, *Hell in a Very Small Place*, which many considered the better book, stronger on tactics, more businesslike, with none of the high-level staff gossip that made the Roy book so dramatic. And as the first Marine briefings on Khesanh took place in Marine headquarters at Danang or Dong Ha, the name Dienbienphu insinuated itself like some tasteless ghost hawking bad news. Marines who had to talk to the press found references to the old French disaster irritating and even insulting. Most were not interested in fielding questions about it, and the rest were unequipped. The more irritated they became, the more the press would flaunt the irritant. For a while it looked like nothing that had happened on the ground during those weeks seemed as thrilling and sinister as the recollection of Dienbienphu. And it had to be admitted, the parallels with Khesanh were irresistible.

To begin with, the ratio between attackers and defenders was roughly the same, eight to one.. The terrain was hauntingly similar, although Khesanh was only two square miles inside its perimeter, as opposed to the sprawl of Dienbienphu. The weather conditions were the same, with the monsoons favoring the attackers by keeping American air activity at a minimum. Khesanh was now encircled, as Dienbienphu had been, and where the initial attacks of March, 1954, had been launched from Vietminh trenches, the N.V.A. had begun digging a network of trenches that would soon approach to within a hundred yards of the Marine wire. Dienbienphu had been the master plan of General Vo Nguyen Giap; rumors splintered from American Intelligence suggested that Giap himself was directing the Khesanh operation from a post somewhere above the D.M.Z. Given the fact that a lot of Marine officers did not understand what we were doing at Khesanh in the first place, the repeated evocations of Dienbienphu were unnerving. But then, on what briefers liked to call 'our side of the ledger,' there were important differences.

The base at Khesanh was raised, if only slightly, on a plateau which would have slowed a ground attack and given the Marines a gentle vantage from which to fire. The Marines also had a massive reaction force to count on, or at least to hope for. For publication, this consisted of the First Air Cavalry Division and elements of the 101st Airborne, but in fact the force numbered almost a quarter of a million men, men at support fire bases across the D.M.Z., planners in Saigon (and Washington) and most important of all, pilots and crews from headquarters as far away as Udorn, Guam and Okinawa, men whose energies and attentions became fixed almost exclusively on Khesanh missions. Air support was everything, the cornerstone of all our hopes at Khesanh, and we knew that once the monsoons lifted, it would be nothing to drop tens of thousands of tons of high explosives and napalm all around the base, to supply it without strain, to cover and reinforce the Marines.

It was a comfort, all of that power and precision and exquisitely geared clout. It meant a lot to the thousands of Marines at Khesanh, at the base, to officials in the Pentagon. We could all sleep easier for it; lance corporals and General Westmoreland, me, and the President, Navy medics and the parents of all the boys inside the wire. All any of us had to worry about was the fact that Khesanh was vastly outnumbered and entirely surrounded; that, and the knowledge that all ground evacuation routes, including the vital Route 9, were completely controlled by the N.V.A., and that the monsoons had at least six weeks more to run.

There was a joke going around that went like this: 'What's the difference between the Marine Corps and the Boy Scouts?' 'The Boy Scouts have adult leadership.' Dig it! the Grunts would say, digging it just as long as they didn't have to hear it from outside, from 'nonessential personnel' like the Army or the Air Force. For them it was only good as a joke when it also had that touch of fraternal mystery. And what a fraternity! If the war in I Corps was a matter for specialization among correspondents, it was not because it was inherently different as war, but because it was fought almost exclusively by the Marines, whose idiosyncrasies most reporters found intolerable and even criminal. (There was a week in the war, one week, when the Army lost more men killed, proportionately, than the Marines, and Army spokesmen had a rough time hiding their pride, their absolute glee.) And in the face of some new variation on old Marine disasters, it didn't much matter that you knew dozens of fine, fine officers. Something almost always went wrong somewhere, somehow. It was always something vague, unexplainable, tasting of bad fate, and the results were always brought down to their most basic element — the dead Marine. The belief that one Marine was better than ten Slopes saw Marine squads fed in against known N.V.A. platoons, platoons against companies, and on and on, until whole battalions found themselves pinned down and cut off. That belief was undying, but the Grunt was not, and the Corps came to be called by many the finest instrument ever devised for the killing of young Americans. There were always plenty of stories about entire squads wiped out (their mutilated bodies would so enrage Marines that they would run out 'vengeance patrols' which often enough ended the same way), companies taking seventy-five percent casualties. Marines ambushing Marines, artillery and airstrikes called in on our own positions, all in the course of routine Search-and-Destroy operations. And you knew, sooner or later, if you went with them often enough, that it would happen to you, too.

And the Grunts themselves knew: the madness, the bitterness, the horror and doom of it. They were hip to it, and more; they savored it. It was no more insane than most of what was going down, and often enough it had its refracted logic. 'Eat the apple, fuck the Corps,' they'd say, and write it up on their helmets and flak jackets for their officers to see. (One kid tattooed it on his shoulder.) And sometimes they'd look at you and laugh silently and long, the laugh on them and on you for being with them when you didn't have to be. And what could be funnier, really, given all that an eighteen-year-old boy could learn in a month of patrolling the Z? It was that joke at the deepest part of the blackest kernel of fear, and you could die laughing. They even wrote a song, a letter to the mother of a dead Marine, that went something like, 'Tough shit, tough shit, your kid got greased, but what the fuck, he was just a Grunt. . . .' They got savaged a lot and softened a lot, their secret brutalized them and darkened them and very often made them beautiful. It took no age, seasoning or education to make them know exactly where true violence resided.

And they were killers. Of course they were; what would anyone expect them to be? It absorbed them, inhabited them, made them strong in the way that victims are strong, filled them with the twin obsessions of Death and Peace, fixed them so that they could never, never again speak lightly about the Worst Thing in the World. If you learned just this much about them, you were never quite as happy (in the miserable-joyous way of covering the war) with other outfits. And, naturally, the poor bastards were famous all over Vietnam. If you spent some weeks up there and afterwards joined an Army outfit of, say, the 4th or 25th Divisions, you'd get this:

'Where you been? We ain't seen you.'

'Up in I Corps.'

'With the *Marines?*'

'That's what's up there.'

'Well, all I got to say is Good Luck! Marines. Fuck that.'

'Khesanh is the Western Anchor of our defense,' the Commanding General offered.

'Who told you that?' the Examining Angels replied.

'Why . . . everybody!'

No Marine ever called it that, not even those officers who believed in it tactically, just as no Marine ever called what happened there for seventy-six days a 'siege.' Those were M.A.C.V. conceits, often taken up by the press, and they angered Marines. As long as the 26th Marines could maintain a battalion outside the wire (the garrison at Khesanhville was withdrawn and the town bombed flat, but Marines still patrolled beyond the perimeter and lived on nearby hilltops), as long as planes could resupply the base, it could not be a siege. Marines may get beleaguered, but not besieged. Whatever one chose to call it, by the

time of the Tet Offensive, a week after the shelling of Khesanh began,
it looked as though both sides had committed themselves on such a
scale that engagement would be inevitable. No one I knew doubted that
it would come, probably in the form of a massive ground attack, and
that when it came it would be terrible and great.

Tactically, its value to the Command was thought so great that
General Westmoreland could announce that the Tet Offensive was
merely Phase II of a brilliant Giap strategy. Phase I had been revealed
in the autumn skirmishes between Locninh and Dakto. Phase III ('the
capstone,' the General called it) was to be Khesanh. It seems impossible that anyone, at any time, even in the chaos of Tet, could have
actually called something as monumental (and decisive?) as that offensive a mere diversion for something as negligible as Khesanh, but all of
that is on record.

And by then Khesanh was famous, one of the very few place-names
in Vietnam that was recognized by the American public. Khesanh said
'seige,' it said 'encircled Marines,' and 'heroic defenders.' It could be
understood by newspaper readers quickly, it breathed Glory and War
and Honored Dead. It seemed to make sense. It was good stuff. One
can only imagine the anxiety which the Commander-in-Chief suffered
over it. Lyndon Johnson said it straight out, he did not want 'any damn
Dinbinfoo,' and he did something unprecedented in the history of war-
fare. The Joint Chiefs of Staff were summoned and made to sign a
statement 'for the public reassurance,' asserting that Khesanh could
and would be held at all costs. (Apparently, *Coriolanus* had never been
required reading at the Point. Noncoms in the field, even Grunts with
no career ambitions, felt the professional indignity of the President's
gambit, talked of it as something shameful.) Perhaps Khesanh would
be held, perhaps not; the President had his statement now, and it was
signed clearly. If Khesanh stood, he would presumably be available for
a grin in the victory picture. If it fell, it would not be on his head.

More than any other Americans in Vietnam, Khesanh's defenders
became hostages, nearly eight thousand Americans and Vietnamese
who took their orders not from the Regimental Commander in the
T.O.C., nor from General Cushman in Danang nor General Westmoreland in Saigon, but from a source which one intelligence officer I knew
always called 'downtown.' They were made to sit and wait, and Marines defending are like anti-Christs at vespers. Somehow, digging in
seems a soft thing to do, fighting from a hole is like fighting on your
knees. ('Digging,' General Cushman said, 'is not the Marine way.')

Most of the defenses against artillery were built entirely or substantially reinforced after the heavy shelling began, when the Tet Offensive diverted supply from the air and made Khesanh even more isolated. They were built on the scrounge and so haphazardly that the lines of sandbagging had a sensuous, plastic drift to them as they stretched away into the filtered light of mist and dust, the shapes growing dimmer in the distance. If all of the barbed wire and all of the sandbags were taken away, Khesanh would have looked like one of those Colombian valley slums whose meanness is the abiding factor, whose despair is so palpable that for days after you leave you are filled with a vicarious shame for the misery you have just tripped through. At Khesanh, most bunkers were nothing more than hovels with inadequate overhead cover, and you could not believe that Americans were living this way, even in the middle of a war. The defenses were a scandal, and everywhere you could smell that sour reek of obsolescence that followed the Marines all over Vietnam. If they could not hear their own dead from Conthien, only three months past, how could they ever be expected to hear the dead from Dienbienphu?

Not a single round had fallen inside the perimeter. The jungled slopes running up from the bowl of the base were not yet burned over and hung with the flare-chutes that looked like infants' shrouds. Six shades of green, mother-fucker, tell me that ain't something beautiful. There were no heaps of shredded, blood-soaked jungle fatigues outside the triage room, and the wires were not cluttered each dawn with their dead. None of it had happened yet when Khesanh became lost forever as a tactical entity. It is impossible to fix the exact moment in time when it happened, or to know, really, why. All that was certain was that Khesanh had become a passion, the false love-object in the heart of the Command. It cannot even be determined which way the passion traveled. Did it proceed from the filthiest ground-zero slit trench and proceed outward, across I Corps to Saigon and on (taking the true perimeter with it) to the most abstract reaches of the Pentagon? Or did it get born in those same Pentagon rooms where six years of failure had made the air bad, where optimism no longer sprang from anything viable but sprang and sprang, all the way to Saigon, where it was packed and shipped north to give the Grunts some kind of reason for what was about to happen to them? In its outlines, the promise was delicious: Victory! A vision of as many as 40,000 of them out there in the open, fighting for once like men, fighting to no avail. There would be a battle, a set-piece battle where he could be killed by the numbers, killed wholesale, and if we killed enough of him, maybe he would go away. In the face of such a promise, the question of defeat could not even be considered, no more than the question of whether, after Tet, Khesanh might have become militarily unwise and even absurd. Once it was all locked in place, Khesanh became like the jar in Wallace Stevens' poem. It took dominion everywhere.

4

When I think of it quickly, just seeing the name somewhere or being asked what it was like, I see a flat, dun stretch of ground running out in an even plane until the rim of the middle-distance takes on the shapes and colors of jungled hills. I had the strangest, most thrilling kind of illusion there, looking at those hills and thinking about the death and mystery that was in them. I would see the thing I knew I actually saw: the base from the ground where I stood, figures moving across it, choppers rising from the pad by the strip, and the hills above. But at the same time I would see the other, too; the ground, the troops and even myself, all from the vantage of the hills. It was a double vision that came to me more than once there. And in my head, sounding over and over, were the incredibly sinister words of the song we had all heard for the first time only days before. 'The Magical Mystery Tour is waiting to take you away,' it promised, 'Coming to take you away, dy-ing to take you away. . . .' That was a song about Khesanh: we knew it then, and it still seems so. Inside the bunker, one of the Grunts has been saying hideous things in his sleep, laughing a bad laugh and then going more silent than even deep sleep permits before starting it up again, and it is more terrible in there than anyplace I can even imagine. I got up then and went outside, anyplace at all was better than this, and stood in the dark smoking a cigarette, watching the hills for a sign and hoping none would come because, hell, what could be revealed except more fear? Three in the morning, and my blood is intimate with the chill, host to it, and very willing, too. From the center of the earth there is a tremor that shakes everything, running up through my legs and body, shaking my head, yet no one in the bunker wakes up. We called them 'Archlights,' he called them Rolling Thunder, and it was incessant during the nights. The bombs would release at 18,000 feet and the planes would turn and fly back to Udorn or Guam. Dawn seems to last until late morning, dusk falls at four. Everything I see is blown through with smoke, everything is on fire everywhere. It doesn't matter that memory distorts; every image, every sound comes back out of smoke and the smell of things burning.

Some of it, like smoke from an exploding round in the air, breaks cleanly and at a comfortable distance Some of it pours out of large tubs of shit being burned off with diesel fuel, and it hangs, hangs, taking you full in the throat even though you are used to it. Right there on the strip a fuel ship has been hit, and no one who has heard that can kill the shakes for an hour. (What woke you? ... What woke you?) A picture comes in, absolutely still for a moment, and then resumes the motion it once had: a heat tablet, burning in high-intensity, covered by a tiny, blackened stove, a Marine had made for me two weeks before in Hué out of the small dessert can from a ration box. From this little bit of light I can see the outlines of a few Marines, all of us in a bunker filling with the acrid smoke of the tablet, glad for it because the rations will be hot tonight, glad because we know how safe the bunker is and because we are both private and together, and find a lot of things to laugh about. I brought the tablets with me, stole them from a colonels' aide in Dong Ha, supercilious prick, and these guys hadn't had any in days, weeks. I also have a bottle. ('Oh man, you are welcome here. You are definitely welcome. Let's wait for Gunny.') The beef and potatoes, the meatballs and beans, the ham and Mothers, all that good stuff will be hot tonight, and who really gives a shit about tomorrow night anyway? Somewhere above ground now, in full afternoon light, there is a four-foot stack of C-ration cartons, the cardboard burned away from the metal binding wire, the cans and utility packs lying all around, and on top of it all there is the body of a young A.R.V.N. Ranger who had just come over to Bravo Recon to scrounge a few cans of American food. If he'd succeeded, he would have gone back to his unit a celebrity, but as it was he didn't make out. Three rounds had come in very quickly, neither killing nor wounding any of the Marines, and now two lance corporals are arguing. One wants to put the dead Ranger into a green body bag, the other just wants to cover the body somehow, anyhow, and run it over to the Dink compound. He's very pissed off. 'We keep tellin' them fuckin' people to stay with their own fuckin' outfits,' he says, over and over. Fires eat at everything. There are fires at night, trees on hillsides kilometers away erupting in smoke and burning. At late morning, the sun burns off the last of the chill and early mist, making the base visible from above until late afternoon, when the chill and mist return. Then it is night again, and the sky beyond the western perimeter is burning with slowly dropping magnesium flares. Heaps of equipment are on fire, terrifying in their jagged black massiveness, burning prehistoric shapes like the tail of a C-130 sticking straight up in the air, dead metal showing through the grey-black smoke. *God, if it can do that to metal, what will it to do me?* And then something very near me is smoldering, just above my head, the damp canvas coverings on the sandbags lining the top of a slit trench. It is a small trench, and a lot of us have gotten into it in a hurry. At the end farthest from me there is a young guy who has been hit in the throat, and he is making sounds a baby will make who is trying to work up the breath for a good scream. We were on the ground when those rounds came, and a Marine nearer the trench had been splattered badly across the legs and groin. I sort of took him into the trench with me. It was so crowded I couldn't help leaning on him a little, and he kept saying, 'You motherfucker, you cocksucker,' until someone told him that I wasn't a Grunt, but a reporter. Then he started to say, very quietly, 'Be careful, mister. Please be careful.' He'd been wounded before, and he knew how it would hurt in a few minutes. People would just get ripped up in the worst ways there, and things were always on fire. Far up the road that skirted the T.O.C. was a dump where they burned the gear and uniforms that nobody needed anymore. On top of the pile I saw a flak jacket so torn apart that no one would ever want it again. On the back, its owner had listed the months he had served in Vietnam. 'March, April, May' (each month written out in a tentative, spidery hand), 'June, July, August, September, Octobler, Novembler, December, Janurary, Feburary,' the list ending right there like a clock stopped by a bullet. A jeep pulled up to the dump and a Marine jumped out carrying a bunched-up fatigue jacket held out away from him. He looked very serious and scared. Some guy in his company, some guy he didn't even know, had been blown away right next to him. He held the fatigues up and I believed him. 'I guess you couldn't wash them, could you?' I said. He really looked like he was going to cry as he threw them into the dump. 'Man,' he said, 'you could take and scrub them fatigues for a million years, and *it would never happen.*'

I see a road. It is full of ruts made by truck and jeep tires, but in the passing rains they never harden, and along the road there is a two-dollar piece of issue, a poncho which had just been used to cover a dead Marine, a blood-puddled, mud-wet poncho going stiff in the wind. It has reared up there by the road in a horrible, streaked ball. The wind doesn't move it, only setting the pools of water and blood in the dents shimmering. I'm walking along this road with two black Grunts, and one of them gives the poncho a vicious, helpless kick. 'Go easy, man,' the other one says, nothing changing in his face, not even a look back. 'That's the American flag you gettin' your foot into.'

During the early morning of February seventh, something so horrible happened in the Khesanh sector that even those 'of us who were in Hué when we heard news of it had to relinquish our own fear and despair for a moment to acknowledge the horror and pay some tribute to it. It was as though the very worst dream any of us had ever had about the war had come true; it anticipated nightmares so vile that they could take you off shuddering in your sleep. No one who heard it was able to smile that bitter, secret, survivor's smile that was the reflex to almost all news of disaster. It was too awful even for that.

Five kilometers southwest of the Khesanh Combat Base, sitting above the river which forms the border with Laos, there was a Special Forces A Camp. It was called Langvei, taking its name from the small Montagnard village nearby which had been mistakenly bombed a year before by the Air Force. The camp was larger than most Special Forces camps, and much better built. It was set on twin hills about 700 meters apart, and the vital bunkers holding most of the troops were on the hill nearest the river. It was manned by twenty-four Americans and over four hundred Vietnamese troops. Its bunkers were deep, solid, with three feet of reinforced concrete overhead, seemingly impregnable. And sometime after midnight, the North Vietnamese came and took it. They took it with a style that had been seen only once before, in the Ia Drang, attacking with weapons and tactics which no one imagined they had. Nine light tanks, Soviet T-34's and 76's, were deployed east and west, closing on the camp so suddenly that the first sound of them was mistaken by the Americans for a malfunction of the camp generator. Satchel charges, bangalore torpedoes, tear gas and – ineffable horror – napalm were all hurled into the machine-gun slits and air vents of the bunkers. It took very little time. An American colonel who had come on an inspection visit to Langvei was seen charging the tanks with nothing but hand grenades before he was cut down. (He survived. The word 'miracle' doesn't even apply.) Somewhere between ten and fifteen Americans were killed, and as many as three hundred of the indigenous troops. The survivors traveled all night, most of them on foot through N.V.A. positions (some were picked up later by choppers), arriving at Khesanh after dawn, and it was said that some of them had become insane. At the same time that Langvei was being overrun, Khesanh received the most brutal artillery barrage of the war: 1500 rounds that night, six rounds a minute for more minutes than anyone could bear to count.

The Marines at Khesanh saw the Langvei survivors come in. They saw them and heard about them up in their Special Forces compound, holding off all visitors at rifle point, saw their faces and their unfocused stares, and they talked quietly among themselves about it. Jesus, they had tanks. Tanks! ... After Langvei, how could you look out of your perimeter at night without hearing the treads coming? How could you patrol in the dark without remembering every story you ever heard about ghostly enemy helicopters flying the fringes of the Z? About the trails cut in the floor of the A Shau Valley, big enough to hold trucks? About the complete fanaticism of attackers who were doped to the eyeballs (Sure they smoke dope, it gets them crazy), who ran pushing civilian shields forward, who chained themselves to their machine-guns and died right there rather than fail, who had No Regard For Human Life?

Officially, the Marines admitted no relevance between the Langvei attack and Khesanh. Confidentially, they said something awful about Langvei having been bait — bait which the poor, desperate bastards took, exactly as we hoped they would. But everyone knew better, much better, and the majors and colonels who had to tell reporters about it were met with embarrassed silence. One hated to bring it up, one never really did, but there was a question that had everything in the world to do with Khesanh after Langvei fell. I wanted to ask it so badly that my hesitance made me mad for months. Colonel (I wanted to ask), this is purely hypothetical, I hope you understand: But what if all of those Gooks that you think are out there are *really* out there? And what if they attack before the monsoons blow south, some mist-clogged night when our planes just cannot get up there? What if they really want Khesanh, want it so badly that they are willing to maneuver over the triple lines of barbed wire, the German razor-wire too; over barricades formed by their own dead (a tactic, colonel, favored by your Gook in Korea), coming in waves, *human* waves, and in such numbers that the barrels of our .50-calibers overheat and melt and all the M-16's are jammed, until all of the death in all of the Claymore mines on our defenses has been spent and absorbed? What if they are still coming, moving towards the center of a base so smashed by their artillery that those pissy little trenches and bunkers that *your* Marines half got up are useless, coming as the first MIG's and IL-28's ever seen in this war bomb out the T.O.C. and the strip, the med tent and the control tower (People's Army my ass, right, colonel?) coming at you twenty to forty thousand strong? And what if they pass over every barricade we can put in their way . . . and kill every living thing, defending or retreating . . . and take Khesanh?

Some strange things would happen. One morning, at the height of the monsoons, the sun came up brightly at dawn and shone all day. The early morning skies were clean, brilliant blue, the only time before April that anyone saw that at Khesanh, and instead of waking and coming out shivering from their bunkers, the Grunts stripped down to boots, pants and flak jackets; biceps, triceps and tattoos all out for breakfast. Probably because the N.V.A. knew that American surveillance and bombers would be working overtime on a morning like this, there was almost no shelling, and we all knew we could count on it. For those few hours, Khesanh had the atmosphere of reprieve. I remember passing a chaplain named Stubbe on the road and seeing his incredible pleasure at the miracle of this morning. The hills did not seem like the same hills that had given off so much fear the night before and all the days and nights before that. In the early-morning light they looked sharp and tranquil, as though you could take some apples and a book and go up there for an afternoon.

I was walking around by myself in the First Battalion area. It was before eight in the morning, and as I walked I could hear someone walking behind me, singing. At first I couldn't hear what it was, only that it was a single short phrase being sung over and over at short intervals, and that every time someone else would laugh and tell the singer to shut up. I slowed down and let them catch up.

'I'd rather be an Oscar Mayer weiner,' the voice sang. It sounded very plaintive and lonely.

Of course I turned around. There were two of them, one a big Negro with a full moustache that drooped over the corners of his mouth, a mean, signifying moustache that would have worked if only there had been the smallest trace of meanness anywhere on his face. He was at least six-three and quarter-back thick. He was carrying an AK-47. The other Marine was white, and if I'd seen him first from the back I would have said that he was eleven years old. The Marines must have a height requirement; whatever it is, I don't see how he made it. Age is one thing, but how do you lie about your height? He'd been doing the singing, and he was laughing now because he'd made me turn around.

His name was Mayhew, it was written out in enormous red letters across the front of his helmet: MAYHEW — You'd better believe it! I'd been walking with my flak jacket open, a stupid thing to do even on this morning, and they could see the stitched tag above my left breast pocket with the name of my magazine on it.

'Correspondent?' the Negro said. Mayhew just laughed.

'I'd – a rather be – a Oscar Mayer.... weenieeee,' he sang. 'You can write that, man, tell 'em all I said so.'

'Don't pay no attention to him,' the Negro said. 'That's Mayhew. He's a crazy fucker, ain't you Mayhew?'

'I sure hope so,' Mayhew said. 'I'd rather be an Oscar Mayer weiner. . . .'

He was young, nineteen, he later told me, and he was trying to grow a moustache. His only luck with it so far were a few sparse, transparent blond clumps set at odd intervals across his upper lip, and you couldn't see that unless the light was right. The Negro was called Day Tripper. It was on his helmet, along with DETROIT CITY. And on the back, where most guys just listed the months of their tours, he had carefully drawn a full calendar where each day served was marked off with a neat X. They were both from Hotel Company of the Second Battalion, which was dug in beyond the northwest perimeter, but they were taking advantage of the day to visit a friend of theirs, a mortarman with 1/26.

'The lieutenant ever hear 'bout this, he know what to do,' Day Tripper said.

'Fuck the lieutenant,' Mayhew said. 'You remember from before he ain't wrapped too tight.'

'Well, he wrapped tight enough to tear *you* a new asshole.'

'Now what's he gonna do to me? Send me to Vietnam?'

We walked past the battalion C.P., piled five feet high with sandbags, and then we reached a giant ring of sandbagging, the mortar pit, and climbed down. In the center was a large four-point-deuce mortar piece, and the inside of the pit was stacked completely around with ammunition, piled from the ground to just below the sandbags. A Marine was stretched out in the dust with a war comic spread over his face.

'Hey, where's Evans?' Mayhew said. 'You know a guy named Evans?'

The Marine took the comic off of his face and looked up. He'd been asleep.

'Shit,' he said. 'I thought you was the Old Man for a second. Beg your pardon.'

'We're looking for this guy Evans,' Mayhew said. 'You know him?'

'I – uh – no, I don't guess so. I'm pretty new.'

He looked it. He was the kind of kid that would go into the high-school gym alone and shoot baskets for the half hour before the basket-ball team took it over for practice, not good enough yet for the team, but determined.

'The rest of the crew'll be down here right away. You can wait if you want.' He looked at all the rounds. 'It's probably not too cool,' he said, smiling. 'But you can if you want.'

Mayhew unbuttoned one of the pockets in the leg of his fatigues and took out a can of crackers and cheddar cheese spread. He took the P-38 opener from a band around his helmet and sat down.

'Might as well eat some of this crap while we wait. You get hungry, it ain't so bad. I'd give anything for a can of fruit now.'

I always scrounged fruit from rear areas to bring forward, and I had some in my pack. 'What kind do you like?' I asked.

'Any kind's good,' he said. 'Fruit cocktail's really good.'

'No, man,' Day Tripper said. 'Peaches, baby, peaches. All that syrup. Now that's some good shit.'

'There you go, Mayhew,' I said, tossing him a fruit cocktail. I gave a can of peaches to Day Tripper and kept a can for myself.

We talked while we ate. Mayhew told me about his father, who 'got greased in Korea,' and about his mother, who worked in a department store in Kansas City. Then he started to tell about Day Tripper, who got his name because he was afraid of the night – not the dark, but the night – and who didn't mind who knew it. There wasn't anything he wouldn't do during daylight, but if there was any way at all to fix it he liked to be deep in his bunker by nightfall. He was always volunteering for the more dangerous daylight patrols, just to make sure he got in by dusk. (This was before daylight patrols, in fact almost all patrols around Khesanh, were discontinued.) There were a lot of white guys, especially junior officers trying to be cool, who were always coming on to Day Tripper about his hometown, calling it Dodge City or Motown and laughing. ('Why they think somethin's special about Detroit?' he said. 'Ain't nothin' special, ain't nothin' so funny, neither.') He was a big bad Spade gone wrong somehow, and no matter how mean he tried to look something constantly gentle showed. He told me he knew guys from Detroit who were taking mortars back, breaking them down so that each one could get a piece in his duffel and then reassembling them when they got together back on the block. 'You see that four-oh-deuce?' he said. 'Now; that'll take out a police station for you. I doan need all that hassle. But maybe nex' year I gonna need it.'

Like every American in Vietnam, he had his obsession with Time. (No one ever talked about When-this-lousy-war-is-over. Only 'How much time you got?') The degree of Day Tripper's obsession, compared with most of the others, could be seen in the calendar on his helmet. No metaphysician ever studied Time the way he did, its components and implications, its per-second per-seconds, its shadings and movement. The Space–Time continuum, Time-as-matter, Augustinian Time; all of that would have been a piece of cake to Day Tripper whose brain cells were arranged like jewels in the finest chronometer. He had assumed that correspondents in Vietnam *had* to be there. When he learned that I had asked to come here he almost let the peaches drop to the ground.

'Lemmee.... lemmee jus' hang on that a minute.' he said. 'You mean you doan' *have* to be here? An' you're *here?*'

I nodded.

'Well, they gotta be payin' you some tough bread.'

'You'd get depressed if I told you.'

He shook his head.

'I mean, they ain' got the bread that'd get me here if I didn' have t' be here.'

'Horse crap,' Mayhew said. 'Day Tripper loves it. He's short now, but he's comin' back, ain't you, Day Tripper?'

'Shit, my momma'll come over here and pull a tour before I fuckin' come back.'

Four more Marines dropped into the pit.

'Where's Evans?' Mayhew demanded. 'Any of you guys know Evans?'

One of the mortarmen came over.

'Evans is over in Danang,' he said. 'He caught a little shit the other night.'

'That right?' Mayhew said. 'Evans get wounded?'

'He hurt bad?' Day Tripper said.

'Took some stuff in the legs. Nothing busted. He'll be back in ten days.'

'That ain' bad enough, then,' Day Tripper said.

'No,' Mayhew said. 'But ten days, sheeit, that's better'n nothin'.'

* * *

A Chinook, forty feet long with rotors front and back, set down on the airstrip by Charlie Med, looking like a great, gross beast getting a body purchase on some mud, blowing bitter gusts of dust, pebbles and debris for a hundred yards around. Everywhere within that circle of wind men turned and crouched, covering their necks against the full violence of it. The wind from those blades could come up strong enough to blow you over, to tear papers from your hands, to lift tarmac sections weighing a hundred pounds in the air. But it was mostly the sharp fragments, the stinging dirt, the muddy, pissed-in water, and you acquired the second sense of when it would reach you, learned to give it only your back and your helmet. The Chinook had flown in with its rear hatch down and a gunner with a .50-caliber machine gun stretched out flat on his stomach, peering over the edge of the hatch. Neither he nor the door gunners would relax their weapons until the chopper touched the strip. Then they let go, the barrels of the big guns dropping down like dead weights in their mounts. A bunch of Marines appeared on the edge of the strip and ran to the chopper, through the ring of harsh, filthy wind, toward the calm at the center. Three mortar rounds came in at three-second intervals, all landing in a cluster two hundred meters down the strip. No one around the chopper stopped. The noise from the Chinook drowned out the noise of the rounds, but we could see the balls of white smoke blowing out away from the strip in the wind, and the men were still running for the chopper. Four full litters were carried at a run from the rear of the Chinook to the med tent. Some walking wounded came out and headed for the tent, some walking slowly, unaided, others moving uncertainly, one being supported by two Marines. The empty litters were returned and loaded with four poncho-covered figures which were set down near some sandbagging in front of the tent. Then the Chinook reared up abruptly, dipped horribly, regained its flight and headed north and west, toward the covering hills.

'One-nine,' Mayhew said. 'I'll bet anything.'

Four kilometers northwest of Khesanh was Hill 861, the hardest-hit of all the sector outposts after Langvei, and it seemed logical to everyone that the First Battalion of the Ninth Marine Regiment should have been chosen to defend it. Some even believed that if anyone but 1/9 had been put there, 861 would never have been hit. Of all the hard-luck outfits in Vietnam, this was said to be the most doomed; doomed in their Search-and-Destroy days before Khesanh, known for a history of ambush and confusion and for a casualty rate which was the highest of any outfit in the entire war. That was the kind of reputation that takes hold most deeply among the men of the outfit itself, and when you were with them you got a sense of dread that came out of something more terrible than just a collective loss of luck. All the odds seemed somehow sharply reduced, estimates of your own survival were revised horribly downward. One afternoon with 1/9 on 861 was enough to bend your nerves for days, because it took only a few minutes up there to see the very worst of it: the stumbles, the simple motions of a walk suddenly wracked by spasms, mouths sand-dry seconds after drinking, the dreamy smiles of total abdication. Hill 861 was the home of the thousand-yard stare, and I prayed hard for a chopper to come and get me away from there, to fly me over the ground fire and land me in the middle of a mortar barrage on the Khesanh pad – whatever! Anything was better than this.

On a night shortly after the Langvei attack, an entire platoon of 1/9 was ambushed during a patrol and wiped out. Hill 861 had been hit repeatedly, once for three days straight during a perimeter probe that turned into a siege that really was a siege. For reasons that no one is certain of, Marine helicopters refused to fly missions up there, and 1/9 was cut off from support, resupply or medical evacuation. It was bad, and they had to get through it any way they could, alone. (The stories from that time became part of the worst Marine legends; the story of one Marine putting a wounded buddy away with a pistol shot because medical help was impossible, or the story of what they did to the N.V.A. prisoner taken beyond the wire; stories like that. Some of them may have even been true.) The old hostility of the Grunt toward Marine Air became total on 861: when the worst of it was over and the first UH-34 finally showed over the hilltop, the door gunner was hit by enemy ground fire and fell out of the chopper. It was a drop of over two hundred feet, and there were Marines on the ground who cheered when he hit.

Mayhew, Day Tripper and I were walking near the triage tent of Charlie Med. In spite of all the shrapnel that had fallen into that tent, no way had been found to protect it. The sandbagging around it was hardly more than five feet high, and the top was entirely exposed. It was one reason why Grunts feared even the mildest of the Going Home wounds. Someone ran out of the tent and took photographs of the four dead Marines. The wind from the Chinook had blown the ponchoes from two of them, and one had no face left at all. A Catholic chaplain on a bicycle rode up to the entrance of the tent and walked inside. A

Marine came out and stood by the flap for a moment, an unlighted
cigarette hanging from his mouth. He had neither a flak jacket nor a
helmet. He let the cigarette drop from his lips, walked a few steps to
the sandbags and sat down with his legs drawn up and his head hanging down between his knees. He threw one limp arm over his head and
began stroking the back of his neck, shaking his head from side to side
violently, as though in agony. He wasn't wounded.

We were here because I had to pass this way to reach my bunker,
where I had to pick up some things to take over to Hotel Company for
the night. Day Tripper wasn't liking the route. He looked at the bodies
and then at me. It was that look which said, 'See? You see what it
does?' I had seen that look so many times during the past months that
I must have had it too now, and neither of us said anything. Mayhew
wasn't letting himself look at anything. It was as though he were walking by himself now, and he was singing in an odd, quiet voice. 'When
you get to San Francisco,' he sang, 'be sure and wear some flowers in
your hair.'

We passed the control tower, that target that was its own aiming-
stake, so prominent and vulnerable that climbing up there was worse
than having to run in front of a machine gun. Two of them had already
been hit, and the sandbags running up the sides didn't seem to make
any difference. We went by the grimy admin buildings and bunkers, a
bunch of deserted 'hardbacks' with crushed metal roofs, the T.O.C.,
the Command Latrine and a post-office bunker. There was the now-
roofless beer hall and the collapsed, abandoned officers' club. The Seabee bunker was just a little further along the road.

It was not like the other bunkers. It was the deepest, safest, cleanest
place in Khesanh, with six feet of timbers, steel and sandbags overhead, and inside it was brightly lit. The Grunts called it the Alamo
Hilton and thought it was candy-assed, while almost every correspondent who came to Khesanh tried to get a bed there. A bottle of
whisky or a case of beer would be enough to get you in for a few
nights, and once you became a friend of the house, gifts like that were
simply a token and very deeply appreciated. The Marines had set up a
press 'facility' very, very near the strip, and it was so bad that a lot of
reporters thought there was a conscious conspiracy working to get
some of us killed off. It was nothing more than a narrow, flimsily
covered, rat-infested hole, and one day when it was empty an incoming
152 shell sewed part of it up.

I went down into the Seabee bunker, picked up a bottle of Scotch and a field jacket, and told one of the Seabees to give my rack to anyone who needed it that night.

'You ain't mad at us or anything?' he said.

'Nothing like that. I'll see you tomorrow.'

'Okay,' he said as I left. 'If you think so.'

As the three of us walked toward the 2/26 positions, two batteries of Marine artillery started firing 105's and 155's from the other side of the base. Every time a round was fired I'd flinch a little, and Mayhew would laugh.

'Them're outgoing,' he said.

Day Tripper heard the deep sliding whistle of the other shells first. 'That ain' no outgoin',' he said, and we ran for a short trench a few yards away.

'That ain't outgoing,' Mayhew said.

'Now what I jus' say?' Day Tripper yelled, and we reached the trench as a shell landed somewhere between the 37th A.R.V.N. Rangers' compound and the ammo dump. A lot of them were coming in, some mortars too, but we didn't count them.

'Sure was some nice mornin',' Day Tripper said. 'Oh man, why they can' jus' leave us alone one time?'

'Cause they ain't gettin' paid to leave us alone,' Mayhew said, laughing. 'Sides, they do it cause they know how it fucks you all up.'

'Tell me you ain' scared shit!'

'You'll never see me scared, motherfucker.'

'Oh no. Three nights ago you was callin' out for your momma while them fuckers was hittin' our wire.'

'Boo-sheeit! I ain't never gettin' hit in Vietnam.'

'Oh no? Okay, mothafucker, why not?'

'Cause,' Mayhew said, 'it don't exist.' It was an old joke, but this time he wasn't laughing.

By now, the trenchline circled the camp almost completely. Most of the northern perimeter was held down by the Second Battalion of the 26th Marine Regiment, and Hotel Company was along this sector, in its westernmost part. It was opposed by North Vietnamese trenches that ended just three hundred meters away. Farther to the east 2/26 sat above a narrow river, and beyond that was Hill 950, three kilometers to the north, which was held by the N.V.A. and whose highest ridge ran exactly parallel to the Khesanh airstrip. The bunkers and connecting trenchworks sat on a rise that ran up from the riverbank, and the hills

began a couple of hundred meters from the far side of the river. Two
hundred meters away, facing the Marine trenches, there was an N.V.A.
sniper with a .50-caliber machine gun who shot at the Marines from a
tiny spider hole. During the day he fired at anything that rose above
the sandbags, and at night he fired at any lights he could see. You could
see him clearly from the trench, and if you were looking through the
scope of a Marine sniper's rifle you could even see his face. The Marines
fired on his position with mortars and recoilless rifles, and he would
drop into his hole and wait. Gunships fired rockets at him, and when
they were through he would come up again and fire. Finally, napalm was
called in, and for ten minutes the air above the spider hole was black
and orange from the strike, while the ground around it was galvanized
clean of every living thing. When all of it cleared, the sniper popped up
and fired off a single round, and the Marines in the trenches cheered.
They called him Luke the Gook, and after that no one wanted anything
to happen to him.

Mayhew had a friend named Orrin from somewhere in Tennessee,
from the mountains there where his family owned three small trucks
and did a short-haul business. On the morning that Mayhew and Day
Tripper had gone over to 1/26 to find Evans, Orrin received a letter
from his wife. It told him straight off that her pregnancy was not seven
months along, as he had believed, but only five. It made all the difference in the world to Orrin. She had felt so awful all the time (she
wrote) that she went to see the minister, and the minister had finally
convinced her that the Truth was God's one sure key to a beautiful
conscience. She would not tell him who the father was (and Honey,
don't you never, never try and make me tell), except to mention that it
was someone Orrin knew well.

When we got back to the company, Orrin was sitting on top of the
sandbags above the trench, alone and exposed, looking out toward the
hills and Luke the Gook. He had a beefy, sulky kid's face, a perpetual
mean squint and a pouting mouth that would break into a dull smile
and then a dry, soundless laugh. It was the face of someone who would
hunt the winter out and then let the meat go to rot, a mean Southland
aberration of a face. He just sat there, working the bolt of a freshly
cleaned .45. No one in the trench would go near him or say anything to
him, except to yell out, 'Come on down, Orrin. You'll get greased for
sure, Motherfucker.' Finally, the Gunnery Sergeant came along and
said, 'If you don't get your ass down off that berm I'll shoot you
myself.'

'Listen,' Mayhew said. 'Maybe you better go and see the Chaplain.'
'Real good,' Orrin said. 'What's that cocksucker gone to do for me?'
'Maybe you could get an emergency leave.'

'No,' someone said. 'There's gotta be a death in the family before you'll get out like that.'

'Oh, don't worry,' Orrin said. 'There's gone be a death in my family. Just soon's I git home.' And then he laughed.

It was a terrible laugh, very quiet and intense, and it was the thing that made everyone who heard it believe Orrin. After that, he was the crazy Grunt who was going to get through the war so he could go home and kill his Old Lady. It made him someone special in the company. It made a lot of guys think that he was lucky now, that nothing could happen to him, and they stayed as close to him as they could. I even felt some of it, enough to be glad that we would be in the same bunker that night. It made sense. I believed it too, and I would have really been surprised if I had heard later that anything had happened to him. But that was the kind of thing you seldom heard after you left an outfit, the kind of thing you avoided hearing if you could. Maybe he was killed or maybe he changed his mind, but I doubt it. When I remembered Orrin, all I could think of was that there was going to be a shooting in Tennessee.

Once on a two-day pass to Danang, Mayhew had gone off limits and into the black market looking for grass and an air mattress. He never found the grass, and he had been scared to death when he finally bought the mattress. He told me that nothing that had ever happened at Khesanh had scared him the way he had been scared that day. I don't know what he had been told the M.P.'s would do to him if they'd caught him in the market, but as he told the story it had been the best adventure he'd had since the day two years back when the game warden had used a helicopter to chase him and a friend out of the woods after deer season had closed. We were sitting in the mingy damp of the eight-man bunker where Mayhew and Day Tripper both slept. Mayhew had been trying to make me use his mattress for the night and I'd refused it. He said that if I didn't sleep on it he was just going to take it and throw it outside into the trench and leave it there until morning. I told him that if I'd wanted an air mattress I could have picked one up any time in Danang, and that the M.P.'s wouldn't have even hassled me about it. I said I liked sleeping on the ground, it was good training. He said that that was all horse crap (he was right), and he swore to God the mattress would just lie out there all night with the rest of the rubbish that collects on trench floors. Then he got very mysterious and told me to think about it while he was gone. Day Tripper tried to find out where he was going, but Mayhew wouldn't tell him.

During those brief moments when the ground all around you was not rumbling, when there were no airstrikes on the hills, no incoming or outgoing or firing from the perimeter, you could sit inside and listen to the rats running across the bunker floor. A lot of them had been poisoned, shot, caught in traps or killed by the lucky toss of a combat boot, and they were here in the bunker, too. There was the smell of urine, of old, old sweat, C-ration decay, moldy canvas and private crud, and that mixing up of other smells that were special to combat zones. A lot of us believed that exhaustion and fear could be smelled and that certain dreams gave off an odor. (We were regular Hemingway Gypsies about some things. No matter how much wind a chopper would put out as it landed, you could always tell when there were body bags around an LZ, and the tents where the Lurps, the Long Range Reconaissance Patrol troops lived, smelled unlike any other tents anywhere in Vietnam.) This bunker was at least as bad as any I'd ever been in, and I gagged in there once, the first time. Because there was almost no light, you had to imagine most of what you smelled, and that became something like a pastime. I hadn't realized how black Day Tripper was until we walked inside the bunker.

'It *defi*nitely stinks somethin' fierce in here,' he said. 'I gotta be gettin' me a mo' — uh — ef*fec*tive deodorant.' He paused. 'Any kinda shit come up tonight, you jus' keep with me. You be lucky Mayhew don't think you a Zip an' blast your head off. He'll go pretty crazy sometimes.'

'You think we'll be hit?'

He shrugged. 'He might try an' do a probe. He did that number 'gainst us three nights ago an' kill one boy. Kill a Brother.' He smiled. 'That ain' no easy trick. But this here's a real good bunker. We took some stuff right on top here. All kindsa dirt come down on top of our heads, but we'se all right.'

'Are guys sleeping in their flak jackets?'

'Some do. I doan'. Mayhew, crazy fucker, he sleeps bare-ass. He's so tough, man, the hawk is out, an' he's in here bare-ass.'

'What's that? About the hawk?'

'That means it's a co-o-old motherfucker.'

Mayhew had been gone for more than an hour now, and when Day

Tripper and I stepped out on the ammocrate planking that made the trench floor we saw him outside, talking to some Grunts. He started walking toward us, laughing, looking like a little boy dressed in a man's combat gear, swimming in his flak jacket, and the Grunts sang after him, 'Mayhew's a lifer.... 'Ray for him.'

'Hey, Day Tripper!' he called. 'Hey, you hear it, motherfucker?'

'I hear *what*?'

'I just went over and extended.'

The smile vanished on Day Tripper's face. He looked like he didn't understand for a second, and then he looked angry, almost dangerous.

'Say again?'

'Yeah,' Mayhew said. 'I just saw the Old Man about it.'

'Uh-huh. How long you extend for?'

'Just four months.'

'Jus' four months. Tha's real fine, Jim.'

'Hey, man....'

'Don' talk to me, Jim.'

'Oh come on, Day Tripper, Don't be a hard ass. It gets me outta the Corps three months early.'

'Whatever. Jim.'

'Oh man, don't call me that.' He looked at me. 'Every time he gets pissed off he calls me that. Listen, motherfucker, I get outta the *Marine Corps* early. And I get a home leave. The Old Man says I can go next month.'

'You *cain't* be talkin to *me*. I jus' don' hear nonna that. I don' hear one word you sayin', Jim.'

'Aw....'

'You jus' another dumb Grunt. What I gotta talk to you for? It's like you never hear one word I say to you, ever. Not one word. An' I *know* ... oh man, I jus' *know* you already sign that paper.'

Mayhew didn't say anything. It was hard to believe that the two were around the same age.

'What I gonna do with you, poor fucker? Why ... why, you jus' don' go runnin' out over th' wire there? Let 'em gun you down an' get it over with. Here, man, here's a grenade. Why you jus' don' go up backa the shithouse an' pull the pin an' lie down on it?'

'You're unbe*liev*able! Man, it's just four months!'

'Four months? Baby, four *seconds* in this whorehouse'll get you greased. An' after your poppa an' all that. An' you jus' ain't *learn*ed. You're the sorriest, *sorriest* Grunt mother I ever seen. No, man, but the *sorriest!* Fuckin' Mayhew, man. I feel sorry for you.'

'Day Tripper? Hey, it'll be okay. Y'know?'

'Sure, baby. Jus' don' talk to me right away. Clean your rifle. Write your momma. Do *somethin'*. Talk to me later.'

'We can smoke some bullshit.'

'Okay, baby. Say later.' He walked back into the bunker and lay down. Mayhew took off his helmet and scratched out something written on the side. It had read, '20 April and OUTTA SIGHT!'

# Truman Capote from
# In cold blood

Capote's determination to reproduce the techniques of the novel in nonfiction is obvious in this passage from In Cold Blood. He uses the technique of parallel narratives that John Steinbeck was so fond of. The following passage comes toward the end of the book. The two ex-convicts, Perry and Dick, have slaughtered all four members of a Kansas farm family, the Clutters, and are drifting across the country. Christmas finds them in a third-rate pensioner's hotel in Miami Beach. In the parallel narratives – one being the story of the two murderers and the other being the story of the good folks-at-home in Kansas – Capote switches very pointedly from the Low Rent Noxema by-the-pool Yule in Miami to the Apple Cider Blowy Snow Off-to-Grandma's-we-go Christmas in Wholesome Holcomb.

For all his attention to novelistic technique, however, Capote does not use point of view in as sophisticated a way as he does in fiction. One seldom feels that he is really inside the minds of the characters. One gets a curious blend of third-person point of view and omniscient narration. Capote probably had sufficient information to use point of view in a more complex fashion but was not yet ready to let himself go in nonfiction. Another weakness is one that is inherent in reconstructed crime stories: the dialogue is confined to short takes; i.e., it is seldom extended enough to develop character fully. The reason is obvious. The reporter could not be present for the events themselves and has to reconstruct the dialogue from what his subjects can remember, and one's recollection of dialogue is almost invariably confined to highlights. On the other hand, Capote's use of status details is quite effective, as in the sketching in of the scene out back of the Somerset Hotel and the account of Dick's covetousness at the Eden Roc. T.W.

In Miami Beach, 335 Ocean Drive is the address of the Somerset Hotel, a small, square building painted more or less white, with many lavender touches, among them a lavender sign that reads, 'VACANCY – LOWEST RATES – BEACH FACILITIES – ALWAYS A SEABREEZE.' It is one of a row of little stucco-and-cement hotels lining a white, melancholy street. In December, 1959, the Somerset's 'beach facilities' consisted of two beach umbrellas stuck in a strip of sand at the rear of the hotel. One umbrella, pink, had written upon it, 'We Serve Valentine Ice-Cream.' At noon on Christmas Day, a quartet of women lay under and around it, a transistor radio serenading them. The second umbrella, blue and bearing the command 'Tan with Coppertone,' sheltered Dick and Perry, who for five days had been living at the Somerset, in a double room renting for eighteen dollars weekly.

Perry said, 'You never wished me a Merry Christmas.'

'Merry Christmas, honey. And a Happy New Year.'

Dick wore bathing trunks, but Perry, as in Acapulco, refused to expose his injured legs – he feared the sight might 'offend' other beach-goers – and therefore sat fully clothed, wearing even socks and shoes. Still, he was comparatively content, and when Dick stood up and started performing exercises – headstands, meant to impress the ladies beneath the pink umbrella – he occupied himself with the Miami *Herald*. Presently he came across an inner-page story that won his entire attention. It concerned murder, the slaying of a Florida family, a Mr. and Mrs. Clifford Walker, their four-year-old son, and their two-year-old daughter. Each of the victims, though not bound or gagged, had been shot through the head with a .22 weapon. The crime, clueless and apparently motiveless, had taken place Saturday night, December 19, at the Walker home, on a cattle-raising ranch not far from Tallahassee.

Perry interrupted Dick's athletics to read the story aloud, and said, 'Where were we last Saturday night?'

'Tallahassee?'

'I'm asking you.'

Dick concentrated. On Thursday night, taking turns at the wheel, they had driven out of Kansas and through Missouri into Arkansas and over the Ozarks, 'up' to Louisiana, where a burned-out generator stopped them early Friday morning. (A second-hand replacement, bought in Shreveport, cost twenty-two fifty.) That night they'd slept parked by the side of the road somewhere near the Alabama–Florida border. The next day's journey, an unhurried affair, had included several touristic diversions – visits to an alligator farm and a rattlesnake ranch, a ride in a glass-bottomed boat over a silvery-clear swamp lake, a late and long and costly broiled-lobster lunch at a roadside seafood restaurant. Delightful day! But both were exhausted when they arrived at Tallahassee, and decided to spend the night there. 'Yes, Tallahassee,' Dick said.

'Amazing!' Perry glanced through the article again. 'Know what I wouldn't be surprised? If this wasn't done by a lunatic. Some nut that read about what happened out in Kansas.'

Dick, because he didn't care to hear Perry 'get going on that subject,' shrugged and grinned and trotted down to the ocean's edge, where he ambled awhile over the surf-drenched sand, here and there stooping to collect a seashell. As a boy he'd so envied the son of a neighbor who had gone to the Gulf Coast on holiday and returned with a box full of shells – so hated him – that he'd stolen the shells and one by one crushed them with a hammer. Envy was constantly with him; the Enemy was anyone who was someone he wanted to be or who had anything he wanted to have.

For instance, the man he had seen by the pool at the Fontainebleau. Miles away, shrouded in a summery veil of heat-haze and sea-sparkle, he could see the towers of the pale, expensive hotels – the Fontainebleau, the Eden Roc, the Roney Plaza. On their second day in Miami he had suggested to Perry that they invade these pleasure-domes. 'Maybe pick up a coupla rich women,' he had said. Perry had been most reluctant; he felt people would stare at them because of their khaki trousers and T-shirts. Actually their tour of the Fontainebleau's gaudy premises went unnoticed, amid the men striding about in Bermuda shorts of candy-striped raw silk, and the women wearing bathing suits and mink stoles simultaneously. The trespassers had loitered in the lobby, strolled in the garden, lounged by the swimming pool. It was there that Dick saw the man, who was his own age – twenty-eight or thirty. He could have been a 'gambler or lawyer or maybe a gangster from Chicago.' Whatever he was, he looked as though he knew the glories of money and power. A blonde who resembled Marilyn Monroe was kneading him with suntan oil, and his lazy, beringed hand reached for a tumbler of iced orange juice. All that belonged to him, Dick, but he would never have it. Why should that sonofabitch have everything, while he had nothing? Why should that 'big-shot bastard' have all the luck? With a knife in his hand, he, Dick, had power. Big-shot bastards like that had better be careful or he might 'open them up and let a little of their luck spill on the floor.' But Dick's day was ruined. The beautiful blonde rubbing on the suntan oil had ruined it. He'd said to Perry, 'Let's pull the hell out of here.'

Now a young girl, probably twelve, was drawing figures in the sand, carving out big, crude faces with a piece of driftwood. Dick, pretending to admire her art, offered the shells he had gathered. 'They make good eyes,' he said. The child accepted the gift, whereupon Dick smiled and winked at her. He was sorry he felt as he did about her, for his sexual interest in female children was a failing of which he was 'sincerely ashamed' – a secret he'd not confessed to anyone and hoped no one suspected (though he was aware that Perry had reason to), because other people might not think it 'normal.' That, to be sure, was something he was certain he was – a 'normal.' Seducing pubescent girls, as he had done 'eight or nine' times in the last several years, did not disprove it, for if the truth were known, most real men had the same desires he had. He took the child's hand and said, 'You're my baby girl. My little sweetheart.' But she objected. Her hand, held by his, twitched like a fish on a hook, and he recognized the astounded expression in her eyes from earlier incidents in his career. He let go, laughed lightly, and said, 'Just a game. Don't you like games?'

Perry, still reclining under the blue umbrella, had observed the scene and realized Dick's purpose at once, and despised him for it; he had 'no respect for people who can't control themselves sexually,' especially when the lack of control involved what he called 'pervertiness' – 'bothering kids,' 'queer stuff,' rape. And he thought he had made his views obvious to Dick; indeed, hadn't they almost had a fist fight when quite recently he had prevented Dick from raping a terrified young girl? However, he wouldn't care to repeat that particular test of strength. He was relieved when he saw the child walk away from Dick.

Christmas carols were in the air; they issued from the radio of the four women and mixed strangely with Miami's sunshine and the cries of the querulous, never thoroughly silent seagulls. 'Oh, come let us adore Him, Oh, come let us adore Him': a cathedral choir, an exalted music that moved Perry to tears – which refused to stop, even after the music did. And as was not uncommon when he was thus afflicted, he dwelt upon a possibility that had for him 'tremendous fascination': suicide. As a child he had often thought of killing himself, but those were sentimental reveries born of a wish to punish his father and mother and other enemies. From young manhood onward, however, the prospect of ending his life had more and more lost its fantastic quality. That, he must remember, was Jimmy's 'solution,' and Fern's, too. And lately it had come to seem not just an alternative but the specific death awaiting him.

Anyway, he couldn't see that he had 'a lot to live for.' Hot islands and buried gold, diving deep in fire-blue seas toward sunken treasure – such dreams were gone. Gone, too, was 'Perry O'Parsons,' the name invented for the singing sensation of stage and screen that he'd half-seriously hoped some day to be. Perry O'Parsons had died without having ever lived. What was there to look forward to? He and Dick were 'running a race without a finish line' – that was how it struck him. And now, after not quite a week in Miami, the long ride was to resume. Dick, who had worked one day at the ABC auto-service company for sixty-five cents an hour, had told him, 'Miami's worse than Mexico. Sixty-five cents! Not me. I'm white.' So tomorrow, with only twenty-seven dollars left of the money raised in Kansas City, they were heading west again, to Texas, to Nevada – 'nowhere definite.'

Dick, who had waded into the surf, returned. He fell, wet and breathless, face down on the sticky sand.

'How was the water?'

'Wonderful.'

The closeness of Christmas to Nancy Clutter's birthday, which was right after New Year's, had always created problems for her boy friend, Bobby Rupp. It had strained his imagination to think of two suitable gifts in such quick succession. But each year, with money made working summers on his father's sugar-beet farm, he had done the best he could, and on Christmas morning he had always hurried to the Clutter house carrying a package that his sisters had helped him wrap and that he hoped would surprise Nancy and delight her. Last year he had given her a small heart-shaped gold locket. This year, as forehanded as ever, he'd been wavering between the imported perfumes on sale at Norris Drugs and a pair of riding boots. But then Nancy had died.

On Christmas morning, instead of racing off to River Valley Farm, he remained at home, and later in the day he shared with his family the splendid dinner his mother had been a week preparing. Everybody – his parents and every one of his seven brothers and sisters – had treated him gently since the tragedy. All the same, at mealtimes he was told again and again that he must please eat. No one comprehended that really he was ill, that grief had made him so, that grief had drawn a circle around him he could not escape from and others could not enter – except possibly Sue. Until Nancy's death he had not appreciated Sue, never felt altogether comfortable with her. She was too different – took seriously things that even girls ought not to take very seriously: paintings, poems, the music she played on the piano. And, of course, he was jealous of her; her position in Nancy's esteem, though of another order, had been at least equal to his. But that was why she was able to understand his loss. Without Sue, without her almost constant presence, how could he have withstood such an avalanche of shocks – the crime itself, his interviews with Mr. Dewey, the pathetic irony of being for a while the principal suspect?

Then, after about a month, the friendship waned. Bobby went less frequently to sit in the Kidwells' tiny, cozy parlor, and when he did go, Sue seemed not as welcoming. The trouble was that they were forcing each other to mourn and remember what in fact they wanted to forget. Sometimes Bobby could: when he was playing basketball or driving his car over country roads at eighty miles an hour, or when, as part of a self-imposed athletic program (his ambition was to be a high-school gymnastics instructor), he took long-distance jog-trots across flat yellow fields. And now, after helping clear the dining table of all its holiday dishes, that was what he decided to do – put on a sweatshirt and go for a run.

The weather was remarkable. Even for western Kansas, renowned for the longevity of its Indian summers, the current sample seemed far-fetched – dry air, bold sun, azure sky. Optimistic ranchers were predicting an 'open winter' – a season so bland that cattle could graze during the whole of it. Such winters are rare, but Bobby could remember one – the year he had started to court Nancy. They were both twelve, and after school he used to carry her book satchel the mile separating the Holcomb schoolhouse from her father's farm ranch. Often, if the day was warm and sun-kindled, they stopped along the way and sat by the river, a snaky, slow-moving, brown piece of the Arkansas.

Once Nancy had said to him, 'One summer, when we were in Colorado, I saw where the Arkansas begins. The exact place. You wouldn't believe it, though. That it was our river. It's not the same color. But pure as drinking water. And fast. And full of rocks. Whirlpools. Daddy caught a trout.' It had stayed with Bobby, her memory of the river's source, and since her death ... Well, he couldn't explain it, but whenever he looked at the Arkansas, it was for an instant transformed, and what he saw was not a muddy stream meandering across the Kansas plains, but what Nancy had described – a Colorado torrent, a chilly, crystal trout river speeding down a mountain valley. That was how Nancy had been: like young water – energetic, joyous.

Usually, though, western Kansas winters are imprisoning, and usually frost on the fields and razory winds have altered the climate before Christmas. Some years back snow had fallen on Christmas Eve and continued falling, and when Bobby set out the next morning for the

Clutter property, a three-mile walk, he had had to fight through deep drifts. It was worth it, for though he was numbed and scarlet, the welcome he got thawed him thoroughly. Nancy was amazed and proud, and her mother, often so timid and distant, had hugged and kissed him, insisting that he wrap up in a quilt and sit close to the parlor fire. While the women worked in the kitchen, he and Kenyon and Mr. Clutter had sat around the fire cracking walnuts and pecans, and Mr. Clutter said he was reminded of another Christmas, when he was Kenyon's age: 'There were seven of us. Mother, my father, the two girls, and us three boys. We lived on a farm a good ways from town. For that reason it was the custom to do our Christmas buying in a bunch — make the trip once and do it all together. The year I'm thinking of, the morning we were supposed to go, the snow was as high as today, higher, and still coming down — flakes like saucers. Looked like we were in for a snowbound Christmas with no presents under the tree. Mother and the girls were heartbroken. Then I had an idea.' He would saddle their huskiest plow horse, ride into town and shop for everybody. The family agreed. All of them gave him their Christmas savings and a list of the things they wished him to buy: four yards of calico, a football, a pincushion, shotgun shells — an assortment of orders that took until nightfall to fill. Heading homeward, the purchases secure inside a tarpaulin sack, he was grateful that his father had forced him to carry a lantern, and glad, too, that the horse's harness was strung with bells, for both their jaunty racket and the careening light of the kerosene lantern were a comfort to him.

'The ride in, that was easy, a piece of cake. But now the road was gone, and every landmark.' Earth and air — all was snow. The horse, up to his haunches in it, slipped sidewise. 'I dropped the lamp. We were lost in the night. It was just a question of time before we fell asleep and froze. Yes, I was afraid. But I prayed. And I felt God's presence ...' Dogs howled. He followed the noise until he saw the windows of a neighboring farmhouse. 'I ought to have stopped there. But I thought of the family — imagined my mother in tears, Dad and the boys getting up a search party, and I pushed on. So, naturally, I wasn't too happy when finally I reached home and found the house dark. Doors locked. Found everybody had gone to bed and plain forgot me. None of them could understand why I was so put out. Dad said, "We were sure you'd stay the night in town. Good grief, boy! Who'd have thought you hadn't better sense than to start home in a perfect blizzard?"'

•    •    •

The cider-tart odor of spoiling apples. Apple trees and pear trees, peach and cherry: Mr. Clutter's orchard, the treasured assembly of fruit trees he had planted. Bobby, running mindlessly, had not meant to come here, or to any other part of River Valley Farm. It was inexplicable, and he turned to leave, but he turned again and wandered toward the house – white and solid and spacious. He had always been impressed by it, and pleased to think his girl friend lived there. But now that it was deprived of the late owner's dedicated attention, the first threads of decay's cobweb were being spun. A gravel rake lay rusting in the driveway; the lawn was parched and shabby. That fateful Sunday, when the sheriff summoned ambulances to remove the murdered family, the ambulances had driven across the grass straight to the front door, and the tire tracks were still visible.

The hired man's house was empty, too; he had found new quarters for his family near Holcomb – to no one's surprise, for nowadays, though the weather was glittering, the Clutter place seemed shadowed, and hushed, and motionless. But as Bobby passed a storage barn and, beyond that, a livestock corral, he heard a horse's tail swish. It was Nancy's Babe, the obedient old dappled mare with flaxen mane and dark-purple eyes like magnificent pansy blossoms. Clutching her mane, Bobby rubbed his cheek along Babe's neck – something Nancy used to do. And Babe whinnied. Last Sunday, the last time he had visited the Kidwells, Sue's mother had mentioned Babe. Mrs. Kidwell, a fanciful woman, had been standing at a window watching dusk tint the outdoors, the sprawling prarie. And out of the blue she had said, Susan? You know what I keep seeing? Nancy. On Babe. Coming this way.'

Perry noticed them first – hitch-hikers, a boy and an old man, both carrying homemade knap-sacks, and despite the blowy weather, a gritty and bitter Texas wind, wearing only overalls and a thin denim shirt. 'Let's give them a lift,' Perry said. Dick was reluctant; he had no objection to assisting hitch-hikers provided they looked as if they could pay their way – at least 'chip in a couple of gallons of gas.' But Perry, little old big-hearted Perry, was always pestering Dick to pick up the damnedest, sorriest-looking people. Finally Dick agreed, and stopped the car.

The boy – a stocky, sharp-eyed, talkative towhead of about twelve – was exuberantly grateful, but the old man, whose face was seamed and yellow, feebly crawled into the back seat and slumped there silently.

The boy said, 'We sure do appreciate this. Johnny was ready to drop. We ain't had a ride since Galveston.'

Perry and Dick had left that port city an hour earlier, having spent a morning there applying at various shipping offices for jobs as able-bodied seamen. One company offered them immediate work on a tanker bound for Brazil, and, indeed, the two would now have been at sea if their prospective employer had not discovered that neither man possessed union papers or a passport. Strangely, Dick's disappointment exceeded Perry's: 'Brazil! That's where they're building a whole new capital city. Right from scratch. Imagine getting in on the ground floor of something like that! Any fool could make a fortune.'

'Where you headed?' Perry asked the boy.

'Sweetwater.'

'Where's Sweetwater?'

'Well, it's along in this direction somewhere. It's somewhere in Texas. Johnny, here, he's my gramp. And he's got a sister lives in Sweetwater. Least, I sure Jesus hope she does. We thought she lived in Jasper, Texas. But when we got to Jasper, folks told us her and her people moved to Galveston. But she wasn't in Galveston — lady there said she was gone to Sweetwater. I sure Jesus hope we find her. Johnny,' he said, rubbing the old man's hands, as if to thaw them, 'you hear me, Johnny? We're riding in a nice warm Chevrolet — '56 model.'

The old man coughed, rolled his head slightly, opened and closed his eyes, and coughed again.

Dick said, 'Hey, *listen*. What's wrong with him?'

'It's the change,' the boy said. 'And the walking. We been walking since before Christmas. Seems to me we covered the better part of Texas.' In the most matter-of-fact voice, and while continuing to massage the old man's hands, the boy told them that up to the start of the present journey he and his grandfather and an aunt had lived alone on a farm near Shreveport, Louisiana. Not long ago the aunt had died. 'Johnny's been poorly about a year, and Auntie had all the work to do. With only me to help. We were chopping firewood. Chopping up a stump. Right in the middle of it, Auntie said she was wore out. Ever seen a horse just lay down and never get up? I have. And that's like what Auntie did.' A few days before Christmas the man from whom his grandfather rented the farm 'turned us off the place,' the boy continued. 'That's how come we started out for Texas. Looking to find Mrs. Jackson. I never seen her, but she's Johnny's own blood sister.

And somebody's got to take us in. Leastways, him. He can't go a lot more. Last night it rained on us.'

The car stopped. Perry asked Dick why he had stopped it.

'That man's very sick,' Dick said.

'Well? What do you want to do? Put him out?'

'Use your head. Just for once.'

'You really are a mean bastard.'

'Suppose he dies?'

The boy said, 'He won't die. We've got this far, he'll wait now.'

Dick persisted. 'Suppose he dies? Think of what could happen. The questions.'

'Frankly, I don't give a damn. You want to put them out? Then by all means.' Perry looked at the invalid, still somnolent, dazed, deaf, and he looked at the boy, who returned his gaze calmly, not begging, not 'asking for anything,' and Perry remembered himself at that age, his own wanderings with an old man. 'Go ahead. Put them out. But I'll be getting out, too.'

'O.K. O.K. O.K. Only don't forget,' said Dick. 'It's your damn fault.'

Dick shifted gears. Suddenly, as the car began to move again, the boy hollered, 'Hold it!' Hopping out, he hurried along the edge of the road, stopped, stooped, picked up one, two, three, four empty Coca-Cola bottles, ran back, and hopped in, happy and grinning. 'There's plenty of money in bottles,' he said to Dick. 'Why, mister, if you was to drive kind of slow, I guarantee you we can pick us up a big piece of change. That's what me and Johnny have been eating off. Re-fund money.'

Dick was amused, but he was also interested, and when next the boy commanded him to halt, he at once obeyed. The commands came so frequently that it took them an hour to travel five miles, but it was worth it. The kid had an 'honest-to-God genius' for spotting, amid the roadside rocks and grassy rubble, the emerald daubs that had once held 7-Up and Canada Dry. Perry soon developed his own personal gift for spying out bottles. At first he merely indicated to the boy the whereabouts of his finds; he thought it too undignified to scurry about collecting them himself. It was all 'pretty silly,' just 'kid stuff.' Nevertheless, the game generated a treasure-hunt excitement, and presently he, too, succumbed to the fun, the fervor of this quest for refundable empties. Dick, too, but Dick was in dead earnest. Screwy as it seemed, maybe this was a way to make some money — or at any rate, a few bucks. Lord knows, he and Perry could use them; their combined finances amounted at the moment to less than five dollars.

Now all three – Dick and the boy and Perry – were piling out of the car and shamelessly, though amiably, competing with one another. Once Dick located a cache of wine and whiskey bottles at the bottom of a ditch, and was chagrined to learn that his discovery was valueless. 'They don't give no refund on liquor empties,' the boy informed him. 'Even some of the beers ain't no good. I don't mess with them usually. Just stick with the surefire things. Dr. Pepper. Pepsi. Coke. White Rock. Nehi.'

Dick said, 'What's your name?'

'Bill,' the boy said.

'Well, Bill. You're a regular education.'

Nightfall came, and forced the hunters to quit – that, and lack of space, for they had amassed as many bottles as the car could contain. The trunk was filled, the back seat seemed a glittering dump heap; unnoticed, unmentioned by even his grandson, the ailing old man was all but hidden under the shifting, dangerously chiming cargo.

Dick said, 'Be funny if we had a smash-up.'

A bunch of lights publicized the New Motel, which proved to be, as the travelers neared it, an impressive compound consisting of bungalows, a garage, a restaurant, and a cocktail lounge. Taking charge, the boy said to Dick, 'Pull in there. Maybe we can make a deal. Only let me talk. I've had the experience. Sometimes they try to cheat.' Perry could not imagine 'anyone smart enough to cheat that kid,' he said later. 'It didn't shame him a bit going in there with all those bottles. Me, I never could've, I'd have felt so ashamed. But the people at the motel were nice about it; they just laughed. Turned out the bottles were worth twelve dollars and sixty cents.'

The boy divided the money evenly, giving half to himself, the rest to his partners, and said, 'Know what? I'm gonna blow me and Johnny to a good feed. Ain't you fellows hungry?'

As always, Dick was. And after so much activity, even Perry felt starved. As he later told about it, 'We carted the old man into the restaurant and propped him up at a table. He looked exactly the same – thanatoid. And he never said one word. But you should have seen him shovel it in. The kid ordered him pancakes; he said that was what Johnny liked best. I swear he ate something like thirty pancakes. With maybe two pounds of butter, and a quart of syrup. The kid could put it down himself. Potato chips and ice cream, that was all he wanted, but he sure ate a lot of them. I wonder it didn't make him sick.'

During the dinner party, Dick, who had consulted a map, announced that Sweetwater was a hundred or more miles west of the route he was driving – the route that would. take him across New Mexico and Arizona to Nevada – to Las Vegas. Though this was true, it was clear to Perry that Dick simply wanted to rid himself of the boy and the old man. Dick's purpose was obvious to the boy, too, but he was polite and said, 'Oh, don't you worry about us. Plenty of traffic must stop here. We'll get a ride.'

The boy walked with them to the car, leaving the old man to devour a fresh stack of pancakes. He shook hands with Dick and Perry, wished them a Happy New Year, and waved them away into the dark.

# Joe Eszterhas
# Charlie Simpson's apocalypse

*Over the past three years no periodical has achieved a more spectacular success with the New Journalism than Jann Wenner's Rolling Stone. One of Wenner's great strengths as an editor is that he insists on detailed reporting in a field — Rock, Pop, Hip, Underground — where many editors give in to writers who want to work strictly from off the top of the head. Wenner has discovered and encouraged many talented young writers, among them, Joe Eszterhas. Eszterhas's 'Charlie Simpson's Apocalypse' brought him immediate and wide attention from editors, book publishers and other writers.*

*The structure of the story is similar to that of In Cold Blood: first the sketching in of a small-town scene, then a rapid progress to the moment of the murder, then an elaborate backtracking to develop the character of the killer and account for the crime — all of it told by an invisible narrator. But unlike Capote, who was determined above all to write nonfiction according to the conventions of the twentieth-century novel, Eszterhas winds up by doing something that, I think, demonstrates the flexibility of the New Journalism. He suddenly introduces himself, the reporter, as a character. He tells how he came to town, how he dressed up one way to talk to the town's more solid burghers and another way to talk to the freaks. In other words, he suddenly, at the very end, decides to tell you how he put the story together. Far from being like an epilogue or anticlimax, however, the device leads to a denouement of considerable power. T.W.*

Right after the sun comes up, first thing folks do around Harrisonville, Missouri, is go up to the barn and see if the mare is still there. Horse-thieves drive around the gravel roads and brushy hills in tractor-trailers looking to rustle lazyboned nags. Then they grind them up into bags of meat jelly for the dogfood people. It's getting so that a man can't live in peace anywhere, not even on his own plot of land.

Harrisonville is 40 miles southeast of Kansas City along Interstate 71, just down the blacktop from the red-brick farmhouse where Harry

S. Truman, haberdasher and President, was born. The little town is filled with weeping willows, alfalfa, Longhorn steer, and Black White-face cows. Life should be staid and bucolic, a slumbering leftover of what everyone who buys the $3.00 Wednesday-night Catfish Dinner at Scott's Bar B-Q calls Them Good Old Days. But it isn't like that any-more. There's always some botheration to afflict a man these days and if it isn't the horse-thieves or the velvetleaf that plagued the soybeans last year, then it's them vagrant tornadoes.

They call this lush area Twister Alley. Of all the woebegone acreage in America, Harrisonville and the fast-blink single-gas-station towns clustered about it — Peculiar, Lone Jack, Gunn City — attract more funnel clouds and 90 mph whirlwinds each hardluck year than anyplace else. The whirlwinds sweep down across greenbacked rows of wheat and corn, tottering power lines and flame onto dried haystacks — rais-ing hell two or three times a season with the insurance rates and the little money a farming man has left after Uncle Sam takes his share. For some reason the land provokes these killer-storms and, out around a bonfire on a warm spring night, a man can sit around with his Mail Pouch and wait for jagged strips of angry lightning to neon the wisteria and the hollyhock.

Except for the twisters, the horse-thieves and the velvetleaf, it is like any other tacky, jaundiced Southern town. It carries a weighty but atrophied Dixie tradition, having once been a proud link of the Con-federacy, although it is not very far from the Kansas border-town where John Brown, saintly revolutionary murderer, launched his blood-bath a century ago. Its most famous citizen is a machinist named Jerry Binder, who won a ballyhooed $5000 suggestion award from Trans World Airlines for improving the turbine of the JT3D jet engine. Billy Quantrill's Civil War raiders once raped and ravaged here to historical acclaim and Harry 'Harricula' Truman, or just plain 'Harry S.' (as they say at Scott's Bar B-Q) visited here one Appreciation Day not long after he dropped the Aye-Tomic Bomb. Harry S. chewed saucy chicken wings on the courthouse steps and told the folks the White House was nothin' but a big white jail.

Harrisonville serves as Cass County's seat — population 4700 — and by 1980 will be only a few miles south of the exact demographic center of America. It will be at the very heart of the calcified Heartland, a patriotic footnote which pleases the town's flaccid watery-eyed mayor and dentist, Dr. M. O. Raine, to no end.

This spring the last snowfall was shoveled away on April Fool's Day and folks started getting ready for the summer: The Harrisonville Fire Department tested its six Civil Defense Air Raid-Tornado Warning sirens and even the 89-year-old Harrisonville Hotel, the oldest building in town, its roof damaged by generations of funnelclouds, got a homey face-lift. Its eroded brick was scraped and washed down. The Missouri Turkey Shoot Season was opening; the American Legion Building at 303 Pearl Street, a mausoleum of cigar butts, housed a nightly clap-happy gospel meeting — 'Do You Want To Be Saved?' — and the Peculiar Panthers knocked off the favored Harrisonville Wildcat basketball team 66–55. The Chamber of Commerce announced 'real-big, real-good' news — the long-delayed acquisition of a shiny new cherry-topped 1972 ambulance.

Less than a month later on a muggy thunderheaded warm day, Friday, April 21st, at 5:55 PM, the Civil Defense sirens let out a high-pitched scream that cut across the wheatfields for miles around. Folks hurried to their citizens' band radios to await emergency instructions.

They thought it was another goddamn tornado.

They couldn't understand the breathless disjointed words which G. M. Allen, town banker and fire chief, garbled at his white-helmeted Civil Defense volunteers in the hamlets and hollows around town.

*What in tarnation was G. M. talking about?* 'Hippies . . . Killed two policemen . . . Dead . . . M-1 carbine . . . Blood all over the place . . . the Simpson boy . . . Come on into town . . . Bring your guns . . . There's more of 'em . . . Yo, a revolution.'

## 1 Charlie Simpson's mad-dog dance

On Friday, April, 21st:

Astronaut John W. Young leaped up off the moondust and exuberantly saluted the American flag. At North Carolina State University, a thousand kids danced around a hand-painted sign that said: NIXON'S MACHINE IS FALLING. In Lawrence, Kansas, 600 persons met in front of Strong Hall to plan an anti-war march.

At 5:55 PM on the town square in Harrisonville, Missouri, Charles Simpson, 24 years old, 6'3", 180 pounds, flowing shoulder-length gun-metal black hair, known to his friends as 'Ootney,' leaped out of a red Volkswagen. He was an asthmatic who liked Henry David Thoreau and had eyes like razor slits. The car was driven by a friend, John Risner, 26, a pallid Navy veteran, the son of a former deputy sheriff, beer-bellied, wire-bearded, blue-jeaned, wearing a picaresque black felt English derby hat. The car had a peace symbol on its windshield.

Charles Simpson jumped out of the car on Independence Avenue, less than a thousand feet across the street from the Allen Bank and Trust Company, a modernized plate-glass structure facing the courthouse. It was minutes away from closing. Simpson was a farmboy who grew up in the apple-knocker village of Holden 24 miles away, the son of a totally disabled World War II combat veteran. He started walking south on Independence Avenue. He was wearing knee-popped bell-bottoms, a waist-length Army fatigue jacket, and yellowed dry-goods boots caked with mud and cowflop. He had high jutting cheekbones, a hooked and fist-kissed nose, a swarthy complexion, and uneven calcimine-white teeth. His eyes were coal-black and slanted. There was whipcord in his muscles but he looked a little funny when he suddenly crossed the street and started running.

As he loped across Independence onto Pearl Street, he reached under his patched Army jacket and took out an M-1 semi-automatic carbine with clip and over 140 rounds of ammunition. It was the same weapon which National Guardsmen used at Kent State University in 1970, killing four students and wounding nine. He had used the combat-regulation weapon in the fields around town with his friend Rise Risner, target-shooting overfed squirrels, moonlighting packrats, and nonreturnable bottles of Budweiser beer.

On this Friday afternoon, as Charles Simpson reached for the M-1 under his fatigue jacket, he saw two brown-uniformed members of the Harrisonville Police Department — Donald Marler, 26, and Francis Wirt, 24, a Vietnam veteran, back from the war only four months and a policeman less than a month. They were part of the department's foot-patrol, recently pressured by the town's businessmen to keep an ever-alert eye on the square. Both men were armed with holstered police-regulation .38s. Both men knew Simpson.

As Friday afternoon traffic backed up around the square — the shops were closing and each of the town square's four corners is red-lighted — Charles Simpson leaned into a crouch and aimed his semi-automatic carbine waist-high at the two policemen. They were less than 100 feet away. He fired a quick burst of bullets. The two policemen went down poleaxed. A lady 20 feet from the gunfire fainted and her car rammed into the Happiness-Is-Tastee-Freeze delivery truck in front of her.

Simpson ran toward the two policemen sprawled on the concrete. Both were moaning, bleeding badly, unable to return fire. He stood rigidly over both men, pointed the muzzle down over first one and then the other, and fired two more staccato bursts into their bodies at point-blank range. The bullets, made for warzones, ripped into and through the bodies. Patrolman Marler was hit twice in the chest, twice in the abdomen, and once in each hand. Wirt was shot twice in the abdomen and three times in the right arm. His elbow looked as if it had been fragged.

Simpson spinned, turning to the Allen Bank and Trust Company, and ran inside. He didn't say anything. He didn't aim the carbine at anyone. He pointed it willy-nilly toward a rear wall covered with advertising slogans — INVEST IN AMERICA, BUY U.S. SAVING BONDS — and fired again. Bullets ricocheted around the floor and walls, wounding two cashiers. Simpson turned again, ran outside, waving the rifle in front of him, and ran west on Pearl, heading toward the town's water tower — HI THERE! CLASS OF '69 — and the Cass County Sheriff's Office. He was a death-dealing whirligig. He had a shitfire grin on his face.

The sheriff's office is about a thousand feet west on Pearl Street from the Allen Bank. Across the street from it is the Capitol Cleaners, which hold a monopoly on the town's laundry trade, offers STARCH BARGAINS.

As Charles Simpson dashed from the bank to the sheriff's office down the narrow street, a 58-year-old man with boils on his neck named Orville T. Allen was getting out of his battered pick-up truck in front of the cleaners. He had operated a dry-cleaning store in nearby Garden City for 27 years and was there to pick up some part-time weekend laundry.

Charles Simpson saw Orville Allen across the street, a man in faded khaki pants he had never seen before, and aimed his carbine. The burst caught Allen in the chest. He dropped to the pavement, twisted on the ground, turned his bleeding chest to the sky, and clasped his hands in prayer. 'God,' he moaned. A trail of blood trickled across the street toward the sheriff's office.

Sheriff Bill Gough, 46, a hulking and slow-footed man, had just taken off his holstered .38 revolver and was sitting down reading that week's issue of the Democrat-Missourian. The paper had come out that noon and carried a front-page story about an 18-year-old Kansas kid the sheriff's deputies had arrested for possession of marijuana. Gough heard something rat-tat-tat outside his office as he scanned the paper, but he didn't think it was gunfire. He thought it was some fool beating a piece of tin with a stick. He went outside, unarmed, to see what all the commotion was about.

As he got outside, he saw Simpson coming toward him, the M-1 aimed head-high. He tried to duck but wasn't quite fast enough (although the savage reflex twist of his big body probably saved his life). He was hit in the right shoulder and the left leg but staggered inside his office. His wife, sitting at a desk, screamed. He knocked her to the floor, grabbed his revolver, and flung himself behind a desk with such force that his elbows were purple for weeks. Covered with his own blood, Sheriff Gough aimed the revolver at the door and waited for Simpson to open it. His hands shook. He was afraid he'd lose control and wildly pull the trigger before Simpson stuck his head inside.

But when he hit Gough in the street, Simpson spinned around and, waving the gun wildly in the air, started trotting back toward the square. Allen's body lay a few feet away from him. Suddenly, in front of the Harrisonville Retirement Home, a dim gray-slab matchbox of a building across the street from Allen's bleeding body, he stopped. He bent down, put the carbine inside his mouth, sucked the barrel. He fired his last burst. He blew the top of his head off. His mad-dog dance was over.

He had fired more than 40 rounds. Four people were dead, three wounded. The town's shiny new Chamber of Commerce ambulance drove around the square and collected bodies. As the Civil Defense sirens screamed and G. M. Allen's volunteer firemen hosed down the bloodstains, gun-wielding deputies and policemen grabbed all the longhairs around the square and took them to Bill Gough's jail.

## 2 The hippies, and G. M. Allen

All roads lead to the square, an editorial in J. W. Brown's shopping-news weekly, the Cass County Democrat-Missourian, once said with prophetic innocence. 'At least that's what it seems like to outsiders. The Square seems to us to be a big chunk out of the past, sitting in the middle of the present. The cobblestone streets, the old hotel and courthouse, are probably taken for granted by the townspeople.' Charles Ootney Simpson's fierce assault on the town square was the final escalation of a guerrilla war of raw nerves and icy glares. It was fought for control of a seemingly insignificant logistical area: courthouse steps, shrubbery encircling it, and sidewalks facing its entrances on Wall and Pearl Streets. To understand the fated intensity of this cornpone guerrilla war, one must understand the uniquely claustrophobic architecture of the square itself and its place in Harrisonville's rustic-schizoid tradition.

The courthouse anchors the square, surrounded on four sides by contrasting clapboard and imitation brick shops. It is the epicenter of a tight and walled-in rectangle decorated by butterflies and honey-bees. The cobblestoned pavement on the four streets surrounding it — Wall to the south, Lexington to the east, Pearl to the north, Independence to the west — is chokingly narrow. It is less than 30 feet from the courthouse curb to any of the businesses on its sides. The streets were designed for horses and buggies, not delivery trucks. All the streets are one-way in a looping arc; you have to drive through Lexington and Pearl to get to Independence. Since the streets are so narrow, the shops on all sides — like South Side Prescriptions, Felix Hacker's Paint Supplies, Ballon's Dry Goods and Wright's Shoe Palace — are literally but steps away from whatever is happening around the courthouse. If someone sitting on the courthouse steps shouts an epithet — 'Off the pigs,' for example — the shout will echo dramatically, reverberating through the little stores where, in years past, only the cash registers made noise.

The courthouse was built in the first decade of the 20th century. It is red-brick, three stories tall, topped by a cupolaed belltower and a flagpole. The bells ring once a year — on the Fourth of July. The flagpole is bare; a new one splits the grass in front of the War Veterans statue and flies the flag 24 hours a day. The building sits atop a mound-like elevation exactly 16 steps above the neatly-swept sidewalk. A black iron railing leads to the south side doors, which are flanked by four columnar graystone pillars. The elevation transforms the courthouse steps into a stage. If Old Lloyd Foster, for example, who ebulliently runs South Side Prescriptions, glances out his store window at the courthouse, he is looking up. The building is at the tip of his nose.

On the Wall Street side of the courthouse there is a fixed metal sign that says: LEARN TO LEAD! ARMY NCO CANDIDATE SCHOOL. The same kind of sign on the Independence Street side in blue and red says: THE MARINE CORPS BUILDS MEN — 2735 B TROOP. Six feet of manicured grass and shrubbery surround the building on all sides. The clock atop the belltower is dead. It's been stuck for more than a decade. For some bizarre reason, the clock's hand paralyzed at different times — it is 2:20 to the south, 6:25 to the east, 1:20 to the west. The northern clock face has been removed — pigeons flutter there. A deeply-carved inscription above the southern door says: A PUBLIC OFFICE IS A PUBLIC TRUST.

The courthouse steps and the town square have served for generations as a place of public lolling. Saturday-night hoedowns were cele-

brated there; its four streets were barricaded and strung with multi-
colored lightbulbs. Three times a year there was a carnival. And gradually the town fathers — meaning the bankers, aldermen, and Chamber
of Commerce officials (the mayor was always a yoyo) — accepted too
that the courthouse steps and shrubbery served as a haven for grizzled
lushes to gulp their pints of Missouri corn whiskey. Every small town
has its drunks, but they always become harmless and somewhat valuable characters, walking examples to contrast with Godfearing lives.
The old bullshit artists are happy enough just to be left alone. They
exude alcohol and sour courtesy, never fuss anyone, and the judges and
deputies avert their eyes and walk smugly past them to wood-paneled
chambers where decanters of aged bourbon are kept out of sight.

In the late summer of 1971, the town drunks abandoned the courthouse steps and claimed they were being spooked out. The figures now
lazing in the shade and dangling their legs were a bewildering new
phenomenon and no one knew quite what to make of them. They were
townie kids who had grown up around Cass County and played for the
Harrisonville Wildcats, getting their first fifths of sourmash from tight-
mouthed Old Lloyd Foster. But when Old Lloyd looked across at these
homegrown kids now, they gave him a fright. They were different.
They had changed. They were their own kids but ... somehow they
weren't their own kids anymore. They wore their hair long and un-
trimmed and grew chinbound moustaches and billowing beards. They
wore all manners of beegum strawhats and cropduster clothes — always
bluejeans and a lot of Army jackets, engineer's boots, and $2 teeny-
shoes which Old Lloyd's son, Don, sold them at the Sears Country
Catalog Store. They played riotous Frisbee in the middle of the street
and collected wilted flowers in back of Vann's Florist Shop and decked
themselves out with dead roses and carnations. They wore 'love
crosses' around their necks from which Jesus' body had been blas-
phemously ripped away.

Some of the women who came in once a week to Connie's Beauty
Salon said they called them filthy names and scratched their privates.
Some of the policemen said they called them 'Pigs' face to face and
were always talking about their godalmighty 'Civil Liberties.' Some of
the businessmen claimed the one word they heard echoing around the
square from morning 'til closing was a four-letter word they couldn't
even repeat out loud what with women and children in town. 'There
was no doubt about it,' said 60-year-old J. W. Brown, editor and publisher of the Democrat-Missourian, a flatulent pipe-smoking country

gentleman. 'What we had here were our own hippies, settin' up there, raisin' hell, callin' our women names, drinkin' wine and smokin' some of that marijuana. I even heard they was right up there in the bushes havin' sexual intercourse. Yes sir. Sex-You-All intercourse. Now those old drunks who used to set up there, those old boys never did any of that.'

Sex-You-All debauchery 16 steps above ground level right at the nosetips of righteous town merchants is not what the new courthouse squatters had in mind. Not at all. They were there in the beginning because there was no other place to go. Where could you go in Harrisonville? – this small time place haunted by homilies, platitudes, and bushwah. Into Guido's Pizza Parlor? Well, maybe, but couldn't stay there too long. As time went by Win Allen, the kingpin, Rise Risner, Ootney Simpson, George Russell, Harry Miller, and the Thompson Brothers hung around the square because it got to be an entertaining mock-serious game. They were liberating Harrisonville, Missouri, showing the Sho-Me State some puffed-up balls. They were fighting their revolution against people they had cowedly called 'Sir' all their teenage lives.

Beer-bellied Rise Risner and Gary Hale, a reedy and subdued James Taylor look-alike, went off to the Navy as cowlicked country boys and came back dazedly turned-on, rejecting everything around them. They were home but home sure as hell didn't feel like home.

Liberating Harrisonville meant a lot of mind-blowing. They soon found themselves romantic figures, idolized by some of the high school kids. They conducted hoohawing teach-ins in front of the War-Vets statue as Legionnaires stood around on the sidewalk in their peaked caps and called it 'jackrollin' the blind.' They'd read selections from Abbie Hoffman, Timothy Leary, and Bobby Seale in stentorian tones, lifting their voices to phrases like 'Off the pigs!' and 'Up against the wall, motherfucker!'

They had Dylan and Jimi Hendrix tapes in their cars and boomed 'Stone Free' and 'Lay Lady Lay' in the night. They smoked as much dope as was available and there was always more than enough. The Army had planted crops of hemp during World War II and five-foot high marijuana plants shadowed the wheatfields.

Snake-charmed, the high school kids started imitating them, of course, using words like 'motherfucker' and acting heavylidded in civics class just for the aggravation of it. The principal, an ex-Marine, freaked, naturally, and zeroed-in on the new villains at council meetings when the school budget was discussed and the vandalism dollar-damage was counted. Only the year before, the principal fired a matronly English teacher who made *Stranger in a Strange Land* required reading. The townspeople picked up the taboo; the lady was once seen going into a liquor store and the town's elders were soon saying she was fucking and sucking all the seniors in her classes.

So these plowboy hippies – who were convinced, perhaps from experience, that their elders still cornholed cows when they got horny – came to dominate the town's consciousness and its square. And of all the revolutionaries and sugartits cavorting around the square, two seemed the most frightening – the Simpson boy, who'd always rub his pecker when a woman went by, and The Nigger, one of the town's six blacks. Win Allen, 24, frail and bird-like, with bloodshot eyes and a habit of slurring his words, made no secret of the fact he was shanghaied into Uncle Sam's Army, went AWOL, and managed to con himself a dishonorable discharge. He was a Bad Nigger as opposed to his younger brother, Butch, 17, a walking bowling ball who played forward for the Harrisonville Wildcats scoring an average 15 points a game. Butch was a Good Nigger. But Win (short for Edwin) had an Afro popout hairdo and was always up there on the steps, holding hands with a white girl, talking about Love, and waving books like *The Fire Next Time* and *Do It!*

Every time one of Bill Davis' policemen or Bill Gough's deputies passed the square, Win Allen would cheerfully yell: 'Hey, here comes The Pigs.' He even spoke his special blackevil language, and pretty soon half the kids in the high school were using this garbled childrenese, not just ordinary hippie words the townspeople heard in television commercials but words they'd never heard before. Words like 'bro' and 'gritting down' (eating) and 'Crib' and 'P-ing down' (sexual intercourse) and 'bogosity' (anything he disagreed with). But the single phrase which all the kids were using was just gibberish for anything that Win liked. When Win liked something as much as he liked P-ing down, he said: 'Most ricky-tick.' 'Most ricky-tick' was being heard all over town. A high school senior even used it in an essay on 'The Prospect of Marriage.' The townspeople would go home at night, after having to endure the raucous courthouse shenanigans all day, and their own kids would say bogosity and gritting down and most ricky-tick.

Some action clearly had to be taken. G. M. Allen, fire-chief, got up at a special Chamber of Commerce meeting and said with hawkshaw eloquence: 'I'm an American, damn it, and I'm proud to be an American and I don't go for all this hangin' the flag upside-down stuff.'

G. M. Allen had another reason for urging civic action, a pocketbook reason. Rise Risner and Charles Simpson and Win Allen and the rest of that pestiferous crew had become an economic menace. Business was off all over town, from the Capot Department Store to alderman Luke Scavuzzo's grocery. Some of the people who shuffled in to make their monthly mortgage payments to G. M. Allen's bank told him they were afraid to come into town. The hippies. The hippies were scaring business away. Harrisonville just couldn't sit around and let itself get overrun, G. M. Allen said.

The aldermen agreed that action had become a matter of local survival, although one of them, sucking his teeth, pointed out alternatives – 'Don't stretch the blanket, now, G. M.' – explaining the financial setback. There was a nationwide economic crisis and wage–price freeze and 11 miles down Interstate 71 one of those deluxe glass and chromium shopping centers, calling itself Truman Corners, had just opened up. Maybe folks were shopping there.

'Maybe so,' G. M. Allen told the tooth-sucker, 'but they'd be leavin' their money here if it weren't for them hippies,' and the Chamber of Commerce spring offensive, to recapture the town square for the old drunks, was under way.

## 3 The battle of the town square

Actually, the aldermen had two offensives to mount at the same time, and they were both G. M. Allen's hardnosed command: Operation Hippie and Operation Tornado.

To facilitate the war against tornadoes, G. M. Allen thought it would be a civic coup if the Fire-Fighters Association of Missouri – tornadowatchers of the entire state – held their annual convention in Harrisonville. The aldermen, perhaps contemplating the weekend revenue from 500 firefighters and their wives gratefully applauded G. M.'s boosterism. G. M. lined the convention up for Friday, April 21st. There would be a tornado committee meeting Saturday morning and a brass-band parade Saturday afternoon. Doris' House of Charm announced it would offer a 'Fireladies' Shampoo Special' for its beehive-headed lady tourists. As a further step, G. M. ran off hundreds of emergency doomsday leaflets and distributed them in the stores around the square. His directive began: 'When a tornado is spotted in the Harrisonville area, six sirens around the city will sound a long *blast* for three minutes. Our air-raid emergency *bombing warning* differs from a storm warning by sounding an up-and-down warbling *blast* rather than a long continuing *blast*. BE ALERT, G. M. ALLEN, FIRE CHIEF.'

To facilitate the offensive against hippies, G. M. figured it was necessary that everyone in town understand the critical nature of the crisis. He arranged with the Kiwanis Club to import a 'drug addict expert.' The 'drug addict expert' was Robert Williams, the police chief from Grandview. Chief Williams, a man of profound second-hand insight, heard about drugs and hippies all the time from his police friends in Kansas City.

'It's approaching a crisis stage,' he told the Kiwanians. 'Police can't even eliminate the problem. We've got to wake up and take a hard stand. What we've got to do is stand up and inject some old-fashioned moral values before all our young fall victim to those older marauders who prey on them.' The Harrisonville Community Betterment Council appointed a Drug-Abuse Committee.

Late at night on March 23rd, G. M. Allen, a delegation of town businessmen, and members of the city council met with police officials at G. M.'s Citizens National Bank on Wall Street. A list of crimes the hippies were suspected of was compiled. Someone broke into the courthouse one night by forcing open a window and crept up three flights to the belltower. Nothing was damaged, or stolen, but three marijuana cigarette butts were found on the floor. Several merchants claimed to have received anonymous threatening phone calls. The caller always used the word 'motherfucker' and threatened 'torching.' In nearby Archie, a carload of the hippies — Risner, Simpson, Win Allen — were seen driving through and that same day bomb threats were reported at the Archie State Bank and the Archie Elementary School. And they all knew, G. M. Allen scowlingly said, about the obstruction of traffic in the square.

The mobilization meeting agreed on some immediate measures: The shrubbery around the courthouse would be trimmed so there couldn't be anymore sexual intercourse going on up there. Superwatted bright lights, the kind used in urban high-crime areas, would be erected around the square. Chief Davis promised a new foot patrol, two of his nine men acting as roving beatmen, walking in circles around the square 12 hours a day. A list of city ordinances — 'Ordinances, man,' Win Allen would say, 'dig?' — was drawn up for city council approval.

'Vulgar, profane, or indecent' language in public was punishable by a $500 fine or 60 days in the county jail or both. Picketing and parades were illegal unless authorized by the city attorney or Chief Davis. And the topper, a declaration of virtual martial law: Any assembly of three or more persons in the town square was declared an illegal assembly punishable by a $1000 fine.

G. M. Allen, the little man with bifocals and Alfred E. Newman haircut that stopped a full inch above his red-veined ears, was happy as a clam. He had a responsibility as fire chief and Civil Defense coordinator and he intended to live up to it. 'You listen to TV, it used to be cowboys and Indians, now it's "Kill the Cops," ' he'd say. He was a World War II combat veteran who'd raised four decent law-abiding kids and, even though his youngest daughter had gone to school with Risner and Win Allen and had liked them, even though she was 'a little bit oversold on Civil Rights,' G. M. Allen was convinced that what they'd decided in his bank that night was for the betterment not only of Harrisonville but of America too. 'If they don't believe in America,' he told the meeting, 'they should get the hell out.'

Hours after the anti-hippie-frisbee-promiscuity meeting ended, a 30-pound slab of concrete was tossed through the $495 plate-glass window fronting G. M. Allen's bank. He sputtered down half a block to see J. W. Brown at the Democrat-Missourian and ordered a boldset black-bordered ad. He was petrified with emotion. The Citizens National Bank was offering a $500 reward for 'information leading to the arrest and conviction of the person or persons who maliciously broke our window.'

For Rise Risner, Gary Hale, Win Allen, and Ootney Simpson, the 'shit coming down from the black sky' was a routine part of 'life in the Hick City.'

During the second week of April, as the footpatrols made ten minute reconnaisance sorties around the square, Win Allen came up with what he told Charles Simpson was 'Dee-Vine Inspiration.' Saturday, the 22nd, would be a national day of protest against the War in Vietnam. Win Allen decided he was going to organize Harrisonville's own anti-war march, a ragamuffin parade of cow-dunged kids screaming anti-imperialist slogans right under the Harrisonville brownshirts' noses. On Wednesday, April 19th, Win Allen and Ootney Simpson, friendly, grinning, and wary, marched to the office of the city attorney and asked for a parade permit. They were told they didn't need one. 'We want somethin' in writin', not jive,' Win said. 'Go ahead and march,' the ferret-faced attorney smiled. But he'd give them no paper.

Charles Simpson, who trusted his instincts, was sure it was a booby-trap. 'The fuckers'll just bust us,' he said.

But Win's dreams escalated: The march would protest not only the war but the new town ordinances. Win would carry a sign that said DOWN WITH NIXON'S WAR and Ootney would carry a sign that said DOWN WITH G. M. ALLEN'S WAR.

'It's gonna be most ricky-tick,' Allen said.

'Crazy fuckin' niggers,' Simpson laughed.

G. M. Allen heard about the anti-war march. The Nigger and the hippies were planning and went to see Chief Davis about it. He wasn't going to have his big weekend spoiled. The Fire-Fighters Association of Missouri would be in town and each of the forty departments was going to bring its fire engine. At two o'clock Saturday afternoon, after they finished caucusing over the tornadoes, all those beautiful firetrucks, their sirens blasting, would be driven around the square.

All the firefighters would be in their starched parade outfits and the sidewalks would be filled with farmers who'd come into town to see the firetrucks and would spend a few dollars while they were there. It would be the biggest thing on the square since the horseshoe-pitching contests they used to hold. G. M. Allen was damned if he was going to let those spitshined firetrucks be set upon by an army of crablice — hometown purvoids spewing filth, contumely, and treason.

The day after the haggling session with the city attorney was spent coordinating Saturday's anti-war march. Win Allen and Ootney Simpson discussed logistics with Rise, Gary Hale and the others — and just about everyone agreed that it was a trap, the march certain to end inside Sheriff Gough's roach-crawling jail. But no one cared. They were high on their own daydreams. They'd march anyway. Fuck it: The theatrical aspects were simply too tempting, too ricky-tick to worry about the whip and thud of the brownshirts' new Japanese billyclubs. They would march up Wall Street, gathering at Guido's Pizza Place minutes before the firefighters' cortege was to assemble near the Missouri Farm Association silo. The square would be decked with bunting and the farmers would be tip-toeing around the sidewalks waiting for the sirens when, led by Win Allen, led by a nigger, the outlaws would shamble into that red-white-blue arena, blowing minds, ruining everything, filling the square with clenched fists and that eyeteeth-rattling cry: 'ONE TWO THREE FOUR WE DON'T WANT YOUR FUCKIN' WAR.'

Word went out Thursday to the timid and sheepish 'Teeny Bros' at the high school that all those interested in coming to jail for the war should come down to the square after school and Win or Rise or Ootney would give them the lowdown. A lot of kids showed up because the Teeny Bros themselves were in the process of launching a guerrilla action of their own, a pep-rally protest against Bar B-Q Ham on Cheese Bun, Chicken Fried Steak-w-cream-gravy, and Cheeseburger Noodle Loaf. The Teeny Bros were actually threatening to take to the streets carrying big signs that said, NO MORE BAR B-Q HAM and waving the signs in front of the struck-dumb principal's office.

The Teeny Bros drifted into town that afternoon, keeping a paranoid eye out for the footpatrols, and organized themselves into action groups. The freshmen and sophomores — 'The Snots' — would all paint signs. The Snots were more than anxious to paint words like NO MORE WAR and demonstrate their militance. As the day wore on and the footpatrols told Chief Davis there seemed to be a pow-wow of outlaws in town, some of the outlaws got bored and went home while other part-time badmen slouched by, having heard about Win's Dee-Vine Inspiration from some squiggly-excited Teeny Bro. Charles Simpson went home around 4 o'clock to his Holden farmhouse, reluctantly, going along with Win's fantasy, noting the ironies offered by the prospect of the two parades. The firefighters would be cheered because they drove shiny engines; the outlaws would go to jail because they dreamed of a warless world. 'Fuck it, they'll just bust us,' Ootney told Win Allen again, 'the whole shit just turns my teeth sour.' Ootney was tired. He was going home and he was going to mowdown some squirrels with his itty-bitty machine gun.

Harry Miller was one of the hangers-on who slouched by — about an hour after Ootney left to do battle with his doomed squirrels. Harry Miller drove into the square, nodding respectfully at the brownshirts, and then catfooted over to Rise and Win and some of the others. Everything looked cool: Win was chasing dragonflies.

Harry Miller is 24 years old and his jeans are too tight because there is a gut bulging at his belt. His face is puffy and there is a Brando-like sluggishness, a hovering petulance, about him. He doesn't rattle very easily and he looks like he can take care of himself — a veteran of bicep-building Army infantry training. He looks like a young Bill Haley. His hair is parted in the middle and shoved to the sides but his hair isn't long enough and sometimes a few hairs dangle into the forehead forming perfect curleycues.

It was near 5:30. The air was stuffed with heat and they were thirsty. Win and Rise and Gary Hale and Harry Miller and George Russell and John Thompson, their smart-cracking court-jester, walked across the street to Lloyd Foster's drug store. One of the Teeny Bros whose mother had given him allowance money that day was sent inside to spend it on a carton of Pepsi-Cola.

'Here we are,' Harry Miller says, 'standin' not exactly under the drug store's roof but out in front, near the Sears store, which Old Lloyd's boy, Don, runs. So we're waitin' for this kid to bring us some belly-wash. We are standin' right beside a mailbox which is public property. OK, out of nowhere, Don Foster drives up. Man, I seen that car comin', you could tell he was gonna do somethin', it was in his eyes, like he already knew he was gonna do this. OK, when he comes over there, there were already police parked on the other side of the square so we couldn't see 'em. Don Foster pulls up and he immediately jumps out and storms up. He's a big guy, wears nice cowboy boots, got sideburns, carries a pencil behind his ear, walks around wantin' everybody to cut down trees.

'So he storms up and he starts sayin', "Get away from my store." He says to Win, "Get your black ass out of here." So he starts violently throwin' shit and John Thompson says, "Listen, man, we pay taxes, I'm not gettin' out of here." So the Foster dude says, "Oh, you wanna fight, I'll fight you." So he pushes John with both hands, just pushes John and knocks him back. John weighs about 40 pounds less than the dude and most of his weight is stuck up on top of his head in his hair. Well, right then I caught a sense, I knew exactly what was gonna happen. OK, so then the old man, Old Lloyd, comes runnin' out and starts throwin' some bogus shit. I don't know what he was sayin', just yellin' and screamin'. Somehow Don Foster got a hold of John again and pushed him again.

'So I got in between them. I says to Foster, "Man, leave us alone, you're tryin' to fight us, you wanna get us throwed in jail, just leave our asses alone, we're not goin' to jail for you." And he says: "You get out of the way or I'll smack your ass, buddy." So I got out of the way and they got off by theirselves again and started pilin' at it. So his father, Old Lloyd, says: "By Gawd, I'm gonna call the police." So he walks back to his store, takes about four steps, doesn't even get to his phone, turns back out again watchin' them hassle, and here comes the police already turnin' the corner of the courthouse, boogeyin' from the courthouse. OK, after they turn the courthouse, it is like 50 feet before the first one gets to the fight – here's John and this Don Foster on the ground.

'The Foster dude is on top smackin' John beside the head. John's on the bottom gettin' ahold of him by the neck and ear. So here's Sgt. Jim Harris, the police officer, the other two pigs are behind him. OK, so Harris is 500 feet away, his club in the air, runnin' right at him. Here's John at the bottom with Foster on top of him. So Harris twists around and leans down so he can hit John even with Foster on top of him. He hits John in the shoulder and across the side of the face. Foster jumped off and the other two policemen picked up Foster's jacket for him. Foster got his jacket and walked up beside his old man and Old Lloyd starts pointin' at us, sayin' "Him and him and him" and points to Win and says: "The Nigger, The Nigger, The Nigger," over and over again. So the pigs put us all under arrest for disturbin' the peace and start walkin' us over to the jail in the sheriff's office. Eight of us: Rise and Win and Gary Hale and John Thompson and George Russell and some of the others.

'On the way over there, one of the pigs decides he's gonna have a little fun with Win, so he sticks Win in the spine with his nightstick as hard as he can. When Win turns around the pig yells, "The Nigger's resistin' arrest." When we get to the jail we says, "We wanna file a complaint against the Foster dude for pushin' John," 'cause I mean, if they're gonna play that game on you, you might as well play it back on them. Chief Davis is there and the sheriff is there and Sgt. Jim Harris is there and they all said they didn't have the authority for us to file a complaint.

'So we had to just scream, say, *"Goddamnit, I want a damn report! I wanna file a complaint!"* I mean we had to scream for 15, 20 minutes. Finally they brought the city attorney down and he gives us two sheets of paper with nothin' on it except the top says "Municipal Court" and some bogus printed stuff. But all they had us do was sign our names on it and that couldn't – man, when you file a complaint there's somethin' wrote down there and you read it, so that couldn't have been any real complaint form. OK, so that was just to get us to shut up. They throw us in jail and we knew it was bogus, we just took it as it was, $110 apiece. Then our Nigger, he was about the last one to come in. We hollered across the monkeybars over to his cell and we say – "Hey, Win' how we gonna get out?" And he says: "You know, I don't know, my bail's $1100."

'That jail is like the inside of a toilet bowl in a place where everybody's got the backdoor trots, know what I mean? We had to take a shit, well, we had to get a Look Magazine and tear the pages and put it on the seat it was so grubby. The shitter didn't really have a seat on it.

They had some drunks over in the bullpen but they didn't say nothin' to us, nobody said nothin'.

'There were cops crawlin' out of the ratholes, we must have scared the pricks off of 'em. Here's eight guys in jail, right? They had six Highway Patrolmen there, they had five guys from the city police department, they had five guys from the sheriff's department, about seven policemen from the surrounding towns in the county.'

The chief of the fire department, Harry Miller says, 'Yes siree, G. M. Allen comes in all aflutter. Had this little red firehat on, Number 4. He says, "Did you get 'em all? Anybody hurt?" G. M. walks up and down real slow, lookin' at us, lookin' us over, lookin' us in the hair, and then he says: "Where's The Nigger? I got somethin' to say to The Nigger."'

Win Allen says: 'Dig, here I am, under arrest, in the clink. And this dude comes up to me in his little cute firehat and I expect him to say somethin' to me about what happened. So he comes up to me, gets really friendly allasudden and whispers, "Win, I want you to come see me tomorrow about that bill you owe me." He has the fuckin' audacity to come to me in the clink and talk to me about a loan my family owes him.'

A 16-year-old dimple-cheeked high school dropout named Robin Armstrong, a strangely vague and muted farmgirl whose father blew his brains out two years ago — 'I'm fed up with everything; people are just so fuckin' ignorant anymore' — was standing in front of the firetruck. All of her friends were in jail and she was screaming, 'You fuckin' pigs!' and the firemen were clutching their gleaming hatchets.

Her mother drove up then and Robin Armstrong, trembling with fear and fury, started running like a panicked jackrabbit down an alley.

'I saw it from the window,' Harry Miller says. 'Robin starts boogeyin' in between the jail and the rest home, she's gonna run down this old road because she don't want her mother to capture her ass. So the firetruck has a tank with 200 pounds of pressure in it and you know that big hose they have — well, they open that big hose up and hit Robin in the back with it and knocked her on the ground. They skidded her face across the gravel.'

Mrs. Armstrong, 40ish and sagging but dressed as if she still knew how to please, went up to her sobbing daughter whose mouth was bleeding, and slapped her hard. She called her daughter a 'little hoor' and then she sashayed back to the fireman who was still holding the hose. And then she thanked him.

The outlaws spent their night in the crabseat wiping their asses with Look Magazine and organizing their Saturday parade, wondering all the time how they'd make bail. One of their bros was up all night, making phone calls and asking the parents to bail their kids out and getting nowhere. They didn't want to spend their money.

As the sun came up, red-eyed Ootney Simpson had figured out only one way to get his friends out of jail. At 11 o'clock Friday morning, Ootney Simpson, smiling like a dimwit fool, worn down to the edge, showed up at the sheriff's office. The outlaw looked the sheriff in the eye and put $1500 in cash on the counter. It was his life's savings, the bankroll for the plot of land he dreamed about. His dream was dead. A sweat of fatigue caked his face.

'Simpson's the name,' the dreamer said, 'revolution's my game. Free The People!'

## 4 Ootney Simpson's dream

They called him 'Ootney' because of a shriveled old geezer named Jimbob Jones who runs a carry-out grocery on Number Seven Highway about four miles from town. Jimbob Jones took a weird shine to Charles Simpson and whenever he and his friends would wander in for their quarts of strawberry wine and sixpacks of beer, Jimbob Jones would cackle: 'Well, looky here, Rootin' Tootin' Mr. Simpson.' So Rise and Win called him 'Rootin' Tootin' ' at first, and then 'Tootney' and gradually bastardized it into Ootney.

When Ootney showed up at the jail that Friday morning with his packet of liberating $100 bills, Rise and Win weren't surprised. It was just like Ootney – whenever something had to be done, Ootney was there to do it. As his father says, 'All his life he'd go out there in the hayfield and keep up with the best of 'em.'

He was of the hayfield and the barn, grew to manhood there and loved it. He lived in Holden, a town smaller and even more backwoods than Harrisonville, a place where the cemetery is still called 'the boneyard,' a police station is a 'booby hutch,' and the mentally retarded are 'cabbageheads.'

Ootney's father, Charles B. Simpson, is 53 years old and looks 75. He looks like a man who is going to die and has looked that way for years. He stands 5'9", weighs 102 pounds, sports a Hitler moustache, a red baseball cap, and a cardigan sweater which the moths have savored for years. He walks with face-twisted pain and a briar walking stick with a vulcanized rubber tip, his leg having been broken into pieces by shrapnel on the African front in WWII. He raised three kids and supported a wife, did as much work as he could, pinched pennies, lived on hot dogs and beans, and waited for the disability checks. Four years ago his wife left him and, except for Charles, the kids got married and left him too.

The corpse-faced veteran and his boy were never too close and it was only in the past year or so that they did much talking. It was hard for the old man to move and he spent long hours sitting in his rocking chair in the room with the calico rug and the big calendar filled with bone-chilling winter scenes. He sat in the rocking chair with his baseball cap pulled over his grey eyes, the cane draped over a thigh, staring at the walls and the dates on the calendar. The boy would come into the room, his long hippie hair in his face, squat down on the rug, and they would talk. They talked about the land and the crops and the war, about policemen and guns and steer, about Henry David Thoreau and Abbie Hoffman and General of the Army Douglas MacArthur. 'The boy expressed his feelings too plain,' the old man says, 'you can't do that.'

He was always telling the old man about Thoreau and although the old man didn't know too much about him, he listened. Thoreau lived by a pond and his friends were plants and animals. He didn't pay his taxes because he wouldn't support a government which practiced slavery.

The old man didn't have too much to say about Henry David Thoreau but a man talking to his son has to have something to say, so he told the boy stories about General Douglas MacArthur. The old man admired General Douglas MacArthur as much as the boy admired Henry David Thoreau. So he told his stories. How General MacArthur won the Philippines from the Japs. How he could have beat the Chinese across the Yalu River if Harry S. Truman hadn't had stopped him. How Harry S. Truman once wanted to be a piano player in a whorehouse and that's where he belonged. How General Douglas MacArthur should have been President and the country wouldn't be in the fix that it's in.

The old man didn't know exactly what the boy did all the time in Harrisonville. One time Al Wakeman, the Holden police chief, came over and told the old man to keep his damn boy the hell out of trouble. Charles was always roaring up and down the streets on his motorcycle. 'Disturbing the peace,' the chief said.

Ever since he was a kid, Ootney had a bad case of asthma. He'd have an attack and his nose and throat would swell up, shutting most of his breathing off. That kept him out of the Army. 'One shot-to-hell veteran's enough in the family,' the old man says. 'He went to high school but he didn't graduate — he had mumps real bad his senior year.' Rise Risner adds: 'He just farted school off. He said, "Man, you fuckers are just teachin' me a bunch of lies, you're not teachin' me anything I wanna learn." He finally got into a big hassle with a teacher one day, just never did go back. He was real intelligent, he could see through shit. He'd always tell you the truth, even if it hurt. He'd say, "Look you motherfucker, you've been layin' down some phony shit." '

When he dropped out of high school, Ootney Simpson went to work at a foundry in Kingsville. He was bored with the job but worked at it for more than a year. He said he wanted to save enough money to build himself the world's most souped-up drag racer. 'He saved up a bunch of money,' Rise says, 'and he got fired 'cause he took off one weekend. He told his supervisor, "Well, I'm not gonna be at work a few days." So he came back and they said, "Well, you know, since you didn't notify anybody that you were gonna be haulin' ass for these few days, you're fired." So he started thinkin'. He went back raisin' hell. He went right into the personnel department and said, "Look you mother-fuckers, I did notify you. I want this changed. I still wanna be fired but I want this to read that I notified you and you let me go," and so after that he started collectin' unemployment.'

Ootney was spending a lot of time in those days with his younger brother, Elwyn, 23. 'Bubber' looks like a chunkier Ootney — the same coal-black eyes, hair as long and parted the same way down the middle. Bubber also worked at the foundry and, together, they were building their dream drag racer, blowing most of their money on new manifolds and sparkling chrome treasures.

Win Allen says, 'Like the cat and Bubber, they used to race their drags in Kansas City, makin' cars and doin' some racin' and then one day Bubber says, "We're just gettin' screwed, people are just takin' our money," and so they stopped racin'.' Rise adds: 'They put $10,000 into their dream car, Ootney was just floatin' along, searchin', he broke his back on that car. And they put ten grand into it and that's when Bubber got married and Bubber's wife said, "All right, you gotta get rid of that race car." Well, Ootney and Bubber were in a partnership, you know, he says to his wife, "OK, honey, I'll get rid of that racin' machine for you." And they sold the major part of it for $1000. So they took a $9000 beatin' right there.

'Bubber and Ootney broke bad after that, like Bubber's wife was always hasslin' Charles even. Bubber picked up all this pseudo-shit —

shit like trailers and pickup trucks. Like he was working 16 hours a day in two different foundries. He worked at one in Harrisonville and he got off work there at 3:30 and he had to haul ass to punch in on time to get to the other foundry by 4. Just to feed his wife. Well, that's about when Ootney's head started to spin. He didn't give a fuck about the money, but he just knew that whatever he was searchin' for he couldn't find at a drag strip. That's when he started showin' up around the square with us and gettin' into readin'.

'After a while he started talkin' to us about Thoreau,' Rise says, 'and he said the only thing he and Thoreau differed on was women. Like Ootney man, he dug on women. I mean he didn't fall in love with 'em or get stuck on 'em he just dug to fuck, just P-down, man. He just loved it. He could fuck all night and he still couldn't have enough. He was crazy about it. But he said he had to have women around him all the time and that's the only thing he and Thoreau differed on because Thoreau says in one of his books, he goes, "A Woman would be a foe to my career," and Ootney goes, "Old Henry David, he must not have liked to fuck."

'If Ootney felt like takin' off his clothes, he didn't give a fuck who was there, no, he'd take his clothes off and jump in a river and take a bath or somethin'. Nothin' embarrassed him, nothin' natural. And he was crazy-good with women. Any woman you ever seen in your life, Ootney Simpson could scheme her into the fuckin' bedroom. It was like he was above women, they owed it to him to fuck him. He was a peach, true beautifulness. He had this long black hair and he had this big beard for a while that was like right under his eyes, hair all over him, skinny. His eyes had a sparkle, the whites were real big, this hooked nose, a real freak, a freak all the way. When he let his beard grow, the only thing you could see was the eyes — just the whites of 'em, 'cause the rest of him was dark. Sometimes he wore great big baggy Army pants. He was a real killer, man.

'He was real weird in a lot of healthy ways. Like he hated telephones. He'd fuckin' drive 40 miles to tell a dude some little-ass thing rather than call him on the phone. He hated phones. He said, "If you can't look a man in the eyes when you're talkin' to him to tell him somethin', it ain't worth nothin'. " He said, "Anything that you lay on somebody that you feel is a part of you, you gotta look them in the eyes, feel their soul right there." '

Harry Miller says, 'He was full of feelings, just look at him and you could tell. Just look at his face and you'd say, "Man, that guy there, he'll give me a dollar to get somethin' to eat.'" It seems like anytime somebody was depressed, he was around to help them out. His feelings were so sensitive, like you couldn't gross him out, but he had such feeling for his friends. He could stand 50 feet away and somebody would jump up on you and the vibes from Ootney would knock him down. If we were havin' a hassle in town, fuckin' Ootney would pick up the vibes 30 miles away.

'Some of his fuckin' acts you could never forget,' says Harry. 'One time an ex-Marine from out of Vietnam, been home three months, comes up to Pat and Ernie's Bar and drinks 15 beers and an old guy that we used to know in high school brings him over to Rise's house, we called it the Hippie House, and Ootney is there. So they come in and the Marine starts throwin' down shit about — "Gawddamn, you don't faaght for your country, ya oughta be shawt." I was in bed but Ootney heard it. This guy was gonna fire on Rise's ass. Ootney gets up stark nekid, walks in there, and comes down into shit like Rubin jumpin' a Chicago pig's ass or somethin'. And jumps all over the Marine. He looks the dude back about three steps and he grabs his prick and shakes it at the Marine and turns around and just shoots him the moon and then he gives him the finger. Man, that Marine, he ran away.'

Rise says, 'But he was always gettin' into some shit. Like there was a cloud over him and it rained pigs everytime Ootney made a move. Like even when he wanted to do nothin' but listen to a rock and roll concert. He dug Black Sabbath. Black Sabbath cost him $150. He went up to Kansas City to see 'em and, first, he lost his ticket so he had to buy another ticket when he got up there and there was another dude there, a friend of ours who didn't have any money and didn't have a ticket either. So Ootney bought him a ticket. Plus all the other shit, miscellaneous money bullshit from that day. Then after the concert he was takin' a piss outside, you know, in the street, and he got busted for his piss and it cost him $100.

'Another time he was with a dude and the dude was drivin' through Kingsville, the town where the foundry is, and the pigs busted this guy for a faulty exhaust or somethin'. And so they were sittin' in the pig's cruiser and they had to wait for the county pigs to get there and give them the ticket because those pigs were just flunkies or somethin'. So Ootney says to the pig, "Am I under arrest?" And the pig goes, "No, you're not under arrest." So Ootney gets the keys from the dude who drove the car and he just jumps in and speeds away at like 100 mph,

makin' a U-turn and givin' the pigs the finger and everythin'. He keeps
racin' on at 100 mph and the pigs put out a roadblock for him 'cause
he's tearin' up the countryside. He stops off at his place in Holden and
puts his brother Bubber's motorcycle helmet on and some gloves and
comes roarin' back to Kingsville 'cause he knows the pigs must be after
him. Well, he roars right around that roadblock at 100 mph and drives
right back up to where his friend is sittin' in the pig's car. One of the
pigs pulls out his gun and he was pointin' the gun and shakin' and
sayin', "Get your ass over here, Simpson," And Ootney has on his
helmet and gloves and he just freaked them out. 'Course he spent that
night in jail too.'

Win Allen says, 'Like the time we were over in Holden and I was
found guilty of contempt of court, that was an outtasight scene right
there. Like Rise and Ootney and I and his brother Bubber were there
and Bubber had a traffic violation that he was found guilty of and he
didn't do nothin' wrong. So when the judge tells him that he's guilty,
seeing that I dig on freedom of speech, I say, "Bullshit" and the judge
fined me. After a while the judge calls me up there and he says, "Do
you know the prior defendant?" And I say, "Yeah, I know him, he's a
citizen of America." So after a while one of the pigs says, "Boy, come
along with me." "Boy," dig? And I was gonna slide with him you know.
So Ootney says, "Stop the music, I'll pay the nigger's fine." They
freaked out. They didn't know how to react. They smiled. And Ootney
says, "We'll teach the nigger a lesson once we got him into his cage."
Sheeit, we laughed all the way out of town. The judge musta thought
Ootney was gonna cut my dick off and put it down my throat or somethin'.'

Over and over again, in the past few months, Charles Simpson told
his friends about the plot of land that he was going to buy. 'I'm gonna
live just like Thoreau,' he told them, 'just like old Henry David.' He'd
laugh. 'Fuck all you longhaired hippie dudes.'

'He was gonna buy these 12 acres,' Rise says, 'aww, fuck, that's all
he did for a couple of months — just dream about and plan his land.
That's all he wanted and the fuckin' redneck farmer told him, "Yeah,
I'll sell it to you." It is a shitty piece of land but Ootney liked it, just
rocks and all barren, real freak's land. The redneck tells him, "All we
gotta do now is send off to the capital and get a few papers, make out
the forms and everything" and so Charles, he had the money, he made
all the arrangements, all he had to do is give the redneck the money
and take over. It would be his land. He used to take us out there and

we'd sit around on the rocks and smoke a few joints and Ootney would say, "Welcome to my land, this is my land." Well, somethin' happens and the redneck goes, "Aw, hell, I don't wanna sell it, there's too much red tape and I don't wanna sell it to no hippie anyway." That broke Ootney's back.'

On Wednesday, April 19th, Charles Simpson found out he couldn't have his barren rock-filled dreamworld. On Friday, the 21st, he withdrew his dream money to bail out his outlaw friends.

He went home and told his father he'd gotten the money from the bank and the shot-apart, ashen-faced old man sitting in the rocking chair said:

'What about the land?'

'It don't matter now.'

He reached into a closet and took out the M-1 semi-automatic carbine he had bought from a friend and said he was leaving for Harrisonville to get his friends out of jail.

'What you takin' the gun for?' the old man asked.

'Gonna shoot me some targets,' his boy said.

## 5 The shit comes down from the sky

'Simpson's my name, revolution's my game' didn't go over very well with Sheriff Bill Gough, but he didn't say anything about it. Those longhairs were making noise all morning and driving him batty. It would be a real pleasure to get them out of his jail. He'd take those friendly old juiceheads any day. It looked like a long weekend was cropping, what with the fire-fighters coming in that night and those crazy longhairs still talking – right in jail – about holding their protest march tomorrow.

So he didn't give the Simpson boy any trouble when he said, 'Free The People!' in a shade louder voice than the sheriff liked to hear in his office. He counted the stacks of bills and looked up just how much the bond was and told his deputy to start getting the longhairs out of their cells. Simpson had a big grin on his face, but he looked like he hadn't slept for weeks. The whites of his eyes were more red than white and his hands were skittery. When the Anderson boy came in, Simpson looked at him as if he were going to kill him and before the sheriff could do anything, Simpson had the Anderson boy by the lapels. 'Now listen here,' the sheriff said, 'you fight in here, both of you are gonna go to jail. I don't care how much money you got.'

Rise Risner had just been brought out of his cell and was standing next to the counter when John Anderson walked through the door. 'Anderson works at TWA with some computers, but he always made out that he was a friend of ours, rappin' to us and stuff. Anderson was there the night before, Thursday, when we were being taken to jail. Well, he had enough money on him to get some of us out and he didn't do it. He didn't want to spend his damn money. Ootney found out about it and when he saw Anderson he said, "Look you fucker, you're supposed to be a friend of ours. I don't want you to ever fuck me over like that." '

Ootney looked strungout to everyone. 'He was tired, yeah,' Win Allen says, 'but it was more. He was pissed off bad. I think the money had a lot to do with it – like, this was the money he was gonna buy his land with, dig, and it had turned into jail money. And he was pissed off about me, too. Like Charles really dug me. So when he found out my bond was so high, a thousand dollars more than the others, that really pissed him off bad. He told me after he got us out, he said, "Nigger, if your face was as white as my ass, you wouldn't be havin' all this shit." He goes, "These fuckin' crackers, they gonna lynch you up against a tree one night." Then he laughed. Ootney was like that. He was jolly and jivin' but the vibes were like off center, it was like there was a bomb inside his head.'

Standing around the watertower outside the jail, they decided it was more important than ever to stage their antiwar march. They went to George Russell's house, where Ootney 'leaned up against a wall and looked like he was gonna fall asleep.'

'You fuckin' jailbirds kept me up all night,' he said.

'Ootney lost his beauty sleep,' they hooted.

Rise says, 'We were real determined we had to be in that square the next day marchin' with those signs and screamin'. The bust was the best example of the kind of shit we had all felt. Old Lloyd just had to point his finger and say "Him and Him" and it was enough to send us all to the crabseat.'

Win Allen decided they'd hand pamphlets out Saturday as they marched around the square 'so the Truth can be put up on the walls.' Hasty essays had to be written about war, repression, racism, and the new town ordinances.

'Come on, Ootney,' Win said. 'Help us write some of this shit.'

'OK,' Simpson said. 'I'll write how much I like fuckin'.'

They raspberried him and threw him lip-smacking mock farts, figuring, as Rise says, 'We better leave old Ootney alone 'cause he looked pretty tired.' But Simpson brightened after a while and, before the meeting ended, offered to help after all. A friend of his in Holden had a mimeo-machine and he would take the essays over there and have them run off.

'Ootney's the production manager,' Rise yelled, and, as the others laughed, Simpson came alive, dancing around, his fists flying, shadow-boxing Rise's belly.

'Come on, come on,' he yelled, 'Charles Simpson's gonna take on all you creepo fuckers.'

Rise says, 'After a while we split up and Ootney took the stuff we wrote up and he was gonna take it over to Holden to the friend of his that had the machine. He asked me if I wanted to go over there with him and I said sure. We piled on into his 1952 Chevy. That was Oot-ney's batmobile. It was an old, fallin' apart car that made a lot of noise. He loved the car, said it was a real Hippie car. So we drove on and out and we got outside a place called Strasburg and the goddamn car blows up. So we sat there not believin' it, you know, here we are and I just got out of jail and Ootney didn't get any sleep and now the goddamn car blows. Well, we couldn't believe it. We were so pissed off we couldn't do nothin' but stand there and mumble and say fuck it and laugh.

'So we decided we were gonna hitchhike into Holden and then hitch-hike back to Harrisonville. Ootney had his sleeping bag in the back and the M-1 but I didn't think nothin' of it 'cause he and I were always goin' target shootin' with the thing. So he puts the rifle into his sleepin' bag and we're standin' there hitchhikin' and the car's still smokin'. Then this dude from Harrisonville that we know comes along and picks us up. He's goin' back to Harrisonville so he drives us back there and we get my car. We drive into Holden and drop the shit off with the mimeo guy and then we had nothin' to do. So Ootney says, "Let's just take the gun and shoot some target practice." We were gonna spend the night out in the woods.'

As Charles Simpson and Rise Risner drove from Holden to Harrison-ville late Friday afternoon, they talked. The radio was thumping and Rise only half-listened. The conversation was like a hundred others they had had. 'Nothing much,' Rise says, 'Just a lot of shit, rap talk. Maybe he was trying to tell me somethin', but if he did, maybe I wasn't listenin' that close.'

They talked about astrology. Ootney was a Pisces and as they speeded past the wheatfields and around the greening countryside, he talked to Rise about being a Pisces, about how he'd read a book that said he'd be nothing but a dreamer all his life and he'd never make any money. He said that this book said a Pisces was 'self-destructive.'

'So what does that mean?' Rise asked.

'I don't know,' Ootney laughed. 'Maybe it means I'm fucked up.'

'Yeah, it means you'll fuck yourself to death,' Rise said.

They talked, too, about dope. Ootney said he hadn't done any dope for some time and didn't want to do any dope, 'because everytime I smoke a joint I think about how everybody's fuckin' us over and I get all depressed and down.'

As Rise drove into town, he heard Charles Simpson say a few quiet sentences that would forever stick in his mind.

*Everytime I turn around, I'm gettin' fucked up somehow. My old man's dyin' and my old lady leaves and the pigs are always hasslin' me. Shit, I can't buy a piece of land even when I got the money. I can't drive around without my car blowin' up on me. It's always the same shit. Ain't it ever gonna stop?*

'When we got into town,' Rise says, 'We were stopped at the red light and the radio was playin' the new Stones song. I was beatin' on the dash and sayin' "Tumblin'-tumblin'," and all of a sudden Charles jumps out of the car and runs up the street. He was out of the car and halfway up the street before I even knew what happened. And I freaked right there. What the fuck was he doin'? He had the fuckin' gun. What the fuck was he runnin' up the street for with that fuckin' gun in his jacket?'

Rise panicked. He made a U-turn, stepped on the gas, and 'started boogeyin' out of Harrisonville, goin' the other direction.'

When Simpson jumped out of the car, Charles Hale, Gary's younger brother, saw him and ran up to him. He asked Simpson if he had seen Gary.

'He just shook his head,' Charles Hale says, 'the only thing I noticed was, he had this great big beautiful smile on his face.'

Gary Hale was on the other side of the square with Win Allen and some of the others. 'So all of a sudden,' Win says, 'We heard this *rat-tat-tat-tat-tat* like. And I said, "Hey Gary, that sound like some caps, man, like somebody bustin' some caps," and he said, "That's what it sounds like to me." We looked at one another and we got vibes instantly, we said, "Wait a minute, man, who's all here?" So then we see people startin' to run and we started boogeyin' and we heard these two pigs were shot. And then we heard, "There's a dirty hippie down there, dead," and we all — like we saw Charles' body — and like we couldn't identify with that blood.'

Rise drove around for a while, scared, and then, finally, drove back to the square. 'By the time I got there the two dead pigs had been taken off the street but Charles was still layin' in the street where he had shot himself, all covered up. All I could see was his boots stickin' out from under the plastic bag. My knees just kind of buckled and I was leaned up against this building and I just kind of went down. I just passed out on the sidewalk and I lay there a few seconds. There's this woman who runs the cleaners and I've known her all my life and she goes:

' "Well, he tried to shoot me, Johnny" and I didn't say anything.

' "Why did he try to shoot me, Johnny? I didn't do anythin' to him," and I just screamed, "Shut up, goddamn you, just shut up." '

G. M. Allen was about to leave the bank for the day when he saw people running and heard the police sirens. He ran over to the other side of the square, saw the people in front of the Allen Bank and Trust Company, and heard about the two policemen killed and the Simpson boy in the alley with his head blown off. He wasn't surprised. He expected something like this all along. He felt it in his bones. He turned and headed back to his office as fast as he could. He had to activate the Civil Defense sirens and get on the CB band and tell his volunteers to get into town. Gary Hale saw him rushing across the square and went up to him.

'You satisfied now?' Gary Hale said, 'You see what you've done?'

'Get out of my way, you little bastard,' G. M. Allen said.

He got to his office and as he pushed the button and the sirens started screaming, G. M. Allen had a comforting thought.

It was 6 o'clock and the firefighters coming for their convention would be checking into their motels. They'd have more than enough manpower in Harrisonville that night to handle whatever would happen. 500 firefighters from all across the State of Missouri would be there.

And right then G. M. Allen said a prayer. He thanked the Lord for giving him the wisdom to plan the convention for the right time — 'when the hippies started doing their killing.'

## 6 Life among the razorbacks

Firefighters watchdogged the street corners that night with hatchets and shotguns in their hands. The square was barricaded and police cruisers shadowed all the streets leading into town. A rifleman armed with a carbine very much like Charles Simpson's perched in the courthouse belltower, which commands an overview and a clear shot to every cranny of the square. Around 11 o'clock a thunderstorm rolled in with its gnarled bolts of field-lightning and the rain sent the gunmen scurrying to their cars.

About an hour after the shooting, Win Allen was walking across the square and a policeman went up to him and said, 'You got two of ours, now it's time we get some of you.' When a curfew was announced that night, Win and Rise and the others got out of town fast and decided to stay out.

'There was blood in those people's eyes,' Rise says, 'It was like we'd all pulled that trigger, not just Ootney. They couldn't do anything to Ootney because he was smart and blew his brains out, but we were still there. I was really scared. Those people were crazy. The pigs were lookin' at us like they could hardly wait to tickle their triggers. We knew that if any of us like made the smallest wrong move, one of us would be dead and they'd just make up some bogosity and get away with callin' it justifiable murder.'

G. M. Allen says, 'I was just happy we had all those men in town. Besides that, we had policemen come from as far as 50 miles away. We didn't know what to expect, but we were ready. We thought some of the hippies might wanna shoot some more policemen or some innocent people. It didn't make sense, not any of it, unless you figure the whole thing was planned and Simpson was just talked into killin' those policemen for the sake of their revolution.'

On Saturday, the 22nd, the national day of protest to end the Vietnam War, the curfew was lifted – but only during the day, until six o'clock that night. Some of the firefighters and policemen got some rest, but gunmen still patrolled all sides of the square and a rifleman still stood guard in the belltower, using binoculars to scan the alleys and the rooftops. Harrisonville's first anti-war protest was, naturally, canceled, and after only brief debate, the firefighters decided to cancel their parade.

'You mean we drove those trucks all the way out here for nothin'?' a firefighter asked G. M. Allen.

'It ain't fair, sure,' G. M. Allen said, 'but I figure a lot of people are gonna be too scared to come into town.'

He was wrong. Except for the longhairs, everyone within a hundred miles seemed to drive to Harrisonville that day. Traffic was backed up for half a mile, all the way to the FINA gas station, and people stood in clusters around the spots which had been pools of blood the day before.

In the course of florid descriptions, rumor fed upon rumor. The Simpson boy had eaten LSD just before he did his killing. The gun was traced to the Black Panther Party in Chicago. Simpson had belonged to a Communist hippie group in Kansas City. FBI men were coming into town. The longhairs had decided to kill the whole town, just like Charlie Manson had killed those people in California. They found some dynamite hidden in the MFA silo. The courthouse would be burned that night. The hippies had a list with the names of townspeople who were going to be killed on it. The National Guard was coming in.

And the pickup trucks carrying whole families of people who hardly ever came to town kept coming in on this day. Excited little kids stood by the Retirement Home's grey walls and asked, 'Is this where he killed himself, mommy?'

Saturday night, the gunman in the belltower saw something move on the roof of the Harrisonville Hotel. He yelled to the firefighters across the street and, within minutes, the hotel was surrounded by dozens of men carrying all sorts of weapons – from Colt .45s to mail-order Lee Harvey Oswald specials.

'Give yourself up,' a deputy's bullhorn echoed. 'You're surrounded.'

There was a crash on the pavement and an old wino who'd found a comfortable place for the night yelled, 'Don't shoot, don't shoot, I'm comin',' and miraculously no shots were fired. The doddering old drunk had dropped his pint of whiskey from the rooftop in pants-pissed fear and a deputy was assigned to sweep the glass off the street.

The burials were held Monday. Patrolman Donald Lee Marler's was the first. More than 50 policemen came to the funeral, some of them from Kansas City. Marler's open casket was in the church foyer but was closed minutes before his wife and family got there. The minister said, 'The fact that everyone dies is proof that all have sinned. But God says it does not end there. Our friend took the short cut home.' The city council held a meeting before Marler's funeral and voted to pay for both Marler's and Wirt's funerals. A reporter asked if the curfew would be extended and Mayor M. O. Raine, the dentist who'd once pulled one of Charles Simpson's teeth, said, 'This is a black day and I don't like to have too many decisions made when people are so emotional, so I'm not gonna make that decision now.'

Charles Simpson was buried last – in Chilhowee, a tiny town not far from Holden, where his grandparents are buried. Rise Risner, who was one of the pallbearers, says, 'There was a whole lot of people there. I think about half of 'em were pigs because a lot of 'em had cameras. This dude, this minister, like you could tell he wasn't too happy about havin' to bury Ootney. He was just goin' through the motions, like he was the one who got stuck with buryin' a sack of shit. That's what the vibe was, that's what his face said. The minister was talkin' about how Jesus died and all this shit and he didn't say one fuckin' thing about Charles. They didn't have anything about him even, they didn't say one fuckin' thing about his life. Nothin'. He was rappin' shit about fuckin' buryin' Jesus and "He rose" and all this shit. I thought he was talkin' about Charles for a long time until I figured out what he was talkin' about. John Thompson was singin' "Blowin' in the Wind" and we all chimed in.'

After the ceremony, as they were bringing the casket out of the church, in the glare of television cameras and wire service photographers, the pallbearers clenched their fists and held them to the sky, their other hand on the wooden box that had Charles Simpson's body in it. 'We gave the power fist 'cause we figured that would be a way of showin' everyone that Ootney was a brother,' Rise says, 'No matter what kind of shit they were sayin' about him. He was one of us. We did it 'cause we loved him.'

Some of the townspeople saw and others heard about the pallbearers' clenched fists and, at first, no one knew what to make of it. But then G. M. Allen told Mayor Raine he heard it meant someone else was going to die and Mayor Raine told some of the councilmen and by nightfall the word was out all over town: The hippies were going to kill another policeman. So the curfew was extended still another night and the rifleman still crouched in the bell-tower.

The curfew was lifted, finally, the next day, but Win Allen and Rise Risner and Gary Hale and the others still didn't feel safe going into town. They drove out to the City Park about a mile from town and were surrounded by guns within minutes.

'You gonna get your asses outta here,' a policeman told Rise Risner, 'or we gonna get even.'

Win and Rise collected all of their friends and left town, camping out in an open and nearly inaccessible field about six miles away. 'I was afraid they'd come to one of our houses like one of those lynching parties on TV and just take us,' Rise says. 'It was cold out there and it rained and we were wet as hell, but we were alive.'

By Friday, feelings ran so ugly that the Rev. W. T. Niermeier, who had sermonized at Patrolman Marler's funeral, wrote a column for the Democrat-Missourian that said:

'A word of God for our community at this time. Recompense to no man evil for evil. Live peaceably with all men. Dearly beloved, avenge not yourselves. Thou shalt not follow a multitude to do evil.'

That day's Democrat-Missourian carried a news story about the shooting but nothing about the circumstances. 'Well, I didn't want to write too much about Simpson,' said J. W. Brown, the editor, 'not after all the trouble he caused us. I figured folks just wouldn't want to read about him and if folks don't want to read about somethin', I don't print it.' That same day, the newspaper was awarded its 16th Blue Ribbon Weekly Newspaper citation by the Missouri Press Association — for 'outstanding performance in the field of journalism.'

The next issue of the paper carried a new two-column ad. The ad was the result of all the funerals J. W. Brown had to attend that week. He talked to some of the directors and they determined that the funeral homes didn't do much advertising in the Democrat-Missourian and the next week, the bold black-bordered ad, which in a perverse way Charles Simpson had solicited, said

## A HOUSE WITHOUT A WOMAN

is like a body without soul or spirit. Benjamin Franklin's words of wisdom recognize that a house becomes a home through the loving touch of a woman and the warm glow of a friendly hearth. Likewise, we believe, a funeral director becomes more than a business man since his prime object is to be of service to those in need. It is with humble pride that we serve the citizens of this community.

Friday afternoon, a week after the shooting, G. M. Allen was talking to one of his friends about the list the hippies were supposed to have with the names of the people they were going to kill on it. G. M. Allen said he heard that he was Number One on that list. 'I don't hold too much by it,' G. M. Allen said, 'maybe there isn't even any list – but, by God, they try somethin' – well, I was in the Infantry during the War, they better think about that.'

A few days after that, Luke Scavuzzo, who runs Scavuzzo's Grocery and is an alderman, was doing a radio talk in Kansas City and he said: 'Maybe some people in town pushed those kids too much.' Now, Luke Scavuzzo said, 'Some people have learned they better *ease up*.' By nightfall, town scuttlebutt held that Luke Scavuzzo was saying they were going to '*give up*.' The next day about 20 people came in to tell Luke Scavuzzo they weren't going to buy his groceries anymore because of what he said.

'Luke had to go around for a whole week tellin' everybody he never said that,' G. M. Allen says, 'He should have known better. Nobody's gonna give up or ease up. Are we supposed to wait around till someone else gets killed?'

A few weeks after Ootney Simpson fired his M-1 on the town square, the Civil Defense sirens screamed again and people ran to their citizens' band radios expecting to hear the worst of their fears confirmed. More trouble. Another killing. The voice of G. M. Allen was as breathless and garbled as the last time. But this time there was little to worry about. It came out of the east and overturned a mobile home and knocked down some outhouses and then it was gone.

Just another goddamn tornado.

I got into Harrisonville about two weeks after the shooting. The first person I saw was Win Allen. He was lying on the courthouse steps, pressed flat with his face to the cement. He didn't move and he stayed that way, as still as the pennies on a dead man's eyes. Win and Rise and the others had decided it was safe enough to go back into town. The old mock-heroic game for the town square would go on. Four dead men weren't going to get in the way.

I got out of the car and walked into the drug store for a pack of Luckies and an old man behind the counter was staring out the window at Win Allen. He watched me get out of the car and his eyes must have picked out the Missouri plates on it because when I walked in his tone was conspiratorial and trusting. 'See that nigger boy up there,' Lloyd Foster said, 'he's been climbin' those steps every day for four days now and just layin' down up there. He goes up there and he looks around and he puts his fist up in the air and then he lays down on top of his face. He pretends he's dead. They say it's a way of rememberin' the crazy hippie that killed our policemen.'

I was wearing a tie and a blue blazer and the next few days I wore the same get-up, exaggerating the effect, walking around with a fat Special Corona 77 cigar sticking out of my mouth. I sought out townspeople in the most razor-backed bars in town, buying them beer and malt liquor and getting them to talk. I slicked my hair back above my ears and bought a bottle of gooey hair-oil and – with cigar and coat and tie – I must have looked respectable enough to them because pretty soon they were buying me beers. I told them I was from a magazine in San Francisco and forgot to say which one. I think the cigar and the slick hair got through. When I got back to the motel at night and looked in the mirror I saw some guy I remembered from somewhere but I couldn't place him.

When I was finished talking to the townspeople I drove back to my motel and washed my hair and changed. I put my jeans on and let my hair fall down over my ears and put on my leather jacket and drove back into town. I was getting pretty tired of cigars anyway. I found Win Allen and told him I was from ROLLING STONE and wanted to talk about Charles Simpson, and Win Allen almost cried he was so happy. 'Man,' Win said, 'we been watchin' you watchin' us and we figured you was FBI. With that cee-gar.' We laughed.

That night we gathered near the square — one of the cops I'd talked to spotted me and gave me a fixed hard glare — and drove about ten miles out of town into the middle of a wheatfield. We found a clearing that suited us and built a bonfire. It was a cloudy spring night, about 70 degrees, and the lightning was already playing patterns off to the east. There were about a dozen of us and we had eight or nine bottles of red wine and a dozen six-packs of beer. We also had a bagful of tongue-burning Missouri weed.

The fire was roaring and Rise Risner's red Volkswagen, which had been pulled as close as possible, played Dylan, Hendrix, and, what the hell, Jose Feliciano. The people here were Charles Simpson's best friends. We were talking about a man who had killed three innocent people in cold blood. They were calling him a brother and telling me how much he loved people and how he believed in The Cause.

'Sometimes Ootney said he thought violence was the only kind of revolution there was,' Rise said. 'But dig,' Win said, 'as far as violent revolution — anytime someone infringes on me and fucks me, it makes me mad, that's the way Charles was thinkin' too.'

'A lot of freaks you meet in places,' Rise said, 'somebody will rip them off or something and they'll haul ass. But we're not that way. We're country boys. We're willin' to fight the motherfuckers if they wanna fight us.'

'Ootney was smart,' Rise said, 'he killed himself to keep the pigs from havin' the satisfaction of killin' him or lockin' him up in some honky jail. He was into so much cosmic shit, man. He was so heavy with that, it was a religion to him. Like some religions say self-destruction is the best thing you can do for your God, that's why they burn themselves. I know Ootney had to feel the same thing.'

'One time Ootney was in a black neighborhood,' Win said; 'and somebody said somethin' about Jesus to him and Ootney said, "The only way that Jesus and I differ is that he was willin' to die for the people around him and I'm not ready for that yet."'

'I think he was Jesus,' Rise said, 'as far as I'm concerned he was Jesus.'

'Because that cat just laid down truth, man,' Win said. 'Everything that came out of his mouth was truth and supposedly like Jesus laid down the same thing. And when he got up the stuff to die for The Cause, Charles became of the same instance. He was groovy, outta-sight, he had so much compassion for people, sentimental about a lot of things, sensitive.'

It had been a long few days and I had scrutinized too many vivid details of four vicious killings and something in my mind flailed out now — Jesus Simpson, murderer, cold-blooded killer, compassionate, sensitive, sentimental. It could have been the fatigue or the Missouri weed or the beer mixed with wine, but I saw too many grotesqueries leaping about in that blazing bonfire.

'As far as I'm concerned,' Rise said, 'Charles isn't dead. It is just somethin' Charles wanted to do and if Charles wanted to do it, I can't say anything about it.'

'Yeah,' I said, 'but what about the people killed and their wives and kids? Don't you care about that?'

'Well, you know,' Rise said, 'how can I criticize it. It's Charles' thing. Like it was a far-out thing to do.'

We were gathered around this bonfire on a spring night in Missouri and the date was the fourth of May, 1972. I've never had much luck with the fourth of May. On this day in 1971, I was standing around a green field at Kent State University listening to requiems and eulogies. And on this day in 1970 I was running dazedly around those same lush fields looking at pools of blood and asking National Guardsmen why they had killed four innocent kids.

And now I was talking to some kids asking them why one of their best friends killed three innocent people with the same kind of gun the Guardsmen used and all they could say to me was:

*Like it was a far-out thing to do.*

I told them the story of my May 4ths and Win Allen said:

'Well, dig, man, now it's four to three.'

'Right on,' Rise said.

'Old Ootney,' Win said. 'Old Ootney. That gun was outtasight, man. Like the first time I went to his crib I saw it and I said, "Ootney, is that yours?" and he said, "Yeah, a friend of mine gave it to me," and I said: "Wow, man, sometime when you and I go fishin' and out in the woods, maybe I can dig on it." Like Charles had this big Buck knife with a holster on it and this most beautiful fishin' pole and he said — he said whenever he went home, he just fondled the stuff all the time, felt it up and dug it.'

'Yeah,' Rise said, 'Ootney loved nature.'

# Terry Southern from
# Red dirt marijuana and other tastes

*Terry Southern was an editor at* Esquire *and not yet well known as a novelist when he wrote 'Twirling at Ole Miss.' It was the first example I noticed of a form of journalism in which the writer starts out to do a feature assignment ('Go to Mississippi and see what happens when five hundred pubescent baton twirlers meet in earnest competition') and ends up writing a curious form of autobiography. It is not autobiography in the customary sense, because the writer has put himself in the situation for no other reason than to write something. The supposed subject (e.g., baton twirlers) becomes incidental; and if the writer has the wit to make his own reactions that fascinating, the reader doesn't care. Hunter Thompson has become the maestro of this form and calls it Gonzo Journalism. T.W.*

### Twirling at Ole Miss

In an age gone stale through the complex of bureaucratic interdependencies, with its tedious labyrinth of technical specialization, each contingent upon the next, and all aimed to converge into a single totality of meaning, it is a refeshing moment indeed when one comes across an area of human endeavor absolutely sufficient unto itself, pure and free, no strings attached – the cherished and almost forgotten *l'art pour l'art*. Such is the work being carried forward now at the Dixie National Baton Twirling Institute, down at the campus of Ole Miss – a visit to which is well worthwhile these days, if one can keep one's wits about.

In my case, it was the first trip South in many years, and I was duly apprehensive. For one thing, the Institute is located just outside Oxford, Mississippi – and, by grotesque coincidence, Faulkner's funeral had been held only the day before my arrival, lending a grimly surreal aura to the nature of my assignment ... namely, to get the story on the Baton Twirling Institute. Would reverting to the Texas twang and callousness of my youth suffice to see me through?

Arriving in Oxford then, on a hot midday in July, after the three-hour bus ride from Memphis, I stepped off in front of the Old Colonial Hotel and meandered across the sleepy square toward the only sign of life at hand — the proverbial row of shirt-sleeved men sitting on benches in front of the county courthouse, a sort of permanent jury.

'Howdy,' I say, striking an easy stance, smiling friendly-like. 'Whar the school?'

The nearest regard me in narrow surmise: they are quick to spot the stranger here, but a bit slow to cotton. One turns to another.

'What's that he say, Ed?'

Big Ed shifts his wad, sluices a long spurt of juice into the dust, gazes at it reflectively before fixing me again with gun-blue-cold eyes.

'Reckon you mean, "Whar the school *at*?", don't you, stranger?'

Next to the benches, and about three feet apart, are two public drinking fountains, and I notice that the one boldly marked 'For Colored' is sitting squarely in the shadow cast by the justice symbol on the courthouse façade — to be entered later, of course, in my writer's notebook, under 'Imagery, sociochiaroscurian, hack.'

After getting directions (rather circuitous, I thought — being farther put off by what I understood, though perhaps in error, as a fleeting reference to 'the Till case') I decided to take a cab, having just seen one park on the opposite side of the square.

'Which is nearer,' I asked the driver, 'Faulkner's house or his grave?'

'Wal,' he said without looking around, 'now that would take a little studyin', if you were gonna hold a man to it, but offhand I'd say they were pretty damn near the same — about ten minutes from where we're sittin' and fifty cents each. They're in opposite directions.'

I sensed the somehow questionable irony of going from either to the Baton Twirling Institute, and so decided to get over to the Institute first and get on with the coverage.

'By the way,' I asked after we'd started, 'where can a man get a drink of whiskey around here?' It had just occurred to me that Mississippi is a dry state.

'Place over on the county line,' said the driver, 'about eighteen miles; cost you four dollars for the trip, eight for the bottle.'

'I see.'

He half turned, giving me a curious look.

'Unless, of course, you'd like to try some "nigger-pot." '

'Nigger-Pot? Great God yes, man,' I said in wild misunderstanding, 'Let's go!'

It soon developed, of course, that what he was talking about was the unaged and uncolored corn whiskey privately made in the region, and also known as 'white lightning.' I started to demur, but as we were already in the middle of the colored section, thought best to go through with it. Why not begin the sojourn with a genuine Dixieland experience – the traditional jug of corn?

As it happened the distiller and his wife were in the fields when we reached the house, or hut as it were, where we were tended by a Negro boy of about nine.

'This here's a mighty fine batch,' he said, digging around in a box of kindling wood and fetching out unlabeled pints of it.

The taxi driver, who had come inside with me, cocked his head to one side and gave a short laugh, as to show we were not so easily put upon.

'Why, boy,' he said, 'I wouldn't have thought you was a drinkin' man.'

'Nosuh, I ain't no drinkin' man, but I sure know how it suppose to taste – that's 'cause times nobody here I have to *watch* it and I have to *taste* it too, see it workin' right. We liable lose the whole batch I don't know how it suppose to taste. You all taste it,' he added, holding out one of the bottles and shaking it in my happy face. 'You see if that ain't a fine batch!'

Well, it had a pretty good taste all right – a bit edgy perhaps, but plenty of warmth and body. And I did have to admire the pride the young fellow took in his craft. You don't see much of that these days – especially among nine-year-olds. So I bought a couple of bottles, and the driver bought one, and we were off at last for the Institute.

The Dixie National Baton Twirling Institute holds its classes in a huge, sloping, fairyland grove on the campus of Ole Miss, and it resembles something from another age. The classes had already begun when I stepped out of the cab, and the sylvan scene which stretched before me, of some seven hundred girls, nymphs and nymphets all, cavorting with their staffs in scanty attire beneath the broadleaf elms, was a sight to spin the senses and quicken the blood. Could I but have donned satyr's garb and rushed savagely among them! But no, there was this job o'work to get on with – dry, factual reportage – mere donkey work, in fact. I decided the correct procedure was to first get some background material, and to this end I sought out Don Sartell, 'Mister Baton' himself, Director of the Institute. Mr. Sartell is a handsome and personable young man from north of the Mason-Dixon line, highly intelligent, acutely attuned to the needs of the young, and, need-less to say, extremely dexterous *avec les doigts*. (By way of demon-strating the latter he once mastered a year's typing course in a quick six hours – or it may have been six days, though I do recall that it was an impressive and well-documented achievement.)

'Baton twirling,' he tells me straight off, 'is the second largest girls' youth movement in America – the first, of course, being the Girl Scouts.' (Veteran legman, I check this out later. Correct.) 'The popu-larity of baton twirling,' he explains, 'has a threefold justification: (1) it is a sport which can be practiced alone; (2) it does not, unlike other solo sports (sailing, skiing, shooting, etc.), require expensive equip-ment; and (3) it does not, again like the aforementioned, require travel, but, on the contrary, may be practiced in one's own living room or backyard.'

'Right,' I say. 'So far, so good, Mister Baton – but what about the intrinsics? I mean, just what is the point of it all?'

'The point, aside from the simple satisfaction of mastering a com-plex and highly evolved skill, is the development of self-confidence, poise, ambidexterity, disciplined coordination, et cetera.'

I asked if he would like a drink of nigger-pot. He declined graci-ously: he does not drink or smoke. My place, I decided, is in the grove, with the groovy girls – so, limbering up my 600-page, eight-dollar copy of *Who's Who in Baton Twirling*, I take my leave of the excellent fellow and steal toward the sylvan scene below, ready for anything.

The development of American baton twirling closely parallels the his-tory of emancipation of our women. A larger version of this same baton (metal with a knob on the end) was first used, of course, to direct military marching bands, or, prior to that, drum corps – the baton being manipulated in a fairly straightforward, dum-de-dum, up-and-down manner. The idea of *twirling* it – and finally even *flinging* it – is, obviously, a delightfully girlish notion.

Among those most keenly interested in mastering the skill today are drum majorettes from the high schools and colleges of the South and Midwest, all of which have these big swinging bands and corps of majorettes competing during the half at football games. In the South, on the higher-educational level, almost as much expense and training goes into these groups as into the football team itself, and, to persons of promise and accomplishment in the field, similar scholarships are available. Girls who aspire to become majorettes – and it is generally considered the smartest status a girl can achieve on the Southern campus — come to the Institute for preschool training. Or, if she is already a majorette, she comes to sharpen her technique. Many schools send a girl, or a small contingent of them, to the Institute to pick up the latest routines so that they can come back and teach the rest of the corps what they have learned. Still others are training to be professionals and teachers of baton twirling. Most of these girls come every year — I talked to one from Honey Pass, Arkansas, a real cutie pie, who had been there for eight consecutive years, from the time she was nine. When I asked if she would like a drink of pot, she replied pertly: 'N ... o ... spells "No"!' Such girls are usually championship material, shooting for the Nationals.

Competitions to determine one's degree of excellence are held regularly under the auspices of the National Baton Twirling Association, and are of the following myriad categories: *Advanced Solo; Intermediate Solo; Beginners Solo; Strutting Routine; Beginners Strutting Routine; Military Marching; Flag; Two-Baton; Fire Baton; Duet; Trio; Team; Corps; Boys; Out-of-State;* and others. Each division is further divided into age groups: 0–6, 7–8, 9–10, 11–12, 13–14, 15–16, 17 and over. The winner in each category receives a trophy, and the first five runners-up receive medals. This makes for quite a bit of hardware riding on one session, so that a person in the baton-twirling game does not go too long without at least token recognition — and the general run of *Who's Who* entries ('eight trophies, seventy-three medals') would make someone like Audie Murphy appear rudely neglected.

The rules of competition, however, are fairly exacting. Each contestant appears singly before a Judge and Scorekeeper, and while the Judge observes and relays the grading to the Scorekeeper, the girl goes through her routine for a closely specified time. In Advanced Solo, for example, the routine must have a duration of not less than two minutes and twenty seconds, and not more than two and thirty. She is scored on general qualities relating to her degree of accomplishment — including *showmanship, speed,* and *drops,* the latter, of course, counting against her, though not so much as one might suppose. Entrance fees average about two dollars for each contestant. Some girls use their allowance to pay it.

In the Institute's grove — not unlike the fabled Arcadia — the groups are ranged among the trees in various states of learning. The largest, most central and liveliest of these groups is the one devoted to the mastery of Strutting. Practice and instruction in Strutting are executed to records played over a public-address system at an unusually loud volume – a sort of upbeat rock and roll with boogie-woogie overtones. *Dixie*, *The Stripper*, and *Potato Peel* were the three records in greatest use for this class – played first at half speed, to learn the motions, then blasted at full tempo. Strutting is, of course, one of the most fantastic body-movement phenomena one is likely to see anywhere. The deliberate narcissistic intensity it requires must exceed even that of the Spanish flamenco dancer. High-style (or 'all-out') Strutting is to be seen mainly in the South, and what it resembles more than anything else is a very contemporary burlesque-house number – with the grinds in and the bumps out. It is the sort of dance one associates with jaded and sequin-covered washed-out blondes in their very late thirties – but Ole Miss, as is perhaps well known, is in 'the heartland of beautiful girls,' having produced two Miss Americas and any number of runners-up, and to watch a hundred of their nymphets practice the Strut, in bathing suits, short shorts, and other such skimp, is a visual treat which cuts anything the Twist may offer the viewer. It is said, incidentally, that the best Strutting is done at the colored schools of the South, and that of these the greatest of all is to be seen at Alabama State Teachers College. That jazz trends have decisively influenced the style of Strutting in recent years is readily acknowledged, and is highly apparent indeed.

At the Institute, the instructor of the Strut stands on a slightly raised platform facing her class, flanked by her two assistants. She wears dark glasses, tight rolled shorts, and looks to be about 34–22–34. She's a swinger from Pensacola, Florida, a former National Senior Champion and Miss Majorette of America, now turned pro. When not at the Dixie Institute at the University of Mississippi, or a similar establishment, she gives private lessons at her own studio, for four to six dollars an hour, and drives a Cadillac convertible.

As for other, more academic, aspects of baton twirling, an exhibition was given the first evening by members of the cadre – all champions, and highly skilled indeed. It is really quite amazing what can be done with a baton, and no one could have been more surprised than your correspondent. The members of the cadre can literally walk those sticks over every inch of the body, almost it seems without touching them. This is especially effective at night when they use a thing called the 'fire baton,' with a torch flaming at each end.

Instruction in speed and manipulation of this sort is a long and nerve-racking process. There is something almost insane about the amount of sheer effort and perseverance which seems to go into achieving even a nominal degree of real excellence – and practice of four hours a day is not uncommon. And yet the genuine and really impressive skill which is occasionally displayed makes it difficult to consider the art as so totally ridiculous as one would have previously believed – though, of course, another might argue that such achieved excellence only makes it more ridiculous – or perhaps not so much ridiculous as absurd. In fact, in the existentialist sense, it might well be considered as the final epitome of the absurd – I mean, people starving in India and that sort of thing, and then others spending four hours a day skillfully flinging a metal stick about. *Ça alórs!* In any case it has evolved now into a highly developed art and a tightly organized movement – though by no means one which has reached full flower. For one thing, a nomenclature – that hallmark of an art's maturity – has not yet been wholly formalized. Theoretically, at least, there should be a limit to the number of possible manipulations, each of which could legitimately be held as distinct from all others – that is to say, a repertory which would remain standard and unchanged for a period of time. The art of baton twirling has not yet reached that stage, however, and innovations arise with such frequency that there does not exist at present any single manual, or similarly doctrinaire work, on the subject. Doubtless this is due in large part to the comparative newness of the art as a large and intensively active pastime – the Dixie National Baton Twirling Institute, for example, having been founded as recently as 1951. The continuous evolution of the art as a whole is reflected in the names of the various manipulations. Alongside the commonplace (or classic) designations, such as *arabesque, tour-jeté, cradles,* etc., are those of more exotic or contemporary flavor: *bat, walk-over, pretzel,* and the like ... and all, old or new, requiring countless hours of practice.

During the twirling exhibition I fell into conversation with a couple of graduate law students, and afterward went along with them to the campus coffee shop, 'Rebel Devil' or whatever it is called – nearly all shops there have the word 'Rebel' in them – and we had an interesting talk. Ole Miss prides itself, among other things, on having the only law school in the state which is accredited by the American Bar Association – so that these two graduate law students were not without some claim to representing a certain level of relative advancement in the community of scholars. They were clean-cut young men in their mid-twenties, dressed in summer suits of tasteful cut. In answer to a question of mine, we talked about Constitutional Law for ten minutes before I realized they were talking about *State* Constitutional Law. When it became apparent what I was driving at, however, they were quick to face the issue squarely.

'*We* nevuh had no Negra problem heah,' said one of them, shaking his head sadly. He was a serious man wearing glasses and the mien of a Harvard divinity student. 'Theah just *weren't* no problem — wasn't till these *agi-ta-tors* came down heah started all this problem business.'

They were particularly disturbed about the possible 'trouble, an' I mean *real* trouble' which would be occasioned by the attempted registration of a Negro student [James Meredith] which was threatening to take place quite soon, during that very summer session, in fact. As it happened, the authorities managed to delay it; I did, however, get a preview of things to come.

'Why they'll find *dope* in his room the first night he's heah,' the other student said, 'dope, a gun, something — *anything*, just plant it in theah an' *find* it! And out he'll go!'

They assured me that they themselves were well above this sort of thing, and were, in fact, speaking as mature and nonviolent persons.

'But now these heah young *unduh* graduates, they're hot-headed. Why, do you know how *they* feel? What *they* say?'

Then to the tune of *John Brown's Body*, the two graduate law students began to sing almost simultaneously: '*Oh we'll bury all the niggers in the Mississippi mud . . .*', singing it rather loudly it seemed to me — I mean if they were just documenting a point in a private conversation — or perhaps they were momentarily carried away, so to speak. In any event, and despite a terrific effort at steely Zen detachment, the incident left me somewhat depressed, so I retired early, to my comfortable room in the Alumni House, where I sipped the white corn and watched television. But I was not destined to escape so easily, for suddenly who should appear on the screen but old Governor Faubus himself — in a gubernatorial campaign rant — with about six cross-purpose facial tics going strong, and in general looking as mad as a hatter. At first I actually mistook it for a rather tasteless and heavy-handed parody of the governor. It could not, I thought, really be Faubus, because why would the network carry an Arkansas primary campaign speech in Mississippi? Surely not just for laughs. Later I learned that while there is such a thing in television as a *nation*wide hookup for covering events of national importance, there is also such a thing as a *South*wide hookup.

• • •

The Institute's mimeographed schedule, of which I had received a copy, read for the next day as follows:

| | |
|---|---|
| 7:30 | Up and at 'em |
| 8–9 | Breakfast – University Cafeteria |
| 9–9:30 | Assembly, Limber up, Review – Grove |
| 9:30–10:45 | Class No. 4 |
| 10:45–11:30 | Relax – Make Notes |
| 11:30–12:45 | Class No. 5 |
| 1–2:30 | Lunch – University Cafeteria |
| 2:30–4 | Class No. 6 |
| 4–5:30 | Swim Hour |
| 6:30–7:30 | Supper – University Cafeteria |
| 7:30 | Dance – Tennis Court |
| 11 | Room Check |
| 11:30 | Lights Out (NO EXCEPTIONS) |

The 'Up and at 'em' seemed spirited enough, as did the 'No EXCEPTIONS' being in heavy capitals; but the rest somehow offered little promise, so, after a morning cup of coffee, I walked over to the library, just to see if they really had any books there – other than books on Constitutional Law, that is. Indeed they did, and quite a modern and comfortable structure it was, too, air-conditioned (as was, incidentally, my room at the Alumni House) and well-lighted throughout. After looking around for a bit, I carefully opened a mint first-edition copy of *Light in August*, and found 'nigger-lover' scrawled across the title page. I decided I must be having a run of bad luck as, a few minutes later, I suffered still another minor trauma on the steps of the library. It was one of those incredible bits of irony which sometimes do occur in life, but are never suitable for fiction – for I had completely put the title-page incident out of my mind and was sitting on the steps of the library, having a smoke, when this very amiable gentleman of middle age paused in passing to remark on the weather (102°) and to inquire in an oblique and courteous way as to the nature of my visit. An immaculate, pink-faced man, with pince-nez spectacles attached by a silver loop to his lapel, nails buffed to a gleam, he carried a smart leather briefcase and a couple of English-literature textbooks which he rested momentarily on the balustrade as he continued to smile down on me with what seemed to be extraordinary happiness.

'My, but it's a mighty warm day, an' that's no lie,' he said, withdrawing a dazzling white-linen handkerchief and touching it carefully to his brow, '...an' I expect you all from up Nawth,' he added with a twinkle, 'find it especially so!' Then he quite abruptly began to talk of the 'natural tolerance' of the people of Mississippi, speaking in joyfully objective tones, as though it were, even to him, an unfailing source of mystery and delight.

'Don't mind nobody's business but yoah own!' he said, beaming and nodding his head – and it occurred to me this might be some kind of really weirdly obscured threat, the way he was smiling; but no, evidently he was just remarkably good-natured. ' "Live an' let live!" That's how the people of Mississippi feel – always have! Why, look at William Faulkner, with all his notions, an' him livin' right ovah heah in Oxford all the time an' nobody botherin' him – just let him go his own way – why we even let him teach heah at the University one yeah! That's right! I know it! Live an' let live – you can't beat it! I'll see you now, you heah?' And his face still a glittering mask of joviality, he half raised his hand in good-by and hurried on. Who was this strange, happy educator? Was it he who had defaced the title page? His idea of tolerance and his general hilarity gave one pause. I headed back to the grove, hoping to recover some equilibrium. There, things seemed to be proceeding pretty much as ever.

'Do you find that your costume is an advantage in your work?' I asked the first seventeen-year-old Georgia Peach I came across, she wearing something like a handkerchief-size Confederate flag.

'Yessuh, I *do*,' she agreed, with friendly emphasis, tucking her little blouse in a bit more snugly all around, and continuing to speak in that oddly rising infection peculiar to girls of the South, making parts of a reply sound like a question: 'Why, back home near Macon ... Macon, Georgia? At Robert E. Lee High? ... we've got these outfits with *tassels!* And a little red-and-gold skirt? ... that, you know, sort of *flares out?* Well, now they're awful pretty, and of course they're *short* and everything, but I declare those tassels and that little skirt get in my way!'

The rest of the day passed without untoward incident, with my observing the Strut platform for a while, then withdrawing to rest up for the Dance, and perhaps catch the Faub on video again.

The Dance was held on a boarded-over outdoor tennis court, and was a swinging affair. The popular style of dancing in the white South is always in advance of that in the rest of white America; and, at any given moment, it mostly resembles that which is occurring at the same time in Harlem, which is invariably the forerunner of whatever is to become the national style. I mused on this, standing there near the court foul line, and (in view of the day's events) pursued it to an interesting generalization: perhaps *all* the remaining virtues, or let us say, positive traits, of the white Southerner – folk song, poetic speech, and the occasional warmth and simplicity of human relationships – would seem rather obviously to derive from the colored culture there. Due to my magazine assignment, I could not reveal my findings over the public-address system at the dance – and, in fact, thought best to put them from my mind entirely, and get on with the coverage – and, to that end, had a few dances and further questioned the girls. Their view of the world was quite extraordinary. For most, New York was like another country – queer, remote, and of small import in the scheme of things. Several girls spoke spiritedly of wanting to 'get into television,' but it always developed that they were talking about programs produced in Memphis. Memphis, in fact, was definitely the mecca, yardstick and *summum bonum*. As the evening wore on, I found it increasingly difficult, despite the abundance of cutie pieness at hand, to string along with these values, and so finally decided to wrap it up. It should be noted too, that girls at the Dixie National are under extremely close surveillance both in the grove and out.

The following day I made one last tour, this time noting in particular the instruction methods for advanced twirling techniques: *1-, 2-, 3-finger rolls, wrist rolls, waist roll, neck roll,* etc. A pretty girl of about twelve was tossing a baton sixty feet straight up, a silver whir in the Mississippi sunlight, and she beneath it spinning like an ice skater, and catching it behind her back, not having moved an inch. She said she had practiced it an hour a day for six years. Her hope was to become 'the best there is at the high toss and spin' – and she was now up to seven complete turns before making the catch. Was there a limit to the height and number of spins one could attain? No, she guessed not.

After lunch I packed, bid adieu to the Dixie National and boarded the bus for Memphis. As we crossed the Oxford square and passed the courthouse, I saw the fountain was still shaded, although it was now a couple of hours later than the time before. Perhaps it is always shaded – cool and inviting, it could make a person thirsty just to see it.

# Hunter S. Thompson
# The Kentucky Derby is decadent and depraved

*Hunter Thompson's career as a 'Gonzo Journalist' began after he wrote his first book,* The Hell's Angels, a Strange and Terrible Saga. *Infuriated because* Playboy *wouldn't run a story they had commissioned him to do on Jean-Claude Killy's career as a celebrity huckster for Chevrolet, Thompson rewrote the story for Warren Hinckle's* Scanlan's Monthly, *throwing in his hassle with* Playboy *as part of the saga. The upshot was a manic, highly adrenal first-person style in which Thompson's own emotions continually dominate the story. This approach seldom grates in Thompson's hands, probably because Thompson, for all his surface ferocity, usually casts himself as a frantic loser, inept and half-psychotic, somewhat after the manner of Céline. This story on the Kentucky Derby gave Thompson a chance to polish the comic medium he had invented in his Killy story and led to his longest piece of Gonzo, the book* Fear and Loathing in Las Vegas. *All three — the Killy piece,* Fear and Loathing, *and this one on the Derby — began as routine magazine assignments and ended up as quite something else. It is only after finishing 'The Kentucky Derby Is Decadent and Depraved' that one realizes how much of Thompson's description of the Derby has come in the form of Céline-like fantasies he presents to the artist, Ralph Steadman, in conversation. T.W.*

## Welcome to Derbytown

I got off the plane around midnight and no one spoke as I crossed the dark runway to the terminal. The air was thick and hot, like wandering into a steam bath. Inside, people hugged each other and shook hands ... big grins and a whoop here and there: 'By God! You old *bastard!* Good to see you, boy! *Damn* good ... and I *mean* it!'

In the air-conditioned lounge I met a man from Houston who said his name was something or other — 'but just call me Jimbo' — and he was here to get it on. 'I'm ready for *anything*, by God! Anything at all. Yeah, what are you drinkin?' I ordered a Margarita with ice, but he wouldn't hear of it: 'Naw, naw ... what the hell kind of drink is that for Kentucky Derby time? What's *wrong* with you, boy?' He grinned and winked at the bartender. 'Goddam, we gotta educate this boy. Get him some good *whiskey....*'

I shrugged. 'Okay, a double Old Fitz on ice.' Jimbo nodded his approval.

'Look.' He tapped me on the arm to make sure I was listening. 'I know this Derby crowd, I come here every year, and let me tell you one thing I've learned — this is no town to be giving people the impression you're some kind of faggot. Not in public, anyway. Shit, they'll roll you in a minute, knock you in the head and take every goddam cent you have.'

I thanked him and fitted a Marlboro into my cigarette holder. 'Say,' he said, 'you look like you might be in the horse business ... am I right?'

'No,' I said. 'I'm a photographer.'

'Oh yeah?' He eyed my ragged leather bag with new interest. 'Is that what you got there — cameras? Who you work for?'

'Playboy,' I said.

He laughed. 'Well goddam! What are you gonna take pictures of — nekkid horses? Haw! I guess you'll be workin' pretty hard when they run the Kentucky Oaks. That's a race just for fillies.' He was laughing wildly. 'Hell yes! And they'll all be nekkid too!'

I shook my head and said nothing; just stared at him for a moment, trying to look grim. 'There's going to be trouble,' I said. 'My assignment is to take pictures of the riot.'

'What riot?'

I hesitated, twirling the ice in my drink. 'At the track. On Derby Day. The Black Panthers.' I stared at him again. 'Don't you read the newspapers?'

The grin on his face had collapsed. 'What the *hell* are you talkin about?'

'Well ... maybe I shouldn't be telling you....' I shrugged. 'But hell, everybody else seems to know. The cops and the National Guard have been getting ready for six weeks. They have 20,000 troops on alert at Fort Knox. They've warned us — all the press and photographers — to wear helmets and special vests like flak jackets. We were told to expect shooting....'

'No!' he shouted; his hands flew up and hovered momentarily between us, as if to ward off the words he was hearing. Then he whacked his fist on the bar. 'Those sons of bitches! God Almighty! The Kentucky Derby!' He kept shaking his head. 'No! *Jesus!* That's almost too bad to believe!' Now he seemed to be jagging on the stool, and when he looked up his eyes were misty. 'Why? Why *here?* Don't they respect *anything?*'

I shrugged again. 'It's not just the Panthers. The FBI says busloads of white crazies are coming in from all over the country – to mix with the crowd and attack all at once, from every direction. They'll be dressed like everybody else. You know – coats and ties and all that. But when the trouble starts ... well, that's why the cops are so worried.'

He sat for a moment, looking hurt and confused and not quite able to digest all this terrible news. Then he cried out: 'Oh ... Jesus! What in the name of God is happening in this country? Where can you get away from it?'

'Not here,' I said, picking up my bag. 'Thanks for the drink ... and good luck.'

He grabbed my arm, urging me to have another, but I said I was overdue at the Press Club and hustled off to get my act together for the awful spectacle. At the airport newsstand I picked up a Courier-Journal and scanned the front page headlines: 'Nixon Sends GI's into Cambodia to Hit Reds' ... 'B-52's Raid, then 2,000 GI's Advance 20 miles' ... '4,000 U.S. Troops Deployed Near Yale as Tension Grows Over Panther Protest.' At the bottom of the page was a photo of Diane Crump, soon to become the first woman jockey ever to ride in the Kentucky Derby. The photographer had snapped her 'stopping in the barn area to fondle her mount, Fathom.' The rest of the paper was spotted with ugly war news and stories of 'student unrest.' There was no mention of any protest action at a small Ohio school called Kent State.

I went to the Hertz desk to pick up my car, but the moon-faced young swinger in charge said they didn't have any. 'You can't rent one anywhere,' he assured me. 'Our Derby reservations have been booked for six weeks.' I explained that my agent had confirmed a white Chrysler convertible for me that very afternoon but he shook his head. 'Maybe we'll have a cancellation. Where are you staying?'

I shrugged. 'Where's the Texas crowd staying? I want to be with my people.'

He sighed. 'My friend, you're in trouble. This town is flat *full.* Always is, for the Derby.'

I leaned closer to him, half-whispering: 'Look, I'm from Playboy. How would you like a job?'

He backed off quickly. 'What? Come on, now. What kind of a job?'
'Never mind,' I said. 'You just blew it.' I swept my bag off the
counter and went to find a cab. The bag is a valuable prop in this kind
of work; mine has a lot of baggage tags on it — SF, LA, NY, Lima,
Rome, Bangkok, that sort of thing — and the most prominent tag of all
is a very official, plastic-coated thing that says 'Photog. Playboy Mag.' I
bought it from a pimp in Vail, Colorado, and he told me how to use it.
'Never mention Playboy until you're sure they've seen this thing first,'
he said. 'Then, when you see them notice it, that's the time to strike.
They'll go belly up every time. This thing is magic, I tell you. Pure
magic.'

Well ... maybe so. I'd used it on the poor geek in the bar, and now,
humming along in a Yellow Cab toward town, I felt a little guilty about
jangling the poor bugger's brains with that evil fantasy. But what the
hell? Anybody who wanders around the world saying, 'Yes, I'm from
Texas,' deserved whatever happens to him. And he had, after all, come
here once again to make a 19th century ass of himself in the midst of
some jaded, atavistic freakout with nothing to recommend it except a
very saleable 'tradition.' Early in our chat, Jimbo had told me that he
hasn't missed a Derby since 1954. 'The little lady won't come anymore,' he said. 'She just grits her teeth and turns me loose for this one.
And when I say "loose" I do mean *loose!* I toss ten-dollar bills around
like they were goin' outa style! Horses, whiskey, women ... shit,
there's women in this town that'll do *anything* for money.'

Why not? Money is a good thing to have in these twisted times.
Even Richard Nixon is hungry for it. Only a few days before the Derby
he said, 'If I had any money I'd invest it in the stock market.' And the
market, meanwhile, continued its grim slide.

*Waiting for Steadman*

The next day was heavy. With 30 hours to post time I had no press
credentials and — according to the sports editor of the Louisville
Courier-Journal — no hope at all of getting any. Worse, I needed two
sets; one for myself and another for Ralph Steadman, the English illustrator who was coming from London to do some Derby drawings. All I
knew about him was that this was his first visit to the United States.
And the more I pondered that fact, the more it gave me fear. Would he
bear up under the heinous culture shock of being lifted out of London
and plunged into a drunken mob scene at the Kentucky Derby? There
was no way of knowing. Hopefully, he would arrive at least a day or so

ahead, and give himself time to get acclimated. Maybe a few hours of peaceful sightseeing in the Bluegrass country around Lexington. My plan was to pick him up at the airport in the huge Pontiac Ballbuster I'd rented from a used car salesman named Colonel Quick, then whisk him off to some peaceful setting to remind him of England.

Colonel Quick had solved the car problem, and money (four times the normal rate) had bought two rooms in a scumbox on the outskirts of town. The only other kink was the task of convincing the moguls at Churchill Downs that *Scanlan's* was such a prestigious sporting journal that common sense compelled them to give us two sets of the best press tickets. This was not easily done. My first call to the publicity office resulted in total failure. The press handler was shocked at the idea that anyone would be stupid enough to apply for press credentials two days before the Derby. 'Hell, you can't be serious,' he said. 'The deadline was two months ago. The press box is full; there's no more room ... and what the hell is *Scanlan's Monthly* anyway?'

I uttered a painful groan. 'Didn't the London office call you? They're flying an artist over to do the paintings. Steadman. He's Irish, I think. Very famous over there. I just got in from the Coast. The San Francisco office told me we were all set.'

He seemed interested, and even sympathetic, but there was nothing he could do. I flattered him with more gibberish, and finally he offered a compromise: he could get us two passes to the clubhouse grounds.

'That sounds a little weird,' I said. 'It's unacceptable. We *must* have access to everything. *All* of it. The spectacle, the people, the pageantry and certainly the race. You don't think we came all this way to watch the damn thing on television, do you? One way or another we'll get inside. Maybe we'll have to bribe a guard — or even Mace somebody.' (I had picked up a spray can of Mace in a downtown drugstore for $5.98 and suddenly, in the midst of that phone talk, I was struck by the hideous possibilities of using it out at the track. Macing ushers at the narrow gates to the clubhouse inner sanctum, then slipping quickly inside, firing a huge load of Mace into the governor's box, just as the race starts. Or Macing helpless drunks in the clubhouse restroom, for their own good. . . .)

By noon on Friday I was still without credentials and still unable to locate Steadman. For all I knew he'd changed his mind and gone back to London. Finally, after giving up on Steadman and trying unsuccessfully to reach my man in the press office, I decided my only hope for credentials was to go out to the track and confront the man in person, with no warning – demanding only one pass now, instead of two, and talking very fast with a strange lilt in my voice, like a man trying hard to control some inner frenzy. On the way out, I stopped at the motel desk to cash a check. Then, as a useless afterthought, I asked if by any wild chance Mr. Steadman had checked in.

The lady on the desk was about fifty years old and very peculiar-looking; when I mentioned Steadman's name she nodded, without looking up from whatever she was writing, and said in a low voice, 'You bet he did.' Then she favored me with a big smile. 'Yes, indeed. Mr. Steadman just left for the racetrack. Is he a friend of yours?'

I shook my head. 'I'm supposed to be working with him, but I don't even know what he looks like. Now, goddammit, I'll have to find him in that mob at the track.'

She chuckled. 'You won't have any trouble finding him. You could pick that man out of any crowd.'

'Why?' I asked. 'What's wrong with him? What does he look like?'

'Well . . .' she said, still grinning, 'he's the funniest looking thing I've seen in a long time. He has this . . . ah . . . this *growth* all over his face. As a matter of fact it's all over his *head*.' She nodded. 'You'll know him when you see him; don't worry about that.'

Great creeping Jesus, I thought. That screws the press credentials. I had a vision of some nerve-rattling geek all covered with matted hair and string-warts showing up in the press office and demanding *Scanlan's* press packet. Well . . . what the hell. We could always load up on acid and spend the day roaming around the grounds with big sketch pads, laughing hysterically at the natives and swilling mint juleps so the cops wouldn't think we're abnormal. Perhaps even make the act pay: set up an easel with a big sign saying, 'Let a Foreign Artist Paint Your Portrait, $10 Each. Do It NOW!'

### A huge outdoor loony bin

I took the expressway out to the track, driving very fast and jumping the monster car back and forth between lanes, driving with a beer in one hand and my mind so muddled that I almost crushed a Volkswagen full of nuns when I swerved to catch the right exit. There was a slim chance, I thought, that I might be able to catch the ugly Britisher before he checked in.

But Steadman was already in the press box when I got there, a bearded young Englishman wearing a tweed coat and HAF sunglasses. There was nothing particularly odd about him. No facial veins or clumps of bristly warts. I told him about the motel woman's description and he seemed puzzled. 'Don't let it bother you,' I said. 'Just keep in mind for the next few days that we're in Louisville, Kentucky. Not London. Not even New York. This is a weird place. You're lucky that mental defective at the motel didn't jerk a pistol out of the cash register and blow a big hole in you.' I laughed, but he looked worried.

'Just pretend you're visiting a huge outdoor loony bin,' I said. 'If the inmates get out of control we'll soak them down with Mace.' I showed him the can of 'Chemical Billy,' resisting the urge to fire it across the room at a rat-faced man typing diligently in the Associated Press section. We were standing at the bar, sipping the management's scotch and congratulating each other on our sudden, unexplained luck in picking up two sets of fine press credentials. The lady at the desk had been very friendly to him, he said. 'I just told her my name and she gave me the whole works.'

By midafternoon we had everything under control. We had seats looking down on the finish line, color TV and a free bar in the press room, and a selection of passes that would take us anywhere from the clubhouse roof to the jockey room. The only thing we lacked was unlimited access to the clubhouse inner sanctum in sections 'F&G' ... and I felt we needed that, to see the whiskey gentry in action. The governor would be in 'G.' Barry Goldwater would be in a box in 'G' where we could rest and sip juleps, soak up a bit of atmosphere and the Derby's special vibrations.

The bars and dining rooms are also in 'F&G,' and the clubhouse bars on Derby Day are a very special kind of scene. Along with the politicians, society belles and local captains of commerce, every half-mad dingbat who ever had any pretensions to anything within 500 miles of Louisville will show up there to get strutting drunk and slap a lot of backs and generally make himself obvious. The Paddock bar is probably the best place in the track to sit and watch faces. Nobody minds being stared at; that's what they're in there for. Some people spend most of their time in the Paddock; they can hunker down at one of the many wooden tables, lean back in a comfortable chair and watch the ever-changing odds flash up and down on the big tote board outside the window. Black waiters in white serving jackets move through the crowd with trays of drinks, while the experts ponder their racing forms and the hunch bettors pick lucky numbers or scan the lineup for right-sounding names. There is a constant flow of traffic to and from the pari-mutuel windows outside in the wooden corridors. Then, as post time nears, the crowd thins out as people go back to their boxes.

Clearly, we were going to have to figure out some way to spend more time in the clubhouse tomorrow. But the 'walkaround' press passes to F&G were only good for 30 minutes at a time, presumably to allow the newspaper types to rush in and out for photos or quick interviews, but to prevent drifters like Steadman and me from spending all day in the clubhouse, harassing the gentry and rifling an odd handbag or two while cruising around the boxes. Or Macing the governor. The time limit was no problem on Friday, but on Derby Day the walkaround passes would be in heavy demand. And since it took about 10 minutes to get from the press box to the Paddock, and 10 more minutes to get back, that didn't leave much time for serious people-watching. And unlike most of the others in the press box, we didn't give a hoot in hell what was happening on the track. We had come there to watch the *real* beasts perform.

*View from Thompson's Head*

Later Friday afternoon, we went out on the balcony of the press box and I tried to describe the difference between what we had seen today and what would be happening tomorrow. This was the first time I'd been to a Derby in 10 years, but before that, when I lived in Louisville, I used to go every year. Now, looking down from the press box, I pointed to the huge grassy meadow enclosed by the track. 'That whole thing,' I said, 'will be jammed with people; fifty thousand or so, and most of them staggering drunk. It's a fantastic scene — thousands of people fainting, crying, copulating, trampling each other and fighting with broken whiskey bottles. We'll have to spend some time out there, but it's hard to move around, too many bodies.'

'Is it safe out there? Will we *ever* come back?'

'Sure,' I said. 'We'll just have to be careful not to step on anybody's stomach and start a fight.' I shrugged. 'Hell, this clubhouse scene right below us will be almost as bad as the infield. Thousands of raving, stumbling drunks, getting angrier and angrier as they lose more and more money. By midafternoon they'll be guzzling mint juleps with both hands and vomiting on each other between races. The whole place will be jammed with bodies, shoulder to shoulder. It's hard to move around. The aisles will be slick with vomit; people falling down and grabbing at your legs to keep from being stomped. Drunks pissing on themselves in the betting lines. Dropping handfuls of money and fighting to stoop over and pick it up.'

He looked so nervous that I laughed. 'I'm just kidding,' I said. 'Don't worry. At the first hint of trouble I'll start Macing everybody I can reach.'

He had done a few good sketches but so far we hadn't seen that special kind of face that I felt we would need for the lead drawing. It was a face I'd seen a thousand times at every Derby I'd ever been to. I saw it, in my head, as the mask of the whiskey gentry – a pretentious mix of booze, failed dreams and a terminal identity crisis; the inevitable result of too much inbreeding in a closed and ignorant culture. One of the key genetic rules in breeding dogs, horses or any other kind of thoroughbred is that close inbreeding tends to magnify the weak points in a bloodline as well as the strong points. In horse breeding, for instance, there is a definite risk in breeding two fast horses who are both a little crazy. The offspring will likely be very fast and also very crazy. So the trick in breeding thoroughbreds is to retain the good traits and filter out the bad. But the breeding of humans is not so wisely supervised, particularly in a narrow Southern society where the closest kind of inbreeding is not only stylish and acceptable, but far more convenient – to the parents – than setting their offspring free to find their own mates, for their own reasons and their own ways. ('Goddam, did you hear about Smitty's daughter? She went crazy in Boston last week and married a nigger!')

So the face I was trying to find in Churchill Downs that weekend was a symbol, in my own mind, of the whole doomed atavistic culture that makes the Kentucky Derby what it is.

On our way back to the motel after Friday's races I warned Steadman about some of the other problems we'd have to cope with. Neither of us had brought any strange illegal drugs, so we would have to get by on booze. 'You should keep in mind,' I said, 'that almost everybody you talk to from now on will be drunk. People who seem very pleasant at first might suddenly swing at you for no reason at all.' He nodded, staring straight ahead. He seemed to be getting a little numb and I tried to cheer him up by inviting him to dinner that night, with my brother.

'What Mace?'

Back at the motel we talked for a while about America, the South, England, just relaxing a bit before dinner. There was no way either of us could have known, at the time, that it would be the last normal conversation we would have. From that point on, the weekend became a vicious, drunken nightmare. We both went completely to pieces. The main problem was my prior attachment to Louisville, which naturally led to meetings with old friends, relatives, etc., many of whom were in the process of falling apart, going mad, plotting divorces, cracking up under the strain of terrible debts or recovering from bad accidents. Right in the middle of the whole frenzied Derby action, a member of my own family had to be institutionalized. This added a certain amount of strain to the situation, and since poor Steadman had no choice but to take whatever came his way, he was subjected to shock after shock.

Another problem was his habit of sketching people he met in the various social situations I dragged him into, then giving them the sketches. The results were always unfortunate. I warned him several times about letting the subjects see his foul renderings, but for some perverse reason he kept doing it. Consequently, he was regarded with fear and loathing by nearly everyone who'd seen or even heard about his work. He couldn't understand it. 'It's sort of a joke,' he kept saying. 'Why, in England it's quite normal. People don't take offense. They understand that I'm just putting them on a bit.'

'Fuck England,' I said. 'This is Middle America. These people regard what you're doing to them as a brutal, bilious insult. Look what happened last night. I thought my brother was going to tear your head off.'

Steadman shook his head sadly. 'But I liked him. He struck me as a very decent, straightforward sort.'

'Look, Ralph,' I said. 'Let's not kid ourselves. That was a very horrible drawing you gave him. It was the face of a monster. It got on his nerves very badly.' I shrugged. 'Why in hell do you think we left the restaurant so fast?'

'I thought it was because of the Mace,' he said.

'What Mace?'

He grinned. 'When you shot it at the headwaiter, don't you remember?'

'Hell, that was nothing,' I said. 'I missed him . . . and we were leaving, anyway.'

'But it got all over us,' he said. 'The room was full of that damn gas. Your brother was sneezing and his wife was crying. My eyes hurt for two hours. I couldn't see to draw when we got back to the motel.'

'That's right,' I said. 'The stuff got on her leg, didn't it?'

'She was angry,' he said.

'Yah . . . well, okay . . . let's just figure we fucked up about equally on that one,' I said. 'But from now on let's try to be careful when we're around people I know. You won't sketch them and I won't Mace them. We'll just try to relax and get drunk.'

'Right,' he said. 'We'll go native.'

## Derby morning

It was Saturday morning, the day of the Big Race, and we were having breakfast in a plastic hamburger palace called the Ptomaine Village. Our rooms were just across the road in a foul scumbox of a place called the Horn Suburban Hotel. They had a dining room, but the food was so bad that we couldn't handle it anymore. The waitresses seemed to be suffering from shin splints; they moved around very slowly, moaning and cursing the 'darkies' in the kitchen.

Steadman liked the Ptomaine Village because it had fish and chips. I preferred the 'french toast,' which was really pancake batter, fried to the proper thickness and then chopped out with a sort of cookie cutter to resemble pieces of toast.

Beyond drink and lack of sleep, our only real problem at that point was the question of access to the clubhouse. Finally we decided just to go ahead and steal two passes, if necessary, rather than miss that part of the action. This was the last coherent decision we were able to make for the next 48 hours. From that point on – almost from the very moment we started out to the track – we lost all control of events and spent the rest of the weekend just churning around in a sea of drunken horrors. My notes and recollections from Derby Day are somewhat scrambled.

But now, looking at the big red notebook I carried all through that scene, I see more or less what happened. The book itself is somewhat mangled and bent; some of the pages are torn, others are shriveled and stained by what appears to be whiskey, but taken as a whole, with sporadic memory flashes, the notes seem to tell the story. To wit:

## Unscrambling Derby Day – 1
### Steadman is worried about fire

Rain all nite until dawn. No sleep. Christ, here we go, a nightmare of mud and madness.... Drunks in the mud. Drowning, fighting for shelter.... But no. By noon the sun burns, perfect day, not even humid.

Steadman is now worried about fire. Somebody told him about the clubhouse catching on fire two years ago. Could it happen again? Horrible. Trapped in the press box. Holocaust. A hundred thousand people fighting to get out. Drunks screaming in the flames and the mud, crazed horses running wild. Blind in the smoke. Grandstand collapsing into the flames with us on the roof. Poor Ralph is about to crack. Drinking heavily, into the Haig.

Out to the track in a cab, avoid that terrible parking in people's front yards, $25 each, toothless old men on the street with big signs: Park Here, flagging cars in the yard. 'That's fine, boy, never mind the tulips.' Wild hair on his head, straight up like a clump of reeds.

Sidewalks full of people all moving in the same direction, towards Churchill Downs. Kids hauling coolers and blankets, teenyboppers in tight pink shorts, many blacks ... black dudes in white felt hats with leopard-skin bands, cops waving traffic along.

The mob was thick for many blocks around the track; very slow going in the crowd, very hot. On the way to the press box elevator, just inside the clubhouse, we came on a row of soldiers all carrying long white riot sticks. About two platoons, with helmets. A man walking next to us said they were waiting for the governor and his party. Steadman eyed them nervously. 'Why do they have those clubs?'

'Black Panthers,' I said. Then I remembered good old 'Jimbo' at the airport and I wondered what he was thinking right now. Probably very nervous; the place was teeming with cops and soldiers. We pressed on through the crowd, through many gates, past the paddock where the jockeys bring the horses out and parade around for a while before each race so the bettors can get a good look. Five million dollars will be bet today. Many winners, more losers. What the hell. The press gate was jammed up with people trying to get in, shouting at the guards, waving strange press badges: Chicago Sporting Times, Pittsburgh Police Athletic League ... they were all turned away. 'Move on, fella, make way for the working press.' We shoved through the crowd and into the elevator, then quickly up to the free bar. Why not? Get it on. Very hot today, not feeling well, must be this rotten climate. The press box was cool and airy, plenty of room to walk around and balcony seats for watching the race or looking down at the crowd. We got a betting sheet and went outside.

*Unscrambling D-Day II*
*Clubhouse/Paddock bar*

Pink faces with a stylish Southern sag, old Ivy styles, seersucker coats and buttondown collars. 'Mayblossom Senility' (Steadman's phrase)

... burnt out early or maybe just not much to burn in the first place. Not much energy in these faces, not much *curiosity*. Suffering in silence, nowhere to go after thirty in this life, just hang on and humor the children. Let the young enjoy themselves while they can. Why not? The grim reaper comes early in this league ... banshees on the lawn at night, screaming out there beside that little iron nigger in jockey clothes. Maybe he's the one who's screaming. Bad DT's and too many snarls at the bridge club. Going down with the stock market. Oh Jesus, the kid has wrecked the new car, wrapped it around that big stone pillar at the bottom of the driveway. Broken leg? Twisted eye? Send him off to Yale, they can cure anything up there.

Yale? Did you see today's paper? New Haven is under seige. Yale is swarming with Black Panthers.... I tell you, Colonel, the world has gone mad, stone mad. Why they tell me a goddam woman jockey might ride in the Derby today.

I left Steadman sketching in the Paddock bar and went off to place our bets on the sixth race. When I came back he was staring intently at a group of young men around a table not far away. 'Jesus, look at the corruption in that face!' he whispered. 'Look at the madness, the fear, the greed!' I looked, then quickly turned my back on the table he was drawing. The face he'd picked out to draw was the face of an old friend of mine, a prep school football star in the good old days with a sleek red Chevy convertible and a very quick hand, it was said, with the snaps of a 32 B brassiere. They call him 'Cat Man.'

But now, a dozen years later, I wouldn't have recognized him anywhere but here, where I should have expected to find him, in the Paddock bar on Derby Day ... fat slanted eyes and a pimp's smile, blue silk suit and his friends looking like crooked bank tellers on a binge....

Steadman wanted to see some Kentucky Colonels, but he wasn't sure what they looked like. I told him to go back to the clubhouse men's rooms and look for men in white linen suits vomiting in the urinals. 'They'll usually have large brown whiskey stains on the front of their suits,' I said. 'But watch the shoes, that's the tip-off. Most of them manage to avoid vomiting on their own clothes, but they never miss their shoes.'

In a box not far from ours was Colonel Anna Friedman Goldman, *Chairman and Keeper of the Great Seal of the Honorable Order of Kentucky Colonels*. Not all the 76 million or so Kentucky Colonels could make it to the Derby this year, but many had kept the faith and several days prior to the Derby they gathered for their annual dinner at the Seelbach Hotel.

The Derby, the actual race, was scheduled for late afternoon, and as the magic hour approached I suggested to Steadman that we should probably spend some time in the infield, that boiling sea of people across the track from the clubhouse. He seemed a little nervous about it, but since none of the awful things I'd warned him about had happened so far – no race riots, firestorms, or savage drunken attacks – he shrugged and said, 'Right, let's do it.'

To get there we had to pass through many gates, each one a step down in status, then through a tunnel under the track. Emerging from the tunnel was such a culture shock that it took us a while to adjust. 'God almighty!' Steadman muttered. 'This is a ... Jesus!' He plunged ahead with his tiny camera, stepping over bodies, and I followed, trying to take notes.

*Unscrambling D-Day III*
*The infield*

Total chaos, no way to see the race, not even the track ... nobody cares. Big lines at the outdoor betting windows, then stand back to watch winning numbers flash on the big board, like a giant bingo game.

Old blacks arguing about bets; 'Hold on there, I'll handle this' (waving pint of whiskey, fistful of dollar bills); girl riding piggyback, t-shirt says, 'Stolen from Fort Lauderdale Jail.' Thousands of teenagers, group singing 'Let the Sun Shine In,' ten soldiers guarding the American flag and a huge fat drunk wearing a blue football jersey (No. 80) reeling around with quart of beer in hand.

No booze sold out here, too dangerous ... no bathrooms either. Muscle Beach.... Woodstock ... many cops with riot sticks, but no sign of riot. Far across the track the clubhouse looks like a postcard from the Kentucky Derby.

*Unscrambling D-Day IV*
*'My Old Kentucky Home'*

We went back to the clubhouse to watch the big race. When the crowd stood to face the flag and sing 'My Old Kentucky Home,' Steadman faced the crowd and sketched frantically. Somewhere up in the boxes a voice screeched, 'Turn around, you hairy freak!' The race itself was only two minutes long, and even from our super-status seats and using 12-power glasses, there was no way to see what was really happening.

Later, watching a TV rerun in the press box, we saw what happened to our horses. Holy Land, Ralph's choice, stumbled and lost his jockey in the final turn. Mine, Silent Screen, had the lead coming into the stretch but faded to fifth at the finish. The winner was a 16-1 shot named Dust Commander.

Moments after the race was over, the crowd surged wildly for the exits, rushing for cabs and buses. The next day's Courier told of violence in the parking lot; people were punched and trampled, pockets were picked, children lost, bottles hurled. But we missed all this, having retired to the press box for a bit of post-race drinking. By this time we were both half-crazy from too much whiskey, sun fatigue, culture shock, lack of sleep and general dissolution. We hung around the press box long enough to watch a mass interview with the winning owner, a dapper little man named Lehmann who said he had just flown into Louisville that morning from Nepal, where he'd 'bagged a record tiger.' The sportswriters murmured their admiration and a waiter filled Lehmann's glass with Chivas Regal. He had just won $127,000 with a horse that cost him $6,500 two years ago. His occupation, he said, was 'retired contractor.' And then he added, with a big grin, 'I just retired.'

The rest of that day blurs into madness. The rest of that night too. And all the next day and night. Such horrible things occurred that I can't bring myself even to think about them now, much less put them down in print. Steadman was lucky to get out of Louisville without serious injuries, and I was lucky to get out at all. One of my clearest memories of that vicious time is Ralph being attacked by one of my old friends in the billiard room of the Pendennis Club in downtown Louisville on Saturday night. The man had ripped his own shirt open to the waist before deciding that Ralph wasn't after his wife. No blows were struck, but the emotional effects were massive. Then, as a sort of final horror, Steadman put his fiendish pen to work and tried to patch things up by doing a little sketch of the girl he'd been accused of hustling. That finished us in the Pendennis.

Sometime around 10:30 Monday morning I was awakened by a scratching sound at my door. I leaned out of bed and pulled the curtain back just far enough to see Steadman outside. 'What the fuck do you want?' I shouted.

'What about having breakfast?' he said.

I lunged out of bed and tried to open the door, but it caught on the night-chain and banged shut again. I couldn't cope with the chain! The thing wouldn't come out of the track – so I ripped it out of the wall with a vicious jerk on the door. Ralph didn't blink. 'Bad luck,' he muttered.

I could barely see him. My eyes were swollen almost shut and the sudden burst of sunlight through the door left me stunned and helpless like a sick mole. Steadman was mumbling about sickness and terrible heat; I fell back on the bed and tried to focus on him as he moved around the room in a very distracted way for a few moments, then suddenly darted over to the beer bucket and seized a Colt .45. 'Christ,' I said. 'You're getting out of control.'

He nodded and ripped the cap off, taking a long drink. 'You know, this is really awful,' he said finally. 'I must get out of this place . . .' he shook his head nervously. 'The plane leaves at 3:30, but I don't know if I'll make it.'

I barely heard him. My eyes had finally opened enough for me to focus on the mirror across the room and I was stunned at the shock of recognition. For a confused instant I thought that Ralph had brought somebody with him – a model for that one special face we'd been looking for. There he was, by God – a puffy, drink-ravaged, disease-ridden caricature . . . like an awful cartoon version of an old snapshot in some once-proud mother's family photo album. It was the face we'd been looking for – and it was, of course, my own. Horrible, horrible. . . .

'Maybe I should sleep a while longer,' I said. 'Why don't you go on over to the Ptomaine Village and eat some of those rotten fish and chips? Then come back and get me around noon. I feel too near death to hit the streets at this hour.'

He shook his head. 'No . . . no . . . I think I'll go back upstairs and work on those drawings for a while.' He leaned down to fetch two more cans out of the beer bucket. 'I tried to work earlier,' he said, 'but my hands keep trembling . . . It's teddible, teddible.'

'You've got to stop this drinking,' I said.

He nodded. 'I know. This is no good, no good at all. But for some reason I think it makes me feel better. . . .'

'Not for long,' I said. 'You'll probably collapse into some kind of hysterical DT's tonight – probably just about the time you get off the plane at Kennedy. They'll zip you up in a straitjacket and drag you down to the Tombs, then beat you on the kidneys with big sticks until you straighten out.'

He shrugged and wandered out, pulling the door shut behind him. I went back to bed for another hour or so, and later – after the daily grapefruit juice run to the Nite Owl Food Mart – we drove once again to the Ptomaine Village for a fine lunch of dough and butcher's offal, fried in heavy grease.

By this time Ralph wouldn't even order coffee; he kept asking for more water. 'It's the only thing they have that's fit for human consumption,' he explained. Then, with an hour or so to kill before he had to catch the plane, we spread his drawings out on the table and pondered them for a while, wondering if he'd caught the proper spirit of the thing ... but we couldn't make up our minds. His hands were shaking so badly that he had trouble holding the paper, and my vision was so blurred that I could barely see what he'd drawn. 'Shit,' I said. 'We both look worse than anything you've drawn here.'

He smiled. 'You know – I've been thinking about that,' he said. 'We came down here to see this teddible scene: people all pissed out of their minds and vomiting on themselves and all that ... and now, you know what? It's us. ...'

Huge Pontiac Ballbuster blowing through traffic on the expressway. The journalist is driving, ignoring his passenger who is now nearly naked after taking off most of his clothing, which he holds out the window, trying to wind-wash the Mace out of it. His eyes are bright red and his face and chest are soaked with the beer he's been using to rinse the awful chemical off his flesh. The front of his woolen trousers is soaked with vomit; his body is racked with fits of coughing and wild choking sobs. The journalist rams the big car through traffic and into a spot in front of the terminal, then he reaches over to open the door on the passenger's side and shoves the Englishman out, snarling: 'Bug off, you worthless faggot! You twisted pigfucker! [Crazed laughter.] If I weren't sick I'd kick your ass all the way to Bowling Green – you scumsucking foreign geek. Mace is too good for you. ... We can do without your kind in Kentucky.'

# Norman Mailer from
# The armies of the night

Any time a nonfiction writer uses an autobiographical approach, he is turning himself into a character in the story. This has a better chance of working if the writer was, in fact, a leading character in the events he is describing. If he was not a leading character, the autobiographical approach often fails. Norman Mailer's nonfiction, which invariably takes an autobiographical stance, is a good illustration of both parts of the rule.

The Armies of the Night was genuine autobiography (and the only example of autobiography included in this book, for reasons cited above). Mailer did not cover the march on the Pentagon in 1967 as a reporter. He was one of the major participants in the demonstration, and – in the classic autobiographical pattern – decided only afterward to write about it (at the behest of Willie Morris, who was then the editor of Harper's). Since he was, in fact, a leading character in the event, his autobiographical view is a view from the inside, and his emotions and reactions help suggest the emotional reality of the event itself.

Mailer tried to use the same technique in writing about the first moon shot (Of a Fire on the Moon). Why did it fail so badly? Because this time he was not, in fact, a leading character in the event, and his use of an autobiographical point of view merely set up a clumsy and tedious distraction in the foreground, viz., himself. The main characters during the moon shot were three astronauts in a space capsule. Mailer's autobiographical technique never succeeds in taking the reader inside the capsule, much less inside the points of view or central nervous systems of the astronauts themselves. This is a failure not only in technique but in reporting. Mailer tends to be a very shy reporter, reluctant to abandon the safety of the Literary Gentleman in the Grandstand.

The Armies of the Night, on the other hand, is quite a charming book. Its subtitle is History as a Novel, the Novel as History, and in the following pages one sees how deliberately Mailer, like Capote, has

*gone about creating the effect of 'like a novel.' His use of the omnisci-*
*ent narrator's aside to the reader creates a quaint, nostalgic and alto-*
*gether pleasant mood. Another strength of the book is his use of the*
*third-person autobiographical form first popularized by Henry Adams*
*in* The Education of Henry Adams. *The main character becomes not 'I'*
*but 'Mailer,' a device that successfully takes the edge off what other-*
*wise might seem like an annoying egocentrism. Instead one finds*
*'Mailer' quite lovable. This device will not work, however, unless the*
*writer takes the trouble to describe and develop his own character with*
*at least as much care as he would devote to any other main character.*

*Incidentally, the march on the Pentagon offered Mailer a curious*
*dividend. He has never been able to write convincing dialogue, a fact*
*that has seriously limited him as a novelist. In* The Armies of the
Night, *however, he was able to use transcripts from tapes and movies*
*made of his own participation in the event. T.W.*

## A confrontation by the river

It was not much of a situation to study. The MPs stood in two widely
spaced ranks. The first rank was ten yards behind the rope, and each
MP in that row was close to twenty feet from the next man. The
second rank, similarly spaced, was ten yards behind the first rank and
perhaps thirty yards behind them a cluster appeared, every fifty yards
or so, of two or three U.S. Marshals in white helmets and dark blue
suits. They were out there waiting. Two moods confronted one another, two separate senses of a private silence.

It was not unlike being a boy about to jump from one garage roof to
an adjoining garage roof. The one thing not to do was wait. Mailer
looked at Macdonald and Lowell. 'Let's go,' he said. Not looking again
at them, not pausing to gather or dissipate resolve, he made a point of
stepping neatly and decisively over the low rope. Then he headed
across the grass to the nearest MP he saw.

It was as if the air had changed, or light had altered; he felt immediately much more alive – yes, bathed in air – and yet disembodied
from himself, as if indeed he were watching himself in a film where this
action was taking place. He could feel the eyes of the people behind
the rope watching him, could feel the intensity of their existence as
spectators. And as he walked forward, he and the MP looked at one
another with the naked stricken lucidity which comes when absolute
strangers are for the moment absolutely locked together.

The MP lifted his club to his chest as if to bar all passage. To

Mailer's great surprise — he had secretly expected the enemy to be calm and strong, why should they not? they had every power, all the guns — to his great surprise, the MP was trembling. He was a young Negro, part white, who looked to have come from some small town where perhaps there were not many other Negroes; he had at any rate no Harlem smoke, no devil swish, no black, no black power for him, just a simple boy in an Army suit with a look of horror in his eye. 'Why, why did it have to happen to me?' was the message of the petrified marbles in his face.

'Go back,' he said hoarsely to Mailer.

'If you don't arrest me, I'm going to the Pentagon.'

'No. Go back.'

The thought of a return — 'since they won't arrest me, what can I do?' — over these same ten yards was not at all suitable.

As the MP spoke, the raised club quivered. He did not know if it quivered from the desire of the MP to strike him, or secret military wonder was he now possessed of a moral force which implanted terror in the arms of young soldiers? Some unfamiliar current, now gyro-scopic, now a sluggish whirlpool, was evolving from that quiver of the club, and the MP seemed to turn slowly away from his position con-fronting the rope, and the novelist turned with him, each still facing the other until the axis of their shoulders was now perpendicular to the rope, and still they kept turning in this psychic field, not touching, the club quivering, and then Mailer was behind the MP, he was free of him, and he wheeled around and kept going in a half run to the next line of MPs and then on the push of a sudden instinct, sprinted suddenly around the nearest MP in the second line, much as if he were a back cutting around the nearest man in the secondary to break free — that was actually his precise thought — and had a passing perception of how simple it was to get past the MPs. They looked petrified. Stricken faces as he went by. They did not know what to do. It was his dark pinstripe suit, his vest, the maroon and blue regimental tie, the part in his hair, the barrel chest, the early paunch — he must have looked like a banker himself, a banker, gone ape! And then he saw the Pentagon to his right across the field, not a hundred yards away, and a little to his left, the marshals, and he ran on a jog toward them, and came up, and they glared at him and shouted, 'Go back.'

He had a quick impression of hard-faced men with gray eyes burning some transparent fuel or flame, and said, 'I won't go back. If you don't arrest me, I'm going on to the Pentagon,' and knew he meant it, some

absolute certainty had come to him, and then two of them leaped on
him at once in the cold clammy murderous fury of all cops at the
existential moment of making their bust – all cops who secretly expect
to be struck at that instant for their sins – and a supervising force
came to his voice, and he roared, to his own distant pleasure in new
achievement and new authority – 'Take your hands off me, can't you
see? I'm not resisting arrest,' and one then let go of him, and the other
stopped trying to pry his arm into a lock, and contented himself with a
hard hand under his armpit, and they set off walking across the field at
a rabid intent quick rate, walking parallel to the wall of the Pentagon,
fully visible on his right at last, and he was arrested, he had succeeded
in that, and without a club on his head, the mountain air in his lungs as
thin and fierce as smoke, yes, the livid air of tension on this livid side
promised a few events of more interest than the routine wait to be
free, yes he was more than a visitor, he was in the land of the enemy
now, he would get to see their face.

## Bust 80 beyond the law

One of the oldest devices of the novelist – some would call it a vice – is
to bring his narrative (after many an excursion) to a pitch of excitement where the reader no matter how cultivated is reduced to a beast
who can pant no faster than to ask, 'And then what? Then what happens?' At which point the novelist, consummate cruel lover, introduces
a digression, aware that delay at this point helps to deepen the addiction of his audience.

This, of course, was Victorian practice. Modern audiences, accustomed to superhighways, put aside their reading at the first annoyance
and turn to the television set. So a modern novelist must apologize,
even apologize profusely, for daring to leave his narrative, he must in
fact absolve himself of the charge of employing a device, he must plead
necessity.

So the Novelist now pleads necessity. He will take a momentary
delay in the proceedings – because in fact he must – to introduce a
further element to our history which will accompany us intermittently
to the end. It must now be admitted – the reader does well to expect a
forthright shock – that the Participant was not only a witness and
actor in these proceedings, but was being photographed as well! Mailer
had – in what he considered an inexcusable weak moment – agreed to
the request of a young English filmmaker named Dick Fontaine to have
a documentary made of him for British television. Once before he had

had such a documentary filmed and the experience had been finally not pleasant because it seemed to consist of sitting in a chair and cerebrating for the camera. Mailer, when all was said, was no Arnold Toynbee, no Bertrand Russell (perhaps not even an Eric Goldman) no, with all granted, Mailer as an intellectual always had something of the usurper about him – something in his voice revealed that he likely knew less than he pretended. Watching himself talk on camera for this earlier documentary, he was not pleased with himself as a subject. For a warrior, presumptive general, ex-political candidate, embattled aging enfant terrible of the literary world, wise father of six children, radical intellectual, existential philosopher, hard-working author, champion of obscenity, husband of four battling sweet wives, amiable bar drinker, and much exaggerated street fighter, party giver, hostess insulter – he had on screen in this first documentary a fatal taint, a last remaining speck of the one personality he found absolutely insupportable – the nice Jewish boy from Brooklyn. Something in his adenoids gave it away – he had the softness of a man early accustomed to mother-love. So Mailer stayed away from further documentaries of himself. Talented cinematographers like the Maysles brothers approached him – he had no interest. Fontaine, who had been introduced with the best of credentials by a young English lady in whose personality the novelist took delight, succeeded through sheer bull British perseverance in extracting a promise that Fontaine and his crew could be present at a few of the novelist's more active projects. No speeches.

Therefore, witness the first fulfillment of this promise. It was on the initial night of shooting Mailer's second film (which was most tentatively entitled *Bust 80* and was later to be called *Beyond the Law*) a study of detectives and suspects in a police precinct. Mailer had theories on how to make films. He liked to take people who were able to talk themselves in and out of trouble, and cast them in situations which he tried to make sufficiently intense so that they would not be too aware of the camera. Whether they had ever acted before did not often concern him. It was his theory – not too novel an hypothesis – that many people who had never acted, and could never begin to act on stage without training, still had several extraordinary characterizations they could bring to a film provided they spoke their own words and had no script to remember. It can be seen this is a lively theory which leaves much to the director and takes much away from him; Mailer boosted the ante on the first night of shooting by having three camera crews and several interrogations going on in several rooms at once –

the cries or shouts of one interrogation affected the quiet dialogue of another. The intensity of this process, cameras, actors, and scenes working simultaneously on the same floor (which is about the way matters proceed in a police station) conceivably worked a magic on the actors – Mailer's opinion of the film as it began to come together in the early rushes is that it was not impossible he had divined and/or blundered onto the making of the best American movie about police he had ever seen. It was certainly the first film which had ever bypassed altogether the formal morality of Hollywood crime and punishment. His film brought forth instead the incredible – which is to say existential – life buried in all passing relations between cops and criminals: his police were the most interesting police he had come across in films, his suspects were as vivid as the best faces one sees on a strange street.

But the first night's shooting was chaos, and promised disaster. The director had picked some of his most bullheaded friends to play cops; some of his most complicted buddies to play crooks – action abounded everywhere: confusion kept up with it: cameras, sound men, and still photographers often collided, the tail of one film crew being run into by the lens of another. To this disorder was added a fourth camera, the BBC crew working for Fontaine – more than once that night the Director came close to barring the fourth crew for inevitably they were an active part of the confusion. Yet, at a given moment when an exciting scene was still full of action, the first camera ran out of film. 'Get another camera,' Mailer bawled into the corridor. But the second camera was being loaded; so was the third. 'Well, who's that over there,' roared the Director, 'who's that over there whose camera is going now?'

'Oh, that's the BBC.'

Technological crews generate little élan until their working process has delivered the first joke. 'Oh, that's the BBC,' carried the night, and left Mailer with an impression of a cameraman who loaded so fast he seemed never to run out of film. The next time he saw that cameraman was in the dressing room of a small television studio in New York. Mailer, soon to be interviewed on the approaching March on the Pentagon, was having television cosmetics applied to his face, and looked into the mirror to see the lens of the camera on him. Now he did order the cameraman and his sound man out. 'Do you think I've reached the age of forty-four in order to have movies taken of myself while I'm being made up?'

The next time he saw them was in Washington. As Mailer came off

the stage of the Ambassador Theater, Fontaine and the cameraman,
Leiterman, were beaming. 'We got wonderful stuff of you tonight,' said
Fontaine. They were there the next day at the Department of Justice,
and Mailer had the opportunity to watch Leiterman work. There were
long periods when nothing was occurring which he thought appropriate
to photograph, but he never put his camera down, yet it must have
weighed twenty pounds. All during that long afternoon, Leiterman kept
it cradled in his arms, ready to photograph the first target of opportunity. The next day, out on the March, walking backward over Arling-
ton Memorial Bridge in the center of the hollow square, Leiterman was
photographing the line of notables. Whenever he saw Mailer, he would
smile. This seemed part of his photographic technique: He always
smiled encouragingly at his subject. After a while, one was glad to see
him – even while listening to the Fugs; Mailer had felt Leiterman's
camera on him; as Lowell, Macdonald, and Mailer had approached the
rope they were going to cross in order to be arrested, Leiterman and
Fontaine had been with them.

But now, perambulating around the Pentagon in the first ten seconds
of his arrest, with the U.S. Marshal's hand still full of tremors on his
arm, what pleasant shock to see Leiterman suddenly dart in front of
them, give his great smile of encouragement to Mailer – it had the
spark of something most special now – and with his eye to the optical
finder, start filming the progress of the Marshal and himself from five
feet in front, Leiterman walking backward at the same great rate they
were walking forward, so that he performed a small athletic prodigy
since their path was uneven, they walked up small slopes, down them,
crossed a concrete path, stepped over grass, were on the walks again,
climbed up a ramp without breaking pace, and all the while, five feet
ahead, ten feet ahead, unaware of what was behind him, Leiterman
walking backward at a very fast rate, staggering occasionally and recovering with his heavy camera on his shoulder nonetheless seemed
never to let go of the grip of his lens on his subject, all the while
mustering a beatific encouraging grin, as if he were saying, 'Go man,
you are making it for a touchdown.'

Mailer's arm was being held in the trembling grip of a U.S. Marshal –
this trembling a characteristic physical reaction of the police whenever
they lay hands on an arrest, or at least so Mailer would claim after
noticing police in such a precise state for three out of the four times he
had in his life been arrested – yes they had trembled almost uncontrollably. Whether this was due to a sudden onrush – quote Freud from a

letter to Fliess — of 'unruly latent homosexuality,' or whether from a terror before God that they judged other men sufficiently to make arrest, or whether simply they were cowards, or if to the contrary they trembled from the effort it cost them to keep from assaulting the prisoner, whatever, Mailer could not quite decide — he had sometimes even wondered if it had to do with the incongruities of his own person, whether it was possible he offended some deeps in the police, no matter, the fact, incontrovertible, was that policemen quivered uncontrollably as they laid hands on him. This observation taken and confirmed in the first few steps he made in company with the Marshal after his successful arrest, it had been to his great surprise and pleasure, for, there is a certain loneliness in these first few steps — that he had looked up to see Leiterman.

And now a reporter darted up on the flank of this procession to ask a question of Mailer with that friendly, intimate, solicitous attention reporters project into the dramatic work of getting a quote; done well enough the subject feels sufficiently important to believe his immortal initials are being carved on a buttock of history. 'Why were you arrested, Mr. Mailer?'

The subject was not absolutely calm. To his own excitement was added the tense quivering grip of the Marshal — the sense of breathing mountain air had hardly abated; his lungs seemed to take in oxygen with a thin edge, his throat burned. But his voice, to his surprise, was calmer than himself — for once it came out about the way he wanted it to, quiet and even. 'I was arrested for transgressing a police line.' ('Of course, he was misquoted,' said Mailer's sister later. 'He wouldn't use a word like transgress.' She did not anticipate the solemnity men bring to these matters.) 'I am guilty,' Mailer went on. 'It was done as an act of protest to the war in Vietnam.'

'Are you hurt in any way?' asked the reporter.

'No. The arrest was correct.'

He felt as if he were being confirmed. (After twenty years of radical opinions, he was finally under arrest for a real cause.) Mailer always supposed he had felt important and unimportant in about as many ways as a man could feel; now he felt important in a new way. He felt his own age, forty-four, felt it as if he were finally one age, not seven, felt as if he were a solid embodiment of bone, muscle, flesh, and vested substance, rather than the will, heart, mind, and sentiment to be a man, as if he had arrived, as if this picayune arrest had been his Rubicon. He was secretly altogether pleased with himself at how well he had managed his bust – no cracks on the head, no silly scenes – he was damned if he was going to spoil it with an over-intense speech now, no, just the dry salient statement. (Of course, he did not know that one of the first two reports to go out would have him saying: 'I am guilty, I transgressed a police line,' so that some of the follow-up stories would have him arrested by accident. But for that matter, he had been inaccurate himself – it was a *Military* Police line he had crossed.)

They were walking along now on a path roughly parallel to a side of the Pentagon he learned later was the River Entrance, and to his left he could see water which he assumed was the Potomac – in fact, it was a basin of the Potomac called Boundary Channel, and pleasure craft were anchored at marina within it.

The grip of the Marshal's hand had lightened. Perhaps it was the attention paid to him by the reporters, but the Marshal's features had gone through a small metamorphosis. As his rage and agitation subsided, his face converted back into an intelligent, clean-featured American face, not let us say unlike the pleasant modest appearance of Mr. Fran Tarkenton, quarterback for the New York Giants. Mailer and the Marshal began to descend from their peak of mountain air. About now, a man in plain clothes halted Leiterman. 'You can't come with us,' said the man. So Leiterman signed off with a short wave and a smile and Mailer now alone again in his mind, crossed a ramp over a dual highway below and came onto an asphalt reception area of the Pentagon, seeing objects now with the kind of filtered vision which sometimes comes to a man on drugs in the bleak hour when he is coming down – a glimpse is had of everyday things in their negative aspect, the truth of the object (even the beloved is then an object) stripped of all love, sentiment, or libido. They were coming into a reception area adjacent to the wall; paved in gray asphalt, the air itself in these shadows looked gray, and the soldiers and marshals standing about had a cold professional studied indifference Mailer had not seen in twenty-three years, not since he had come to Leyte as a replacement, and had been apparently invisible to the eyes of the veterans, cavalrymen from Texas overseas thirty months and more. The soldiers here had such a look. Even the indifference of the faces one sees in a New York subway have more reaction, as if the air along this sheltered wall of the Pentagon had been injected with Novocain. A pall covered the tension.

# Nicholas Tomalin
# The General goes zapping Charlie Cong

*Newspaper editors are fond of arguing that the New Journalism cannot be adapted to daily journalism, either on the grounds that it works only with trivial ('Pop') subjects or breaks down under the demands of deadlines. In 1966 Nicholas Tomalin was one of England's leading investigative reporters, a 'hard news' journalist of great repute, when he used the techniques of the New Journalism to write this story. He went on the Zapping mission with the General and wrote the story in a single day. It had the most astonishing impact in England, creating for English readers the emotional reality of the war . . . and a somewhat horrified fascination in it. Tomalin was, in fact, writing for a weekly, the Sunday Times, which takes some of the edge off his feat; nevertheless, writers on dailies could achieve this sort of effect fairly often, I am convinced, if they were trained and encouraged to do so. Jimmy Breslin used to manage it with regularity. Not many newspaper writers have the talent or moxie of Tomalin and Breslin. But there is a worse problem: not many newspaper editors want to know that it can even be done. T.W.*

After a light lunch last Wednesday, General James F. Hollingsworth, of Big Red One, took off in his personal helicopter and killed more Vietnamese than all the troops he commanded.

The story of the General's feat begins in the divisional office, at Ki-Na, twenty miles north of Saigon, where a Medical Corps colonel is telling me that when they collect enemy casualties they find themselves with more than four injured civilians for every wounded Viet Cong — unavoidable in this kind of war.

The General strides in, pins two medals for outstanding gallantry to the chest of one of the colonel's combat doctors. Then he strides off again to his helicopter, and spreads out a polythene-covered map to explain our afternoon's trip.

The General has a big, real American face, reminiscent of every movie general you have seen. He comes from Texas, and is 48. His present rank is Brigadier General, Assistant Division Commander, 1st Infantry Division, United States Army (which is what the big red figure one on his shoulder flash means).

'Our mission today,' says the General, 'is to push those goddam VCs right off Routes 13 and 16. Now you see Routes 13 and 16 running north from Saigon toward the town of Phuoc Vinh, where we keep our artillery. When we got here first we prettied up those roads, and cleared Charlie Cong right out so we could run supplies up.

'I guess we've been hither and thither with all our operations since, an' the ol' VC he's reckoned he could creep back. He's been puttin' out propaganda he's goin' to interdict our right of passage along those routes. So this day we aim to zapp him, and zapp him, and zapp him again till we've zapped him right back where he came from. Yes, sir. Let's go.'

The General's UH 18 helicopter carries two pilots, two 60-calibre machine-gunners, and his aide, Dennis Gillman, an apple-cheeked subaltern from California. It also carries the General's own M 16 carbine (hanging on a strut), two dozen smoke-bombs, and a couple of CS anti-personnel gas-bombs, each as big as a small dustbin. Just beside the General is a radio console where he can tune in on orders issued by battalion commanders flying helicopters just beneath him, and company commanders in helicopters just below them.

Under this interlacing of helicopters lies the apparently peaceful landscape beside Routes 13 and 16, filled with farmhouses and peasants hoeing rice and paddy fields.

So far today, things haven't gone too well. Companies Alpha, Bravo and Charlie have assaulted a suspected Viet Cong HQ, found a few tunnels but no enemy.

The General sits at the helicopter's open door, knees apart, his shiny black toecaps jutting out into space, rolls a filtertip cigarette to-and-fro in his teeth, and thinks.

'Put me down at Battalion HQ,' he calls to the pilot.

'There's sniper fire reported on choppers in that area, General.'

'Goddam the snipers, just put me down.'

Battalion HQ at the moment is a defoliated area of four acres packed with tents, personnel carriers, helicopters and milling GIs. We settle into the smell of crushed grass. The General leaps out and strides through his troops.

'Why General, excuse us, we didn't expect you here,' says a sweating major.

'You killed any 'Cong yet?'

'Well no General, I guess he's just too scared of us today. Down the road a piece we've hit trouble, a bulldozer's fallen through a bridge, and trucks coming through a village knocked the canopy off a Buddhist pagoda. Saigon radioed us to repair that temple before proceeding – in the way of civic action, General. That put us back an hour...'

'Yeah. Well Major, you spread out your perimeter here a bit, then get to killin' VC's will you?'

Back through the crushed grass to the helicopter.

'I don't know how you think about war. The way I see it, I'm just like any other company boss, gingering up the boys all the time, except I don't make money. I just kill people, and save lives.'

In the air the General chews two more filtertips and looks increasingly forlorn. No action on Route 16, and another Big Red One general has got his helicopter in to inspect the collapsed bridge before ours.

'Swing us back along again,' says the General.

'Reports of fire on choppers ahead, sir. Smoke flare near spot. Strike coming in.'

'Go find that smoke.'

A plume of white rises in the midst of dense tropical forest, with a Bird Dog spotter plane in attendance. Route 16 is to the right; beyond it a large settlement of red-tiled houses.

'Strike coming in, sir.'

Two F105 jets appear over the horizon in formation, split, then one passes over the smoke, dropping a trail of silver, fish-shaped canisters. After four seconds' silence, light orange fire explodes in patches along an area fifty yards wide by three-quarters of a mile long. Napalm.

The trees and bushes burn, pouring dark oily smoke into the sky. The second plane dives and fire covers the entire strip of dense forest.

• 'Aaaaah,' cries the General. 'Nice. Nice. Very neat. Come in low, let's see who's left down there.'

'How do you know for sure the Viet Cong snipers were in that strip you burned?'

'We don't. The smoke position was a guess. That's why we zapp the whole forest.'

'But what if there was someone, a civilian, walking through there?'

'Aw come son, you think there's folks just sniffing flowers in tropical vegatation like that? With a big operation on hereabouts? Anyone left down there, he's Charlie Cong all right.'

I point at a paddy field full of peasants less than half a mile away.

'That's different son. We know they're genuine.'

The pilot shouts: 'General, half right, two running for that bush.'

'I see them. Down, down, goddam you.'

In one movement he yanks his M16 off the hanger, slams in a clip of cartridges and leans right out of the door, hanging on his seatbelt to fire one long burst in the general direction of the bush.

'General, there's a hole, maybe a bunker, down there.'

'Smokebomb, circle, shift it.'

'But General, how do you know those aren't just frightened peasants?'

'Running? Like that? Don't give me a pain. The clips, the clips, where in hell are the cartridges in this ship?'

The aide drops a smoke canister, the General finds his ammunition and the starboard machine-gunner fires rapid bursts into the bush, his tracers bouncing up off the ground round it.

We turn clockwise in ever tighter, lower circles, everyone firing. A shower of spent cartridge cases leaps from the General's carbine to drop, lukewarm, on my arm.

'I ... WANT ... YOU ... TO ... SHOOT ... RIGHT ... UP ... THE ... ASS ... OF ... THAT ... HOLE ... GUNNER.'

Fourth time round the tracers flow right inside the tiny sandbagged opening, tearing the bags, filling it with sand and smoke.

The General falls back off his seatbelt into his chair, suddenly relaxed, and lets out an oddly feminine, gentle laugh. 'That's it,' he says, and turns to me, squeezing his thumb and finger into the sign of a French chef's ecstasy.

We circle now above a single-storey building made of dried reeds. The first burst of fire tears the roof open, shatters one wall into fragments of scattered straw, and blasts the farmyard full of chickens into dismembered feathers.

'Zapp, zapp, zapp,' cries the General. He is now using semi-automatic fire, the carbine bucking in his hands.

Pow, pow, pow, sounds the gun. All the noises of this war have an unaccountably Texan ring.

'Gas bomb.'

Lieutenant Gillman leans his canister out of the door. As the pilot calls, he drops it. An explosion of white vapour spreads across the wood a full hundred yards downwind.

'Jesus wept, lootenant, that's no good.'

Lieutenant Gillman immediately clambers across me to get the second gas bomb, pushing me sideways into his own port-side seat. In considerable panic I fumble with an unfamiliar seatbelt as the helicopter banks round at an angle of fifty degrees. The second gas bomb explodes perfectly, beside the house, covering it with vapour.

'There's nothing alive in there,' says the General. 'Or they'd be skedaddling. Yes there is, by golly.'

For the first time I see the running figure, bobbing and sprinting across the farmyard towards a clump of trees dressed in black pyjamas. No hat. No shoes.

'Now hit the tree.'

We circle five times. Branches drop off the tree, leaves fly, its trunk is enveloped with dust and tracer flares. Gillman and the General are now firing carbines side by side in the doorway. Gillman offers me his gun: No thanks.

Then a man runs from the tree, in each hand a bright red flag which he waves desperately above his head.

'Stop, stop, he's quit,' shouts the General, knocking the machine-gun so traces erupt into the sky.

'I'm going down to take him. Now watch it everyone, keep firing roundabout, this may be an ambush.'

We sink swiftly into the field beside the tree, each gunner firing cautionary bursts into the bushes. The figure walks towards us.

'That's a Cong for sure,' cries the General in triumph and with one deft movements grabs the man's short black hair and yanks him off his feet, inboard. The prisoner falls across Lieutenant Gillman and into the seat beside me.

The red flags I spotted from the air are his hands, bathed solidly in blood. Further blood is pouring from under his shirt, over his trousers.

Now we are safely in the air again. Out captive cannot be more than sixteen years old, his head comes just about up to the white name patch – Hollingsworth – on the General's chest. He is dazed, in shock. His eyes calmly look first at the General, then at the Lieutenant, then at me. He resembles a tiny, fine-boned wild animal. I have to keep my hand firmly pressed against his shoulder to hold him upright. He is quivering. Sometimes his left foot, from some nervous impulse, bangs hard against the helicopter wall. The Lieutenant applies a tourniquet to his right arm.

'Radio base for an ambulance. Get the information officer with a camera. I want this Commie bastard alive till we get back ... just stay with us till we talk to you, baby.'

The General pokes with his carbine first at the prisoner's cheek to keep his head upright, then at the base of his shirt.

'Look at that now,' he says, turning to me. 'You still thinking about innocent peasants? Look at the weaponry.'

Around the prisoner's waist is a webbing belt, with four clips of ammunition, a water bottle (without stopper), a tiny roll of bandages, and a propaganda leaflet which later turns out to be a set of Viet Cong songs, with a twenty piastre note (about 1s. 6d.) folded in it.

Lieutenant Gillman looks concerned. 'It's OK, you're OK,' he mouths at the prisoner, who at that moment turns to me and with a surprisingly vigorous gesture waves his arm at my seat. He wants to lie down.

By the time I have fastened myself into yet another seat we are back at the landing pad. Ambulance orderlies come aboard, administer morphine, and rip open his shirt. Obviously a burst of fire has shattered his right arm up at the shoulder. The cut shirt now allows a large bulge of blue-red tissue to fall forward, its surface streaked with white nerve fibres and chips of bone (how did he ever manage to wave that arm in surrender?).

When the ambulance has driven off the General gets us all posed round the nose of the chopper for a group photograph like a gang of successful fishermen, then clambers up into the cabin again, at my request, for a picture to show just how he zapped those VCs. He is euphoric.

'Jeez I'm so glad you was along, that worked out just dandy. I've been written up time and time again back in the State for shootin' up VCs; but no one's been along with me like you before.'

We even find a bullet hole in one of the helicopter rotor blades. 'That's proof positive they was firin' at us all the time. An' firin' on us first, boy. So much for your fellers smellin' flowers.'

He gives me the Viet ᴄong's water bottle as souvenir and proof. 'That's a chicom bottle, that one. All the way from Peking.'

Later that evening the General calls me to his office to tell me the prisoner had to have his arm amputated, and is now in the hands of the Vietnamese authorities, as regulations dictate. Before he went under, he told the General's interpreters that he was part of a hardcore regular VC company whose mission was to mine Route 16, cut it up, and fire at helicopters.

The General is magnanimous in his victory over my squeamish civilian worries.

'You see son, I saw rifles on that first pair of running men. Didn't tell you that at the time. And, by the way you mustn't imagine there could have been ordinary farm folk in that house, when you're as old a veteran as I am you get to know about those things by instinct. I agree there was chickens for food with them, strung up on a pole. You didn't see anything bigger, like a pig or a cow did yuh? Well then.'

The General wasn't certain whether further troops would go to the farmhouse that night to check who died, although patrols would be near there.

It wasn't safe moving along Route 16 at night, there was another big operation elsewhere the next day. Big Red One is always on the move.

'But when them VC come back harassin' that Route 16 why, we'll zapp them again. And when they come back after that we'll zapp them again.'

'Wouldn't it be easier just to stay there all the time?'

'Why, son, we haven't enough troops as it is.'

'The Koreans manage it.'

'Yeah, but they've got a smaller area to protect. Why Big Red One ranges right over – I mean up to the Cambodian Border. There ain't no place on that map we ain't been.

'I'll say perhaps your English generals wouldn't think my way of war is all that conventional, would they? Well, this is a new kind of war, flexible, quickmoving. Us generals must be on the spot to direct our troops. The helicopter adds a new dimension to battle.

'There's no better way to fight than goin' out to shoot VCs. An' there's nothing I love better than killin' 'Cong. No, sir.'

# Tom Wolfe from
# The electric kool-aid acid test

*In this scene in* The Electric Kool-Aid Acid Test *I felt justified in experimenting with a stream of consciousness as well as point of view. The scene shows Ken Kesey in hiding in Mexico after he had been arrested in California for the second time on a narcotics charge (possession of marijuana) and faced a mandatory five-year jail sentence with no chance of parole. Deep into the Halusion Gulp of paranoia, he sits in his hideaway convinced that Mexican federales or FBI agents or California state troopers on vacation are about to pounce on him; for, as the saying goes, even paranoids have enemies.*

*There was an unusually rich record of Kesey's thoughts and feelings during this interlude. He had written at length to his friend Larry McMurtry about it at the time, he had made tapes even while he was in the jungle, and I had interviewed his companions in flight, Zonker and Black Maria, about it, as well as Kesey himself, of course. Much of the direct interior monologue is taken from Kesey's letters to McMurtry. T.W.*

### The fugitive

Haul ass, Kesey. Move. *Scram. Split flee hide vanish disintegrate.* Like run.

Rrrrrrrrrrrrrrrrrrrrrrrrrrrev revrevrevrevrevrevrevrevrev or are we gonna have just a late Mexican re-run of the scene on the rooftop in San Francisco and sit here with the motor spinning and watch with fascination while the cops they climb up once again to *come git you*—

THEY JUST OPENED THE DOOR DOWN BELOW, ROTOR ROOTER, SO YOU HAVE MAYBE 45 SECONDS ASSUMING THEY BE SLOW AND SNEAKY AND SURE ABOUT IT

Kesey sits in a little upper room in the last house down the beach, $80 a month, on paradise-blue Bandarias Bay, in Puerto Vallarta, on the west coast of Mexico, state of Jalisco, one step from the floppy green fronds of the jungle, wherein flourish lush steamy baboon lusts of paranoia – Kesey sits in this little rickety upper room with his elbow on a table and his forearm standing up perpendicular and in the palm of his hand a little mirror, so that his forearm and the mirror are like a big rear-view mirror stanchion on the side of a truck and thus he can look out the window and see them but they can't see him—

COME ON, MAN, DO YOU NEED A COPY OF THE SCRIPT TO SEE HOW THIS MOVIE GOES? YOU HAVE MAYBE 40 SECONDS LEFT BEFORE THEY COME GET YOU

– a Volkswagen has been cruising up and down the street for no earthly reason at all, except that they are obviously working with the fake telephone linesmen outside the window who whistle—

THERE THEY GO AGAIN

– whistle in the slow-brain brown Mexican huarache day-laborer way, for no earthly reason except that they are obviously synched in, finked in, with the Volkswagen. Now a tan sedan comes along the street, minus a license plate but plus a stenciled white number – *exactly like a prison stencil* – police and two coatless guys inside, both in white shirts so they're *not* prisoners—

ONE TURNED LOOKED BACK!

IF YOU WERE WATCHING ALL THIS ON A MOVIE SCREEN YOU KNOW WHAT YOUR REACTION WOULD BE THROUGH A MOUTHFUL OF POPCORN FROM THE THIRD ROW: 'WHAT MORE DO YOU NEED, YOU DOLT! SCRAM OUTTA THERE ...'

– But he has just hooked down five dexedrines and the old motor is spinning and rushing most nice and euphorically in fascination and a man can't depart this nice $80-a-month snug harbor on paradise-blue Bandarias Bay just yet with a cool creek of speed rush in his veins. It is such a tiny little fink scene as he sees it in the hand mirror. He can tilt it and see his own face entropied with the strain and then tilt it – a sign! – a sparrow, fat and sleek, dives through the dwindling sun into a hole in one of the lampposts; home.

MORE TELEFONO TRUCKS! TWO LOUD WHISTLES THIS TIME – FOR NO EARTHLY REASON EXCEPT TO COME GIT YOU. YOU HAVE MAYBE 35 SECONDS LEFT

– Kesey has Cornel Wilde Running Jacket ready hanging on the wall, a jungle-jim corduroy jacket stashed with fishing line, a knife, money, DDT, tablet, ball-points, flashlight, and grass. Has it timed by test runs that he can be out the window, down through a hole in the roof below, down a drain pipe, over a wall and into thickest jungle in 45 seconds – well, only 35 seconds left, but head start is all that's needed, with the element of surprise. Besides, it's so fascinating to be here in subastral projection with the cool rushing dex, synched into *their* minds and his own, in all its surges and tributaries and convolutions, turning it this way and that and rationalizing the situation for the 100th time in split seconds, such as: If they have that many men already here, the phony telephone men, the cops in the tan car, the cops in the Volkswagen, what are they waiting for? why haven't they crashed right in through the rotten doors of this Rat building — But he gets the signal even before he finishes the question:

WAITING! THEY KNOW THEY'VE GOT YOU, FOOL, HAVE KNOWN FOR WEEKS. BUT THEY'RE CERTAIN YOU'RE CONNECTED WITH ALL THE LSD BEING SMUGGLED UP FROM MEXICO AND THEY WANT TO TAKE IN AS BIG A HAUL AS POSSIBLE WHEN THEY FINALLY SLAM IT. LIKE LEARY; THEY MUST HAVE BEEN WATCHING A DREADFUL LONG TIME BEFORE THEY WERE CONTENT THEY HAD SOMETHING WORTH HIS SIZE. THIRTY YEARS. FOR A HARVARD DOCTOR WITH GRASS. THAT'S HOW BAD THEY WANTED THE WHOLE BUSINESS LOCKED AWAY. THAT'S HOW DAN-GEROUS THEY CONSIDER THE WHOLE BUSINESS. AND THEY WERE COM-PLETELY CORRECT — IF NOT IN THEIR FANTASY, THEN AT LEAST IN THEIR EVALUATION OF THE PRESENT AND EVER-GROWING PSYCHEDELIC THREAT

A NOISE DOWN BELOW.

THEM?

30 SEGUNDOS LEFT?

— maybe it's Black Maria, come back with good things for eating and stuff for the new disguise, Steve Lamb, mild-mannered reporter and all-around creep—

RUN, FOOL!

— Shhhhhhhhhhhhhhhhh. Such a quiet secret muffled smile will be on Black Maria's face.

Rrrrrrrrrrrrrrrrrrrrevrevrevrevrevrevrevrevrevrev It could have been all so quiet, just him and Zonker and the smoldering Black Maria in this $80-a-month paradise-blue Bandarias Bay in Puerto Vallarta. If the suicide ruse and the rest of the main Fugitive fantasy had but worked.

The trip into Mexico was easy, because everything with Boise was easy. Boise always *knew*. They picked up Zonker in L.A., and then Jim Fish, and they coasted on over the line at Tijuana. No hassle to cross over into Mexico. The border at Tijuana is like a huge superhighway toll station, a huge concrete apron and ten or fifteen custom booths in a row for all the cars pouring over into Tijuana from San Diego and points north, all plastic green and concrete like part of suburban superhighway America. So they rolled on over the line with Kesey hidden in the back of Boise's old panel truck and heart don't even thump too bad. Spirits up, a little of the Prankster élan back in the cosmos. In true Prankster fashion they spent one third their money stash on a Madman Muntz autostereo rig to go along with all the other valuables, like tape recorders and many tapes.

The next likely hassle is visas, because this shapes up as a long stay. Might be hot to try to get Kesey one in Tijuana, because Tijuana is just a California annex, really, the slums of San Diego, and they just might very well know about the case.

'We'll do it in Sonoita, man,' says Boise. 'They don't give a shit there. Put down a couple of bucks and they can't see anything else.'

Sonoita is almost due east of Tijuana, just south of the Arizona border. Kesey uses his good shuck ID there and all is jake in Sonoita. Fugitive! – real-life and for sure now.

Then south down so-called Route 2 and so-called Route 15, bouncing and grinding along through the brown dust and scrawny chickens and animal dung brown dust fumes of western Mexico, towns of Coyote, Caborca, Santa Ana, Querobabi, Cornelio, El Oasis, hee, Hermosillo, hah, Pocitos Casas, Cieneguito, Guaymas, Camaxtli, Mixcoatl, Tlazolteotl. Quetzalcoatl, Huitzilopochtli, Tezcatlipoca haunting the Dairy Queen Rat Queen crossroads in the guise of a Rat, a Popoluactli-screeing rat, Tetzcotl, Yaotl, Titlacahuan he whose slaves we are, Ochpaniiztl priesty Angel-freaked out in a motorcycle made from the vaseline skin of Gang Bang Girl Meets White Trash ... A confetti of skulls and death in western Mexico, the Rat lands. Not one inch of it is picturesque burros and shawls or nova Zapata hats or color-TV pink chunks of watermelon or water lilies or gold feathers or long eyelashes or high combs or tortillas and tacos and chili powder or fluty camote vendors or muletas or toreros or olés or mariachi bands or water lilies or blood of the dahlia or tinny cantinas or serapes or movie black marias with shiny black hair and steaming little high round pubescent bottoms. None of the old Mexico we know and love on the 21-day excursion fare. Just the boogering brown dust and bloated rat corpses by the road, goats, cows, chickens with all four feet up in the air at the Tezcatlipocan skull rot crossroads of Mexico.

To kesey it was a hopeless flea-bitten desert he was fleeing into. But Boise made it bearable. Boise always *knew*. Boise was wizened and thin-faced and he had the awfulest New England high flat whine, and he didn't belong anywhere near here, but he was *here*, *now*, and he *knew*.

The truck breaks down for the fourteenth time—

'No hassle, man. We just back it up on a rock, man ... Then we just take the tire off and fix it.'

More flat, Rat country, mosquito and flea, into total nothing, like the lines of perspective in a surrealist painting, but Boise makes you realize it is all the same, here as anywhere. Boise lecherously scanning the streets as they bounce through the dead chicken towns just like it was only Saturday night on Broadway in North Beach, spotting a good looking gringa muchacha padding along the side of the road with honest calves,

25 SECONDS LEFT, FOOL!

and he says, 'Shall we get her over and *ball* her, man?' all in the same New England whine, as if he were saying, Wanna Coke, or not? Kesey looks at Boise's lined face and his thin lips, looks ancient, only a glitter comes out of the eyes, nice and lecherous, dead certain and crazy alive at the same time. And Boise in that moment is in the tiny knot of Perfect Pranksters, the inner circle, ascending into the *sangha* for good.

In Guaymas, on the gulf, Jim Fish wants out. *An early attack of paranoia, Jim Fish?* and catches a bus back to the U.S., leaving Kesey, Boise and Zonker and the equipment. But was it not ever so? You're either on the bus or off the bus. Kesey's spirits were picking up. Boise was pulling everything together : : : this crazy New Englander is *here* in these Rat lands.

'Hey, man ...' Boise points at a construction scene they're going by. '...*see that?*' as if to say, There's the whole thing, right there.

A whole gang of workmen are trying to put the stucco on the ceiling of a building they're finishing up. One fat man is mixing up the stucco in a washtub. One skinny one is scooping the stucco out of the tub with a little trowel and pitching it up underhanded at the ceiling. A little of it sticks -- and three or four guys stand on a plank scaffolding taking stabs at smoothing it out -- but most of it falls down on the floor and three or four more are hunkered down there scraping it up off the floor and shoveling it back in the tub and the skinny guy skinnies up another little gob with his skinny trowel and they all stare again to see what happens. They are all hunkering around in huaraches, worthless flat Rat woven sandals, up on the scaffolding, down on the floor, waiting to see what happens, how fate brings it off with this little gob of nothing pitched up at the Rat expanse ...

And it's all there -- the whole Mexico Trip—

'They have a saying, "Hay tiemp—" ' Boise honks the steering wheel to get around an ice-cream vendor in the middle of the road ' "– o," "There is time." '

20 SECONDS, IDIOT!

Huaraches, which are *the* Rat shoe. It all synches. Mexico is the Rat paradise. But of course! It is not worthless – it is perfection. It is as if the Rat things of all the Rat lands of America, all the drive-ins, mobile-home parks, Dairy Queens, superettes, Sunset Strips, auto-accessory stores, septic-tank developments, souvenir shops, snack bars, lay-away furniture stores, Daveniter living rooms, hot-plate hotels, bus-station paperback racks, luncheonette in-the-booth juke-box slots, raw-concrete service-station toilets with a head of urine in the bowl, Greyhound bus toilettes with paper towels and vomit hang-ing over the hockey-puckblack rim, Army–Navy stores with Bikini Kodpiece Briefs for men, Super Giant racks with matching green twill shirts and balloon-bottom pants for honest toilers, $8,000 bungalows with plastic accordion-folding partitions and the baby asleep in there in a foldaway crib of plastic net, picnic tables with the benches built onto them used in the dining room, Jonni-Trot Bar-B-Q sandwiches with a carbonated fruit drink, aluminum slat awnings, aluminum sid-ings, lukewarm coffee-'with' in a china mug with a pale brown pool in the saucer and a few ashes, a spade counter chef scraping a short-order grill with a chalky Kitchy-Brik and he won't take your order till he's through, a first-come-first-serve doctor's waiting room with mod-est charwomen with their dresses stuck on the seats of shiny vinyl chairs and they won't move to get loose for fear you'll look up their dress, plaid car coats from Sears and a canvas cap with a bill, synthetic dresses for waitresses looking like milky cellophane, Rat cones, Rat sodas, Rat meat-salad sandwiches, Rat cheezis, Ratburgers – it is as if the Rat things of all the Rat lands of America had been looking for their country, their Canaan, their Is-ra-el, and they found it in Mexico. It has its own Rat aesthetic. It's hulking beautiful ...

Then they reached Mazatlan, the first full-fledged resort you reach on the west coast of Mexico, coming down from the States. Every-body's trip was fishing in Mazatlan. Along the old Avenida del Mar and the Paseo Claussen, white walls with nice artistic Rat fishing scenes and hotel archways with great shiny blue marlins hanging inside the arches and gringos with duckbill caps here to catch some marlin. Mari-achi music at last, with the trumpets always breaking and dropping off the note and then struggling up again. Zonker has the bright idea of going to O'Brien's Bar, on the beach front, place he got beat up out back of once by thirteen Mexican fags. Zonker enjoys revisiting scenes of previous debacles. *Like also spends hours on the beach telling them how his true and fiercest fear is of being attacked by a shark while swimming ... as he picks flea-bite scabs until his legs stream blood to the luscious world ... then goes swimming.*

O'Brien's brings on the paranoia right away. It is a break in the Rat movie. It is dark and a Mexican band plays — signaling to the Rat sensibility that it will cost too much. Rat souls everywhere fear dark, picturesque restaurant, knowing instinctively they will pay dearly for the bullshit ambiance, dollar a drink probably. O'Brien's was crowded, and then through the cocktail gloom: *heads.* A bunch of kids with the jesuschrist hair, the temple bells and donkey beads, serape vests, mandalas; in short, American heads. Zonker recognizes them immediately. They're not only American heads, but from San Jose, and some had been to the Acid Tests. *Just what the Fugitive needs to blow the whole suicide ruse. 'Guess who I saw in Mexico ...'* Naturally. Zonk, with his zest for debacle, hails them over, Kesey is introduced as 'Joe,' and nobody pays him much mind except for one dark little girl, Mexican-looking, with long black hair.

'When were you born?' she says to Kesey. She doesn't sound Mexican. *She sounds like Lauren Bacall speaking through a tube.*

'I'm a Virgo.' *No sense hitting a ball three hits you can see coming if you can cut across the fourth.*

'I thought so. I'm a Scorpio.'

'Beautiful.'

The black Scorpio obviously knows Zonk best. She knows him when. But Zonk belongs to the ages and it comes to pass that Zonk or no Zonk, she and Kesey relax out in the open air on the pier one night down by a Mazatlan Rat beach, all dirt and scrabble, but the waves and the wind and the harbor lights do it up right and the moon hits some kind of concrete shaft there, putting her in the dark, in the shadow, and him in the light, lit up by the moon, as if some designer drew a line precisely between their bodies. *Black Maria,* he decides.

So Black Maria joins the Fugitive band and they go off to Puerto Vallarta. Puerto Vallarta is out of the Rat lands. All picture-book Mexico. Paradise-blue Bandarias Bay and a pure white beach and white latino cottages right up against the jungle, which is a deep raw green, and clean. Fat green fronds lapping up against the back of the houses on the beach. Macaw sounds, or very near it. Secret poisonous orchid and orange pops and petals winking out when the foliage moves. A nice romantic Gothic jungle. Zonker hassles with an oily little real-estate man and gets the last house on the edge of town for $80 a month. The rent is low because the jungle is too close for the tourists, the jungle and too many Mexican kids and chickens and the rural dung dust. Boise heads back to the U.S. and Kesey, Zonker and Black Maria move in. They have the upper half of the house, one floor and a spiral staircase up to the roof. Up on the roof is a kind of thatched hut, the highest perch around, a perfect lookout post and a snug harbor. Kesey decides to risk a phone call to the States to let Faye and everybody know he's O.K. He goes into town and calls Peter Demma in the Hip Pocket Book Store in Santa Cruz. A little metallic clanking about by the telefonista señoritas down at central. And then,

'Peter?'

From many Rat miles away: 'Ken!' Very surprised, naturally...

So Kesey whiled the time sitting in the snug hacienda on the edge of Puerto Vallarta sipping beer and smoking many joints and writing in a notebook occasionally. He wanted to get a little of all this down and send it to Larry McMurtry.

'Larry:

'Phone calls to the states 8 bucks apiece besides was ever a good board to bound my favorite ball of bullshit prose often, it was you...'

Like all about Black Maria. In many ways she was so great. She is quiet and has a kind of broody beauty. She cooks. She looks Mex and speaks Mex. She can even hassle Mex. She sounds out the mayor of Puerto Vallarta as to how safe Kesey will be here in town. Hay tiempo, he says. The extradition takes forever. Very nice to know...

And yet Black Maria is not completely a Prankster. She wants to be a part of all this, she wants to do this thing, but *she does it without belief*. It is like the Mexican part of her Black Maria thing. She has all the trappings of Mexican – she looks it, she speaks it, her grandfather was even Mexican – but she is not Mexican. She is Carolyn Hannah of San Jose, California, under everything else, even the blood. He wrote in the notebook:: *Moving the dark Indian*

10 SECONDS LEFT, YOU FREAKING EE-JOT!!!!

*body out of the Indian land weakened the Indian blood with chicken soup and matzoh balls. So much of the fire concealed by the dark and broody beauty lies just that deep. Because she does it without belief.*

And yet it is very nice up here in this thatched perch atop the last house. A car heads up the street — Zonker and Black Maria coming back to the house. He peers over the edge at the car kicking up the dust, then writes in the notebook, it is a perfect lookout, *allowing me to see them without them seeing me*. Many things . . . synch.

Zonker and Black Maria drove down the road, scattering up the kids and the chickens and the dust, and Black Maria pointed up to the top of the house and said to Zonker:

'Look, there's Kesey.' Then she looked out the window and stared at the jungle. 'I bet he thinks we can't see him.'

The jig is up. Zonker brings a telegram from Paul Robertson back in San Jose and it is a bear. It is not even a warning, it

5 SECONDS — 5 SECONDS LEFT — YOU REALLY JES GON' SIT THERE FOR THE SQUASH?

is final. The jig is up, it says. Meaning, it turned out, that the suicide ruse had been exposed and the cops knew he was in Puerto Vallarta. Ex*posed?* — hell, the suicide prank had turned into a goddamn comic opera. For a start, Dee had pulled a sort of Dee-out, as Mountain Girl feared. Dee had driven up looking for a cliff near Humboldt Bay, about 250 miles north of San Francisco, up near Eureka, California, not far from the Oregon border in redwoods country. He got up to the last hill going up there and the panel truck wouldn't pull the hill. So he called into town for a tow truck and the garage man and the tow truck pulled the suicide vehicle up the last mile. Hired and paid for and thanks a lot. Always nice to hire some help to commit suicide. Next Dee dropped Kesey's distinctive sky-blue boots down to the shore below — but they hit the water instead and sank without a bubble. Next, the goddamned romantic suicide desolate foaming cliff was so goddamned desolate, nobody noticed the truck for about two weeks, despite the Ira Sandperl for President sign on the rear bumper. Apparently people figured the old heap had been abandoned. The Humboldt county police finally checked it out on February 11. Next, the suicide note, which seemed so ineluctably convincing as Kesey and Mountain Girl smoked a few joints and soared into passages of Shelleyan *Weltschmerz* — it gave off a giddy scent of put-on, even to the straight cops of the Humboldt. There were certain inconsistencies. Like the part about the truck smashing into a redwood. Well – even in a Dee-out, Dee couldn't exactly ask the tow-truck man, Well, now that you've towed it up here, how about jamming it into a tree for me. Next, the late, happy call to Peter Demma in Santa Cruz. Demma had really been bowled over to hear from Kesey. A lot of people, a lot of people who liked him, had really been worried that he was dead. And now here was Kesey calling him – *alive* – with a message for Faye and the whole thing. That was Saturday. The next night, Sunday, February 13, Demma dropped into Manuel's Mexican Restaurant in Santa Cruz, and there was his old friend Bob Levy. By way of making conversation, Levy says,

'What have you heard from Ken?'

'I just got a *call* from him!' says Demma. 'From Puerto Vallarta!'

That's interesting.

Levy happened to be a reporter for the Watsonville *Register-Pajaronian*, Watsonville being a town near Santa Cruz. The next afternoon, Monday, the lead story in the Watsonville *Register-Pajaronian* carried a five column headline reading:

MISSING NOVELIST TURNS UP
IN MEXICO

The next day, Tuesday, the San Jose *Mercury* picked up the story and put a little more spin on it with a story headlined:

KESEY'S CORPSE HAVING A BALL
IN PUERTO VALLARTA

2 SECONDS, OH CORPSE OF MINE!
THAT'S NO BLACK MARIA SHHHHHHHHUFFLING UP THE STAIRS OUTSIDE
  THE DOOR, DOLT, IT'S A COP CLUMP UP THE STAIRS NO EARTHLY
  SOUND LIKE IT
SHARP WHISTLE FROM THE TELEFONISTAS
VW BACKING DOWN THE STREET
THIS IS TRULY IT, TRULY IT
GRAB THE CORNEL WILDE RUNNING JACKET, FOOL! MAKE THE BRAIN
  CATCH HOLD! RRRRRRRRRRRRRRREVREVREVREV SPINNING AND IN THE
  GIANT PYRAMIDAL CELLS OF BETZ OF PRECENTRAL CEREBRAL CORTEX
  RISE AND HEAVE AND SLIP GANGLIONIC LAYER SHUDDERS AND GIGGLES
  SYNAPSES LIGHT LIKE RANDOM BEATLE FLASHBULBS KHEEWWW BLAST-
  ING OUT SILLY FROM MOTOR HOMUNCULUS YOU MISSED YR FLASH OH
  MIGHTY MASTICATOR, SALIVATOR, VOCALIZER, SWALLOWER, LICKER,
  BITER  SUCKER  BROW-KNITTER  LOOKER  BLINKER  RUBBERNECKER

THUMBER   PRODDER   UPYOURS   FINGERER   RING-WEARER   NOSEPICKER
WAVER   DRINKER   ARMLIFTER   BODYBENDER   HIPSWIVELER   KNEER
SPRINGER RUNNER

Zero: : : : : : : : oooooooo: : : :::: RUN!

Sonbitch! The gears catch at last, he springs up, grabs Cornel Wilde
jacket, leaps through the back window, down through the hole, down
the drainpipe – now vault the wall, you mother, into the jungle floppy—

AWWRRRRRAMM̍MANNNNNNN

WHAZZAT?

His head is down but he can see it

WHAZZAT!

Up there in the window he just jumped out of

BROWN!

He can feel it. There is a vibration on the parasympathetic efferent
fibres behind the eyeballs and it hums

HRRRRRRRRAMANNNNNNNNNNN

Two of them one brown dumpy Mex with gold-handle butt gun one
crewcut American FBI body-snatcher watching him flying like a monkey
over the wall into the jungle the brown Mex holds gold gun but the
brain behind that face too brown moldering Mex earth to worry about
couldn't hit a peeing dog

PLUNGE

into the lapping P.V. fronds bursting orchid and orange the motor
homunculus working perfect now powerful gallop into the picturebook
jungles of Mexico—

A moment later Black Maria walked into the apartment. She found
Kesey gone and the Cornel Wilde jungle running jacket gone. That trip
again. Well, he'll come back when he's ready to, worn out, and things
will be cool for a while. Kesey had gotten paranoid as hell, but that
wasn't the only thing. He *liked* this Fugitive game. Man, he'd scram out
in the jungle and hide out there for two or three days and smoke a lot
of grass and finally straggle in. That started before the telegram even.
There was a whole signal they worked out. Or he worked out. When
the coast was clear, she was supposed to hang up a yellow shirt of
Zonk's on the line outside the back window, facing the jungle. It was a
yellow shirt with a black and brown print on it, on the *faggy* side, if
you asked Black Maria. The flag would go up and finally Kesey would
straggle back home beat, having run himself about to death in the
jungle or along the beach.

And yet it was nice. It was crazy but nice. Kesey was the most magnetic person she had ever met. He radiated something, a kind of power. His thoughts, the things he talked about, were very complex and metaphysical and cryptic but his manner was back-home, almost back-country. Even while he was reeking with paranoia, he seemed to have total confidence. That was very strange. He could make you feel like part of something very . . . He had even given her a new name, Black Maria. She was . . . Black Maria.

As a girl in San Jose, California, she had felt like everything she really was had been smothered under layers and layers of games she couldn't control. Externally there was nothing wrong. Her father and mother were both teachers and life in San Jose was comfortable and serene in the California suburban manner. But half the time nobody ever understands about growing up in this country. Little Penguin Islands full of kids playing Lord of the Flies, a world of pygmy tribes, invisible to the Isfahan adult eye, these little devils, tribes of studs, tribes of rakes, tribes of IntelFinks even, tribes of greasers, and an amorphous mass of hopeless cases left over. Until – psychdelics started around there, mainly grass and acid. The new scene started and suddenly all sorts of . . . well, *beautiful people* blossomed forth from out of the polyglot, people who really had a lot to them only it had been smothered by all the eternal social games that had been set up. Suddenly they found each other.

One night she was high and experienced the unity, the All-one. A light was behind her in the room and hit her body from behind and broke up into beams and shone out before her, hitting the floor and the walls in spokes of light with shadows in between. The room broke up before her eyes and separated in just that pattern with bars of light vibrating. Suddenly it became very clear, the way the room was put together, the way the parts fit, the way the parts of *every*thing fit, as if someone had taken an Indian puzzle ring apart for her. It was clear how *every*thing fit together and it wasn't really a world split up into pointless games and cliques. That was merely the way it looked before you knew the key. And now there were beautiful people who knew the key and this experience could be shared.

Her mother gave her money for the second semester at San Jose State, and although it would hurt her mother at first, she knew what she had to do. She took the money and headed off to Mexico with some beautiful kids. It was a little more complicated than that. She knew Zonk at San Jose State and she knew he was heading for Mexico, for Mazatlan, although she didn't know about the Kesey prank, and so she was following Zonk, for if there were beautiful people, Zonk was one of them.

Mazatlan was just beginning to be the acid heads' favorite spot on the Mexican west coast. It wasn't a place the real hardcore tourists were onto yet. They went on down the coast to Acapulco, generally. At the same time Mazatlan wasn't so unbearably Mexicali ... *sad* ... like the true Acid Central of Mexico, Ajijic, on Lake Chapala. Those poor sad Lake Chapala villages, Ajijic, Chapala, Jocotepec, with the lake drying up and the old suck-smack lily-pad scum mud showing and failed American aesthetes padding around earnestly in sandals, 48-year-old bohos sucking up to young heads of the new generation of Hip. Very sad. It is truly a sad thing when an American boho says fuck this and picks up and leaves this fucking tailfin and shopping plaza and war-crazy civilization and goes to live among real people, the honest folk-type folk, in the land of Earth feelings, Mexico, and the hell with tile baths – and then he *sits* there, in Mexico, amid the hunkering hard-cheese mestizos, and, man, it is honest and real here ... and just as miserable as hell, and he is a miserable aging fuckup with no place else to go.

But Mazatlan – the head scene there was a happy thing and a groove. So she sat down in Mazatlan and wrote her mother a Beautiful People letter ...

And she found Zonk and, unexpectedly, the famous Ken Kesey and beautiful people. But one thing about the beautiful people themselves.... Namely, the Merry Pranksters. She had heard of the fabulous Merry Pranksters even in San Jose. Kesey and Zonk talked about them all the time, of course. The fabulous Babbs, the fabulous Mountain Girl, the fabulous Cassady, Hermit, Hassler and the rest. She had a Prankster name, Black Maria, but she was not yet a Prankster. She was sensitive even to the contours of Kesey's world, too. Sooner or later Kesey would reunite with the Pranksters ...

Well ... put out Zonker's shirt when the coast is clear. Zonker's billowy faggy-looking shirt. Let him stay out on his jungle run for a while. If he enjoys the Fugitive game, why spoil it.

SHHHHHHHHHHWAAAAAAAAAP

flopping lush P.V. fronds Kesey thrashes out of the jungle and across the road—

CARS? ONE MEX ONE AMERICAN COMING IN PALE TAN VW?

no, no cars, man, and then down across the road to rocky scrabble
down by the ocean on the rocks, his heart rattling away, he sinks down
in his Cornel Wilde running jacket listening.

WHOP!

surf hits the rocks, just a little holiday in picturesque P.V. with the sea
kicking up at twilight. He concentrates on the surf – analogy spoken
here? – but the surf is too aimless this way. His heart rattles tachy-
cardiac at this speed, and the surf is synched in to another thing
WHOPping against the rocks

BRANNGGGH

a tin-door sounded up on the road like the ominous tin-car door sounds
in *Hud* always bring on the bad action – like brown Mex and crewcut
drip-dry American up on the road eyes rocketing around, Brown
Mex puffing *I'm-supposed-to-be-off-duty-now-señor*. Kesey faces out
to sea, pulls a tablet out of the jacket. Makes the pink cover visible
as if to prove just an aimless surf artist drawing water swells furl
by furl like Leonardo who *must* have been a head, all the minute
instincts, to sit by the water drawing little furls as the water laps
up on the beach then starts rolling back toward the sea and minute
little churning furls in the lead edge of the water, he drew it all,
furl by furl, like a very meth head plugged into the great God Rotor.
More surf, then

KABOOM!

first – they're FIRING on him. They don't give a shit.

HOT PURSUIT!

we got the guns and the rights, signed on this piece of paper here, one
move blow yr fucking head off and you have *already moved*, Kesey—

HOT PURSUIT!

KABOOM!

but nothing happens. Silence except for the surf.

THAT IS VERY PARANOID, HONDO

why would they try to blast you out of the tub with elephant guns
anyway. It must be workmen using dynamite. So he edges up to the
road and it is workmen all right, sweating and heaving while the
green fronds flap up the hill. He'll just sit here and watch them
dynamite

SURE

just watch them dynamite while every gringo car comes spinning off
the shore drive out here Baskin-Robbins tourist matron lookout and
say 'Hey, Honey, *that's Ken Kee-zee* . . .'

Back into the jungle, Cornel Wilde. Heart still banging up to the edge of fibrillation, through the lush shadowy danks of the jungle. Well, yessir, lookee here a minute, what's this. A three-sided hut in the jungle, some kind of woodsman's hut, with a cot in it and a little hoard of mango papaya, some kind of pallid little fruit. He sinks back on the cot, unzips his fly to air out his sweating nuts and dips into his jacket and pulls out three roaches and wraps a leaf around them like a cone and lights up. He cuts open a fruit and it bleeds meek white and he puts it aside.

A TRAP FOR JUNGLE RUNNERS

this perfect little snug harbor to suck you in, a hut, a cot, meek milk white fruit to eat, a joint of sorts, oh to be back in Baskin-Robbins country just one time facing endless beige tubs of ice cream 31 flavor decisions to make, pointed cone or cup-style

¡PARANOIA!

but this is the real-life jungle, Major. Two-winged flies, dapple-wing Anapholes, Culex tarsalis, verruga-crazed Phlebotomus biting 8-day fever and Oriental sores, greenhead rabbit-fever horseflies, tularemic Loa loa, tsetse mites, Mexican fleas, chinches, chiggers, velvet ants, crab lice crawling up your balls up your belly under your arms right up to your eyelashes for a nice fix of Mexican murine typhus, puss caterpillars, cantharidae beetles, Indian bedbugs, ticks, itch mites nice for scabies and rickety pox, Pacific Coast female tick hiding in the hairs at the base of the head sucking in the death bloat with blood, paralysis coming up from the toes will it reach the lungs before the big blood sausage mother drops off, a blood bag with tiny feet wriggling like worm hairs

DDT!

he gets down and pulls the DDT can out of the jacket and starts dusting all around the ground there around the cot, setting up a mighty defense perimeter against the mites of the jungle – which is very funny, come to think of it – down on all fours in deadly battle with the microscopic mites while

THEY

close in to slam you away for five, eight, twenty years . . . driven at last out onto the edge of your professed beliefs. You believed that a man should move off his sure center out onto the outer edges, that the outlaw, even more than the artist, is he who tests the limits of life and that – The Movie :::: by getting totally into Now and paying total Attention until it all flows together in the *synch* and imagining them all into the Movie, your will will determine the flow and control all jungles great and small.

NEXT TO LAST JOINT IN ALL OF MEXICO

he pulls it out of his pocket and lights up. *Maybe I'll knock off the grass for a while.* Su-u-u-ure.

AND THEN BELIEVE ALL THAT CRAP YOU'VE BEEN CLAIMING ABOUT ALTERING BY ACCEPTING. BELIEVE IT! OR YOU ARE A GONER, AND BOY, A WALKING DEAD MAN FOREVERMORE FADING FINALLY INAUDIBLE LIKE THE VOICES MUMBLING BITONES IN THE CATHEDRAL!

And now that I've got your attention – if he sit very still, the rush lowers in his ears, he can concentrate, pay total attention, an even, even, even world, flowing into *now*, no past terrors, no anticipation of the future horror, only *now*, *this* movie, the vibrating parallel rods, and he can *feel* them drawn into the flow, his, every verruga fly, velvet ant, murine fleas and crabs, every chinch and tick, every lizard, cat, palm, the very power of the most ancient palm, held in his will, and he is immune—

# Barbara L. Goldsmith
# La dolce viva

'La Dolce Viva' is an interview story that is amazing for its candor, even by current standards – so much so that it came close to finishing off the magazine it appeared in. It ran in the spring of 1968 in the fourth issue of New York magazine along with photographs of Viva's 'plucked chicken' (her own term) nude form reclining on a ratty odalisque's sofa with rancid milk cartons and cigarette roaches in the foreground. Thinking the new magazine was taking some hideous twisted-geek turn, advertisers abandoned it in droves. The incident made quite a different impression on me, however.

New York's editor, Clay Felker, was well aware of the commercial risk he ran in publishing the piece – his own advertising people had read it and were screaming – but 'La Dolce Viva' was too good a piece not to run. Felker went ahead and ran it ... and the thermotropic missiles went off. ... From that point on I knew that New York was going to make it.

'La Dolce Viva' was not only startling to read but it also brought a whole side of the art world – personified by Andy Warhol and friends – alive for the first time. Barbara Goldsmith's article became a preface to the incident two months later in which one Valerie Solanas shot Andy Warhol in his Factory and nearly killed him.

The New Journalism's contributions to the interview story have been to answer with greater frankness than ever before the question one is left with after most such stories – 'Yes, but what is So-and-so really like?' – and to depict the entire social setting in which the subject lives; and, where possible, to render the interview in the form of a story. In this case the story develops through such moments as Viva's conversation with Con Edison and her confrontation with Warhol himself.

In reporting the story Barbara Goldsmith used the now-standard New Journalistic technique of staying with her subject continually, until revealing scenes took place before her eyes. T.W.

In Andy Warhol's new loft studio 'The Factory' Viva leaned against the white-washed plaster wall, her cotton-candy hair bright blonde under the spotlights. Her fine-boned face and attenuated body were reminiscent of sepia-tinted photographs, found in an attic trunk, of actresses of the early 1930s. She was wearing an Edwardian velvet coat, a white matelassé blouse and tapered black slacks. 'Do I look OK?' she asked Paul Morrissey, Warhol's technical director. 'Like a star,' he replied grandly.

Underground movies have emerged from Village lofts and moved into uptown movie theatres; consequently underground movie stars have emerged too. Viva, who has appeared in *Bike Boy, The Nude Restaurant* and *Tub Girl*, has been the subject of numerous fashion articles and interviews which present her as gay, hip and glamorous.

*Women's Wear Daily* said, 'Viva's look is fashion ... she is the kind of person who influences today's fashion ... She is a presence. Viva's approach to life ... to clothes ... to everything is individual.' She has been compared to Garbo and Dietrich (*The Village Voice*), Lucille Ball (*Vogue*), an American Rita Tushingham or Lynn Redgrave (*The New York Times*).

The elevator at The Factory opened, discharging members of the press and friends who had been invited to see a screening of Viva's most recent movie, *The Lonesome Cowboy*. Almost immediately Viva was surrounded by people. A small dark-haired girl said admiringly, 'I saw you on TV today, Viva. You were great.' 'Thank you, thank you' said Viva, kissing the air in the manner of a Hollywood movie queen. 'Now let's settle down and watch the movie.' The movie (which lasted about 200 minutes) demonstrated the Warhol cinematic formula. It proved to be a melange of homosexual sex, conversation, rape, conversation, transvestitism, conversation, homosexual incest, conversation, masturbation, conversation, heterosexual seduction, talk, talk, talk and an orgy. Viva, the only female in the picture was, quite naturally, responsible for the heterosexual sex and served as a target for the rape.

During the rape scene Viva nudged a friend and remarked, 'There were about 40 children watching this scene. All the art students from the neighboring universities came and brought their children. I screamed "those children will be shocked out of their minds." You hear me say that in a minute.' Viva hunched in a bewildered shrug. 'No one complained. They were all artists so they thought it was art.'

Andy Warhol is a businessman who is by category an artist. Because of this label, the viewer is either intimidated by what he takes for Art, or, and this is more frequently true, he can indulge the voyeur in his nature in the name of artistic experience. Warhol's studio is accurately named 'The Factory' because here he manufactures a blend of peep and ennui for public consumption. His prototype product was *The Chelsea Girls*, the first underground movie to have an uptown run. It cost about $10,000 to produce and the theatre gross on this movie is now over half a million dollars, causing the taciturn Andy to comment, 'The new Art is Business.'

'I'm really worn out,' said Viva at the end of the movie as she popped a pill in her mouth and washed it down with a glass of red wine. 'Andy and Paul are working me to death with all these interviews. How about dropping by to see me tomorrow when I wake up, say about one o'clock.'

On the third ring Viva opened the door to her East 83rd Street brownstone floor-through apartment. The young woman who stood at the door wore no make-up and her eyes were a spot of intense green color in a face of light brows and invisible eyelashes. She wore red slacks and an unbuttoned red cotton blouse. Her hair was pulled back in a bun. As soon as I entered words started spilling out, 'Oh, God, don't look at this place. I haven't cleaned up or picked up a thing in months. Every night I think I'll die from the smell of dust and that cockroach powder. Just look at those filthy windows. I've got to do something about this, but I don't own a vacuum and I can't buy one. I'm penniless, absolutely penniless. My rent is paid by a man I know.'

Viva stepped gracefully over underwear, dresses, bags of laundry, an iron, some dishes, magazines and papers. She leaned down and from under a laundry bag extracted the velvet coat I had seen her wearing the night before. It was badly burned. 'Look at this – ruined. And all the hours I spent on airplanes sewing that lining. Someone dropped a lighted match on it and I didn't notice until it was all burned up. I was so tired and I took two Midols and a muscle relaxer and drank some wine that I made myself last Easter. Then I had two puffs on a pot cigarette and I was so high I didn't notice. It was my favorite. The only other dress I like is a 1920s dress Andy bought but it smells so of perspiration that I can't wear it. Oh, who cares,' said Viva, walking through the stuffing that was oozing out of a gold chair and past a wall full of scrawled telephone numbers.

Viva led the way back into the bedroom. It contained a sheetless double bed which occupied almost the entire room. On it lay the remains of pancakes in a tinfoil dish, an orange juice container, some sweaters, a make-up mirror, various types of make-up, a copy of *The Little Prince* and some photographs. She scooped up the photographs. 'I got these for you to see. They are of my family.' The first photograph showed a cathedral banked with flowers. 'This is my sister Jeannie's wedding picture. She's 24 – a year younger than I am. There are nine of us. My real name is Susan Hoffmann. Here's my father playing the violin. He has 74 violins. He also has four boats, two houses, one in Syracuse and one on Wellesley Island in the Saint Lawrence Seaway, and a farm in Goose Bay. He made it all himself. He's a lawyer in Syracuse.

'My father had an uncontrollable temper and used to take it out on me. Then there was always the difference between how things looked and how they were. He used to raise horses because he said they looked good on the grass of his summer estate but they were never broken so none of his kids could ride them.'

Viva flipped another picture. 'This is my First Communion picture. The whole atmosphere I was brought up in was absurd. On the one hand my parents were always extremely hospitable, all summer long we had thirty people in the house, but at the same time they were really rigid. My mother was a big Joe McCarthy supporter. She had two looks ... one meant "Shut up" and the other meant "Cross your legs."

'I slept with a cross over my bed – the whole works. My father had a five-foot statue of the Blessed Virgin Mary. At Christmas he put a halo and two spotlights on it. I was with the nuns until I was 20. I was a virgin until I was 21. Then I spent the next two years making up for it. Now I can't stand the whole clergy, Pope, bishop, priest, nun, anti-sex, authoritarian thing about the Catholic Church. But I think that Christ was probably really groovy.

'After high school I went to Marymount College in Tarrytown where the Sisters said I was the best student in the school in art. I wanted to be a fashion illustrator. Then I went to the Sorbonne and the Académie Julian in Paris and all that time I lived at a convent in Neuilly. The last term at the Sorbonne I became so depressed I didn't attend classes. I just walked around and sat in Deux Magots sipping warm vermouth.'

Viva stretched, rubbed her eyes and yawned 'I'm tired out from that Tucson location trip for the movie. I didn't get any sleep. The first two nights I slept with John Chamberlain who is an old lover of mine. I slept with him for security reasons. Well, then, it was a different one every night. One night Allen Midgette and what's his name, Tom

Hompertz, both made it with me. Andy looked in the window and said "What are you doing in there? I told you not to. You're supposed to save it for the camera." Then there was Little Joe (Joe D'Alessandro) who was sweet and Eric (Eric Emerson) who was just so rough.' Viva looked up and said 'Don't look so skeptical. It's the truth. I always tell the truth. People sometimes say I put them on, but I really don't know what a put-on is. I'm just like everybody else. It's just that I'm too frank.

'The whole point is I really don't care — well, I guess I do. Paul Morrissey thinks I'm a nymphomaniac, but I don't. I just like to sleep with people, because I hate to sleep alone. I have nightmares and I like to have someone in bed to cuddle up. Most men don't know what it's about anyway, they're so insensitive and don't concentrate on it. I guess I expected too much from men. Men just cannot affect me anymore. I haven't been upset by a man in six months.

'In Andy movies *women* are always the strong ones, the beautiful ones and the ones who control everything. Men turn out to be these empty animals. Maybe the homosexuals are the only ones who haven't really copped out. They treat me better than any straight men I've known. I was very fond of one girl and we're still friends, but I really like men. Even when I used to make it with that girl, we always wanted a man around, just to watch and everything. You know, if somebody's beautiful, they really turn me on.

'My view of men is that they are pathetic, they are creatures that need help. The only kind of men I like now are men who are fantastically naive and not too bright, like my lover Marco. (For this story Viva was photographed having sexual relations with Marco St. John and his wife Barbara.) I'd rather have somebody teach me but I never found anybody who could. Anyway, I don't care if I make it much any more because I feel there is no point. Like the whole dumb Playboy—Hugh-Hefner—sex philosophy, that sex without love is better than no sex at all. I think that's a lot of nonsense. You're better off masturbating. When you're with somebody who is not really with you, you feel ridiculous.

'When I was young though, I could really get obsessed with a man. Just after I got out of school I had a fight with my father. I had a fight with him about every two months. So I got a job in Boston and then I moved to New York. I moved in with a photographer. He was my first lover. He was twice my age, a sort of classic situation. I was looking for a father. He was the first person I ever met who I could talk to and tell him all the things I had never told anybody. He was my only friend. He was married, but separated. Anyway, he never wanted me to go out anywhere. He was insanely jealous. He even burned all my clothes. We'd have dinner and buy magazines and watch TV and read in bed. He'd make up my face every night. I left him after a year.

'I didn't have a cent and my father didn't give me anything so I got jobs modeling. I worked for three agencies, but I was too disorganized and somehow the word got out that I was unreliable. I guess I was. I kept going back to that photographer and we'd fight because he didn't want me to model for anyone else. It was just a mess. Easily the worst period of my life.

'I had no energy and I just got so depressed. It's not that nobody cares about you; that's only secondary. You're depressed without any reason and that's very scary. I knew I was having a nervous breakdown so I got my sister to drive me to Millbrook, New York, to see Timothy Leary.

'Tim Leary had been the first one to turn me on to drugs. He told me to take Psilocybin, the hallucinogenic mushroom, and I took it out of curiosity. I've tried everything except heroin and opium. I've only taken LSD three times and I don't think I'd take it again because of the health hazard. I don't know about those chromosome changes. The first time I took it, I thought it was a big joke because you think you've got the KEY to the whole universe only you can't remember exactly what it is. I could see someone taking drugs every day looking for the KEY. The last time I took LSD I had a bad experience. I was with a guy who wouldn't make love to me so I smashed his TV set and flipped out and he beat me up.

'I prefer mescaline and peyote to synthetic drugs. I can't see anything wrong with taking something that actually grows out of the ground. But peyote is so nauseating to swallow, I don't know if I could do it again. I never take anything regularly. I'm just not organized enough to get a connection. At least half the kids at The Factory are on drugs. We use them in the movies because they are often the most interesting.

'Under drugs I think the answer is love and the constant orgasm. You just keep coming. That puts you in the Kingdom of Heaven. I guess religion is just a whole sexual sublimation. I get into this whole religious thing – I see black and white movies of Egypt being played on the walls. I can't figure out whether it's too much of the nuns or too much reading of psychiatry or what.'

250 Barbara L. Goldsmith

The phone rang. Viva picked it up and said 'O.K., O.K., I've put the check in the mail. You can't cut off my electricity. I told you, I've been away. It's all taken care of.' She hangs up and says 'I've got to call Andy to pay my Con Edison bill. Andy gives me $100 here and $100 there whenever I need money. I never ask for much. We're all supposed to go on regular salary soon, but Andy says the company is bankrupt.

'Anyway,' she resumed, 'I was telling you about Tim Leary. I stayed with him for about a week but he wouldn't let me have anything except a few sniffs of methedrine from my finger so I painted a mural, walked in the woods and made it with some guys. Then I went home to my family because I knew I wasn't getting any better.

'I told my mother that I wanted to commit myself to an institution so she took me to a place in Auburn, N.Y., but when we went inside, the attendant locked the door behind us and then clamped a name tag on my wrist. I just got hysterical and begged my mother to take me home, so she did. The next week I lay in bed shivering and I didn't want my mother to leave my side. Then I said to myself "I'm going back to the womb. I've just got to get out of here." So I caught a plane back to New York and moved in with my sister Jeannie.

'I took a job at Parsons doing fashion modeling in the morning and nude modeling in the afternoon. It saved all that cabfare I'd have to be paying if I ran around to modeling jobs. After eight months the depression passed. One night I went to see Andy's movie I, A Man and I thought it was fabulous. If I had seen one movie like that when I was young, I might not have felt so shy and different. It's just so honest. People hesitate, a girl covers up her breasts because she is embarrassed to show them to you. In Andy's movies people are honest and frank and open. Most people aren't like that at all. Like my parents, everything in their lives is structured by their religion and their politics and their social relationships and anything that doesn't agree with that they think is wrong. Anyway, this whole Puritan atmosphere has one advantage ... it makes everything seem more exciting when you break away from it.

'I don't put my parents down, though. They had nine kids and the kids are all against everything my parents stand for so they couldn't have done everything wrong. If they had, the kids would just be carbon copies of them.'

Viva stood up, tripped over a cup, kicked at it and said angrily, 'I can't stand this place. You'd think I'd move to the country, right?

Right. But I don't. Who am I going to talk to? Almost all my friends are around The Factory. It's just easier to live here and I'm away on college lecture tours with Andy a lot of the time. We pick up a lot of kids on those college tours. That's where we got Tom Hompertz. We show part of our 25-hour movie and we speak to the kids. We tell them we don't believe in goals, no goals, no purpose. We don't believe in art. Everything is art. The only point is to make a movie to entertain.

'I'm nude because Andy says seeing me nude sells tickets. It's hard to believe. I think I look like a parody, a satire on a nude, a plucked chicken. Since I got an I.U.D. (intrauterine device) and stopped taking birth controls pills, I don't even have any breasts. But lately I've gotten a lot of attention and publicity. Some dumb reporter said "Viva has dropped out of the rat race." A lot she knows. I've just entered the rat race. I want money and I guess a career. Trying to plan ahead puts me in a terrible state. I can tell you what I'm doing at the moment, but if I think about the future I get all neurotic.

'I have Andy now to think ahead and make the decisions. I just do what he tells me to do. Andy has a certain mystique that makes you want to do things for him.' Viva looked up, her eyes blank. Then she said slowly 'Sometimes though when I think about Andy, I think he is just like Satan. He just gets you and you can't get away. I used to go everywhere by myself. Now I can't seem to go anywhere or make the simplest decision without Andy. He has such a hold on all of us. But I love it when they talk about Andy and Viva.'

The names coupled that way made me think of a time when it was Andy and Edie, so I asked 'What happened to "Superstar" Edie Sedgwick?' 'Oh,' said Viva, circling her lips with the point of her tongue in a nervous mannerism, 'Edie looks fabulous. I visited her in the hospital. She's been there for a long time. I brought her a cactus plant because of its shape. They kept a nurse in the room with us the whole time because before I visited somebody gave her an amphetamine.'

Viva stood up and took off her slacks. She kneeled before me, naked from the waist down, and began searching through a pile of clothes on the floor. 'I've got to go as soon as I find something to wear,' she said. '*Eye* magazine is making an official group photograph and they need me.'

At Max's Kansas City, after the photography session, Viva, Warhol and Ingrid Superstar and Brigid Polk, both of whom are featured in Warhol movies, sat at a large round table in the corner. The restaurant accords them celebrity status; Viva sent back her fish, then a steak,

252 Barbara L. Goldsmith

meanwhile sniffing methedrine off a spoon. 'I take it every three hours,' Brigid said. 'Don't let anybody tell you speed kills. I've been on it for years.'

'I just got out of the hospital,' Ingrid Superstar said, 'and I'm all set for action.' She held up a packet of condoms.

Brigid said, 'Excuse me for a minute, it's time to wake myself up,' and she headed for the ladies' room.

Viva put her head on the table. 'I'm so tired and this place is depressing me.' She picked up her bag and left.

Later, Viva returned to The Factory, a loft in a business building. The downstairs door was locked. Viva looked for a telephone to summon someone to open the door. The first five booths had been vandalized and were inoperative. From the sixth she grated 'Listen you bastard, this is Viva. Get down here fast and open that goddamned door.' Incredulous, she stared at the phone. 'He hung up,' she said. Viva then dialed Warhol's home number and got the answering service. The voice asked if she would like to leave a message. 'Yes,' she said and proceeded to express it. The answering service hung up.

Viva flung the phone across the booth and walked back to the locked door to wait for somebody to come in or go out. 'I'll show them,' she raged. 'They locked me out, and I'm going to lock them in.' With a dime and a bobby pin she attempted to remove the doorknob.

During this operation Warhol arrived. 'Why don't I have a key to this place?' Viva shouted. 'I'm not treated with any respect around here.' Warhol regarded her, bland as farina, whereupon she flung her hangbag at him catching him across the side of the face. 'You're crazy, Viva' he said dispassionately. 'What do you think you're doing?'

# Joe McGinniss from
# The selling of
# the President 1968

*This is the opening chapter of* The Selling of the President 1968. *Mc-
Ginniss uses a strategy here that required considerable nerve. He presents the reader the picture of Richard Nixon going through five entire
takes of one political commercial, verbatim, five entire takes of a second one, and two entire takes of a third. I think most writers would
have been tempted to present two or three takes and then simply say
that Nixon repeated this boring process nine or ten more times — for
fear of losing the reader through the monotony. McGinniss's strategy
of slogging through it all, right down to the last word, reminds me
somehow of a tactic Mark Twain used in his lecture appearances. If he
told a joke and it fell flat, he simply told it over . . . and over . . . and
over . . . and over . . . up to half a dozen times . . . until the audience
broke out into laughter, not over the joke, of course, but over the ab-
surdity of the repetition. Something of the sort takes place here. Mc-
Ginniss risked losing every reader in the very first chapter, but the
gamble worked: he captures the reader for good. The very process of
making the political commercials, the sense of calculation implicit in
the repetitions, becomes the heart of the story and not simply an
anecdote or illustration.*

*The* Selling of the President 1968 *is a triumph of reporting, particularly in the recording of dialogue. McGinniss managed to penetrate
Nixon's public relations and advertising corps — as a reporter, not as an
infiltrator — and to stay on the inside through the long haul of the
campaign and record these extraordinary scenes in person. The* Selling
of the President 1968 *is a slanted book, as many have pointed out, but
that does not bother me when the reporting is as thorough as you see
it here. T.W.*

Richard Nixon had taped a set of one- and five-minute commercials at
the Hotel Pierre on Monday morning, October 21. Frank Shakespeare
was not happy with the way they were done. 'The candidate was harassed,' he said. 'Tired and harassed.'

Shakespeare obtained backstage space at the theater on West Forty-fourth Street where the Merv Griffin Show was done, for Friday morning, October 25, and Richard Nixon agreed to do another set.

Mike Stanislavsky, an editor from Teletape, the film studio, was told to design a proper setting. He produced the usual: full bookcase, heavy brown desk – but with something new. A window. His design called for a window between the two bookcases behind the desk. 'It adds lightness,' he said. 'Not just physically, but psychological lightness.'

Harry Treleaven got to the theater at ten after ten Friday morning. The secret service already was there. The day was gray and cold, as so many recently had seemed to be. Treleaven walked to a table at the far end of the backstage area where paper cups were stacked next to a pot of coffee. At twenty minutes to eleven, the secret service received word: he's on his way.

Richard Nixon entered the studio at ten-fifty. He went straight to an enclosed dressing room called the Green Room, where Ray Voege, the quiet, blond makeup man, was waiting with his powders and cloths.

Nixon came out of the Green Room at eleven o'clock. There was a drop of three or four inches from the doorway to the floor of the stage. He did not see it and stumbled as he stepped out the door. He grinned, reflexively, and Frank Shakespeare led him to the set.

He took his position on the front of the heavy brown desk. He liked to lean against a desk, or sit on the edge of one, while he taped commercials, because he felt this made him seem informal. There were about twenty people, technicians and advisers, gathered in a semicircle around the cameras.

Richard Nixon looked at them and frowned.

'Now when we start,' he said, 'don't have anybody who is not directly involved in this in my range of vision. So I don't go shifting my eyes.'

'Yes, sir. All right, clear the stage. Everybody who's not actually doing something get off the stage, please. Get off the stage.'

There was one man in a corner, taking pictures. His flash blinked several times in succession. Richard Nixon looked in his direction. The man had been hired by the Nixon staff to take informal pictures throughout the campaign, for historical purposes.

'Are they stills?' Richard Nixon said. 'Are they our own stills? Well then, knock them off.' He motioned with his arm. 'Can them. We've got so goddamned many stills already.'

Richard Nixon turned back towards the cameras.

'Now when you give me the fifteen-second cue, give it to me right under the camera. So I don't shift my eyes.'

'Right, sir.'

Then Len Garment came out with some figures about the rising crime rate in Buffalo, which also happened to be an area where Nixon was falling far behind. It was felt at this time that the Buffalo margin for Humphrey could be large enough to cost Nixon New York State. Len Garment explained that they would like him to do a special one-minute commercial for Buffalo, concentrating on the rise in crime. He showed Nixon his papers with the statistics.

'Are the figures higher there?' Nixon said. Len Garment told him they were – significantly. Nixon studied the papers for a moment and then handed them back. 'All right,' he said.

Then they were ready to start. Richard Nixon sat at the edge of the desk, arms folded, eyes fixed on the camera lens.

'Now let me know just a second or so before you start,' he said, 'so you don't catch me frozen' – he made a face – 'like this.'

'Yes, sir. Okay, we're ready now.'

'You're going to start now?'

'Right now, sir. Here we go.' The red light on camera one began to glow, the camera made a low, whirring sound, and the tape machine emitted three beeps to indicate it was operating.

'As we enter the last few days of this critical campaign,' Richard Nixon said, 'one issue on which the greatest difference exists between the two candidates is that of law and order in the United States. Mr. Humphrey defends the record of the last four years. He defends the attorney general and his policies. I completely disagree with him in that respect. I say that when crime has been going up nine times as fast as population, when we've had riots in three hundred cities that have cost us two hundred dead and seven thousand injured, when forty-three percent of the American people are afraid to walk in the streets of their cities at night, then it's time for a complete housecleaning, it's time for a new attorney general, it's time to wage an all-out war against crime in the United States. I pledge that kind of activity. And I pledge to you that we will again have freedom from fear in the cities and in the streets of America.'

He turned immediately to a technician.

'Let's try it once more,' he said. 'That was a little too long.'

Frank Shakespeare said something from the side of the stage.

'Well, we won't use that one,' Richard Nixon said. 'Because I have another thought. I have to cut it just a little in the outset.'

Frank Shakespeare said something else. The tape machine beeped three times.

'Yeah, I know, but we want to get another thought in at the last,' Richard Nixon said.

Mike Stanislavsky stepped from behind a camera. 'When you bring your head up and start talking, bring your head up and look at the camera for a moment...'

'Yeah.' Richard Nixon nodded.

'...and then start talking so that we can...'

'Okay, Mike?' a floor man asked.

Mike Stanislavsky turned. 'Let's have quiet on the floor, please. There was a little noise during the last take. Stand by, please, here we go.' He looked at Nixon. 'When you're ready,' he said.

'As we enter the last few days of this critical campaign,' Richard Nixon said, 'there's one issue on which the difference between the candidates is crystal clear. And that's the issue of law and order in the United States. Mr. Humphrey defends the record of the last four years, defends the attorney general and his policies.' Nixon shook his head, to indicate disagreement. 'I completely disagree with him,' he said. 'I say that when crime goes up nine times as fast as population, and when forty-three percent of the American people are afraid to walk on the streets of their cities at night, it's time for a complete housecleaning. I pledge a new attorney general. I pledge an—' He stumbled here as the pledges bumped one against the other in his mind.

'Oh, start again,' he said. 'Can you just keep it rolling?'

There were three beeps from the tape machine.

'Quiet, please, here we go,' Mike Stanislavsky said. 'When you're ready.'

Al Scott and Harry Treleaven were watching from a control room one flight below the stage.

'I wish he'd use a teleprompter,' Treleaven said.

'That's been bugging me for a year,' Scott said. 'People think he's reading anyway.'

Nixon had refused the teleprompter from the start. He kept all the figures -- crime rising nine times as fast ... 300 cities ... 200 dead ... 7,000 injured ... 43 percent of the American people afraid ... He kept them all in his head, like the date of the Battle of Hastings.

Now he was starting again: 'As we enter the last few days of the nineteen sixty-eight campaign, there is one issue on which there is a critical difference of opinion between the two candidates and that's on the issue of law and order in the United States. Mr. Humphrey pledges that he will continue the policies of the last—'

He stopped.

'I don't like that, either,' he said. 'Let's – We'll do another one here.'

Again, three beeps from the machine. Richard Nixon sat at the edge of the desk, looking at the floor. He rested his chin on his fist.

'Thinking of the exact timing on this, and I'll get it right.' He paused, then nodded.

'All right,' he said.

'Okay!' Mike Stanislavsky asked. 'All right. Stand by. Here we go again, please. Quiet.'

'As we enter the last few days of this critical campaign of nineteen sixty-eight, there is one issue on which there is a complete difference of opinion between the two candidates. That's the issue of law and order in the United States. Mr. Humphrey defends the record of the last four years, he defends the attorney general and his policies. I completely disagree. I say that when we have had crime going up nine times as fast as population, and when forty-three percent of the American people are afraid to walk on the streets of their cities at night, it's time for a new policy. I pledge a new attorney general. I pledge an all-out war against organized crime in this country. I pledge that we shall have policies that will restore freedom from fear on the streets of the cities of America, and all over this great land of ours.'

The cameras stopped.

'It's all right if it's a little short,' Richard Nixon said.

'Okay. Good.'

'We'll try it one more,' Nixon said, 'just to give you—' He motioned with his hand to indicate he wanted the cameras on. 'Now, if you want, and then I'll give you a Buffalo.'

Three beeps from the machine. Frank Shakespeare stepped forward, not sure what was happening.

'Yeah, I'll try one more,' Nixon told him.

'We're ready when you are, Mike,' a floor man said.

'Okay, quiet on the floor, please. Here we go. We're ready when you are, sir.'

Nixon had it together now; all the phrases arranged properly in his mind. This was the finished product. This one would have cadence along with the statistics.

'As we enter the last few days of this campaign of nineteen sixty-eight there's one issue on which there is a complete difference of opinion between the two candidates for President. And that's on the issue of law and order in the United States. Mr. Humphrey defends the record of the last four years, he defends the attorney general and his policies. I completely disagree.' The headshake was more pronounced this time. 'I say that when crime's been going up nine times as fast as population, when forty-three percent of the American people indicated in a recent poll that they're afraid to walk on the streets of their cities at night, we need a complete housecleaning in Washington. I pledge a new attorney general. I pledge an all-out war against organized crime in this country. I pledge that the first civil right of every American, the right to be free from domestic violence, will again be recognized and protected in this great country of ours.'

He was finished.

'Okay,' he said. 'That gives you another two to play with. Now we'll try Buffalo.'

Three beeps.

'This is again one minute?' Richard Nixon asked.

'Okay, Mike?' a floor man asked.

'Right, one minute. Quiet on the floor. Here we go, please. Ready when you are, sir.'

Richard Nixon looked at the camera with an expression of concern on his face. '*Are the figures higher there?*' he had asked. 'In reading some recent FBI statistics, I found that Buffalo and Erie County was one of the areas in the nation in which we've had an appalling rise in crime. I think we can do something about it. But we can't do something about it if we continue the old leadership. Mr. Humphrey pledges a continuation of that leadership. He defends the attorney general and his policies. I pledge a new attorney general. We will wage an all-out war against organized crime all over this nation. We're going to make the cities of our country, the streets of our country, free from fear again. With your help on November fifth, the first civil right of every American, the right to be free from domestic violence, will again be a right that you will have.'

That 'first civil right' line had not come back to him until the final version of the first commercial. But it pleased him so, the way it marched out of his mouth, that he was reluctant to abandon it. It was as if an old friend had paid him a surprise visit this gloomy morning.

'Let's try it once more,' Richard Nixon said.

'Damned good,' Frank Shakespeare said.

There were three beeps from the tape machine.

'Well, we can even use that, but we'll try it again,' Nixon said.

Shakespeare stepped forward. 'If you do this, and you end it again, say, "it will again be a right that you will have here in Buffalo," so that you'll have Buffalo—'

Richard Nixon was nodding. 'Uh-huh. That's right.'

'Ready when you are, Mike,' the floor man said.

'Okay? Quiet, please, here we go again.' Mike Stanislavsky looked at Nixon. 'Ready when you are.'

'In reading some recent FBI statistics, I found that Erie County and Buffalo was one of the areas in which there's been an appalling rise of crime over the past few years. I say that we have to stop this. In order to stop it we need new leadership from the top in the United States. Hubert Humphrey pledges to continue the old leadership. He defends the attorney general. And he defends the record of that attorney general. I completely disagree. I say that we need a new attorney general, that we need to wage an all-out war against organized crime in the United States of America. And I pledge that under our new leadership we will again have freedom from fear in America. We will again have for all of the American people the protection of that first civil right, and that is the right to be secure from domestic violence.'

The cameras stopped.

'I think that's good,' Nixon said. 'What was the time on that?'

'Forty-eight.'

But there had been a technical problem. The siren of a police car, trying to get through traffic on the street outside, had been picked up on the tape.

'Cinéma vérité,' someone said.

But Harry Treleaven considered it simply a flaw. From the control room, word was sent up that the commercial would have to be done again.

'Ask him why,' Richard Nixon said.

'Tell him we had a technical problem,' Garment said.

But that was not enough of an explanation.

'We don't want to do it again unless it's absolutely necessary,' Frank Shakespeare said. He could see that Nixon's mood, which had been considered exceptionally sunny until now, was fading.

'It's absolutely necessary,' Garment said from the control room.

'Why?' Shakespeare said.

'You'd better go up and explain it, Len,' Harry Treleaven said.

Len Garment went upstairs. As he was on his way, Nixon said to Shakespeare, 'Make sure you ask him why, so then I'll know what changes to make – if he wants a different tone or something.'

'I don't know that we have to bother—' Shakespeare said.

'No, we'll do it,' Nixon said.

Len Garment explained about the siren, assured Richard Nixon that his tone had been superb, and went back downstairs as Nixon again took his position on the edge of the desk. The tape machine beeped three times.

'Okay, Mike, we're ready.'

'Okay, quiet on the floor, here we go again, please. Any time you're ready, sir.'

'The latest FBI figures indicate that Erie County and Buffalo are one of the areas in which the greatest rise in crime has occurred – No, let's start again. Just keep right on.'

Three beeps.

'Okay,' the floor man said.

'All right,' Richard Nixon said.

'Any time you're ready,' Mike Stanislavsky said.

Nixon began, 'In reading the—' He closed his eyes and winced.

'No,' he said.

Three beeps from the machine.

'All right,' Nixon said. 'In reading the latest FBI figures I found that the most appalling rise in crime— Uh-uh. No.'

He shook his head again. There were three more beeps from the tape machine. He looked at the floor again, steadying himself.

'Once more, then this'll do it,' he said.

'Okay. Quiet, please. Here we go. Whenever you're ready.'

'In reading the most recent FBI figures, one of the most appalling rises in crime in the whole country occurred in Erie County and in Buffalo.' Nixon was impatient now and plunged on despite that syntax. 'I think we can do something about it. Hubert Humphrey pledges to continue the leadership of the past four years. He defends the attorney general and the record of the Department of Justice. I completely disagree. I say that we need a new attorney general. We need to wage an all-out war against organized crime in this country; we need to make secure that first civil right of all Americans, and that's the right to be secure from domestic violence. And to all of my friends in Buffalo, I say to you, you can help secure that right for you, for your neighbors, by your votes on November five. Vote for new leadership. Vote to throw out of office those who have failed to defend that right, the right to be secure from domestic violence.'

He finished, delighted to be rid of the FBI statistics and the people of Buffalo and Erie County and their most appalling rise in crime.

'All right,' he said. 'That isn't important enough to do that often, but that's all right. But it's done now. That last one was a—' But his thought shifted suddenly.

'Now we'll do the southern one,' he said.

'Tell me when you're ready,' Mike Stanislavsky said.

Three beeps from the machine.

'This is another one-minute,' Nixon said. He was feeling the pockets of his suitcoat. Then he began to look around on the desk top where he was sitting.

'Did you take them, Dwight?' he said to his personal aide. 'My little notes I had here?'

Dwight Chapin said he had not.

'They were right on the table here.'

There was a sixty-second pause while the notes were looked for and found. Then three beeps.

'We ready?'

'All right,' Richard Nixon said. 'We'll have to do this one probably twice, but – the timing, because I – Take a crack at it. Okay?'

'Stand by, please. Quiet on the floor. Ready any time you are, sir.'

'There's been a lot of double-talk in the South about what is really at stake in this election in nineteen sixty-eight, and I think it's time for some straight talk. If there were a straight-up-and-down vote as to whether the people in the South wanted to continue for four more years the men who have led us for the last four years, whether they want Hubert Humphrey in the White House, the vote would be three to one against him. Only if that vote divides is it possible for Hubert Humphrey to be elected President of the United States. And that's why I say don't divide your vote on November five. Get the new leadership that America can have with our new team, leadership that will restore law and order, leadership that will bring peace abroad and keep peace abroad, leadership that will bring to America again progress without inflation and prosperity without war. Make your vote count.'

Richard Nixon turned to Stanislavsky.

'What was that, fifty-two?'

'Exactly.'

In the control room, Al Scott sighed with admiration. 'Isn't that something?' he said. 'He knew exactly how long he had gone. Without a watch. What a sense of timing.'

'Yeah, well, you can try that one as one,' Richard Nixon was saying. 'And incidentally, use -- Mix them up a little.'

Shakespeare stepped forward. 'Sure,' he said. 'Do you want to try this again?'

'Yeah, I'll do it again.'

Three were three beeps.

'This is a very important one to get out,' Richard Nixon said.

'Yes, sir.'

'And incidentally, you— Well, all right.'

'Quiet on the floor, please,' Stanislavsky said. 'Here we go. Any time you're ready.'

'There's been a lot of double talk about the role of the South in the campaign of nineteen sixty-eight, and I think it's time for some straight talk. If there were a straight-up-and-down vote as to whether the people of the South wanted to continue in office those that have helped to make the policies of the last four years, in other words, whether they're for Hubert Humphrey for President, the vote would be three to one against him. Only if that vote divides is it possible for Hubert Humphrey to even have a chance to be elected the next President of the United States. And so I say, don't play their game. Don't divide your vote. Vote for the team, the only team that can provide the new leadership that America needs, the Nixon–Agnew team. And I pledge to you we will restore law and order in this country, we will bring peace abroad, and will restore respect for America all over the world. And we will provide that prosperity without war, and progress without inflation that every American wants.'

'That was even better,' Frank Shakespeare said. 'Those were good.'

'Yeah, run them both,' Nixon said. 'Use them both.'

He stood up.

'Now I'm going to go over to the side and get out of the light for a minute before the next.'

He walked to the side of the stage.

'I sweat too much anyway,' he said.

When he returned it was with the announcement that he wanted to do a special one-minute commercial about the New York City teachers' strike.

This had not been scheduled. It was Nixon's own idea, and to Harry

Treleaven and Len Garment in the control room it seemed alarmingly inappropriate. Nixon had returned to the city from the campaign tour only the night before. To speak out suddenly about a local issue – and such a bitter issue as this – just two weeks before Election Day seemed unlikely to improve either the situation or Nixon's own image as a restrained and dispassionate chief executive-in-exile.

He again took his place at the edge of the desk.

'I – I'm going to do another one-minute, which – for New York City now, and—'

'Do that now?' Frank Shakespeare said.

'I'll do it now.'

Shakespeare said something else.

'For New York City,' Nixon said.

Mike Stanislavsky announced, 'There's going to be one more one-minute for New York City.'

'Okay, say when, Mike,' the floor man said.

'Okay, stand by. Quiet on the floor, please, we're recording.' He nodded toward Nixon. 'When you're ready.'

Nixon nodded back. 'Uh-huh.' The camera light came on.

'As I've traveled across the country I've found an immense interest and concern about the teachers' strike in New York City. Naturally, I'm not going to take a side—' No, that was the wrong way to put it.

'No, strike that,' Nixon said. 'I'll start again.'

This time there were only two beeps.

'Okay, any time you're ready, sir.'

'As I've campaigned across America these past few days, I've found immense concern about the teachers' strike in New York City. Now, without getting into the merits of that controversy, I think that one point that should be emphasized that has not been emphasized enough is that the heart of the problem is law and order in our schools. I do not think that we can expect teachers to go into classrooms where there is not discipline and where they are not backed up by local school boards. It seems to me that when we ask somebody to teach our children we should give our teachers the backing that they deserve. Discipline in the classroom is essential if our children are to learn. It's essential if our teachers are to take up the obligation of teaching. Let's see to it that we do have law and order in the classrooms of America in the very best sense of the word. This is the only way for a better education for America's children.'

There were two beeps from the tape machine. Downstairs, in the control room, Len Garment and Harry Treleaven looked at each other. Neither smiled. Garment shook his head back and forth with a quick, nervous motion.

'That's all right, Len,' Treleaven said. 'It'll never get on the air.'

Upstairs, Frank Shakespeare had stepped forward to talk to Richard Nixon.

Nixon looked up at him.

'Yep,' Richard Nixon said, 'this hits it right on the nose, the thing about this whole teacher — It's all about law and order and the damn Negro–Puerto Rican groups out there.'

Shakespeare looked at Richard Nixon.

'I don't care whether they're white or whoever the hell they are,' Nixon said. 'When they hit the teachers over the head, goddammit, they have no right to run the school. It's as simple as that. Okay, now we'll do the five-minute.'

It was after noon when Richard Nixon left the studio. His friend from the Laugh-In show, Paul Keyes, was with him. Dwight Chapin and all the other men in short hair and dark suits who always followed him around also were there.

As he passed through the front lobby, a man from the Merv Griffin Show, a man who had known Nixon from the time he had been a guest on the show, stepped forward to wish him luck.

Richard Nixon stopped, accepted the handshake, and smiled. A man was holding open the door of the theater. Another man was holding open the door of Richard Nixon's car. The police had cleared a path through the small crowd that had formed outside the door.

'Say hi to everyone on the show for me,' Richard Nixon said.

The man said he would.

'Oh, say, is that funny woman still on?'

The man from the show said he did not know what funny woman Richard Nixon meant.

'You know. The one with the funny voice.'

The man gave a little shake of his head. He did not know what to say. Richard Nixon was the only one smiling. Everyone else was starting to get embarrassed.

'You know,' Nixon persisted. 'That funny lady.'

The man looked past Richard Nixon, to the men who were with him. For help.

Paul Keyes stepped forward. From the Laugh-In show. He was a big man with gray hair and rimless glasses. The kind of Republican who thought John Wayne was good for the party.

'Oh, you mean Tiny Tim,' Paul Keyes said to Richard Nixon. And while everyone was laughing — Nixon, too — Paul Keyes motioned to the man at the door and the door was opened wider and Richard Nixon walked through and outside to where the cars were waiting.

# George Plimpton from
# Paper lion

*By living, training and scrimmaging with the Detroit Lions, Plimpton was able to get the athletes to tell him the sort of things they had never divulged to sports writers of the ordinary sort. Plimpton played football very poorly, but he was admitted to the fraternity, as it were, because he had entered the arena himself and taken his punishment. The Lions' star defensive tackle, Alex Karras, told Plimpton how he psyched himself up during games by imagining that the opposing quarter-back was the sort of person he hated most, the sort that didn't smoke, drink or swear, the clean-cut type who came from an Eastern school and had a 'hoity-toity voice.' John Gordy, who blocked for the passer on offense, told Plimpton how he psyched himself up by pretending that the passer was his own six-month-old son asleep in his bassinet with monsters rushing in trying to destroy him.*

*Plimpton always begins his reporting stints in a very low key, retiring to the far corner at first, not coming on and not asking questions. Only the marginal players, the players worried about making the squad at all, have ever seemed to resent his presence. Plimpton takes notes as often as he can, and while working on Paper Lion he kept a notebook and ballpoint pen in his helmet, since the uniforms had no pockets. Many of the players thought that the notebook was a book of plays and that Plimpton was a rookie quarterback with a poor memory. Plimpton disciplined himself to write down each night the things he had been unable to take notes on during the day. Like most journalists involved in long stretches of reporting, he found that memory decay is very rapid.*

*When Plimpton was writing Paper Lion, he remembered E. M. Forster saying (in an interview in Plimpton's magazine, the Paris Review) that in writing a novel you have to have a mountain to lead all the characters to. Plimpton's own appearance in an exhibition game as quarterback for the Detroit Lions was going to be that mountain. When the moment came — and his performance was a debacle, an absolute fiasco — he thought at first that he had ruined the book*

*through his own ineptness. In fact, he had made the book; his per-
formance reinforced the myth that professional athletes are superior to
ordinary men.*

*The following selection includes Plimpton's description of his per-
formance and also the chapter that followed. In terms of technique the
latter was far more difficult to write. He wanted not only to convey his
own sense of humiliation but also to explain what it was that the pros
have that ordinary men don't. This Plimpton manages very skillfully.
The explanation comes in the words of a coach, George Wilson, so that
Plimpton gets across the theoretical core of his book without for a
moment sacrificing the sense of scene that he has so carefully maintained.*

*At the time (1966) Paper Lion seemed like such a marvelous stunt
that I am not sure that Plimpton's sophistication as a writer was fully
appreciated. When the old Paris Review set was going strong in Paris in
the early 1950's, Plimpton was looked upon chiefly as an impresario
and business manager. It is very likely that he will be remembered,
instead, as its only important literary figure. T.W.*

I came up off the bench slowly, working my fingers up into my helmet
to get at my ears. As I crossed the sidelines I was conscious then not
only of moving into the massive attention of the crowd, but seeing
ahead out of the opening of my helmet the two teams waiting. Some of
the defense were already kneeling at the line of scrimmage, their heads
turned so that helmeted, silver, with the cages protruding, they were
made to seem animal and impersonal -- wild-life of some large species
disturbed at a waterhole -- watching me come toward them. Close to,
suddenly there was nothing familiar about them. With the arc lights
high up on the standards, the interiors of their helmets were shadowed
-- perhaps with the shine of a cheekbone, the glint of an eye -- no one
recognizable, nor a word from them. I trotted by the ball. Its trade
name 'Duke' was face up. The referee was waiting, astride it, a whistle
at the end of a black cord dangling from his neck. The offensive team
in their blue jerseys, about ten yards back, on their own twenty-yard
line, moved and collected in the huddle formation as I came up, and I
slowed, and walked toward them, trying to be calm about it, almost
lazying up to them to see what could be done.

Jack Benny used to say that when he stood on the stage in white tie
and tails for his violin concerts and raised his bow to begin his routine

— scraping through 'Love in Bloom' — that he *felt* like a great violinist. He reasoned that, if he wasn't a great violinist, what was he doing dressed in tails, and about to play before a large audience?

At Pontiac I *felt* myself a football quarterback, not an interloper. My game plan was organized, and I knew what I was supposed to do. My nerves seemed steady, much steadier than they had been as I waited on the bench. I trotted along easily. I was keenly aware of what was going on around me.

I could hear Bud Erickson's voice over the loudspeaker system, a dim murmur, telling the crowd what was going on. He was telling them that number zero, coming out across the sidelines was not actually a rookie, but an amateur, a writer, who had been training with the team for three weeks and had learned five plays, which he was now going to run against the first-string Detroit defense. It was like a nightmare come true, he told them, as if one of *them*, rocking a beer around in a paper cup, with a pretty girl leaning past him to ask the hot-dog vendor in the aisle for mustard, were suddenly carried down underneath the stands by a sinister clutch of ushers. He would protest, but he would be encased in the accoutrements, the silver helmet with the two protruding bars of the cage, jammed down over his ears, and sent out to take over the team — that was the substance of Erickson's words, drifting across the field, swayed and shredded by the steady breeze coming up against the open end of Wisner Stadium from the vanished sunset. The crowd was interested, and I was conscious, just vaguely, of a steady roar of encouragement.

The team was waiting for me, grouped in the huddle watching me come. I went in among them. Their heads came down for the signal. I called out, 'Twenty-six!' forcefully, to inspire them, and a voice from one of the helmets said, 'Down, down, the whole stadium can hear you.'

'Twenty-six,' I hissed at them. 'Twenty-six near oh pinch; on three. *Break!*' Their hands cracked as one, and I wheeled and started for the line behind them.

My confidence was extreme. I ambled slowly behind Whitlow, poised down over the ball, and I had sufficient presence to pause, resting a hand at the base of his spine, as if on a windowsill — a nonchalant gesture I had admired in certain quarterbacks — and I looked out over the length of his back to fix in my mind what I saw.

Everything fine about being a quarterback — the embodiment of his power — was encompassed in those dozen seconds or so: giving the instructions to ten attentive men, breaking out of the huddle, walking for the line, and then pausing behind the center, dawdling amidst men poised and waiting under the trigger of his voice, cataleptic, until the deliverance of himself and them to the future. The pleasure of sport was so often the chance to indulge the cessation of time itself – the pitcher dawdling on the mound, the skier poised at the top of a mountain trail, the basketball player with the rough skin of the ball against his palm preparing for a foul shot, the tennis player at set point over his opponent – all of them savoring a moment before committing themselves to action.

I had the sense of a portcullis down. On the other side of the imaginary bars the linemen were poised, the light glistening off their helmets, and close in behind them were the linebackers, with Joe Schmidt just opposite me, the big number 56 shining on his white jersey, jumpjacking back and forth with quick choppy steps, his hands poised in front of him, and he was calling out defensive code words in a stream. I could sense the rage in his voice, and the tension in those rows of bodies waiting, as if coils had been wound overtight, which my voice, calling a signal, like a lever would trip to spring them all loose. 'Blue! Blue! Blue!' I heard Schmidt shout.

Within my helmet, the schoolmaster's voice murmured at me: 'Son, nothing to it, nothing at all ...'

I bent over the center. Quickly, I went over what was supposed to happen – I would receive the snap and take two steps straight back, and hand the ball to the number two back coming laterally across from right to left, who would then cut into the number six hole. That was what was designated by 26 – the two back into the six hole. The mysterious code words 'near oh pinch' referred to blocking assignments in the line, and I was never sure exactly what was meant by them. The important thing was to hang on to the ball, turn, and get the ball into the grasp of the back coming across laterally.

I cleared my throat. 'Set!' I called out – my voice loud and astonishing to hear, as if it belonged to someone shouting into the earholes of my helmet. 'Sixteen, sixty-five, forty-four, *hut* one, *hut* two, *hut* three,' and at three the ball slapped back into my palm, and Whitlow's rump bucked up hard as he went for the defensemen opposite.

The lines cracked together with a yawp and smack of pads and gear. I had the sense of quick, heavy movement, and as I turned for the backfield, not a second having passed, I was hit hard from the side, and as I gasped the ball was jarred loose. It sailed away, and bounced once, and I stumbled after it, hauling it under me five yards back, hearing the rush of feet, and the heavy jarring and wheezing of the blockers fending off the defense, a great roar up from the crowd, and above it, a relief to hear, the shrilling of the referee's whistle. My first thought was that at the snap of the ball the right side of the line had collapsed just at the second of the handoff, and one of the tacklers, Brown or Floyd Peters, had tracked through to make me fumble. Someone, I assumed, had messed up on the assignments designated by the mysterious code words 'near oh pinch.' In fact, as I discovered later, my *own man* bowled me over – John Gordy, whose assignment as offensive guard was to pull from his position and join the interference on the far side of the center. He was required to pull back and travel at a great clip parallel to the line of scrimmage to get out in front of the runner, his route theoretically passing between me and the center. But the extra second it took me to control the ball, and the creaking execution of my turn, put me in his path, a rare sight for Gordy to see, his own quarterback blocking the way, like coming around a corner in a high-speed car to find a moose ambling across the center line, and he caromed off me, jarring the ball loose.

It was not new for me to be hit down by my own people. At Cranbrook I was knocked down all the time by players on the offense – the play patterns run with such speed along routes so carefully defined that if everything wasn't done right and at the proper speed, the play would break down in its making. I was often reminded of film clips in which the process of a porcelain pitcher, say, being dropped by a butler and smashed, is shown in reverse, so that the pieces pick up off the floor and soar up to the butler's hand, each piece on a predestined route, sudden perfection out of chaos. Often, it did not take more than an inch or so off line to throw a play out of kilter. On one occasion at the training camp, practicing handoff plays to the fullback, I had my chin hanging out just a bit too far, something wrong with my posture, and Pietrosante's shoulder pad caught it like a punch as he went by, and I spun slowly to the ground, grabbing at my jaw. Brettschneider had said that afternoon: 'The defense is going to rack you up one of these days, if your own team'd let you *stand* long enough for us defense guys to get *at* you. It's aggravating to bust through and find that you've already been laid flat by your own offense guys.'

My confidence had not gone. I stood up. The referee took the ball from me. He had to tug to get it away, a faint look of surprise on his face. My inner voice was assuring me that the fault in the tumble had not been mine. 'They let you down,' it was saying. 'The blocking failed.' But the main reason for my confidence was the next play on my list — the 93 pass, a play which I had worked successfully in the Cranbrook scrimmages. I walked into the huddle and I said with considerable enthusiasm, 'All right! All *right!* Here we *go!'*

'Keep the voice down,' said a voice. 'You'll be tipping them the play.'

I leaned in on them and said: 'Green right' ('Green' designating a pass play, 'right' put the flanker to the right side), 'three right' (which put the three back to the right), 'ninety-three' (indicating the two primary receivers; nine, the right end, and three, the three back) 'on *three* ... Break!' — the clap of the hands again in unison, the team streamed past me up to the line, and I walked briskly up behind Whitlow.

Again, I knew exactly how the play was going to develop — back those seven yards into the defensive pocket for the three to four seconds it was supposed to hold, and Pietrosante, the three back, would go down in his pattern, ten yards straight, then cut over the middle, and I would hit him.

'Set! ... sixteen! ... eighty-eight ... fifty-five ... *hut* one ... *hut* two ... *hut* three ...'

The ball slapped into my palm at 'three'. I turned and started back. I could feel my balance going, and two yards behind the line of scrimmage I *fell down* — absolutely flat, as if my feet had been pinned under a trip wire stretched across the field, not a hand laid on me. I heard a great roar go up from the crowd. Suffused as I had been with confidence, I could scarcely believe what had happened. Mud cleats catching in the grass? Slipped in the dew? I felt my jaw go ajar in my helmet. 'Wha'? Wha'?' — the mortification beginning to come fast. I rose hurriedly to my knees at the referee's whistle, and I could see my teammates' big silver helmets with the blue Lion decals turn toward me, some of the players rising from blocks they'd thrown to protect me, their faces masked, automaton, prognathous with the helmet bars protruding toward me, characterless, yet the dismay was in the set of their bodies as they loped back for the huddle. The schoolmaster's voice flailed at me inside my helmet. 'Ox!' it cried. 'Clumsy oaf.'

I joined the huddle. 'Sorry, sorry,' I said.

'Call the play, man,' came a voice from one of the helmets.

'I don't know what happened,' I said.

'Call it, man.'

The third play on my list was the 42, another running play, one of the simplest in football, in which the quarterback receives the snap, makes a full spin, and shoves the ball into the four back's stomach – the fullback's. He has come straight forward from his position as if off starting blocks, his knees high, and he disappears with the ball into the number two hole just to the left of the center – a straight power play, and one which seen from the stands seems to offer no difficulty.

I got into an awful jam with it. Once again, the jackrabbit-speed of the professional backfield was too much for me. The fullback – Danny Lewis – was past me and into the line before I could complete my spin and set the ball in his belly. And so I did what was required: I tucked the ball into my own belly and followed Lewis into the line, hoping that he might have budged open a small hole.

I tried, grimacing, my eyes squinted almost shut, and waiting for the impact, which came before I'd taken two steps – I was grabbed up by Roger Brown.

He tackled me high, and straightened me with his power, so that I churned against his three-hundred-pound girth like a comic bicyclist. He began to shake me. I remained upright to my surprise, flailed back and forth, and I realized that he was struggling for the ball. His arms were around it, trying to tug it free. The bars of our helmets were nearly locked, and I could look through and see him inside – the first helmeted face I recognized that evening – the small, brown eyes surprisingly peaceful, but he was grunting hard, the sweat shining, and I had time to think, 'It's Brown, it's *Brown!*' before I lost the ball to him, and flung to one knee on the ground I watched him lumber ten yards into the end zone behind us for a touchdown.

The referee wouldn't allow it. He said he'd blown the ball dead while we were struggling for it. Brown was furious. 'You taking that away from *me*,' he said, his voice high and squeaky. 'Man, I took that ball in there good.'

The referee turned and put the ball on the ten yard line. I had lost twenty yards in three attempts, and I had yet, in fact, to run off a complete play.

The veterans walked back very slowly to the next huddle.

I stood off to one side, listening to Brown rail at the referee. 'I never scored like that befo'. You takin' that away from me?' His voice was peeved. He looked off towards the stands, into the heavy tumult of sound, spreading the big palms of his hands in grief.

I watched him, detached, not even moved by his insistence that I

suffer the humiliation of having the ball stolen for a touchdown. If the
referee had allowed him his score, I would not have protested. The
shock of having the three plays go as badly as they had left me dis-
pirited and numb, the purpose of the exercise forgotten. Even the
schoolmaster's voice seemed to have gone -- a bleak despair having set
in so that as I stood shifting uneasily, watching Brown jawing at the
referee, I was perfectly willing to trot in to the bench at that point and
be done with it.

Then, by chance, I happened to see Brettschneider standing at his
corner linebacker position, watching me, and beyond the bars of his
cage I could see a grin working. That set my energies ticking over once
again -- the notion that some small measure of recompense would be
mine if I could complete a pass in the Badger's territory and embarrass
him. I had such a play in my series -- a slant pass to the strong-sided
end, Jim Gibbons.

I walked back to the huddle. It was slow in forming. I said, 'The
Badger's asleep. He's fat and he's asleep.'

No one said anything. Everyone stared down. In the silence I became
suddenly aware of the feet. There are twenty-two of them in the
huddle, after all, most of them are very large, in a small area, and
while the quarterback ruminates and the others await his instruction,
there's nothing else to catch the attention. The sight pricked at my
mind, the oval of twenty-two football shoes, and it may have been
responsible for my error in announcing the play. I forgot to give the
signal on which the ball was to be snapped back by the center. I said:
'Green right nine slant *break!*' One or two of the players clapped their
hands, and as the huddle broke, some of them automatically heading
for the line of scrimmage, someone hissed: 'Well, the *signal,* what's
the signal, for Chrissake.'

I had forgotten to say 'on two.'

I should have kept my head and formed the huddle again. Instead, I
called out 'Two!' in a loud stage whisper, directing my call first to one
side, then the other, '*two! two!*' as we walked up to the line. For those
that might have been beyond earshot, who might have missed the
signal, I held out two fingers spread like a V, which I showed around
furtively, trying to hide it from the defense, and hoping that my people
would see.

The pass was incomplete. I took two steps back (the play was a
quick pass, thrown without a protective pocket) and I saw Gibbons
break from his position, then stop, buttonhooking, his hand, which I

used as a target, came up, but I threw the ball over him. A yell came up from the crowd seeing the ball in the air (it was the first play of the evening which hadn't been 'blown' — to use the player's expression for a missed play), but then a groan went up when the ball was overshot and bounced across the sidelines.

'Last play,' George Wilson was calling. He had walked over with a clipboard in his hand and was standing by the referee. 'The ball's on the ten. Let's see you take it all the way,' he called out cheerfully.

One of the players asked: 'Which end zone is he talking about?'

The last play of the series was a pitchout — called a flip on some teams — a long lateral to the number four back running parallel to the line and cutting for the eight hole at left end. The lateral, though long, was easy for me to do. What I had to remember was to keep on running out after the flight of the ball. The hole behind me as I lateraled was left unguarded by an offensive lineman pulling out from his position and the defensive tackle could bull through and take me from behind in his rush, not knowing I'd got rid of the ball, if I didn't clear out of the area.

I was able to get the lateral off and avoid the tackler behind me, but unfortunately the defense was keyed for the play. They knew my repertoire, which was only five plays or so, and they doubted I'd call the same play twice. One of my linemen told me later that the defensive man opposite him in the line, Floyd Peters, had said, 'Well, here comes the forty-eight pitchout,' and it *had* come, and they were able to throw the number four back, Pietrosante, who had received the lateral, back on the one yard line — just a yard away from the mortification of having moved a team backward from the thirty yard line into one's own end zone for a safety.

As soon as I saw Pietrosante go down, I left for the bench on the sidelines at midfield, a long run from where I'd brought my team, and I felt utterly weary, shuffling along through the grass.

Applause began to sound from the stands, and I looked up, startled, and saw people standing, and the hands going. It made no sense at the time. It was not derisive; it seemed solid and respectful. 'Wha'? Wha'!' I thought, and I wondered if the applause wasn't meant for someone else — if the mayor had come into the stadium behind me and was waving from an open-topped car. But as I came up to the bench I could see the people in the stands looking at me, and the hands going.

I thought about the applause afterward. Some of it was, perhaps, in appreciation of the lunacy of my participation, and for the fortitude it took to do it; but most of it, even if subconscious, I decided was in *relief* that I had done as badly as I had: it verified the assumption that the average fan would have about an amateur blundering into the brutal world of professional football. He would get slaughtered. If by some chance I had uncorked a touch-down pass, there would have been wild acknowledgment — because I heard the groans go up at each successive disaster — but afterward the spectators would have felt uncomfortable. Their concept of things would have been upset. The outsider did not belong, and there was comfort in that being proved.

Some of the applause, as it turned out, came from people who had enjoyed the comic aspects of my stint. More than a few thought that they were being entertained by a professional comic in the tradition of baseball's Al Schacht, or the Charlie Chaplins, the clowns, of the bullfights. Bud Erickson told me that a friend of his had come up to him later: 'Bud, that's one of the funniest goddamn ... I mean that guy's got it,' this man said, barely able to control himself.

I did not take my helmet off when I reached the bench. It was tiring to do and there was security in having it on. I was conscious of the big zero on my back facing the crowd when I sat down. Some players came by and tapped me on the top of the helmet. Brettschneider leaned down and said, 'Well, you stuck it ... that's the big thing.'

The scrimmage began. I watched it for a while, but my mind returned to my own performance. The pawky inner voice was at hand again. 'You didn't stick it,' it said testily. 'You funked it.'

At half time Wilson took the players down to the band shell at one end of the stadium. I stayed on the bench. He had his clipboards with him, and I could see him pointing and explaining, a big semicircle of players around him, sitting on the band chairs. Fireworks soared up into the sky from the other end of the field, the shells puffing out clusters of light that lit the upturned faces on the crowd in silver, then red, and then the reports would go off, reverberating sharply, and in the stands across the field I could see the children's hands flap up over their ears. Through the noise I heard someone yelling my name. I turned and saw a girl leaning over the rail of the grandstand behind me. I recognized her from the Gay Haven in Dearborn. She was wearing a mohair Italian sweater, the color of spun pink sugar, and tight pants, and she was holding a thick folding wallet in one hand along with a pair of dark glasses, and in the other a Lion banner which she waved, her face alive with excitement, very pretty in a perishable, childlike way, and she was calling, 'Beautiful; it was beautiful.'

The fireworks lit her, and she looked up, her face chalk white in the swift aluminum glare.

I looked at her out of my helmet. Then I lifted a hand, just tentatively.

After the scrimmage, the disappointment stuck, and it was hard to ease. It was quiet in the bus going back; everyone was tired, thinking back on the game. We were a long time blocked in traffic outside Pontiac, but no one complained. It was dark inside. Up áhead a police car had its revolving beacon going, which illuminated the interior of the bus with quick periodic washes of deep rose. I was sitting alone. George Wilson came down the aisle. He sat down, and looked, and began talking easily. I was feeling low, and he knew it.

'God, George,' I said. 'I couldn't get unstuck. Those first three plays, I didn't even get to *complete* them. It was like getting into a car and having the motor drop out on the pavement before you even turn the ignition key.'

'It's not easy, is it?' he remarked. 'You have to be a certain type of person to do it well.' He began talking about the character of the football player. He picked Bobby Layne, the Detroit quarterback, whose teams would take anything from him because he *performed* and was tough, the personification of the football player. At the base of it was the urge, if you wanted to play football, to knock someone down, that was what the sport was all about, the will to win closely linked with contact. Wilson told me that his teammate Jumbo Joe Stydahar once shouted at a losing team when he was a coach: 'No wonder you guys get kicked around. Everyone of you's still got his teeth.' Joe himself had none. He was an enormous man, a compulsive eater, and when the Los Angeles Rams tried to pick him up on their shoulders after he coached them to the '51 championship, they dropped him. That was what it was all about: hitting. Wilson himself would be remembered for perhaps the most vicious block in football history, clearing out two Washington Redskins, Chug Justice and Jimmy Johnston, to uncork his fellow Chicago Bear Osmanski for a touchdown on the second play of the championship game that ended in the 73–0 rout. Wilson was a member of one of the greatest teams ever assembled – George Halas's Monsters of the Midway, the Chicago Bears of the early forties: with Wilson were Norm Standlee from Stanford, Sid Luckman, the quarterback from Columbia, Bill Osmanski of Holy Cross, George McAfee of Duke, Ray Nolting of Cincinnati, and Scooter McLean, who was, of course, still with him, as was Aldo Forte. In the line at center was Clyde 'Bulldog' Turner, who came to the attention of the pros through a publicity photograph supplied by his Texas college, which showed him carrying four-hundred-pound cows around on his shoulders. According to a story Red Grange used to tell, Turner fell out of a four-story window once, for some reason – it was never explained – with a big, heavy thump, and when a policeman rushed up, shouting, 'What's going on around here?' Turner, who was brushing himself off, replied, 'Damned if I know, just got here myself.' Hampton Pool of Stanford was also on that team, and so were Joe Stydahar, Ken Kavanaugh of L.S.U., Danny Fortman of Colgate, Ed Kolman of Temple, and then Ed Sprinkle, an extremely rough player who was known as the 'Iceman.' These players made Chicago a power for over a decade, right up to the war. The year after their 73–0 rout of Washington they beat the New York Giants 37–9 two weeks after Pearl Harbor, with a few more than 13,000 people in the stands, and the winnings to the victorious team only $430 apiece.

Sid Luckman had always said that the only play of all these years that would stay in his mind was Wilson's block. In the car after the game Wilson's wife had innocently asked who it was that had wiped out the two Redskins in the brutal move – her tone implying that one of her husband's teammates was near inhuman.

'Well, I ... ah, I did that,' Wilson told her.

I could hear him laughing in the darkness as he remembered. 'Well, now,' he said. 'I may be wrong. Perhaps you *like* physical contact. After all, you boxed Archie Moore and did some rough things in this series you're doing.'

I said, 'Well, I have these tear ducts which react quickly to being hit. It's an unconscious reflex. There's nothing I can do about it. I suspect it embarrasses my opponents – to see that tear-streaked puss opposite them. I'm told that it's called a sympathetic response – it means in fact that I *don't* like to be hit. It doesn't mean I run away....'

'Of course not,' said Wilson. 'But the love of physical contact happens to be a quality that's suited for football, and you can tell it early. When kids, out in the park, choose up sides for tackle rather than touch, the guys that want to be ends and go out for the passes, or even quarterback, because they think subconsciously they can get rid of the ball before being hit, those guys don't end up as football players. They become great tennis players, skiers, or high jumpers. It doesn't mean they lack courage or competitiveness. But the guys who put up their hands to be tackles and guards, or fullbacks who run not for daylight but for trouble – those are the ones who one day will make it as football players.

'What did you put up your hand for?' he asked.

'Well, end,' I said. 'I always thought that was because I was tall and spindly, and better suited for that position. . . .'

'Sure,' said Wilson. 'You probably were.'

I said half jokingly, 'Do you suppose I can pick up a liking for physical contact before the Cleveland game?'

Wilson laughed. 'One interesting thing,' he said, 'is that you begin to lose your zest for it after a while. Take Bobby Layne. In his great years, when he was knocked over because someone missed a block, he'd shove a friendly elbow into the guy's ribs and tell him to forget it, that he could take it. The fellow'd think, "What a guy!" and the next time he'd do better – out of sheer respect for a quarterback who *could* take it. He'd block a bull elephant for Layne, or run through a brick wall for him. But then after a while it wasn't so easy to take, and Layne began to say, "You son-of-a-bitch, you missed your block." The players said Layne began to flinch. It wasn't that – he just lost his liking for it. So he chewed them out. That was all right if he was infallible, but no quarterback is, or ever could be, and his players began to lose respect for him – and when that was gone, his capability diminished at the same time.

'And when that really happens,' Wilson said, looking out the window, 'you're done, and you have to go on to something else.'

He began talking about coaching, then, about its complexities – almost with regret, as if the pleasures of the game with its fundamental simplicity of physical contact were unavailable to him watching from the sidelines – as if it were a frustration and a nuisance to find self-expression in the actions of others. No matter, he said. It was a tough and absorbing job.

And did the coaches change, I asked, under the rigors of it? As Bobby Layne did as a quarterback?

He nodded. 'After a while the coach can't take the losses out on himself. So he turns on his players. He forgets that his players are men. And also he forgets that once he was a player. Why, Joe Stydahar, my old teammate on the Bears, when he was the Rams coach, once crept around a hotel lobby, sneaking around behind the palms – which was hard for him, being as big as he was – and he jotted down a big number of fines for his players coming in late after losing a night game.

I heard about that and called him up – I knew he wouldn't mind – to recall to him that he'd been a player once, and, what's more, a "rounder" – which was what we called a guy who didn't care too much for the rules and regulations.'

'The players say that of Vince Lombardi of the Packers,' I said. 'That he was once a players' coach, and that the pressure in Green Bay changed him into a martinet ... removed him from his players.'

'It's not easy,' Wilson said.

The bus was clear of the Pontiac traffic jam, and we were moving along swiftly through the dark.

Wilson compared his job as a head coach at moments of stress with that of a baseball manager, Casey Stengel, not in scorn, but to make a point – the Met manager coming slowly up out of the dugout to see to his pitcher, hunched forward but moving for the mound as if hauling a small garden roller behind him, getting his short stumpy stride arranged so as not to step on the foul line, all the time his mind turning on what to do, three or four minutes available to decide whether to bring in another pitcher, which was a decision often made easy for him by reference to the 'book' of percentages. The football coach in a similar situation of stress had to marshal a host of minutiae within seconds, and, applying knowledge of intuition, make a decision which if it went wrong, since only fourteen games were played a season, could cost him his job. Often something would happen – a fumble, a penalty, or an injury – to remove the reins and make the coach as much of a bystander as the fellow ripping tickets in half at the gate, or the hot-dog vendor in the aisles. Yet the disaster on the field was his doing and responsibility.

All of this made my own disaster seem far less important, which Wilson had calculated, I'm sure, and it was easy to sense why his men had such respect for him – a 'player's coach' was how they referred to him.

I was grateful to him, and I felt better as the bus turned off the turnpike and headed down the dark country roads for the school.

The players themselves were also concerned about my well-being. When the bus had pulled up at the gym, and we had showered and changed, a group of them took me along that night – a long tearing night through the Dearborn dance halls, all of them shouting, 'Fawty-fowah, fawty-tew,' from time to time, mimicking my accent, and slapping me on the back and making me feel as though I had really done something more than play the fool in Pontiac, until I began to say, 'No, no ... it was nothing at all, really.'

Perhaps most concerned about my welfare following the game was Harley Sewell. He had been eleven years in the National Football League. He had pale, thinning hair, a rolling gait like a sailor's; he was small in stature for a lineman (his weight was in the record books as 230, though he looked much lighter), but when he put his mind to something he was insistent, and his determination was obviously a major part of his equipment. He was always the first player in the locker room, the first dressed, and on the field he always *ran* from one place to another, never to impress anyone, but because that was his way — to drive himself at a furious tempo. One of the jokes in camp was to speak of Sewell as 'dragging his feet' or 'holding things up,' and often they shouted at him: 'Hey, Harley, can't you never get it up?' and he would keep at what he was doing, not letting on he'd heard. Off the field his manner remained the same. A Texan, born in a place called Saint Jo, he kept after me to come down to his part of the world in the off season and try my hand at riding broncos. He was absolutely determined about it.

He'd say, 'Now *when* you coming down to ride them broncos?'

'Well, Harley, I don't know ...'

'I'd sure like for you to have that experience.'

'Well, Harley ...'

'No trouble 'tall to set it up for you.'

'Harley ...'

'Now *when* you think you can come on down?'

'Sometime in the off season,' I'd say.

He was insistent, for sure. John Gordy told me that in his rookie year Harley liked to hear him sing, and kept after him about it. 'All right now, rook, *I'll* play,' he'd say, picking up his guitar. 'You *sing*.'

'God, Harley ...'

'Sing.'

'I can't sing.'

'Sing, rook.'

So Gordy did. There was nothing else to do.

After my scrimmage and our return to the dormitory, Sewell came looking for me. I would be downcast after my sorry performance and in need of company. For some reason he thought I would like a pizza pie, so he drove off and got one somewhere, which he put in the back seat of his car. Only two or three players were in the dormitory when he got there, chatting in one of the rooms about the scrimmage, and Harley appeared in the door, holding the big pizza in front of him. 'Where's the rook at?' he asked.

They told him they thought I was off at the Gay Haven twist palace with the others. He waited around for a while, and they had some of the pizza, though Harley kept a big piece of it in case I turned up. He left finally.

I didn't get in until six in the morning. I had spent two hours in the Dearborn police station, a gleaming emporium where the police serge-ants sit up behind a bright-colored formica-surfaced desk, to retrieve my car, which I had parked too close to a side crossing. In Dearborn, parking violators, no matter how minor the offense, have their cars towed away. I was not aware of this practice, and when I came out of the Gay Haven, a little dizzy in the head from the smoke and exercise, and walked up a quiet street to find the car gone, I sat on the curb, head in hands, and tried to remember where I'd parked it. A taxi cruised by, and the driver, thinking he had a fare, stopped, and after we'd talked a while about the missing car he drove me to the police station nearly ten miles away. Out in back of the station was a big macadam-surfaced parking lot with the yellow tow trucks and the offending cars parked in rows. Mine, they told me, was among them, and I paid up, furious, with no sense of guilt, and then sat in an absolutely immaculate waiting room, as if in a hospital, until the paperwork on the case was done; when they took me out to the car, I drove off with rattling speed through the parking lot to show the con-tempt I felt.

The sun was up when I reached Cranbrook. It was going to be a hot day. I knew the heat would begin to build up in my room, but the bed looked inviting. I hadn't been asleep for more than what seemed a minute when I heard a voice sing out, 'Up you get there, rook. No time for lying around.'

I looked and it was Harley, standing in the door. I had a sudden premonition that he had some broncos ready for me, waiting outside on the lawn. 'Wha'? Wha'?' I said. I sat up in bed. His two children were with him, staring around from behind him.

'Time to be up,' Harley said.

'What time is it?' I asked.

'Eight,' he said.

'God, Harley, I only just got in. I only had two hours' sleep.'

'Time's a-wasting,' he said. 'We'll go for a drive.'

'Harley, I've been in a police station . .

He disappeared with his children, but they were back after a minute or so with coffee and rolls from the dining room. 'These'll fix you up,' Harley said.

I groaned and got up to dress.

'It's best to keep your mind occupied,' Harley said.

'My God, Harley, I was *asleep*.'

'You would've *waked up* wrong,' Harley said.

We went riding through the country in his station wagon. His children sat quietly in the back seat, flanking a lawnmower that Harley had borrowed and had been meaning to return. When I closed my eyes I could feel sleep rock toward me, so I kept the window down to let the warm air, thick with summer, hit, and I tried to keep my mind on what Harley was saying. He was talking about the tough people he had played against, the enormous defensive tackles and ends he had tried to clear out for the offensive backs, the humiliations he had been forced to suffer. He was trying to make me feel better about my own humiliations the night before. He talked about Big Daddy Lipscomb. Harley said that he had played against him a number of times and that while he was one of the best, and he'd been humiliated by him for sure, he was not as good as Leroy Smith of the Green Bay Packers, who was faster and trickier and much harder on a good day than Big Daddy on an average day. Occasionally, Big Daddy would put his mind to it, and then he was invincible. He talked a lot on the field, announcing to everybody what he was going to do and whom he was going to rack up. Harley's worst day against him was in the 1962 Pro-Bowl game when he just couldn't handle him, so he came out and someone else went in to try, and couldn't, then Forrest Gregg tried and couldn't, so finally they double-teamed on him, two men driving at him, and that helped but not much. He had arrived in the National Football League strong and massive, pupil to Art Donovan of Baltimore, where Lipscomb first played, who taught him just about everything he knew, which was instruction from a powerfully knowledgeable source.

I asked Harley why Baltimore had traded such a valuable property even if he did have a bad day or so, to the Pittsburgh Steelers. Well, they'd had problems with him, Harley told me: he was not an easy man, being prideful and quick-tempered, and on one occasion, the year before he was traded, one of the Colts gave a party to which Big Daddy was not invited, and he prowled around until the *idea* that he was being snubbed got the better of him. He turned up at the party and threw the host through a window. There was a big ruckus, of course, particularly since the host, who was a very fleet scatback, cut a tendon in his ankle going through; after that, they didn't think they could keep Big Daddy around. Harley talked about him as if he were still around. The great tackle had died of an overdose of drugs. I asked Harley about his death, but either he didn't hear me or didn't want to answer. We drove in silence for a while.

'The vision I have of him,' I said dreamily, 'is him sitting in a dentist's chair.'

'What's that?' asked Harley sharply.

'I've read somewhere he couldn't stand pain,' I explained. 'He wouldn't get in a dentist's chair unless he had his wife with him, sitting on his lap, to calm him down at the slightest twinge. I never can think of him without seeing that dentist trying to get his job done with those two people sitting in his chair, and having to work around the girl to get at Big Daddy wearing one of those little bibs.'

'I don't see Big Daddy like that 'tall,' said Harley. 'Regretfully, I see him down across the line from me, maybe that shirt out and hanging down behind him like a tail, and then trying to *move* that boy – like running up agin a barn. He wore those funny special shoes – high on his ankle and made of soft leather – because he had corns, maybe. He had a habit, moving for you, of cracking his palm over the earhole of your helmet, so it sounded like the side of your face was caving in.' Harley shook his head, as if his ears were still singing.

Lipscomb did have one flaw which Detroit was able to take advantage of, which was that he liked to pursue and tackle in the open field, preferably by the sidelines, where he could knock his man down in full view of the great crowds he reckoned had come to watch him do such things. Then he'd reach down and pick his victim up by the shoulder pads, set him on his feet, and whack his rear with a big hand. The ruse was to get Big Daddy to range off toward the sidelines looking to make such a play, and then run the ball through his vacated position. The play was called 47 crossbuck take-off, and it required the guard opposite Big Daddy – Harley, say – to pull from his position, indicating that he was leading the interference in a move toward the end, sucking out Big Daddy with him, and then the four back – Pietrosante – would light out through the seven hole with the ball. Of course, if Big Daddy *didn't* fall for it and stayed there in the seven hole, refusing to trail out after the guard, it suddenly became very unpleasant for Pietrosante. But he was a showboat sort, Big Daddy, and the chances

were – at least at the beginning of his career – that he'd move off
laterally after the guard, the long jersey shirt tail, which always came
out toward the end of a game, trailing behind him.

'He had his bad days, I'll tell you,' said Harley, looking over at me.

'Like mine?' I said, grinning at him.

'Sure,' he said, quite seriously. He thought a while and then he said,
'You know of the guys opposite you play each week there's not an easy
one in the bunch, that's what it comes to, which makes my position a
rough one to play. I worry, and I'm occupied with what I'm doing. I
have to block someone on nearly every play, so I usually wind up on
the ground – I *should* be there, except on pass protection, something
like that – but I kind of like it anyway.' He knocked his hand against
the steering wheel. 'Whenever you move, you got to move quick and
hard, the harder you're going, the less likely it is you're going to be
hurt. It's like two cars coming together – the faster comes out cleaner.
Can't have weak grillwork, of course, I mean there's got to be substance and heft behind the speed.'

'Sure,' I said sleepily.

'When you move, you have to keep your body and muscles tense,
because if you're jogging, you're loose, and if you're clobbered when
you're pussyfooting around loose you can get unjointed.'

'Yes,' I said. 'Unjointed. I suppose the same principle holds true in
bronco riding.'

Harley looked over. 'You're coming down to do that, y'know.'

'Is the man goin' *ride*, Pop ?' asked one of the children from the
back seat.

'Nothing but . . .' said Harley.

I looked back at the children, the handle of the lawnmower between
them, and their eyes seemed to me grave and speculative.

Harley turned off the road and we drove up a short driveway to a
house on a wooded ridge. Friends of his were waiting in a screened-in
porch. He hadn't mentioned we were going there, but it was like him
not to. I was introduced around. Coffee was brought in. They heard
about the game the night before and they were eager for details of my
participation.

I sat down and took some coffee. I rather looked forward to telling
them. 'Well, it was a disaster,' I said. 'Just plumb awful.'

Harley was out in the kitchen overseeing something or other, the
cutting of coffeecake perhaps, and he came hurrying in. He said, 'Well,
hold on now, I don't know about *that*.'

'Come on Harley,' I said, grinning at him. 'I lost near thirty yards in five plays ... fell down without anyone laying a hand on me, then had the ball stolen by Roger Brown, then threw the ball ten feet over Jim Gibbons' head – that's pretty plumb awful. . . .'

Harley said, 'You didn't do too bad ... *considering*...' He was very serious, really trying, consciously, to keep me from being upset and humiliated.

'Harley,' I said, 'you're a poor judge of disasters.'

The others on the porch kept after me for details, but Harley wouldn't let me discuss the subject. 'It don't do any good *dwelling* on such things,' he said.

'Aw come on, Harley,' they said.

'No sir!' he said.

So we humored him and talked about other things, and eventually I managed to get just enough in about the game to satisfy them, though we waited until Harley was off the porch, out on the lawn with his children.

He drove me back to Cranbrook after a while. It had been a pleasant morning, and I told him so, standing in the driveway, hands on the car-door window sill, though Harley, inside, behind the wheel, continued to look preoccupied. He was still worried about my state of mind. 'The thing is not to *fret* on it,' he said. 'Your luck wasn't running too good. Just forget about it, and get yourself going again for the Cleveland game – put your mind on *that* bitch. . . .'

'That won't be hard,' I said. 'Listen, Harley, I really am grateful to you.'

'When you wake up, it'll be all right.'

'Sure,' I said.

# James Mills
# The detective

*James Mills first demonstrated his virtuosity as a reporter when he
lived with a group of junkies for three months in order to write 'The
Panic in Needle Park' for Life. He spent almost five months with Detective George Barrett to do this piece, also for Life. 'The Panic in
Needle Park' was written in a rather conventional magazine feature
style — i.e., it did not resemble the New Journalism except in the remarkable feats of reporting — and 'The Detective' has certain vestiges
of the old feature style, particularly at the outset.*

*'The Detective' is sympathetic to Barrett but also exposes certain
taboo sides of police life. Mills's original agreement with Barrett was
that he would be protected by a pseudonym. After Mills had written it,
his editors decided that the story would mean nothing without using
Barrett's real name. Mills returned to Barrett, explained the problem
and showed him the story. Barrett read it, realized he faced political
ruin in the department, talked the situation over with his wife, and
finally told Mills: 'Que será, será. Run it.' This, as it turned out, was in
keeping with Barrett's code on the street: 'I don't move unless I know
I'm right. But once I move, I go all the way.'*

*'Part of it,' Mills told me, 'was that Barrett cared very deeply about
what he was doing, and this was the one time it was going to be
recorded, the one time his life was going to be taken note of publicly.'*

*I think this is a much stronger impulse generally than most reporters
realize. T.W.*

Every evening George Barrett kisses his four sons goodnight, including
the two oldest who are 17 and 19. It embarrasses the older boys to be
kissed by their father, and he admits that it may seem 'a little weird.'
But, he says, 'I think that the way I live I may never see them again,
and I don't want to be stretched out dying in a street some place
wishing for one more chance to see my family and say goodby. So
every time I kiss them it's like it's the last time I'll ever see them, and
I'm kissing them goodby forever.'

Forever can come very suddenly to Detective George Barrett. He is a hunter of men. And none of those he hunts — thieves, drug pushers, Murphy men, assault and robbery men, killers — wants to confront him on anything resembling even terms. Because when George Barrett hunts for a man, he invariably finds him; and when he finds him, the man is not always arrested, but he is always sorry he was found. George Barrett is a tough cop. His eyes, cold as gun metal, can be looked at but not into. His jaw is hard and square as a brick, and his thin lips are kept moist by nervous darting passes of his tongue. When he laughs, only his face and voice laugh. Inside, George Barrett does not laugh.

'I'm obsessed,' he says, 'with the idea that I've got to win, and these animals can smell it. No one's going to mess with me and win because I've been around, I've been up against the bad guys. These animals on Broadway? I'll eat them up. I've got the tools and I know how to use them. If I can't get the best of the guy with punches, I'll kick him, and if he's a better kicker than I am, I'll go with the stick or the jack, and if I have to, I'll use my gun.'

To some people George Barrett is precisely what's wrong with law enforcement. To others he is all that can save it.

In late evening darkness he stands on New York City's West 52nd Street, the 16th Precinct's northern border, and looks south into the flashing neon fireball of Times Square. This is Broadway, the Great White Way, the fabled street of dreams. Barrett calls it the sewer. Down it flows the worst America has to offer in the way of degenerates, perverts and lawbreakers — to Barrett, 'germs.'

Already on Broadway and on Seventh Avenue, down to the precinct's southern edge at 42nd Street, the prostitutes are prowling. Murphy men (confidence men who pose as pimps, then vanish when they have the money) are hunting for their marks. Car boosters, working close to the curb and nodding as they pass each car to see what they can find inside, walk the side streets, always against the traffic to thwart detectives who might follow them in squad cars. From 8 P.M. to midnight they'll do their biggest business, hitting theatergoers' cars, most with out-of-state plates so that the drivers will not be around to go to court if the thief is caught. No car lock can protect suitcases against the booster's screwdriver (to snap open fly windows on sedans) or his bent fork (stuck between the closed windows of a hardtop or convertible to flip up the lock button).

This early in the evening the Murphy men concentrate near the dance halls and discothèques, looking for men grown bold on beer. And looking with them are their more vicious cousins, the A&R men, assault and robbery specialists, muggers. The gypsy women, dotted around the precinct in little glass-fronted shops with dim lights, velvet chairs and phony flowers, sit seductively, moving occasionally to the doorway to invite some passer-by to taste the delicious intrigues of the back room. If the quarry enters, he will have his pocket picked, and by experts whose fingers can slip the 20s from the inside of a roll without disturbing the outside singles.

On Broadway, between 43rd and 45th streets, the male prostitutes line up like whores in Hamburg — baby-faced youngsters and broad-belted, black-booted toughs, any type the trade demands. Around the corner in the alleylike darkness of 43rd Street, homosexual exhibitionists skip between Broadway and Eighth Avenue, shouting affectionate female curses at each other. On 42nd Street, beneath the brilliant white marquees touting movies called *Orgy at Lil's Place*, *The Dirty Girls*, and *Rape*, flow streams of degenerates of all varieties. And everywhere, up and down the precinct, are the junkies, the pill addicts and the pushers.

George Barrett's precinct is small — 384 acres, 15.8 miles of streets — and you can walk it end to end in 20 minutes. But into its 70 square blocks are packed Rockefeller Center, Radio City, the theater district, the diamond center and Times Square. In it every month are reported 15 robberies, 20 felonious assaults, 20 burglaries, 320 larcencies, two rapes, and more acts of prostitution, perversion and extortion than anyone has ever tried to count. Every day more than a million people flood into it, some to ebb away as the offices, shops, bars and theaters close, others to stay a night or two in hotels that rent from $3 a room in rat-packed havens for whores and junkies to $92 for a suite in the Astor.

Looking south into the chaos of his precinct, Barrett, says, 'This is a fast track, and if you can't stay in the ball game you get farmed out. If you're a little old lady detective, you end up in a little old lady precinct, out in Queens. Over 20,000 guys in uniform want to be detectives, because they want the title, "Detective," and they think they'd like this job — "Broadway Detective," very glamorous.'

Barrett works in a 'block' of four men. They take turns 'catching squeals' (recording and investigating complaints). This evening two of his partners are back in the station house typing out reports and answering phones, while Barrett, who types fast and would rather be on the street, patrols with the fourth partner. Barrett says that he feels 'ambitious,' but he wants to be particularly selective tonight about making an arrest because his 'swing' (days off) begins tomorrow. If he makes an arrest tonight he will have to spend tomorrow in court on his own time, extending his workday to more than 20 straight hours. So he is going to be selective. But there are ways to discourage crime without going to court.

Barrett has walked less than a block when he and his partner stop next to a parking lot and stand there casually continuing their conversation about the New York Giants. Neither has mentioned it to the other, but both have spotted a tall, thin man who started into the empty attendant's shack in the parking lot, then quickly backed out when he saw the attendant looking at him from the lot. Now the thin man walks past them, and they resume their stroll, watching him. He moves fast, looking in cars as he hurries by them. He is down to 47th and Broadway when he stops short at a car, peers in and opens the door. He reaches into the car and comes out with a toy camera which he shakes, listens to and tosses into a trash can. 'That's petty larceny, no matter what the thing's worth,' Barrett says, 'but let's see what develops.' The man eyes sidewalk merchandise, goes in a drugstore and cases the counters. Finally he is coming out of a clothing store with his hands full of ties and Barrett grabs him.

'Hey, man, what you doin' to me, why you grabbin' me, I'm gonna pay for them, I was gonna pay.'

Barrett and his partner take the man back into the store and find the manager, who says he is being robbed blind and will definitely go to court as a complainant. The thief is making a fuss, playing to a crowd of shoppers. 'I'll pay for the ties, man. Let me go home and I'll be good. I promise, man. I'll be good. I wouldn't lie to you.'

'You wouldn't lie,' Barrett says. 'No, you wouldn't lie. What about the toy camera?'

'What toy camera?'

'The one you took out of the car.'

'What car?'

Barrett and his partner take the man to the station house and up the antique spiral staircase to the squad room. The five-story brick building – often condemned but never vacated – has been there since the Civil War. Its scarred walls are flaking off their millionth coat of paint, and the thick wooden floors creak with the burdens of a century. They walk past a small wooden bench for waiting complainants through a waist-high steel swinging gate with a broken latch. Barrett tells the prisoner to sit down and he settles into a broken wooden chair tied together with twine. The five desks are scarred and ancient, one of them steadied with a quarter-inch stack of arrest cards under a short leg. Wastebaskets overflow onto the tobacco-brown floor, littered with discarded forms, cigaret butts, rubber bands and pins that serve for paper clips. Light comes from four ceiling lamps – the broken globe on one has been replaced with a piece of bent cardboard. The green walls are covered with framed pictures of the FBI's 10 most wanted criminals, and smaller shots of teen-age boys and girls who have run away from home to seek the glamor of Times Square (some of them go home after the first taste, others end up as drug addicts or prostitutes).

A wire cage the size of a large closet contains four prisoners in one corner of the room. Three are drug addicts arrested for boosting cars and one is a female impersonator loudly demanding to be separated from 'such riffraff.' A blind boy is explaining to a detective at a desk how someone walked up to him on Seventh Avenue, grabbed the wallet out of his pocket and ran. At another desk a man, his wife and her sister are reporting a burglary, all of them talking at once.

A detective questions a 25-year-old A&R man arrested for attacking a passer-by with a knife on 48th Street. 'What's your name?' he asks.

'Who, me?' The prisoner is a pro at countering interrogation.

'Yeah, you. What's your name?'

'My name?'

'Your name. What's your name?'

'My name's Sonny.'

'What's your last name?'

'My last name?'

'Look! What's your name, all of it?'

'Sonny Davis.'

'Where do you live?'

'Where do I live?'

It goes on like that, and Barrett looks disgusted. He does not interfere, but he would not have put up with it. He is a good interrogator and he knows that you do not get anywhere with a prisoner until you break down the barrier between his world and yours. You are neatly dressed, relaxed, secure, educated and a cop. He is shabby, nervous, defiant and a prisoner. There is no communication until by a soft word, a tough word, a cigaret, a slap in the face – depending on the individual – the gap is bridged and real talk begins.

Not long ago a junkie prostitute and her boyfriend were arrested for robbing and beating to death an old man in a cheap West Side hotel. 'They brought her in,' Barrett says, 'and people started questioning her. Everyone was talking to her like a lady and she was loving it and they were getting nowhere. I looked at her sheet and saw whore, and I decided it was time someone talked to her like a whore. So I took her into the C.O.'s office and I turned out the lights – people find it easier to tell you things in the dark – and I said to her, "Look, you're nothing but a cheap junkie whore and I know that and you know it, so let's just talk to each other that way, okay?" A few minutes later she was crying on my shoulder and clutching my hands and telling me how she went through the old man's pockets while her boyfriend played the anvil chorus on his head with a firehose nozzle.'

Screams – long, piercing female screams – rise up from downstairs. Scuffling sounds on the stairs, and then a tall, attractive blond prostitute arrives with two plainclothesmen. Tears and mascara flow down her cheeks. 'I want to see the captain! You can't lock me up! I didn't do anything! I want to call my lawyer!' The plainclothesman who arrested her is short, fat, bald and looks like anything but a cop. Her eyes flash with the fury of a prostitute whose ability to spot a cop has just been proved defective. The plainclothesman quietly hunts around for the necessary forms and she keeps screaming. 'I knew you were a cop! I didn't say nothing to you! You can't bust me!' A detective fingerprinting the A&R man suddenly turns from the fingerprint table and yells, 'Shut up, will you? We all know how tough it is these days for a whore to make a good honest living and how all your civil rights are being violated and all that, but just shut the hell up!' Surprised by the outburst, she quiets down and sits in a corner muttering through her tears.

A patrolman walks in with a sharply dressed young lawyer who is slightly tipsy. The lawyer and a friend, also drunk, had been creating a disturbance on Broadway and when the cop told them to move, the lawyer informed his friend that he would 'take care of this,' then offered $25 to the cop 'to get lost.' Afraid that the lawyer might later claim that he had succeeded with the bribe, the cop arrested him for attempting it.

'I want to call my lawyer,' the lawyer said, and was given a phone.

He dialed a number and waited for the answer. 'Hello, Charlie? This is Sam. You sitting down, Charlie? . . . Charlie, I've been pinched . . . Charlie . . . Charlie, don't make jokes.'

The lawyer was put in the cage with the others. In a moment a detective he had not seen before walked in and another detective began asking him where he had been. Taking the first detective for a suspect, the lawyer shouted from the cage, 'Don't answer that! You don't have to answer any questions! You want a lawyer? I'll represent you!'

The detective looked at him, incredulous. 'You'll represent me? Buddy, you are the one in the cage. Me, I'm going home.'

'That's too bad, really too bad,' Barrett said, discussing the lawyer's case. 'I mean he was just a little drunk, showing off to his friend, and now he has to go down to court and really feel humiliated in front of the judge and the other attorneys. Not much will happen to him, but it's a shame it ever got this far. It never would have if the cop hadn't suspected he might pull a fast one on him. He did break a law offering the cop money, and the cop had to protect himself.'

Barret was typing up records on his thief when a distinguished looking middle-aged man appeared in the doorway. Barrett looked up and stopped typing, but did not take his fingers from the keys. 'Yes,' he said, 'may I help you?' The man came in and sat in a chair by the desk. He said he had been walking on 47th Street when he felt for his wallet and it was missing. It had had $250 in it. His car was in a garage and he needed five dollars to get it out. He was vice president of a business in New Jersey, where he lived, and was very careful to be polite and agreeable.

Barrett listened to the man without a word. When he was through Barrett sat back and said, 'You just told me what happened. Now, listen, okay? Because I'm going to tell you what really happened. You thought you were going to get something from the Gypsy, right? From the shop there on 47th between Broadway and Eighth Avenue. You had a couple of drinks and she looked good and she hustled you into the place and picked your pocket, right?'

The man looked startled and confused, trying to decide if he should lie or not.

'Look,' Barrett said, 'you're a big boy now. You thought you were going to get something, and what you really got was hustled. So be a man and go over to the phone there and make a reverse call to New Jersey and ask your wife or a friend to come and get you. And don't tell me cute little stories about losing your wallet, you understand? Because I wasn't born yesterday, either.' He paused. 'If you want me to go over and try to get your money back, I'll do that.'

The man stood up and offered his hand to Barrett. 'Thank you,' he said. 'You're a good man, a really good man.' Barrett stared at the typewriter, and did not shake hands. The man went back down the stairs. Barrett sat there looking at the keys, not typing. Finally he said,

'All he wants is five bucks to get home. He never thought of taking a tube for 30c. He comes in here with a phony story like that and he expects me to give him $5.'

A patrolman came up from downstairs and said the man was still there and that he said he had changed his mind and would like Barrett to go over to the Gypsy shop and try to get his money back.

Barrett went with him and on the way the man said, 'You are really very nice. May I ask, sir, what school you went to? I went to Dartmouth.'

'That's fine,' Barrett said. 'I went to PS12.'

They got to the shop and Barrett banged on the door, but the lights were out and no one answered. 'When they make a good score, they move to another shop,' Barrett said. 'If you want to come tomorrow, I'll come back with you and see what I can do.'

'No thanks,' the man said. 'Come back yourself and if you get the money give it away.' He walked off.

'He couldn't care less about locking up someone who just beat him for $250,' Barrett said. 'All he cares about is $5 to get his car.'

Barrett went back and finished the paper work and fingerprinting on his prisoner. He was not about to spend a day off to take a petty thief to court, so he found another detective who had to go to court anyway and asked him to take this prisoner too. The court appearance would only be to set bail and there would be no sworn testimony, but nevertheless the detective would be violating procedure to take in someone else's prisoner. He had never done this before, argued, and finally agreed reluctantly. Leaving the station house to continue patrol, Barrett's partner asked what the problem had been. 'Nothing,' Barrett said, 'he just lost his virginity tonight, that's all. He'll be a good cop.'

Back on patrol, at 2 A.M., they walk from Broadway's bright lights into a cave of darkness on West 43rd Street. The back of a theater, a flat brick wall with iron fire escapes hanging on it, rises high on the left. On the right a dim glow of light comes from the loading platforms of the New York *Times* press room. A few pressmen, wearing hats folded from newspapers, stand by the platforms watching an argument across the street. Two homosexuals are shouting at each other and four others are watching. All are wearing high female wigs, long earrings, false eyelashes and makeup. Barrett stops beside the watching pressmen and listens to the argument. His partner keeps going and says, 'Come on, George, you know you're not going to make an arrest, so why look?' Barrett is not going to make an arrest, but he is not going to ignore an assault either.

Suddenly one of the homosexuals, a Negro, knocks the other into the street and jumps on top, hitting him. Barrett starts toward them, and a pressman says, 'Look out, he has a knife.' Barrett grabs the Negro by the shirt, yanks him off the victim and slams him up against the theater wall. The man's wig goes flying into the gutter.

The one who was on the bottom gets up, a cut under his left eye. The others are walking away, trying to get out of sight before Barrett notices them. Barrett yells for them to come back and he collects them all under a fire escape. The man who had been on top is still against the wall, and Barrett ignores him. The others are all talking at once.

'Quiet!' Barrett orders. 'No one talks unless I ask something. Because I won this little show, right? So we play this ball game my way.' He writes their names and addresses in a notebook and then asks the one who was beaten if he wants to prefer charges. He says, 'No, I just want to leave it where it's at.' Barrett then asks each the same questions and gets from each the same answers:

'Are you male?'

'Yes.'

'Are you a homosexual?'

'Yes.'

'Are you a female impersonator?'

'No.'

They have said no to the last because impersonating a female is a crime, but so long as they do not actually wear female clothes they cannot be arrested.

The man who had been on top walks over to the gutter and retrieves his wig.

'Hey, germ!' Barrett yells at him. 'Come here!'

The man adjusts the wig on his head as Barrett asks him his name and address. The man gives the same answers to the same questions.

'Now,' Barrett says, indicating everyone except the attacker, 'all of you germs walk up this street to Broadway and get lost. Don't come back.' They take off.

Then he starts walking the other way, toward Eighth Avenue, with the last one.

'Now listen to me, germ,' he says as they walk. 'A lot of people saw this little thing and I'd be a lot better off if I locked you up. But I'm not going to.'

'Man, don't lock me up. I didn't do nothing'. That bitch called me a nigger, and I'm not going to take that from her or anyone else.'

'Yeah. Well, I'm a member of the N.A.A.C.P. myself, but I don't go around trying to put knives in people. And you're not listening to me. I'm not going to lock you up. I'm going to walk you around the corner to the subway and you're going to run down into that hole and get out of here and if you ever come back I'm going to drill you right between the eyes, you understand that? You get that? And do you know how unhappy that's going to make me? That's going to make me so unhappy I'm going to go out and eat a big steak dinner and then go home and sleep for 10 hours. So get in that hole and get out of here.'

The man disappears down into the subway.

Later, in a Times Square bar, he felt he should explain about what he had done. 'I have nothing against homosexuals,' he said. 'They're sick, and I understand that, but that doesn't mean they have a right to go around trying to kill each other. I mean, no one said it was open season on fags this week. A lot of detectives wouldn't have done anything about that, especially since the guy was a Negro. They would have been afraid to get involved. Afraid of ending up in front of a grand jury. I got their names and addresses and admissions that they are homosexuals and that no one wants to prefer charges. So tomorrow when one of those guys from the *Times* calls up headquarters and wants to know how come some detective was manhandling a fine upstanding citizen, I'll be prepared to explain myself. But most cops would have been afraid to do that in front of all those witnesses, so they would have either walked away or just stood there and watched a homicide. So I roughed someone up – all right, but at least he won't do life for murder, and the guy he was on top of isn't dead.

'Lawyers spend weeks preparing a case, a judge spends weeks considering it, but I've got to make a decision in a second. Does he have a knife? Does he have a gun? Should I hit him? How hard? If I don't hit him hard enough he can kill me. If I hit him too hard I'm brutal. I don't move unless I know I'm right, but when I do move I'm prepared to move all the way. Most cops today just stand there running the whole legal case over in their minds, and meanwhile someone's being stabbed to death. That's why I like working with Sam Huff [a nickname for an enormous detective named Bob Kenney, one of Barrett's partners]. Because if you're standing outside a door with Sam and there's a real bad guy inside and you say, "Okay, Sam, let's go," he's going to hit that door and go right through it, whereas most guys would start reciting sections of the penal code to you. They know there's a bad guy in there, but they want to try the case out in the hall before they go in. I like to collar [arrest] the guy before he kills someone, and then let them try the case in court.'

The bar he was in was filled with hoods, and for that, Barrett knew, he could get in trouble too. 'Some cops see you talking to known felons and they figure there's a romance going on or something. They say, "What're you talking to him for? He a friend of yours or something?" But then they'll call you up on a homicide and say, "Gee, George, do you think you could talk to that guy about this or that?" When something big breaks they come to me because I know who the actors are.'

A young, short, very heavy man stopped to talk to Barrett. Barrett shook hands and asked how much time the man thought he was going to get.

'I don't know, George. Maybe a year. It looks like maybe a year. But I don't want to do no time at all. It looks tough.' He left and Barrett said, 'He's a real bad guy. For $1,000 he'd take a contract to hit you in the head. My only claim to fame with him and these other animals in here is they know I wouldn't hand them a wrong one. But I lock up enough of them every year so they know Barrett's around. I'll tell you, I really *like* locking these bastards up. People – even cops – say to me, "George, why are you so cynical, why are you so mean?" Well, I've got guys up there doing 20 to life wishing they could cut my heart out, and I sleep like a baby. I don't feel bad about them at all. Because I think of the victims. I went for a long time on a case once, and somewhere near the end of it, the D.A. says to me, "George, what's the name of the victim, the deceased?" Everyone was so deep into litigation that no one could remember the name of the victim. Whenever I start to feel sorry for these animals I think of the victims, and I'm all right again. But most of the cops today don't think of the victims or the bad guys or anything. I don't say all cops are like that, but a lot of them are. They just don't want to get involved. "Don't get involved," they figure, "don't get involved." '

Barrett has been involved since he was 12 years old. He was living with his family in Brooklyn, and he got a brutal taste of what crime can mean. His father, a newspaper pressman, was on his way home from church when he was robbed, beaten and left for dead in a doorway. He lay there for two hours before a neighbor found him and called a doctor. Barrett remembers that the beating was so severe that 'when the doctor arrived I had to help him press on my father's stomach to keep everything in place.'

A year later young Barrett was walking behind his two brothers when he heard two thugs planning to attack them. 'I slipped into a doorway,' he says, 'and grabbed a couple of empty milk bottles. Then when the two guys started to go up on my brothers, I stepped in and tattooed them into the ground with the bottles. I did what had to be done. And ever since, that's been the story of my life. I do what has to be done.'

Barrett began his climb into the detectives' ranks on a December night in 1954, the only time he has ever shot to kill. He was a patrolman then, off duty, on his way to visit an aunt. He heard calls for help and saw a cab driver struggling with three male passengers. Barrett approached the cab, saw a gun in the hand of one of them, and opened fire. The bullet missed, and the passengers piled out. Barrett hit one in the mouth with his gun, shearing off the man's teeth. The other two ran. Barrett rode with the prisoner in the cab to the station house. 'I had him on the back floor of the cab with my gun in his mouth,' Barrett says, 'and he decided to tell me who his friends were.' All three admitted to 22 other stickups and burglaries – one had shot a man just the night before – and were convicted. Barrett won a promotion to detective.

A ring mark on a murdered man's finger produced Barrett's next promotion three years later. A 20-year-old ex-con named Henry Dusablon, working with a 28-year-old friend, robbed and murdered six shopkeepers in five days, four of them in one day. One of the dead men ran a novelty store in the 16th Precinct. Investigating that killing, Barrett noticed the ring mark, assumed that the ring had been stolen by the killers, and from the dead man's wife obtained a description of it. Hoping the killers would try to sell the ring, Barrett and other de-

tectives went to work on pawnshops. They finally found the ring,
pawned by Dusablon under his real name. The pawnbroker said Dusablon had known the exact weight of the stone, indicating he had already had it appraised somewhere else. The detectives canvassed other
shops and finally came up with a clerk who said a man answering
Dusablon's description had tried to sell him the ring. The clerk had
asked him to return later and Dusablon had remarked that he was
staying in a hotel nearby on West 48th Street. The detectives checked
the hotels, found him, and in 1963 Dusablon and his accomplice were
convicted of murder. Barrett was jumped to Detective Second Grade.
He is still second grade, with a salary of $9,714.

The kind of detective Barrett accuses of wanting to play it safe and
shun involvement can easily do so. The city itself has inadvertently
conspired to keep the detective off the streets, to urge him into inacti-
vity. He must spend hours every day typing out forests of forms regarding not only serious crimes but such relatively petty and alien matters
as lost keychains and fountain pens, clearly unsolvable petty thefts, and
the chronic, crank complaints of almost anyone who wants to walk up
the 23 steps to the squad room. If he makes a significant arrest, the
number of reports multiplies. He must fill out forms on everything
from the prisoner's aliases to detailed descriptions of his hair, eyes,
nose, mouth, chin, ears, eyebrows, build and speech ('Check one: gruff,
soft, refined, coarse, accented, effeminate, high-pitched, lisping, stutter-
ing, rapid speaker, slow speaker, mute, tongue-tied'). A juvenile drug addict arrested under anything but the most ordinary circumstances pre-
cipates a flurry of 22 forms and reports, all typed out by the arresting
officer. A detective who could make 10 or 20 vice or narcotics arrests
in one night actually makes only one or two because he knows it will
take him the rest of his time to finish the paper work. And when the
detective is not filling in forms and answering phones, he performs
other nonpolice functions, such as fingerprinting applicants for government jobs and credentials. Many detectives feel like clerks. 'We may
not be fighting crime,' says Barrett, 'but we're sure recording it.'

When the detective is not typing, he is in court. Though many large
cities require the arresting officer's presence in court only when his
testimony is needed, New York demands him there whenever the defendant appears. Criminals and their lawyers, knowing this, sometimes
delay cases repeatedly, waiting for the one morning the detective does
not show up to move for dismissal on the grounds that he is not there

and cannot testify. For every arrest made, the detective spends hours, often days, in court, much of it on his own time.

When the paper work and the court appearances are out of the way, the detective is permitted to be a detective — almost. He goes out on a case with the very certain knowledge that for being too much of a cop he can wreck his career. He knows that he may have to decide between risking his life or his job; and it is this knowledge that pressures him not to be a cop.

This urge to play it safe, not to get involved, not to enforce the law, has had a long, gradual genesis. In the past few years Supreme Court decisions concerning search, seizure of evidence, arrest, and prisoner interrogation have created an atmosphere of confusion and uncertainty among the police. Not sure what they can legally do, the police have frequently responded by doing nothing. And when a policeman does take action, he may find himself subjected to great pressure and criticism, especially if the person he acts against is a Negro. Reasonable police force often is equated with brutality. Two recent and widely publicized killings, which have had a profound effect on the New York police force, show how this can happen.

In July 1964, an off-duty police lieutenant named Thomas Gilligan was in a Manhattan radio repair shop when he heard shouts outside and ran to the sidewalk to investigate. The superintendent of an apartment building had sprayed some summer-school pupils with a hose, and they had responded by throwing bottles and garbage can covers at him. One of the pupils, a Negro teen-age boy, declared that he was going to 'cut' the superintendent. The super ran into a hallway, pursued by the boy. Gilligan arrived, produced his badge and gun, announced that he was a police lieutenant, and ordered the boy to come out of the doorway and drop the knife. The boy lunged at Gilligan with the knife. Gilligan fired a warning shot into the front of the building. The boy then swung with the knife, cutting Gilligan's right arm. The boy attacked again, and Gilligan fired a bullet through his arm into his chest. Still stabbing, the youth once more went at the cop. Gilligan then fired into the boy's abdomen, killing him.

The boy's death sparked six nights of rioting in Manhattan and Brooklyn. Posters displaying Gilligan's picture said, 'WANTED FOR MURDER – GILLIGAN THE COP.' CORE Leader James Farmer accused Gilligan of having killed the boy in cold blood. The policeman's home was picketed and finally he was forced into hiding.

A grand jury ultimately upheld Gilligan's account of the incident and cleared him of improper action. One of two Negroes on the jury revealed that the decision was unanimous and added, 'I did the right thing, and so did the rest of the jury.' But Gilligan's home continued to draw pickets, and he was secretly transferred to another precinct. Today harassment continues and placards still show up around New York with the words, 'When Will Gilligan Kill Again?'

Last July, one year after the Gilligan affair, Patrolman Sheldon Liebowitz was on duty at a crowded corner in a Negro section of Brooklyn when he saw a Negro man acting in 'a loud and boisterous manner.' (Witnesses later testified variously that the man was shadow boxing, pounding on the pavement, crawling in a circle, screaming and yelling.) Liebowitz tried to quiet the man, an ex-convict named Nelson Erby who, it turned out later, had had two convictions for felonious assault, one against a policeman. Erby turned and tried to attack Liebowitz with a stiletto. The patrolman got the knife away from Erby and was trying to handcuff his hands behind his back when Erby charged forward, throwing the patrolman over his back onto the sidewalk. Erby grabbed the patrolman's gun and fired one bullet into his left arm, splintering the bone. Erby kept fighting with the wounded cop until a passing truck driver jumped to the cop's aid and struck Erby with a club. Liebowitz then regained his revolver and in the continuing battle shot Erby and killed him.

That night CORE sponsored a protest rally, and Black Nationalists harangued crowds at the site of the shooting. Threats and abusive phone calls flooded into Liebowitz's hospital room, and police put the hospital under special surveillance and placed a 24-hour-a-day guard outside the patrolman's room. A few days later he was secretly moved to another hospital. The day after the shooting, CORE demonstrators marched on police headquarters chanting, 'Down with the killers in blue,' and 'The next cop's bullet may be yours.'

The grand jury's report supported Patrolman Liebowitz, exonerated him completely and pointed out that Liebowitz was a 'mere child' compared to Erby, who was so powerful he had managed to break handcuffs placed on his wrists. The entire anti-Liebowitz campaign appeared motivated by a growing prejudice against police, rather than by a legitimate protest of brutality. Nevertheless, CORE continued to insist that Liebowitz had acted without justification, and the patrolman himself remained the object of harassment and abuse.

These are not, of course, the only two cases in a year and a half of policemen who have been accused of using improper force. Other less publicized charges have brought punishment to some cops, exoneration to others. But the cases of Gilligan and Liebowitz, because the officers involved were demonstrably innocent and because their persecution was so deliberate and intense, have cut very deeply into the dedication of New York's police. That cases like Gilligan and Liebowitz hurt the feelings of policemen is unimportant; that they subvert effective law enforcement is critical. By these cases, and by the continued public badgering of the police department by pressure groups, both white and Negro, the cops have received a message. They have been told that what they don't see can't hurt them. Rather than be another Gilligan, many off-duty cops would stay in the radio repair shop and let the superintendent get knifed. Rather than be another Liebowitz, many patrolmen would walk quietly to the other end of their post. They have adopted the tactics of look-away waiters.

This state of mind worries and angers Barrett. 'Today,' he says, 'the police are running scared. Over the years the pressure groups have been chipping away at us, chipping away, until before long we'll just be a bunch of lamplighters, a bunch of guys marching up and down with broom handles, and the streets will be full of hoods. Just keep marching, keep marching, that's the idea, and if a body falls in front of you, step over it. These cops are just marchers. A bad guy commits a crime today, and he practically tells the cops what to do. He knows no one wants to get involved.'

A cop who does want to get involved can have trouble with his own colleagues. Early one morning when Barret was in the station house, a young off-duty patrolman in civilian clothes came in with a prisoner. The patrolman told Barrett he had just left the station house and was on his way home when the prisoner, a large man about 25, stopped him on Eighth Avenue and demanded money. The patrolman told him no, and the man threatened him. The patrolman then found a uniformed cop, identified himself and suggested that the cop keep an eye on the man who had accosted him. The off-duty patrolman then continued on his way home, but the man approached him again, angry now for having been reported. The man pulled a knife and said, 'I'll fix you.'

'And then,' the off-duty patrolman told Barrett, 'this man I had talked to who is in uniform, who is *supposed* to be a cop, sort of ambles up and wants to know what the matter is. He does nothing.

Nothing. This guy is standing there with a knife on me, and the cop becomes a spectator. He says to me, "What do you want me to do?" I think he's crazy or something. Then he says, "Do you want the collar?" Like he's not going to do anything just because he doesn't want to get involved, because he's *scared* to get involved. So I say, "You're damned right I'll take the collar." And then he disarms the guy and I bring him in.' He handed Barrett the knife.

'Then,' the patrolman continued, growing more and more frustrated and angry as he relived the story, 'then I get to the station house and the lieutenant down there wants to know what I'm doing. He wants to know if the guy actually *hurt* anyone or not. He knows I put my resignation papers in last week and that I'm leaving soon and so he says to me, "Look, you're leaving anyway, so why bother about it?" Here this guy has just tried to knife someone – just tried to knife *me* – and this guy, a lieutenant, is telling me not to bother.' He turned from Barrett to another man in the room, whom he took to be a detective, and said, 'They give you a shield and they tell you you're a cop and you figure you're supposed to uphold law and order and all that, and then they put you out on the street and castrate you. They make you feel like if you do your job, you're an idiot. Don't get involved everyone says. What is this? Can you just tell me that? What is this?' He turned and looked at his assailant, and his rage exploded.

'Look me in the eye, you son of a bitch,' he shouted. The man looked up, and the cop swung at him. The prisoner ducked, and the cop swung again. He was much smaller than the prisoner and not much of a fighter. But he managed to land a couple of punches, which the prisoner accepted without apparent fear and without striking back. Two hours later the prisoner was sitting quietly waiting to be locked up for the night, and the cop was back from a neighborhood hospital with a sling on his arm, which he had wrenched in his fury of missed punches.

A few nights later Barrett was patrolling in a taxicab (lawbreakers easily spot unmarked squad cars) when he saw five uniformed patrolmen and two plain-clothesmen trying to get three prisoners into patrol cars for the ride to the station house. One of the prisoners, a female impersonator, carried a sharp-pointed umbrella. Barrett told the patrolmen to get the umbrella. He said it three times and finally a cop obeyed. Driving away in the cab again, Barrett was dismayed. 'He could have run someone through with that thing. They didn't want to get it away from him because they were afraid someone in the crowd would think they were manhandling him. But we're still allowed to disarm them. It's not *that* bad, yet.'

Later Barrett was telling a friend about something he had seen happen a few nights ago. 'A woman OD'd [collapsed from a drug overdose] on Broadway and there's a guy there who is built like a cigaret machine and he has six cops at bay, just standing listening to him swear at them. There's a crowd and the cops are afraid to do anything, even question him, because he's yelling about brutality and swearing at them and the crowd is watching and he feels like a great man because everyone's seeing him abuse those six cops who are afraid to go near him. I didn't want to jump into the middle and act like a big hero or something. So I stepped into a doorway and told one of the cops to bring him in to me. Just for openers, I was going to hit him in the stomach. And then what happened after that would depend on what kind of ball game he wanted to get into. But the cop says, "No, George, I can't get him in here. He's too nasty." So I told another cop to go out and bring him in. He went into the street and then he came back and said he couldn't get the guy, that he was too mean, that they had to let him go. So I asked the cop what he was going to say if this woman died of the OD. That guy was the last person to be with her. Maybe he gave her the OD. Maybe he killed her. And the cops didn't even know his name. They wouldn't even talk to him. And I can tell you that now that he's told six cops where to go in public and got away with it, I feel sorry for the next lone cop who sees him making a disturbance and tries to stop him. The cop'll get killed. That was a real bad guy. And the important thing is that those cops weren't afraid of *him* – they were big enough to eat him up – they were afraid of the crowd, of someone who might accuse them of brutality and get them kicked off the force.'

He had grown intense, impassioned, and thought he recognized in his listener a lack of total attention. 'These are not *words* I am using to you,' he pleaded suddenly. 'This is *important*.'

'Bad guys' are always important to George Barrett. He uses the phrase often, and means by it a person who pursues brutal crimes as a way of life. He means armed robbers, killers, professional extortionists – not check forgers and petty thieves. He talks about bad guys with the solemn intensity of a man whose whole soul and being is focused on the pinpoint of a single idea. He does not question who he is, where he is going, what he should do. His mission is the extermination of bad guys. He says, 'I am 45 years old, a cop for 20 years, and I am still a real cops and robbers guy.'

Barrett can detect bad guys as quickly and certainly as they can detect him. He has no more trouble pinpointing a veteran armed robber than a doctor has spotting a smallpox victim. He treats a petty thief who has been arrested for shoplifting as nothing more or less than a petty thief. But let the thief reveal an inclination toward violence, and Barrett can respond violently. His body moves with a powerful, controlled force that in an instant can be released into calculated, thought-through violence. For two hours one night he stalked a Murphy man. Ordinarily he does not bother with petty criminals, but he knows that often a Murphy man unsuccessful at conning money from a victim resorts to assault, usually with a knife. Finally, when he had observed enough to make a case in court, he arrested the man and put him in the back seat of the squad car. He sat next to him. The man was wearing a trench coat and Barrett asked what he had in his pockets. The man said, 'Nothing.' Barrett asked again, and the man, looking defiant and arrogant, again replied, 'Nothing.' Barrett asked once more, got the same answer, then plunged his left hand into the trench coat's right-hand pocket. He came out with a switchblade knife. In an instant, Barrett's right hand flashed up and struck the man across the mouth.

'Nothing!' Barrett said, his face twisted in contempt. 'You had nothing. What were you going to do with this? Cut me? Cut me, germ?' The man wiped his mouth. The arrogance and defiance were gone. 'No, man, I didn't even know it was there. I don't cut people, man. I may be a Murphy man, but I don't cut people.'

A few nights later Barrett was patrolling with another man in a taxicab when he spotted a Murphy man waiting on a corner for a mark. Barrett parked the cab, and two of them walked back past the Murphy man.

'Hey, mister,' he said to Barrett, 'you want some girls?' Barrett played dumb, and the Murphy man fell into step beside him and began, to explain the marvels of the imaginary brothel he worked for. It had scores of girls of all nationalities, it had a bar, a restaurant, a floor show. The three of them walked and talked, and the man continued with his pitch until he realized their stroll was taking him closer and closer to the precinct station house. He stopped talking and so did Barrett. They walked in silence for several minutes, and then the Murphy man said hesitantly, 'I sure do hope I haven't made an error with you gentlemen?'

Barrett put handcuffs on him and took him in. He asked him if he had any arrests for assault. The man said no. Barrett checked his record with headquarters and found he was telling the truth. If he had had a record for assault, Barrett would have booked him and gone to court. Because he did not, Barrett let him go and avoided wasting time in court just to lock up a con man. But before he let him go he warned him not to come back to the precinct. He looked at him hard, and the man seemed impressed. 'I use my eyes more than my jack,' Barrett said later. 'I look at a bad guy with my nasty eyes and I deliver the message. Even my wife says I have mean eyes. The other day someone told my son *he* had mean eyes. Here I am with perfect teeth, and he has to inherit these nasty eyes.'

If Barrett hates the bad guys, he grieves for the good. He walks through the west side of the precinct, among the crowded apartment houses, and he points to the heavy wire screens and bars covering the back windows over the alleys and empty lots. 'Look at that,' he says. 'They have to make prisons for themselves to keep the germs out. They have to hide themselves behind bars.'

It is Sunday and he walks over to a playground where some West Side men, mostly young Irish stevedores, are playing softball. He watches for a while, talks to them, and promises to meet them after the game in their clubhouse. Three hours later he walks over to a first floor room with a small backyard in an apartment house and they are all there. They welcome him with shouts and mugs of beer drawn from a keg behind a bar. In the backyard – a weed and dirt rectangle half the size of a tennis court – they are barbecuing steaks and drinking beer and listening to the second baseman play an electric guitar. Brownstone apartments rise five stories high at the yard's back and front, and at the sides stand 20-foot stone walls topped with broken glass and barbed wire. 'This is the end of the old West Side,' Barrett says sadly. 'They've been backed up into a stockade and this is the end of it. They stand out here drinking beer and singing and telling war stories about the old days, but these walls and the barbed wire tell you it's all over. The streets belong to the germs.'

Another detective is there. He and Barrett talk and then someone asks what they think is the single most important quality in a detective. Barrett answers easily: 'He has to be able to move with people, to move with anyone. He has to talk to a Fifth Avenue businessman and communicate with him, and then go over and talk to some guy who's maybe a janitor or something like that and communicate with him. He has to be able to move with anyone.'

He talks to one of the older men, a stevedore boss with bright, sparkling Santa Claus eyes. The man is not entirely untarnished. He has had his connections with the underworld, and Barrett asks him, 'What do you hear from Tony?'

'Tony? Nothing. I haven't heard anything about him.'

'Oh, yeah? I heard he died.'

'Yeah? Oh, that's right. That's right. Yeah, he died.'

'When did he die?'

'Oh, I don't know. Maybe yesterday. Yeah, maybe yesterday.'

They all laugh and Barrett laughs, too, not really having expected an answer.

It gets dark and they leave the yard for the little clubhouse room with the bar in it. They are almost all stevedores and they talk about the docks and sing old Irish songs. They ask for a song from Barrett, who is not Irish, and in his thick husky voice he sings them one:

Sure me name it tis McGuire
And I'll quickly tell to you
Of the pretty girl I admire
Name of Kitty Donohue

He finishes singing of Kitty Donohue, and they cheer, toast him in beer and demand an encore. He pulls his head down on his neck, cocks it, puts his hands in front of him at the waist, thumbs up, and does an impression in dialect of a Mafia hoodlum. They laugh. Not because he is a cop, but because they know he understands them, because he can move with them.

Many of the people Barrett knows and moves with in the precinct are disillusioned about the law. They have lost faith in cops and in the courts. They see men on the streets around them who have been convicted of murders and assaults, and they cannot take seriously what they consider the duty of cops and courts – to separate criminals from society. And so sometimes when they are in trouble they go to a cop they believe in for help – not for an arrest, but for real help. An old Yugoslav man who owned a small bar on the West Side asked Barrett to come see him. For years the bar had catered to a small but steady clientele of neighborhood Yugoslavs. But lately West Side toughs had starting taking over the place. They sat in it and used the pay phone for taking bets on horse races and were turning it into a bookie joint. His old customers had stopped coming in. When he complained, the toughs threatened him. He was terrified of losing his bar license because of the bookmaking. He told Barrett he knew that if the men were arrested, they would be out of jail in no time and beat him up and ruin his bar.

'So one of my partners and I took the guys – and they were real bad guys, oldtime West Side hoodlums – over to a quiet little place by the docks and we put the bull on them. We told them what the score was, and we used a little muscle to get the message home. And then the next day one of them goes over to the old man's bar and asks him how much he paid to get me to put the bull on him, and that made me mad because no one buys my muscle. So I got him and we went back over to the docks, and now everything's taken care of and he calls me Mr. Barrett.'

In some crimes an arrest does so little good that neither Barrett nor the victim even gives it a thought. He is walking up Sixth Avenue and a junkie girl comes towards him. Hurrying after her is a man in a butcher's apron. Barrett stops to watch. The man grabs the girl, reaches into her purse and pulls out two cellophane-wrapped packages of bacon she had stolen from his store to sell for drugs. He takes them back to his store, without a word, as casually as if he had just borrowed a match. Barrett does not make an arrest. 'The butcher doesn't want to be a complainant,' he says. 'There could have been a uniformed man standing right there and he wouldn't have called him. He gets beat all the time by shoplifters. He knows what kind of a bargain basement that court is down there. She'd be back on the street before his shop closed for the night. He figures he got his bacon back, so he's a winner.'

Another day Barrett had been checking on a case in a 16th Precinct hospital when he ran into another detective. The other man had two drugs addicts with him that he had arrested for possessing barbiturates, and he had brought them to the hospital to withdraw from their stupor. Late that same night Barrett was in Times Square and telephoned the squad to check in. As he spoke, the same two drug addicts who had been in the hospital walked past him. In less than 10 hours' they had been arrested, taken to a hospital, treated, returned to the station house, fingerprinted, booked, taken to court, released, and found their way back to Times Square. Barrett was talking on the phone to the detective who had arrested them. He was still typing up the arrest records.

Some time ago Barrett visited Nevada to pick up a prisoner, and since then he has been telling friends – maybe joking, maybe not – that what he really wants in life is to be sheriff of some quiet Western county where people are not yet so callous to crime. He can remember when he was a teen-ager in Brooklyn 'and the cops always seemed to be the best, the straightest kids around. But now a man comes on the force just because it's a job, because instead of being a carpenter or a plumber or something he figures he'll do 20 easy years, not bothering, just stepping over the bodies, and then relax with a pension. Or maybe he's a kid who's intelligent but never really got street wise – who thinks a criminal is someone with shifty eyes and a hat brim pulled down over his face – and he wants to spend hours thinking over every move, while meantime the body's getting cold. And if you do get a really savvy, bright, ambitious guy, after a period of collaring everyone who's wrong, he's going to find that he's living in court and the germs are the ones on the street. So he'll start getting more selective, just grabbing the really bad guys and forgetting about the others. He finds out that with the courts down there, the bad guys are getting more and more right every day, and it's him – the cop – who is wrong.'

So Barrett thinks about America's less sophisticated areas 'where people still know the difference between cops and robbers.' He is in a motel talking to the security man when a report comes in that a guest has been burglarized. Barrett and the security man go to the room. Someone has entered the room while the guest, a Wyoming business-man, and his wife and little boy were out sight-seeing. The burglar took exactly $2.17.

Barrett and the house detective leave the room and as they walk to the elevator the house man says disgustedly, 'What about that? A crummy $2.17 and he wants to make a big federal case out of it.'

'No, no, you're wrong,' Barrett says. 'He's from Wyoming and some-one was in *his* room. That's what's got him mad. And I subscribe to that completely. We're beginning to take this stuff for granted. "Some-one in my room? Oh, okay." Like it was the standard thing. Well, it shouldn't be the standard thing. I'm with the man from Wyoming. He's one of the good guys – and there aren't too many of us left.'

# John Gregory Dunne from
# The studio

*John Dunne's book about Twentieth Century–Fox is one of the most extraordinary things ever written about the movie business and all the more interesting because it was published at the twilight of that institution known as 'the studio.' The Studio is a triumph of reporting, and Dunne pulled off one of his greatest coups when he gained access to the inside workings of Twentieth Century–Fox in the first place. He had a certain amount of entrée in that he and his wife, Joan Didion, were already well known around Hollywood, and his brother, Dominick Dunne, was a movie producer. Dunne took a hard line from the first, saying he didn't want to write the book unless he were given carte blanche to see whatever he wanted to see at the studio, and his approach worked.*

*For four months Dunne, as a reporter, kept studio hours, arriving at Fox in the morning and coming home at night when the lot closed. The major project at Fox was an eighteen-million-dollar children's movie, Dr. Dolittle, which was coming out at a time when the studio could not afford an eighteen-million-dollar disaster. But a disaster it was to be, as the studio executives themselves began to realize when the film was previewed in Minneapolis. The punchline of the following selection — 'What we had here was your typically sophisticated Friday night Minneapolis audience' — becomes the punchline of the book and is typical of the rich dialogue that Dunne recorded. He got such material only by being on hand as key scenes in the studio's own adventures took place. As a narrator Dunne keeps himself invisible on the assumption, quite correct, I believe, that turning the reporter into a character would only be a distraction in this case. T.W.*

**'That's what we come to Minneapolis for,' Stan Hough said**

There was never any doubt that the Studio would hold its first preview of *Dr. Dolittle* in Minneapolis. Fox considered the Minnesota capital its lucky city; Robert Wise's production of *The Sound of Music* was first sneaked there, and with the enormous success of that picture, the

Studio superstitiously kept bringing its major roadshow attractions to Minneapolis for their first unveiling before a paid theater audience. With so much money at stake – the budget of *Dr. Dolittle* was close to $18 million – the Studio was unwilling to hold a sneak anywhere around Los Angeles, reasoning that it could get a truer audience reaction in the hinterlands, far from the film-wise and preview-hardened viewers who haunt screenings in and around Hollywood. The plan originally had been to go to Minneapolis on Friday, September 8, and to Tulsa the following evening, but early that week the Tulsa screening was canceled. 'If the picture plays, we don't have to go to Tulsa,' Richard Fleischer said. 'If it doesn't play, why go to Tulsa the next night and get kicked in the ass again? You make some changes, then you go to Tulsa.'

Because of the magnitude of *Dr. Dolittle*, the Minneapolis screening attracted twenty-eight Studio personnel from New York and Los Angeles. The major contingent from Los Angeles was booked on Western Airlines Flight 502, leaving at 8:30 A.M. on September 8. Arthur Jacobs, accompanied by Natalie Trundy, arrived at International Airport nearly an hour before flight time. He was tieless and wearing a dark blazer and he lingered around the escalator coming up from the check-in counters on the ground floor, greeting members of the Fox party as they arrived. His salutation never varied. 'I'm not nervous,' Jacobs said. 'I'm not going to Minneapolis. I'm just here to wave you all good-by.'

'Oh, Arthur,' Natalie Trundy said. 'Calm down.'

'Calm down,' Jacobs said. '*Calm down*. You treat me like one of the dogs.' He turned to Fleischer. 'We've got poodles. She treats me like a poodle.'

'You're a very nice-looking poodle, Arthur,' Fleischer said.

They milled around the gate, waiting for Flight 502 to be called, Jacobs, Natalie Trundy, Fleischer, Mort Abrahams, Herbert Ross, the choreographer on *Dr. Dolittle*, and Warren Cowan, who was once a partner of Jacobs in a public relations firm and whose company, Rogers, Cowan & Brenner, was handling the publicity and promotion for *Dolittle*. At last the flight was called. As Jacobs and Natalie Trundy walked up the ramp, Jacobs turned to Fleischer and said, 'I just don't want to go to Minneapolis. Let's go to Vegas instead.'

'It would be less of a gamble,' Fleischer said.

Jacobs and Natalie Trundy took two seats at the rear of the first-class compartment. Cowan, a short, pudgy man with constantly moving eyes and a voice that sounds somewhat like Daffy Duck's, sat by himself in front of them and spread the New York and Los Angeles papers on his lap. Jacobs could not keep still. 'We land at noon,' he shouted up the aisle. 'At twelve-thirty, we visit the public library. At one o'clock, the museum.'

No one laughed except Fleischer, who tried to humor Jacobs. 'At one-thirty, the textile factory,' Fleischer said.

'And then we have a rest period between eight and eleven this evening,' Jacobs said. This was the time scheduled for screening.

'What I like about you, Arthur, is your calm,' Fleischer said.

'Why should I be nervous?' Jacobs said. 'It's only eighteen million dollars.'

The trip to Minneapolis was uneventful. Most of the Fox people slept, except for Jacobs, who kept prowling the aisle looking for someone to talk to. It had just been announced in the trade press that Rex Harrison had bowed out of the musical production of *Good-bye, Mr. Chips* that Gower Champion was scheduled to direct and Jacobs to produce for release by M-G-M. 'It was all set,' Jacobs said sadly. 'Gower and I even went to Paris to see Rex. We drive out to his house in the country and he meets us at the door. "Marvelous day," he says. You know the way he talks.' Jacobs put on his Rex Harrison voice. '"Marvelous day. Bloody Mary, anyone, Bloody Mary." He gets us the Bloody Marys and then he says, "Now let me tell you why I'm not going to do *Mr. Chips*." That's the first we heard about it. It was all set. Well, Gower looks at me, picks up his attaché case and says, "Sorry. I'm going to the airport, I'm going home."' Jacobs gazed out the window at the clouds. 'It was all set,' he said. '*All set.*'

The Fox party was met at the airport in Minneapolis by Perry Lieber, of the publicity department, who had flown in from Los Angeles the day before to supervise the preview arrangements. Lieber approached the task as if it were — and indeed he seemed to equate it with — the annual pilgrimage of the English royal family from Buckingham Palace to Balmoral. There were none of the ordinary traveler's mundane worries about luggage, accommodations and transportation. Lieber had checked the entire twenty-eight man Studio contingent into the Radisson Hotel, ordered a fleet of limousines to transport each planeload of Fox people to the hotel, and arranged that all baggage be picked up at the airport and sent immediately to the proper rooms and suites. He gathered baggage tags and dispensed them to waiting functionaries and gave each new arrival an envelope containing his room key and a card listing that person's flight arrangements to New York or Los Angeles the next day, as well as the time that a limousine would pick him up at the hotel for the trip out to the airport.

Jacobs took his envelope and gave it to Natalie Trundy. For a moment, he peered intently at Lieber's tie pin, a musical staff on which the words 'The Sound of Music' were written in sharps and flats. 'You've got the wrong picture,' he said.

'Are you kidding?' Lieber replied boisterously. 'This is my lucky tie-pin. You know how Sound of Music did and we previewed that here.'

Warren Cowan shook his head slowly. 'This has got to be the most superstitious movie company in the world,' he said.

'If they're so superstitious,' Fleischer said, 'then why didn't they get Bob Wise to direct this picture?'

Outside the airport, standing beside a limousine, Natalie Trundy pulled out a Kodak Instamatic and began snapping pictures of the Fox party. She was dressed all in white and was wearing pale yellow sunglasses. She aimed her camera at Cowan, but her flashbulb misfired and she asked for one more shot.

'Oh, for God's sake, Natalie,' Jacobs said. 'Let's get going.'

Cowan sat on the jump seat and opened a copy of the Minneapolis Tribune to the theater section, where the Studio had placed a teaser advertisement that did not give the name of the picture. The advertisement was headlined 'Hollywood Red Carpet Preview.'

'They're charging $2.60 a ticket,' Cowan said. 'That's a mistake. You want to get the kids at a preview of a picture like this, and at $2.60 a head, it's too steep.'

'They should have made it two bucks a couple,' Jacobs agreed miserably. At this point, he seemed to see disaster in everything. 'To get the Friday night dates.'

'It's a mistake,' Cowan repeated softly.

As the limousine sped toward downtown Minneapolis, the chauffeur began to issue statistics about the city. 'There are fifty-eight lakes and parks within the city limits,' he said. No one paid any attention. Jacobs put out one brown cigarettello and lit another.

'Are you going to stand or sit in the theater tonight?' he asked Fleischer.

The director stared out the window at the early autumn foliage. 'I'm going to lie down,' he said. He patted Jacobs on the knee. 'It's only a preview, Arthur,' he said.

'Of an $18 million picture,' Jacobs said.

Lunch was served in the Flame Room of the Radisson. It was after three o'clock and the dining room was deserted, but the kitchen had been kept open for the Fox group. Many had not yet arrived and others were up in their rooms napping. Jacobs had changed into a dark suit and he bounded from table to table.

'Don't forget we're due at the art museum at three-thirty,' he said.

'Arthur's making jokes,' Lionel Newman said. The head of the Studio's music department, Newman had arranged the score and conducted it on the sound track. He had arrived in Minneapolis the day before with a Studio sound engineer to help set up the theater for the preview. 'Arthur, as a comic, you're a lardass.'

Jacobs looked chagrined.

'You know what I call this hotel?' Newman said. 'Menopause Manor. He smiled at the waitress. 'That's okay, honey, I don't mean you. But you got to admit, there's one or two old people staying here. I mean, this hotel talks about the swinging sixties, they don't mean the year, they mean the Geritol set.'

Suddenly Jacobs raised his arms and shouted, 'The Brinkmans.' Standing in the doorway of the Flame Room, with his wife Yvonne, was Leslie Bricusse, the tall, bespectacled young English writer who had written the screenplay, music and lyrics for *Dr. Dolittle.* Jacobs was beside himself. 'The Brinkmans are here,' he cried to Fleischer. 'Brinkmans' was his nickname for the Bricusses. 'Did you see them?'

'He could hardly miss, Arthur,' Newman said. 'You make it seem like the start of World War III.'

'Sit over here, Leslie,' Jacobs said. He snapped his fingers for the waitress, who was standing right behind him. 'We need chairs. Leslie, you want a sandwich, coffee, a drink?'

The Bricusses were pummeled by the Fox people and diffidently gave their order to the waitress. Yvonne Bricusse, a handsome, dark-haired English actress, slipped into a banquette alongside Natalie Trundy, who kissed her on the cheek. She poured herself a cup of coffee.

'What are you wearing to the opening?' Natalie Trundy said.

'New York?' Yvonne Bricusse said.

'Mmmmm,' Natalie Trundy said.

'A heavenly thing,' Yvonne Bricusse said. 'Leslie bought it for me.

Autumn colors, sort of. Burnt orange, with a bow here.' She patted her bosom.

'Divine,' Natalie Trundy said. 'How about Los Angeles?'

'Nothing yet,' Yvonne Bricusse said, sipping her coffee. 'I thought I'd get something made. What do you think of Don Feld?' Feld is a motion picture costume designer.

'Heavenly,' Natalie Trundy said. She reached over with her fork and speared a piece of steak off Jacobs' plate. 'A lot of feathers, though.'

Yvonne Bricusse brooded for a moment. 'Mmmm,' she said. 'I know what you mean. He *does* like feathers.' She stirred a spoon lazily in her coffee cup. 'What about you?'

'In the works,' Natalie Trundy said. 'They're on the drawing boards, New York, London, Los Angeles, all the openings.' She fluttered her arms like a ballerina. 'I'm going to *float*. I haven't even talked about colors yet. I want to see how they look on the board.'

That evening, before the preview, Richard Zanuck hosted a party for the Fox group at the Minneapolis Press Club on the second floor of the Radisson. Zanuck had just that day returned from Europe, a combination business and pleasure trip to London and Paris, then a week vacationing in the South of France with David and Helen Gurley Brown. He looked tanned and healthy. 'I'm still on Paris time,' he said, dipping a cocktail frankfurter into some mustard. 'Stopped off in New York this morning to see a rough cut of *The Incident*, then back onto a plane out here.'

'You can sleep tomorrow,' Arthur Jacobs said.

Zanuck shook his head. 'I'm going back to Los Angeles at six-thirty in the morning.'

'Why?' Jacobs said.

'I want to go to the Rams game tomorrow night,' Zanuck said.

Jacobs looked incredulous. He filtered through the room, stopping at each little group. 'Dick's leaving for L.A. tomorrow at six-thirty. In the morning. You know why? He wants to go to the Rams game.'

At 7:45, Perry Lieber beat on the side of a glass with a fork. He told the assembled group that the preview started at eight sharp and that after the picture there would be a supper served in Richard Zanuck's suite on the twelfth floor. The picture was playing just down the street from the hotel at the Mann theater, one of a chain owned by a Minnesota theater magnate named Ted Mann. Fox had rented the theater for the night, paying off Universal Pictures, one of whose roadshow films

*Thoroughly Modern Millie*, was playing there. Three rows of seats had been roped off for the Fox contingent, along with three other seats in the back of the house for Jacobs, Mort Abrahams and Natalie Trundy. Jacobs had specially requested these seats because he is a pacer and wanted to be free to walk around the theater without disturbing anyone. As Jacobs walked into the lobby of the theater, his eye caught a large display for *Camelot*, the Warner Brothers-Seven Arts musical that was to be the Christmas presentation at another Mann house. He stopped in his tracks.

'Oh, my God,' he said. He looked at the people spilling into the theater. 'Oh, my God, *Camelot*. That's what they'll think they're going to see. Oh, my God.'

The house lights went down at 8:13. The audience was composed mainly of young marrieds and the middleaged. There were almost no children present. Zanuck sat in an aisle seat, with Barbara McLean, the head of the Studio's cutting department, beside him, a pad on her lap, ready to take notes. The overture was played and then a title card flashed on the screen that said, 'Equatorial Africa, 1845.' The card dissolved into a prologue and Rex Harrison, in frock coat and top hat, rode onto the screen on top of a giraffe. There was no murmur of recognition from the audience. Some of the Studio party began to shift uneasily in their seats. The prologue lasted only a few moments. Harrison, as Dr. Dolittle, the man who could talk to the animals, slipped off the back of the giraffe to treat a crocodile ailing with a toothache. He tied a piece of string to the aching tooth and then tied the other end of the string to the tail of an elephant. At a signal from Dr. Dolittle, the elephant pulled on the cord and the tooth snapped out of the crocodile's mouth. Harrison patted the crocodile on the snout, put its huge molar in his waistcoat pocket, climbed on the back of a passing rhinoceros, and rode through the jungle out of camera range. There was not a whisper out of the audience as the prologue dissolved into the cartoon credits. At the appearance of the title *Dr. Dolittle*, there was a smatter of applause from the Studio contingent, but the clapping was not taken up by those who had paid $2.60 a ticket.

Throughout the first half of the film, the audience were equally unresponsive. Even at the end of the musical numbers, there was only a ripple of approval. At the intermission, David Brown hurried out into the lobby. 'I want to hear the comments,' he said. The noise in the lobby was muted. Most of the people just sipped soft drinks and talked

316 John Gregory Dunne

quietly among themselves. Several of the Fox people blatantly eaves-
dropped on their conversations. Jacobs stood by one of the doors, his
eyes darting wildly. Natalie Trundy leaned against him, her eyes brim-
ming with tears, kneading a Kleenex between her fingers. In the center
of the lobby, a circle of Studio executives surrounded Richard Zanuck.

'This is a real dead-ass audience,' Zanuck said. 'But you've got to
remember, this isn't *Sound of Music* or *My Fair Lady*. The audience
hasn't been conditioned to the songs for five years like they are with a
hit musical.'

'This is an original score,' Stan Hough said.

Zanuck nodded his head vigorously. 'And an original screenplay,' he
said. The muscles in his jaw popped in and out feverishly. 'My God,
these people didn't know what they were going to see when they came
into the theater. The first thing they see is a guy riding a giraffe.'

'It's not like *Sound of Music*,' Hough said.

'Or *My Fair Lady*,' Zanuck said. 'Those songs were famous before
they ever began shooting the picture.'

The second half of the picture did not play much better than the
first. There was only sporadic laughter and desultory applause for the
production numbers. When the house lights finally came on, the only
prolonged clapping came from the three rows where the Studio people
were sitting. In the lobby, ushers passed out preview cards. Tables had
been set up and pencils provided for the members of the audience to
fill in their reactions. These cards were more detailed than most preview
questionnaires. 'PLEASE RATE THE PICTURE,' the cards read. 'Excellent. Good. Fair.' In another section, the questionnaire asked:

How would you rate the performance of the following?
Rex Harrison
Samantha Eggar
Anthony Newley
Richard Attenborough
Which scenes did you like the most?
Which scenes, if any, did you dislike?
*We don't want to know your name, but we would like to know the following
facts about you:*
1 Male—Female
2 Check age group you are in—
between 12 and 17
between 18 and 30
between 31 and 45
over 45
*Thank you very much for your courtesy and cooperation.*

Jacobs wandered through the lobby. His eyes were bloodshot. Natalie Trundy trailed after him. She had stopped crying, but her eyes were red-rimmed.

'I hear the cards are seventy-five per cent excellent,' Jacobs said to no one in particular. He watched a woman chewing on a small yellow pencil as she perused her card. The woman wrote something down, erased it, then wrote something else. Jacobs tried to look over her shoulder, but when she saw him, the woman shielded her comments with her hand.

Ted Ashley, the president of Ashley-Famous Artists, Rex Harrison's agents, came up and clapped Jacobs on the back. 'Arthur, you've got yourself a picture here,' Ashley said. Jacobs waited for him to say something else, but Ashley just slapped him on the back again and went over to talk to Zanuck.

'The audience was kind of quiet,' Zanuck said.

Ted Mann, the theater owner, a large blocky man at one of whose theaters Dr. Dolittle was going to play when it opened in Minneapolis, elbowed his way to Zanuck's side. 'I want you to know, Dick, a year's run,' he said. 'A year minimum.'

'I thought the audience was a little quiet,' Zanuck repeated.

'Yes, it was, Dick,' Mann said. 'But it's the kids who are going to make this picture, and we didn't have many kids here tonight.' Mann seemed to search for the proper words. 'You've got to realize,' he said, 'that what we had here tonight was your typically sophisticated Friday night Minneapolis audience.'

Zanuck seemed not to hear. 'They weren't conditioned to it like Sound of Music,' he said.

'That's my point, my point exactly,' Mann said. 'But they'll be hearing this score for the next four months until the picture opens. By the time December rolls around, they'll know what they're going to see, don't you worry about that, don't you worry at all.'

Jacobs looked over at Zanuck. 'Over fifty per cent excellent,' he said.

The theater emptied and the Fox party slowly walked back to the Radisson half a block away. There was little enthusiasm as they rode up the elevator to the party in Zanuck's Villa Suite. The suite was enormous, on two levels, with a large living room and two bedrooms on the balcony above it. A bar had been set up on the balcony and a buffet beside it. The food had not yet arrived. There were only two large bowls of popcorn which were quickly emptied. The room was quiet, with only a slight hum of conversation. Jacobs, Abrahams, Bricusse, Natalie Trundy and Barbara McLean sat around a coffee table totting up the cards, stacking them into piles of 'Excellent,' 'Good' and 'Fair.' There were 175 cards in all – 101 'excellent,' 47 'Good' and 27 'Fair.' One viewer had written 'Miserable' and another noted that Rex Harrison played Dr. Dolittle 'like a male Mary Poppins.' Two women objected to a scene with white mice and five to another scene in which Anthony Newley drinks whiskey out of a bottle.

'Those broads are all over forty-five, right?' Jacobs said.

'The "Fairs" are all over forty-five,' Abrahams said.

Ted Mann peered down at the cards. 'You've got to realize that this was a typically sophisticated Friday night Minneapolis audience,' he repeated.

'What we needed was a lot of kids,' Natalie Trundy said. She dabbed at her eyes with a handkerchief and asked someone to bring her a Scotch on the rocks.

It was obvious that the Studio was distressed by the results of the preview. It was not just that the cards were bad – though with $18 million riding on the film, they were considerably less favorable than the Studio might have liked. But what disturbed them even more was the muted reaction of the audience during the screening of the picture.

'I think it's damn silly to come all the way to Minneapolis and then not tell people what they're going to see,' Zanuck said. 'It's all right to have a sneak in Los Angeles. But you come this goddamn far to get away from that inside audience. So tell them what they're going to see. Get the kids out.'

Richard Fleischer nursed a drink, stirring it slowly with his finger. 'That's right, Dick,' he said. 'Tell them in the ads.' He moved his hand as if he were reading from an advertisement. ' "Dr. Dolittle – the story of a man who loved animals." '

'Right,' Zanuck said. 'They know what they're seeing, they'll break the goddamn doors down.' He gave his glass to Linda Harrison and asked her to get him another drink. 'When we run it next, in San Francisco, maybe, we'll tell them what they're going to see. No goddamn teaser ads.'

'I'd be mystified,' Fleischer said, 'if I came into the theater and didn't know what the picture was and the first scene was a guy riding a giraffe.'

Jonas Rosenfield, the Studio's vice president in charge of publicity, who had come from New York for the screening, edged up beside Zanuck. 'It's all true,' he said. 'But we've all got to admit that this was an invaluable preview. We know now how to promote this picture to make it the big success we still know it's going to be.'

'This is what previews are for,' Owen McLean said.

'Right,' Stan Hough said. 'This is what we come to Minneapolis for, to find out things like this.'

Waiters arrived and laid out a supper of filet mignon on hamburger rolls. Calls were placed to Harrison in France, where he was making another Studio picture, *A Flea in Her Ear*, and to Darryl Zanuck in New York. When the call to Darryl Zanuck came through, Richard Zanuck and David Brown went into a bedroom and closed the door. The party seemed to settle in. Jacobs still went through the cards, one by one.

'No kids,' he said. 'Everyone is over thirty.'

'It's the kids who'll make this picture a hit,' Harry Sokolov said.

In a corner of the room, Owen McLean sat down on a couch beside David Raphel, the Studio's vice president in charge of foreign sales. 'Well, David,' McLean said, 'What did you think?'

Raphel, a distinguished-looking middleaged man with a slight foreign accent, wiped a piece of hamburger bun from his lips. 'A very useful preview,' he said carefully. 'This picture will take very special handling to make it the success we all know it's going to be. We mustn't forget the older people. They're the repeaters. The children won't get there unless their grandparents take them. The grandparents, they're the repeaters. Look at *The Sound of Music*.'

'There are people who've seen *Sound of Music* a hundred times,' McLean said.

'My point,' Raphel said. 'My point exactly.'

Slowly the party began to break up. It was after one A.M. and a number of the Studio people were leaving for Los Angeles at 6:30 the next morning. At the door of Zanuck's suite, Ted Ashley shook hands with Jacobs.

'You've got yourself a picture, Arthur,' Ashley said. 'It's all up there on the screen.'

'It'll work,' Jacobs said. 'Cut a few things, switch a few things.'

'It's going to be great, Arthur,' Rosenfield said. He patted Jacobs on the arm. 'None of us has any doubts about that.'

Zanuck's suite cleared by one-thirty in the morning. At four A.M. he called Harry Sokolov and told him to round up Hough, McLean and David Brown for a meeting in his room. They convened in Zanuck's suite at 4:45 A.M., and for the next hour Zanuck went over the picture reel by reel. Before the meeting broke up, shortly before six, it was tentatively agreed to cut the prologue. A decision was deferred on whether to cut any of the musical numbers. Arthur Jacobs was not present at this meeting.

# John Sack from
# M

*John Sack interviewed the soldiers of M Company about what had been going through their minds during certain adventures, then made these thoughts and feelings part of the action itself as he described it. Sometimes this took the form of brief interior monologues. M first ran in Esquire, and Esquire's lawyers threw their hands up over this use of other people's thoughts on the grounds that it opened the way to invasion-of-privacy suits unless Sack could get written consent from each soldier involved. It is an indication of Sack's perseverance, not to mention his accuracy, that he thereupon backtracked and got in touch with every living soldier who was mentioned — they were spread out from Maine to Vietnam — showed them the manuscript and got their OKs. T.W.*

Thursday, Williams, the gentle Florida periscope operator, achieved immortality of sorts: he really saw a communist, large as life and twice as spunky, an experience that no other trooper in M's alert battalion was to enjoy throughout this Operation. This special communist was staring at Williams from a bush no farther than the other side of a ping-pong table, staring at him down the gray barrel of a rifle, in fact. 'Ho!' Williams shouted in consternation: but to begin at the beginning.

On Thursday, Demirgian's deserving platoon had given itself a siesta as Williams's company and Morton's company walked through the dark of Sherwood forest, slow going, all sorts of tangly things, little red ants, their mission being to destroy Charlie's source of strength: the communist stores of rice. Every time Williams's snail-paced friends came to one they burned it — two or three tons of this brown river-like stuff could keep Charlie's battalion marching on its stomach a week, the idea being. A gay little Vietnamese soldier went along to sanction any or all burnings or blowings up, first having satisfied himself that the rice was truly communist, the soldier having been trained in this mystic art. Once as their machetes cut through the bushes, Williams's company came to a stock of Vermont-like maple candy in laundry-soap sized bars. But being in a cave it just wouldn't burn. An inventive sergeant began to throw the sugary stuff to the ants – but no, too time-consuming. Hand grenades? Now he had maple candy with holes. Nausea-inducing gas? Nothing doing, it might be against the Geneva convention. At last the patient sergeant radioed the Army engineers, who blew up the maple candy with TNT. Bigalow was on this safari in his flack capacity, *a story!* he told himself but he couldn't write it, a public information sergeant having told him these predatory doings do not pass Army censorship. 'You're not going to win friends among Vietnamese farmers,' Bigalow's sergeant had explained.

Even with machetes, moving in this jungle was like searching in a big attic closet on a summer morning, old moist bathrobes drawing across one's face and rusty old clothes hangers snagging in one's hair, corrugated cardboard beneath one's feet. Furthermore, in this wildwood there were snipers shooting at people, a rustling in the leaves and a *slap!* But what really bedeviled Williams's and Morton's companies as they pushed along weren't their human enemies but ants, little red ants which hadn't seen juicy Westerners in a quarter century, even the French army hadn't dared go to this treacherous place. Morton would tell himself, *Oh—! here comes another one*, as still another cackling ant threw itself out of the foliage onto his neck, and Morton would roll it off with sweating fingers, his black rifle in his other hand, pressing it to instant death. Morton felt guilty about his extraordinary acts of self-assertiveness; a Baptist, he didn't think God set anything on this earth without having His reason, maybe in little red ants was a liquid to cure malaria, cancer, doctors would find it some day, Morton piously believed. For weeks he would justify his steady slaughter by telling himself, *it didn't make any difference – there were so many of them.* He would remonstrate with Russo, the young desperado of sixteen who swore that if *he* had been in those insect-infested woods that day (he hadn't, he had fainted from the heat) – that *he* would cry, *'Die!'* to every ant he butchered, laughing like Mephistopheles. Morton would smile at Russo tolerantly, saying that all God's ants should be killed with kindness.

Bigalow – now Bigalow was a soldier first, a PIO reporter second, and squeezing his ants between thumb and index finger he mechanically cast their lifeless bodies to the jungle floor. But as Bigalow inched along he also speculated whether there mightn't be a story in them, *How to Kill Ants, by PFC Vaughan A. Bigalow.* He thought, *One way is to throttle your ant by pushing a grain of sand into its throat with a toothpick.* A *second way* ... a microscopic punji pit, a careless ant expiring horribly on a point of a pin. In practice Bigalow killed his ants conventionally: indifferently, paying no mind to their dying agonies while he walked along with the friend who once had twitted him about his ball-point pen, I stabbed! I stabbed! I stabbed! 'Bigalow,' the boy remembered in this incongruous place, 'tell Dubitsky he owes me five dollars.'

'All right,' said Bigalow, slapping a neck-ant.

'And Bigalow. You've got a pair of my khakis.'

'You're right,' said Bigalow, dropping his dead ant down.

'And Bigalow? If the captain doesn't get us out of here, you can have the other pair too.'

But Williams——! It never occurred to Williams's gentle mind to kill these ants: if one of them bit he just brushed it off without taking his grim revenge. And that was Williams's nonbelligerent temper when he had that sudden brush with his communist, a Vietnamese with a white shirt and *hair* – black hair, Williams would never forget his bushy hair. Resting in a little jungle hole, a gully, hearing a twig crack, turning around, Williams saw this black-haired intruder and shouted, '*Ho*,' ducking into his hole. A bullet burned across his shoulder blade and Williams cried out, '*Oh*,' burying his startled face in the dirt, holding his rifle high above him like an African's spear, shooting it at the trees one-handed, bang! bang! bang! and crying, '*Sergeant! sergeant! sergeant! come here!*' My kingdom for a periscope!

'What's the matter?' Williams's sergeant called as he hurried to this clamorous scene.

'*Keep shooting!*' Williams shouted while he did exactly that, his face still plowing into the dirt. '*I seed one!*'

'Where?'

'*Out there! He shot me*,' jerking his head up, spying the evergreen trees but no more communist.

'Whereabouts?'

'*Here – in the shoulder!*'

'Nothing. Maybe a ricochet breezed across it.'

'*Sergeant, that was no ricochet! I'm hit, I know I'm hit!*'

'Rock steady!' said Williams's unruffled sergeant. 'You aren't hit, you've nothing to worry about, you're okay. Rock steady.'

Williams got dazedly to his feet and stared around. He told his sergeant, 'Okay, I'll try.'

'Can you make it through the jungle?'

'I'll try.'

But as Williams resumed his death-march through the tangled vines, the tendrils plucking at his shoulders, pulling at his feet, he feared to see that blackhaired man staring at him from every bush, he imagined the vines to be black hair, black hair to be condensing from the shadowy air. Red ants fell on Williams's sleeve, and Williams duly brushed them off. *I get through this I'm never going back – never!*

His black-haired nemesis or someone else was shooting Americans all of their arduous way through the forest, *slap!* and *slap!* killing two of them, wounding many. Coming to the bright paddies at last, Williams's friends were plenty mad at communists – believe it! Taking their wild revenge, the irrepressible privates went through a yellow Vietnamese village like Visigoths, like Sherman's army, burning the houses, ripping the clothes, breaking the jars, the rice running out on the muddy floors. *'I won't leave this to the goddam gooks!'* One private shot him a dog, when a sergeant said, *'You're a real good goddam soldier,'* he only laughed. Somebody lit a lighter, *'The lieutenant doesn't want you to,' 'Fuck the lieutenant,'* the house was in black-tongued flames. Somebody used a grenade launcher, there was nothing left.

The following calm morning, Williams went along the foxholes to talk to his sergeant and declare himself *hors de combat.* A young-looking boy from the East, Williams's sergeant had earned his reputation for infinite patience as leader of the bowl patrol when the bowl thing happened back on M's cool rubber plantation. Next to each rubber tree was a sort of white cereal bowl, in late afternoon the Vietnamese tree-tappers were to leave it rightside-up to gather rubber or upside down if it threatened rain. But going above and beyond the call of duty, the Vietnamese had always put certain bowls in a third – un-authorized – attitude: tilted, the rubber sap in the moonlight showing the communist snipers which way to shoot to kill American soldiers best. Evening after evening, Williams's patient sergeant had taken his bowl patrol into the shadowy trees to tilt the white bowls back to proper horticultural angle. Williams could have no more compassionate audience than the saint he was telling today. 'Now, I don't want you to think I'm a comprehentious objector.'

'Do you mean a com – conscientious objective?'

'I don't want you to think I'm one of those. I'll do anything you want me to: exceptin' to kill somebody.'

'Well,' said Williams's sergeant gently. 'Don't you think you're giving up too easy?'

'No, serge, I've tried, I've tried, I've made up my mind. I haven't got it in me to kill, I found that yesterday.'

'Well, there ain't none of us wants to kill somebody. But if it's something got to be done, somebody's got to do it, that's all.'

'Serge, I'm just no use in the jungle unlessin' I can kill someone. I ain't going back to the jungle – I just ain't going back.'

'Well, *somebody* got to go back in that jungle, Charlie ain't coming out,' Williams's patient sergeant concluded.

In the weeks after that at M's sylvan rubber plantation, the soft light slipping through the tall trees, the birds in the leaves, a monkey – the weeks after that, Williams's sergeant made sweet remonstrances, Williams's first sergeant made terrible threats, a courtmartial, six years at hard labor, a dishonorable discharge, but neither the stick nor carrot could change Williams's simple belief, kill or be killed was a law of that jungle and he wanted neither of them. 'The spunkless wonder,' his bitter lieutenant called him at dinner in the officers' tent, thinking, *he's selfish, he's unpatriotic, he says he's scared – well, so everyone is scared,* and Williams's captain remembered his Goethe class at college, *he only earns his freedom and existence who daily conquers them anew.* Amen to that, the diners in the officers' tent would say, telling themselves *there's a war on but Williams won't do his part!* The officers had learned to tolerate this in the Vietnamese army, but Williams – he was an American!

An ambulance having been called for, Williams was taken to the rubber plantation's bright landing strip. Then a red-crossed helicopter and a second Army ambulance took him to the dusty, insufferably hot little tent where his division's psychiatrist sat, engrossedly patting a handkerchief on his sweat-soaked arms and elaborately folding it into quarters and sixteenths prior to his sliding it into his pocket. 'Well, Williams? What's your problem?' the psychiatrist began. He was a red-headed captain.

'I don't want no part of this killing people,' Williams replied.

'Now how did this come about?' Distantly the psychiatrist was thinking, *autism – association – ambivalence – affect,* the four signs of schizophrenia they had taught him at Colorado. One of those telltale *a's* – well, we're none of us perfect. Two of them, uh-oh, three of them, *zap!* a medical discharge for poor old psychotic Williams.

Williams sat in a chair by the doctor's little desk, the same catty-corner furniture arrangement at which he had once sought work at the VC, the Virginia Carolina Mining Corporation, $1.97 an hour. All that

Williams knew of psychiatrists he had acquired on television: he believed that his red-headed doctor would give him some bright-colored blocks to put together in two minutes, schizophrenia he hadn't heard of, three of those *a*'s would be gibberish to Williams, *association* might mean the Knights of Pythias or the NAACP, neither of which he had joined. In all innocence he sat in that sweltering tent and answered the doctor's friendly questions. Williams's father had drowned. Williams had had headaches for a month after that. He lived with his mother, but he had a girl. Kathernell was her name. Williams wanted to marry her, and some day he would. Ten minutes later the doctor wrote 'No *illness found*' on Williams's mimeographed form and sent him back to his rifle company, where the captain made him a cook instead of a combat soldier and where he learned to mix water, flour, lard, and dark brown gravy base to make gravy.

But back to Friday of the Operation.

Friday the long awaited happened — M's battalion killed somebody, at last. 'What's the spirit of the bayonet?' those wild-eyed sergeants had cried to M in training, in America. '*To kill!*' M had learned to shout fiercely back. 'The enemy is dedicated — he won't scare away,' old Smoke, its battalion commander, had said to M, eyes aflame. '*You've got to kill him.*' And on Friday morning M inevitably killed, doing its climactic job with mixed feelings, one understands, some of its soldiers queasy in the presence of waxy death, some of them impassive. M had guessed it would be this way — in training camp, Hofelder would think of a communist running at him savagely, he had asked himself, *could I really kill him?* but a buddy of Hofelder's had simply laughed, saying, 'Shucks. I'm me and he's he,' meaning that if I kill a fellow that is his worry, not mine.

The episode was again the doing of Demirgian's platoon, again it had climbed on those hot APCs and had driven *bump — bounce — bump* to Sherwood forest and beyond, burning more yellow houses as it went. In actual fact, the cavalry's big lieutenant colonel had given his captains the order, *insure that positive identification is made:* a sniper in the house destroy it, otherwise spare it. But through the iteration of imperatives and the abolition of qualifiers and wise apprehension that the colonel couldn't be serious, his order had been almost unrecognizable when it got through channels to Demirgian's Sergeant Gore. Gore had heard the order as, 'Kill everything. Destroy everything. Kill the cows, the pigs, the chickens — *everything.*'

'Well, sir. You can't destroy *everything*,' Gore had told the glum second lieutenant who relayed this.

'That's what the cavalry said,' the lieutenant had answered unenthusiastically.

'Sir, I won't kill the women and children,' Gore had told him.

But as their APCs rolled by the doomed villages, there were no women or children to be seen, men neither – they'd fled. The burly cavalrymen and Demirgian's platoon had been travelling since 7 – *weird*, Sullivan thought as the morning got hotter, observing that his steel vehicle was always in sunshine, never in shade, although there were scores of white sheepclouds in the blue above him: a Vietnamese weather mystery. But the wonder of wonders was Demirgian. An unaccustomed competence seemed to have stolen across Demirgian's features: his eyes level, his rifle at a steady angle of attack, he reminded one of that paragon of infantrymen that had been painted like a rampant lion on each of their training camp's objets d'art, even on the insides of teacups at the officers' mess. Wednesday had satisfied Demirgian's romantic heart, it had confirmed Demirgian's faith: if he didn't stand in lines but stayed in cavalry columns, if he didn't shoulder a rifle to salute with but to shoot with, ah – then the American army needn't be closed to life's grander moments. Getting into the spirit of his fierce orders, Demirgian shot at a water buffalo and heartily he fired tracers into the yellow haystacks to kindle them. Newman, M's old philosophical alligator trapper, a boy to whom the essence of old country stores, of apple barrels and mackinaws, adhered – Newman climbed from his APC to set fire to one yellow farmhouse, but since he had seen women and children running from it one minute earlier he had serious doubts about the propriety of his task. He said to his sergeant, 'Now, why should I do this? They'll just build another tomorrow,' but really he was thinking, *I burn their farmhouse down, that'll just make them communists, won't it*, Smoke himself had asserted so. Still, Newman obeyed his orders, using his Army matches, closing the cover before striking them, the cover inscribed, 'Where liberty is, there is my home – Benjamin Franklin,' the apocalypse drove on.

Then it was that the incident happened. A cavalry sergeant, seeing a sort of bunker place, a hut above, hole below, and hearing some voices inside it, told Demirgian to throw a grenade in. Demirgian hesitating, —, a soldier we have met before, though not by name, jumped from his APC and flipped in a hand grenade himself. It rolled through the door hitting a sort of earthen baffle before it exploded, and — gasped as ten or a dozen women and children came shrieking out in their crinkled pajamas: no blood, no apparent injuries, though, and — got onto his carrier again, it continued on. The next APC in the column, with Yoshi-oka aboard, drove up to this hovel, and a Negro specialist-four, his black rifle in his hands, warily extended his head in, peering through the darkness one or two seconds before he cried, 'Oh my God!'

'What's the matter,' said a second specialist.

'They hit a little girl,' and in his muscular arms the Negro specialist brought out a seven-year-old, long black hair and little earrings, staring eyes — eyes, her eyes are what froze themselves onto M's memory, it seemed there was no white to those eyes, nothing but black ellipses like black goldfish. The child's nose was bleeding — there was a hole in the back of her skull.

Needless to say, America hadn't sent M into battle without having taught it the principles of first aid. Sergeants had spun around like T-formation quarterbacks to slap hypothetical wounds into the torso, arms, and legs of talented volunteers, who rolled their eyes to the ceiling in Stanislavskian agonies as their persecutors cried, 'Okay! He is wounded — right? He got a big bad wound — right?' Later in its oral examination of the tenets of first aid, M had been questioned soldier by soldier, 'Somebody's bleeding, tell me the four things you'd do,' and there had been few trainees who couldn't list two or three, at least: (a) elevate the bleeding part, (b) apply a pressure bandage, (c) press on a pressure point, and (d) apply a tourniquet — of course, a tourniquet wouldn't be indicated in the accident today. Nor could it be argued that M was all surgical competence with no human heart, not in the least. If its oral exams had proved anything, it was that M would try to be Nightingales as well as Galens whenever bleeding occurred, many of its tenderhearted boys reciting the Army's four iatrical measures and adding a fifth of their own, 'I'd first make him real comfortable,' or 'I'd talk to him ... I'd talk to him.' Providence had placed the first of those compassionate soldiers at the door to this morning's bunker, but an injury as massive as that staring girl's went far beyond his earnest abilities, and even a PFC medic was saying sadly, 'There's nothing to be done.'

A cavalry sergeant pressed his thumb on the press-to-talk switch of his radio and reported to his captain, 'Sir, there's a little girl, a civilian girl, who is wounded. Can we have a dust-off?' The sergeant hoped for a helicopter to bring the gazing child to one of Vietnam's civilian hospitals; where the patients lie three to a bed with weird afflictions like missing arms and legs and holes in parts of their bodies.

'Roger,' said the cavalry captain, but then the seven-year-old shuddered and died.

'Sir,' said the cavalry sergeant, 'the little girl died.'

'Roger,' said the captain and the APCs moved on, pausing only for specialist number two to give the other children chewing gum and to comfort the girl's mother as best he could, 'We're sorry,' the mother shaking her head embarrassedly as though to say *please – it could happen to anyone*, a piece of shrapnel sticking out of her shoulder; the medic gave her a bandage before he left.

One doesn't doubt, in the many months to come M would see operations with a greater share of glory (and it would see many, the Army would need fifteen hundred operations as vast as this to cover all Charlie's territory, and Charlie might still be back the following evening) – more glorious operations, but this first Operation of M's had come to its melancholy close, and M's tired battalion was to kill, wound, or capture no other Vietnamese, communist or otherwise, estimated or actual, in the day-and-a-half remaining. Some of M was truly ashamed about the seven-year-old. Sullivan was annoyed with her, *dammit*, he thought, *she should have known we didn't want to hurt her. Why was she hiding out?* Much of M agreed with him, *ignorant people*, they thought. A lieutenant of the cavalry had no misgivings, thinking, *these people don't want us here anyhow, why should I care about them?* a thought that he bitterly volunteered in conversation. In his innocent past, the lieutenant had gone through the empty-looking villages without taking care to destroy them first, a man, a woman, a *boy* opening fire and killing those for whose lives he was responsible. Vietnam had shown to the lieutenant's satisfaction the line where compassion must end, caution begin.

Yoshioka had stood by the bunker watching the girl die. He felt no special affinity toward Asia's troubles, though he was Oriental and his mother had been at Hiroshima, but being an American he did like children – he turned away, his face waxily paralyzed. Life hadn't taught him to phrase his thoughts with any great felicity, and Yoshioka simply told himself his favorite vivid word and promised himself to think of other things. But that he couldn't do, for three Fridays later, jumping from a dusty Army truck, seeing a glistening wire between two bushes, declaring, quite phlegmatically, 'There's a mine,' a sergeant reaching his hand out to keep soldiers back, reaching his hand out, reaching his hand, reaching – three Fridays later in the black explosion Yoshioka was freakishly wounded the same way as that staring child. The sergeant who touched the trip-wire was killed, the Negro who'd found the little girl was killed, M's old alligator trapper, Newman, was ripped in his arms and legs by the whistling pieces of steel and evacuated, and 'Yokasoka's dead,' the soldiers were saying that night at their rubber plantation, still not getting his name right, not knowing how Yoshioka lay in a Saigon hospital vegetally alive, huge Frankenstein stitches on his shaven head, his acne caked with blood, a hole in his throat to breathe through, bubbles between his lips, the soles of his feet a queer pale yellow, his head thrashing right and left as though to cry no-no-no, his hand slapping his thigh as though he'd heard some madcap story, a sheet around the bedframe to hold him in – a jar of clear liquid dripping into him, a brownish-yellow liquid dripping out, a PFC shooing the flies away and sucking things out of him with a vacuum machine, a Navaho nurse pulling the sheet up over his legs for modesty's sake, a doctor leaning over him whispering, 'Bob? You're in a hospital. You're going to be on your litter a while. You're going to be traveling some. First you'll be on a plane. . . .'

It chanced that the bed next to Yoshioka's was a crib, inside it a stuffed red polka-dot puppy and a wide-eyed Vietnamese girl of two. Tiny white plaster casts like dinner candles kept her from picking her moist upper lip, where Yoshioka's gentle and good-samaritan doctor had operated to correct a cleft, an ugly defect since her birth.

Saturday, the last scheduled day of the Operation and the fiftieth since the day when Milett had told M, 'I got a wife, three kids at home . . .,' Saturday, M had nothing to do but push little squares of cotton through its rifle barrels. Demirgian said, 'I cleaned it yesterday,' and with a specialist-four he sat crosslegged on the grass by his foxhole doing the crossword puzzle in Stars and Stripes, his curved back to the communists, if any. 'Appellation of Athena. That's a good one,' Demirgian murmured.

'Room in a harem,' the specialist countered softly.

'Ten down?' Demirgian.

'Nine down,' the specialist.

'Ten down is girl's name is Ann.'

'Nine down.'

'Nine down is room in a harem.'

'Like a bedroom?'

'Nine down is what?' Demirgian asked the elements.

Sullivan sat reading *The Unanswered Questions About President Kennedy's Assassination.* Russo was lying down: his beloved bowie knife had vanished in the woods like Excalibur in the lake, he had heat exhaustion besides, and under a coconut tree he whispered his secret age to his friends in arms, hoping they might betray him to the authorities. Morton sat in his foxhole and ate his C-rations, pleasantly he asked his friends about why they burned down the Vietnamese houses – *he* felt funny about it. Friday morning Morton had asked a squad leader, 'Sergeant, should I burn this house?' 'Here, this'll help it,' the sergeant had answered, giving him a jar of kerosene from the kitchen shelf. All right: an order's an order, Morton had accepted that, but then the sergeant had said, 'That's enough,' and Morton's disobedient friends had lazily stayed behind and burned the whole village into a tiny replica of Lidice – now, Morton was good-naturedly wondering why. His friends, all of them old-timers, guaranteed to Morton that he would be less studious of the sensitivities of Vietnamese after a few experiences of their trying to kill him. One of his friends said, 'All these people, the VC come and take their brothers and fathers away, so if they've got family in the VC of course they'll be VC sympathizers.' Another friend said, 'Look at it this way. You burn their house, if they're not a VC now they'll be one after you've burned their house,' by which he meant go ahead and burn it, a tight little circle of reasoning that made even Morton blink. A third of his friends said simply, 'I burn because I hate. I hate Vietnam. I hate it because I'm here. I hate every house, every tree, every pile of straw and when I see it I want to burn it.' He seemed surprised to learn that the rest of Morton's friends had intellectual reasons, as well.

'Well,' said Morton, laughing, 'I guess in a few months I'll be burning houses too!' But that wasn't to happen. For walking down the road two weeks later, there was a noise and Morton died, he was killed by one of Charlie's mines, his legs in the dusty dirt at raggedy-ann angles – Morton seemed to have three or four legs. 'We held divine memorial services in his honor,' the Chaplain wrote to Morton's mother and father in Texas. 'Many were the generous tears as we reflected upon this profound truth, *Greater love hath no man than this, that a man lay down his life for his friends.* It may,' the Chaplain wrote in his standard letter, 'also be of comfort for you to remember that Billy was serving a noble cause, helping good people to live in freedom here and all over the world. You remain in my prayers,' the Chaplain wrote to

Morton's parents, who buried him in his one-button suit.

'Site of Taj Mahal,' the specialist-four was saying.

'India! India!' Demirgian cried.

'Too many letters,' the specialist told him. Once they were through with the puzzle, they turned to the news and discovered a story on the Operation, several days old, on page one.

'Gee,' Demirgian said, 'I didn't think they'd write so much about this.'

'*The division*,' the specialist said, reading out loud, '*was in the midst of its biggest campaign of the Vietnam war*, hey I didn't know that, *after pouring thousands of troops into a rugged wooded area ...*'

'Wooded!' Sullivan looked up and cried.

'*The battle-hardened division ...*'

'Battle-hardened! Ha!'

'*... relying heavily on the element of surprise to catch a huge Viet-cong force believed to be holing up in the district, launched its drive with lightning speed at daybreak Monday morning. Troops and tanks, along with armed personnel carriers, have swept into the area to close off the entire circle. Another force of troops is sweeping through the woods to the east. ...*'

'Caught in the crossfire!' Sullivan cried.

'Whenever the VC duck we shoot each *other*,' the specialist said.

And so M's merriment continued until a sergeant came marching up to this perimeter to tell its defenders to quit goofing off, 'Demirgian! Police up those papers – pick up those Ç-rations!' And out into no-man's-land Demirgian walked, telling himself that the Army is the Army is the Army ... but thinking it with a new-found equanimity and getting himself an old C-ration peanut butter lid, a C-ration chicken and noodles can, and an empty carton of Marlboro cigarettes that had been brutally ripped open, and six months later Demirgian was—

Six months later, Sullivan was in Washington in the hospital – *bang*, he had accidentally shot off an inch of his index finger. Yoshioka was in California with a steel plate where his skull had been, and Morton was in Texas with a black carnation in his lapel. Prochaska was on the Riviera on leave, he was dating girls in yellow bikinis. Smith was in Panama a PFC, he had busted out of officer candidate school, *lack of mental adaptability*, and Mason had never become a green beret. A convert to candor, Russo was in Yonkers with his honorable discharge. McCarthy was on a leave in Islip seeing his lawyer and – *stop the presses!* He wasn't in Islip any longer, he was awol, he was over the hill. McCarthy at last was WANTED by the military police – but Demirgian was still in Vietnam. Newman was on the rubber plantation driving a jeep, he was limping and didn't have to fight, and Williams was in the kitchen making gravy and waiting – waiting – *why doesn't Kathernell write?* Bigalow had reenlisted till 1970, a bonus of $500. Some of M had medals, a third of M's expeditionary force had been killed or severely wounded, some of M had malaria, M, at times, had been accidentally napalmed or rocketed or shot in the head by sergeants, a second wave of M was upon the waters, Hofelder with it: all aboard to South Vietnam! But Demirgian—

Demirgian was still in his fighting squad, the General had chosen it *best in battalion*. The infantryman *terrible*, terror of sergeants, had himself become an acting sergeant, the leader of five eager privates. While he still had seen no communists, neither had he met a Vietnamese who cared a fig about communists or a feather about his fighting them. On operations, Demirgian shot at the pigeons and people's chickens, he stared at the high yellow flames, he found the American army good. Without any shilly-shallying he told his squad, *'I'd like to burn the whole country down and start again with Americans.'* Half of Demirgian's tour of duty was safely over and done.

# Joan Didion from
# Slouching towards Bethlehem

*Joan Didion was gathering material for a novel when she became interested in the murder case she describes here. It was the environment of the city of San Bernardino, rather than the case itself, that attracted her. She portrays a combination of tedium, anxiety, and restlessness in the midst of Sunset luxury – all of which is somehow symbolized by the hot breath of the Santa Ana winds – the same atmosphere that later was to give her novel* Play It As It Lays *an impact far beyond anything that happens in the story itself. Joan Didion does not regard herself primarily as a journalist, but her collection of magazine articles entitled* Slouching Towards Bethlehem *established her as a ranking New Journalist in 1968. She considers herself too shy to be a good reporter, but photographers she has worked with say her shyness sometimes makes her subjects so nervous they blurt out extraordinary things in their eagerness to fill up the conversational vacuum. T.W.*

### Some dreamers of the golden dream

This is a story about love and death in the golden land, and begins with the country. The San Bernardino Valley lies only an hour east of Los Angeles by the San Bernardino Freeway but is in certain ways an alien place: not the coastal California of the subtropical twilights and the soft westerlies off the Pacific but a harsher California, haunted by the Mojave just beyond the mountains, devastated by the hot dry Santa Ana wind that comes down through the passes at 100 miles an hour and whines through the eucalyptus windbreaks and works on the nerves. October is the bad month for the wind, the month when breathing is difficult and the hills blaze up spontaneously. There has been no rain since April. Every voice seems a scream. It is the season of suicide and divorce and prickly dread, wherever the winds blows.

The Mormons settled this ominous country, and then they abandoned it, but by the time they left, the first orange tree had been planted and for the next hundred years the San Bernardino Valley would draw a kind of people who imagined they might live among the talismanic fruit and prosper in the dry air, people who brought with them Midwestern ways of building and cooking and praying and who tried to graft those ways upon the land. The graft took in curious ways. This is the California where it is possible to live and die without ever eating an artichoke, without ever meeting a Catholic or a Jew. This is the California where it is easy to Dial-A-Devotion, but hard to buy a book. This is the country in which a belief in the literal interpretation of Genesis has slipped imperceptibly into a belief in the literal interpretation of *Double Indemnity*, the country of the teased hair and the Capris and the girls for whom all life's promise comes down to a waltz-length white wedding dress and the birth of a Kimberly or a Sherry or a Debbi and a Tijuana divorce and a return to hairdressers' school. 'We were just crazy kids,' they say without regret, and look to the future. The future always looks good in the golden land, because no one remembers the past. Here is where the hot wind blows and the old ways do not seem relevant, where the divorce rate is double the national average and where one person in every thirty-eight lives in a trailer. Here is the last stop for all those who come from somewhere else, for all those who drifted away from the cold and the past and the old ways. Here is where they are trying to find a new life style, trying to find it in the only places they know to look: the movies and the news-papers. The case of Lucille Marie Maxwell Miller is a tabloid monument to that new life style.

Imagine Banyan Street first, because Banyan is where it happened. The way to Banyan is to drive west from San Bernardino out Foothill Boulevard, Route 66: past the Santa Fe switching yards, the Forty Winks Motel. Past the motel that is nineteen stucco tepees: 'SLEEP IN A WIGWAM — GET MORE FOR YOUR WAMPUM.' Past Fontana Drag City and the Fontana Church of the Nazarene and the Pit Stop A Go-Go; past Kaiser Steel, through Cucamonga, out to the Kapu Kai Restaurant-Bar and Coffee Shop, at the corner of Route 66 and Carnelian Avenue. Up Carnelian Avenue from the Kapu Kai, which means 'Forbidden Seas,' the subdivision flags whip in the harsh wind. 'HALF-ACRE RANCHES! SNACK BARS! TRAVERTINE ENTRIES! $95 DOWN.' It is the trail of an intention gone haywire, the flotsam of the New California. But after a while the signs thin out on Carnelian Avenue, and the houses are no longer the bright pastels of the Springtime Home owners but the faded bungalows of the people who grow a few grapes and keep a few chickens out here, and then the hill gets steeper and the road climbs and even the bungalows are few, and here — desolate, roughly surfaced, lined with eucalyptus and lemon groves — is Banyan Street.

Like so much of this country, Banyan suggests something curious and unnatural. The lemon groves are sunken, down a three- or four-foot retaining wall, so that one looks directly into their dense foliage, too lush, unsettlingly glossy, the greenery of nightmare; the fallen eucalyptus bark is too dusty, a place for snakes to breed. The stones look not like natural stones but like the rubble of some unmentioned upheaval. There are smudge pots, and a closed cistern. To one side of Banyan there is the flat valley, and to the other the San Bernardino mountains, a dark mass looming too high, too fast, nine, ten, eleven thousand feet, right there above the lemon groves. At midnight on Banyan Street there is no light at all, and no sound except the wind in the eucalyptus and a muffled barking of dogs. There may be a kennel somewhere, or the dogs may be coyotes.

Banyan Street was the route Lucille Miller took home from the twenty-four-hour Mayfair Market on the night of October 7, 1964, a night when the moon was dark and the wind was blowing and she was out of milk, and Banyan Street was where, at about 12:30 a.m., her 1964 Volkswagen came to a sudden stop, caught fire, and began to burn. For an hour and fifteen minutes Lucille Miller ran up and down Banyan calling for help, but no cars passed and no help came. At three o'clock that morning, when the fire had been put out and the California Highway Patrol officers were completing their report, Lucille Miller was still sobbing and incoherent, for her husband had been asleep in the Volkswagen. 'What will I tell the children, when there's nothing left, nothing left in the casket,' she cried to the friend called to comfort her. 'How can I tell them there's nothing left?'

In fact there was something left, and a week later it lay in the Draper Mortuary Chapel in a closed bronze coffin blanketed with pink carnations. Some 200 mourners heard Elder Robert E. Denton of the Seventh-Day Adventist Church of Ontario speak of 'the temper of fury that has broken out among us.' For Gordon Miller, he said, there would be 'no more death, no more heartaches, no more misunderstandings.' Elder Ansel Bristol mentioned the 'peculiar' grief of the hour. Elder Fred Jensen asked 'what shall it profit a man, if he shall gain the whole world, and lose his own soul?' A light rain fell, a blessing in a dry season, and a female vocalist sang 'Safe in the Arms of Jesus.' A tape recording of the service was made for the widow, who was being held without bail in the San Bernardino County Jail on a charge of first-degree murder.

Of course she came from somewhere else, came off the prairie in search of something she had seen in a movie or heard on the radio, for this is a Southern California story. She was born on January 17, 1930, in Winnipeg, Manitoba, the only child of Gordon and Lily Maxwell, both school-teachers and both dedicated to the Seventh-Day Adventist Church, whose members observe the Sabbath on Saturday, believe in an apocalyptic Second Coming, have a strong missionary tendency, and, if they are strict, do not smoke, drink, eat meat, use makeup, or wear jewelry, including wedding rings. By the time Lucille Maxwell enrolled at Walla Walla College in College Place, Washington, the Adventist school where her parents then taught, she was an eighteen-year-old possessed of unremarkable good looks and remarkable high spirits. 'Lucille wanted to see the world,' her father would say in retrospect, 'and I guess she found out.'

The high spirits did not seem to lend themselves to an extended course of study at Walla Walla College, and in the spring of 1949 Lucille Maxwell met and married Gordon ('Cork') Miller, a twenty-four-year-old graduate of Walla Walla and of the University of Oregon dental school, then stationed at Fort Lewis as a medical officer. 'Maybe you could say it was love at first sight,' Mr. Maxwell recalls. 'Before they were ever formally introduced, he sent Lucille a dozen and a half roses with a card that said even if she didn't come out on a date with him, he hoped she'd find the roses pretty anyway.' The Maxwells remember their daughter as a 'radiant' bride.

Unhappy marriages so resemble one another that we do not need to know too much about the course of this one. There may or may not have been trouble on Guam, where Cork and Lucille Miller lived while he finished his Army duty. There may or may not have been problems in the small Oregon town where he first set up private practice. There appears to have been some disappointment about their move to California: Cork Miller had told friends that he wanted to become a doctor, that he was unhappy as a dentist and planned to enter the Seventh-Day Adventist College of Medical Evangelists at Loma Linda, a few miles south of San Bernardino. Instead he bought a dental practice in the west end of San Bernardino County, and the family settled there, in a modest house on the kind of street where there are always tricycles and revolving credit and dreams about bigger houses, better streets. That was 1957. By the summer of 1964 they had achieved the bigger house on the better street and the familiar accoutrements of a family on its way up: the $30,000 a year, the three children for the Christmas card, the picture window, the family room, the newspaper photographs that showed 'Mrs. Gordon Miller, Ontario Heart Fund Chairman. . . .' They were paying the familiar price for it. And they had reached the familiar season of divorce.

It might have been anyone's bad summer, anyone's siege of heat and nerves and migraine and money worries, but this one began particularly early and particularly badly. On April 24 an old friend, Elaine Hayton, died suddenly; Lucille Miller had seen her only the night before. During the month of May, Cork Miller was hospitalized briefly with a bleeding ulcer, and his usual reserve deepened into depression. He told his accountant that he was 'sick of looking at open mouths,' and threatened suicide. By July 8, the conventional tensions of love and money had reached the conventional impasse in the new house on the acre lot at 8488 Bella Vista, and Lucille Miller filed for divorce. Within a month, however, the Millers seemed reconciled. They saw a marriage counselor. They talked about a fourth child. It seemed that the marriage had reached the traditional truce, the point at which so many resign themselves to cutting both their losses and their hopes.

But the Millers' season of trouble was not to end that easily. October 7 began as a commonplace enough day, one of those days that sets the teeth on edge with its tedium, its small frustrations. The temperature reached 102° in San Bernadino that afternoon, and the Miller children were home from school because of Teachers' Institute. There was ironing to be dropped off. There was a trip to pick up a prescription for Nembutal, a trip to a self-service dry cleaner. In the early evening, an unpleasant accident with the Volkswagen: Cork Miller hit and killed a German shepherd, and afterward said that his head felt 'like it had a Mack truck on it.' It was something he often said. As of that evening Cork Miller was $63,479 in debt, including the $29,637 mortgage on the new house, a debt load which seemed oppressive to him. He was a man who wore his responsibilities uneasily, and complained of migraine headaches almost constantly.

He ate alone that night, from a TV tray in the living room. Later the Millers watched John Forsythe and Senta Berger in *See How They Run*, and when the movie ended, about eleven, Cork Miller suggested that they go out for milk. He wanted some hot chocolate. He took a blanket and pillow from the couch and climbed into the passenger seat of the Volkswagen. Lucille Miller remembers reaching over to lock his door as she backed down the driveway. By the time she left the Mayfair

Market, and long before they reached Banyan Street, Cork Miller appeared to be asleep.

There is some confusion in Lucille Miller's mind about what happened between 12:30 a.m., when the fire broke out, and 1:50 a.m., when it was reported. She says that she was driving east on Banyan Street at about 35 m.p.h. when she felt the Volkswagen pull sharply to the right. The next thing she knew the car was on the embankment, quite near the edge of the retaining wall, and flames were shooting up behind her. She does not remember jumping out. She does remember prying up a stone with which she broke the window next to her husband, and then scrambling down the retaining wall to try to find a stick. 'I don't know how I was going to push him out,' she says. 'I just thought if I had a stick, I'd push him out.' She could not, and after a while she ran to the intersection of Banyan and Carnelian Avenue. There are no houses at that corner, and almost no traffic. After one car had passed without stopping, Lucille Miller ran back down Banyan towards the burning Volkswagen. She did not stop, but she slowed down, and in the flames she could see her husband. He was, she said, 'just black.'

At the first house up Sapphire Avenue, half a mile from the Volkswagen, Lucille Miller finally found help. There Mrs. Robert Swenson called the sheriff, and then, at Lucille Miller's request, she called Harold Lance, the Millers' lawyer and their close friend. When Harold Lance arrived he took Lucille Miller home to his wife, Joan. Twice Harold Lance and Lucille Miller returned to Banyan Street and talked to the Highway Patrol officers. A third time Harold Lance returned alone, and when he came back he said to Lucille Miller, 'O.K. . . . you don't talk any more.'

When Lucille Miller was arrested the next afternoon, Sandy Slagle was with her. Sandy Slagle was the intense, relentlessly loyal medical student who used to baby-sit for the Millers, and had been living as a member of the family since she graduated from high school in 1959. The Millers took her away from a diffificult home situation, and she thinks of Lucille Miller not only as 'more or less a mother or a sister' but as 'the most wonderful character' she has ever known. On the night of the accident, Sandy Slagle was in her dormitory at Loma Linda University, but Lucille Miller called her early in the morning and asked her to come home. The doctor was there when Sandy Slagle arrived, giving Lucille Miller an injection of Nembutal. 'She was crying as she was going under,' Sandy Slagle recalls. 'Over and over she'd say,

"Sandy, all the hours I spent trying to save him and now what are they trying to *do* to me?" '

At 1:30 that afternoon, Sergeant William Paterson and Detective Charles Callahan and Joseph Karr of the Central Homicide Division arrived at 8488 Bella Vista. 'One of them appeared at the bedroom door,' Sandy Slagle remembers, 'and said to Lucille, "You've got ten minutes to get dressed or we'll take you as you are." She was in her nightgown, you know, so I tried to get her dressed.'

Sandy Slagle tells the story now as if by rote, and her eyes do not waver. 'So I had her panties and bra on her and they opened the door again, so I got some Capris on her, you know, and a scarf.' Her voice drops. 'And then they just took her.'

The arrest took place just twelve hours after the first report that there had been an accident on Banyan Street, a rapidity which would later prompt Lucille Miller's attorney to say that the entire case was an instance of trying to justify a reckless arrest. Actually what first caused the detectives who arrived on Banyan Street toward dawn that morning to give the accident more than routine attention were certain apparent physical inconsistencies. While Lucille Miller had said that she was driving about 35 m.p.h. when the car swerved to a stop, an examination of the cooling Volkswagen showed that it was in low gear, and that the parking rather than the driving lights were on. The front wheels, moreover, did not seem to be in exactly the position that Lucille Miller's description of the accident would suggest and the right rear wheel was dug in deep, as if it had been spun in place. It seemed curious to the detectives, too, that a sudden stop from 35 m.p.h. – the same jolt which was presumed to have knocked over a gasoline can in the back seat and somehow started the fire – should have left two milk cartons upright on the back floorboard, and the remains of a Polaroid camera box lying apparently undisturbed on the back seat.

No one, however, could be expected to give a precise account of what did and did not happen in a moment of terror, and none of these inconsistencies seemed in themselves incontrovertible evidence of criminal intent. But they did interest the Sheriff's Office, as did Gordon Miller's apparently unconsciousness at the time of the accident, and the length of time it had taken Lucille Miller to get help. Something, moreover, struck the investigators as wrong about Harold Lance's attitude when he came back to Banyan Street the third time and found the investigation by no means over. 'The way Lance was acting,' the prosecuting attorney said later, 'they thought maybe they'd hit a nerve.'

And so it was that on the morning of October 8, even before the doctor had come to give Lucille Miller an injection to calm her, the San Bernardino County Sheriff's Office was trying to construct another version of what might have happened between 12:30 and 1:50 a.m. The hypothesis they would eventually present was based on the somewhat tortuous premise that Lucille Miller had undertaken a plan which failed: a plan to stop the car on the lonely road, spread gasoline over her presumably drugged husband, and, with a stick on the accelerator, gently 'walk' the Volkswagen over the embankment, where it would tumble four feet down the retaining wall into the lemon grove and almost certainly explode. If this happened, Lucille Miller might then have somehow negotiated the two miles up Carnelian to Bella Vista in time to be home when the accident was discovered. This plan went awry; according to the Sheriff's Office hypothesis, when the car would not go over the rise of the embankment. Lucille Miller might have panicked then – after she had killed the engine the third or fourth time, say, out there on the dark road with the gasoline already spread and the dogs baying and the wind blowing and the unspeakable apprehension that a pair of headlights would suddenly light up Banyan Street and expose her there – and set the fire herself.

Although this version accounted for some of the physical evidence – the car in low because it had been started from a dead stop, the parking lights on because she could not do what needed doing without some light, a rear wheel spun in repeated attempts to get the car over the embankment, the milk cartons upright because there had been no sudden stop – it did not seem on its own any more or less credible than Lucille Miller's own story. Moreover, some of the physical evidence did seem to support her story: a nail in a front tire, a nine-pound rock found in the car, presumably the one with which she had broken the window in an attempt to save her husband. Within a few days an autopsy had established that Gordon Miller was alive when he burned, which did not particularly help the State's case, and that he had enough Nembutal and Sandoptal in his blood to put the average person to sleep, which did: on the other hand Gordon Miller habitually took both Nembutal and Fiorinal (a common headache prescription which contains Sandoptal), and had been ill besides.

It was a spotty case, and to make it work at all the State was going to have to find a motive. There was talk of unhappiness, talk of another man. That kind of motive, during the next few weeks, was what they set out to establish. They set out to find it in accountants' ledgers and double-indemnity clauses and motel registers, set out to determine what might move a woman who believed in all the promises of the middle class – a woman who had been chairman of the Heart Fund and who always knew a reasonable little dressmaker and who had come out of the bleak wild of prairie fundamentalism to find what she imagined to be the good life – what should drive such a woman to sit on a street called Bella Vista and look out her new picture window into the empty California sun and calculate how to burn her husband alive in a Volkswagen. They found the wedge they wanted closer at hand than they might have at first expected, for, as testimony would reveal later at the trial, it seemed that in December of 1963 Lucille Miller had begun an affair with the husband of one of her friends, a man whose daughter called her 'Auntie Lucille,' a man who might have seemed to have the gift for people and money and the good life that Cork Miller so noticeably lacked. The man was Arthwell Hayton, a well-known San Bernardino attorney and at one time a member of the district attorney's staff.

In some ways it was the conventional clandestine affair in a place like San Bernardino, a place where little is bright or graceful, where it is routine to misplace the future and easy to start looking for it in bed. Over the seven weeks that it would take to try Lucille Miller for murder, Assistant District Attorney Don. A. Turner and defense attorney Edward P. Foley would between them unfold a curiously predictable story. There were the falsified motel registrations. There were the lunch dates, the afternoon drives in Arthwell Hayton's red Cadillac convertible. There were the interminable discussions of the wronged partners. There were the confidantes ('I knew everything,' Sandy Slagle would insist fiercely later. 'I knew every time, places, everything') and there were the words remembered from bad magazine stories ('Don't kiss me, it will trigger things,' Lucille Miller remembered telling Arthwell Hayton in the parking lot of Harold's Club in Fontana after lunch one day) and there were the notes, the sweet exchanges: 'Hi Sweetie Pie! You are my cup of tea!! Happy Birthday – you don't look a day over 29!! Your baby, Arthwell.'

And, toward the end, there was the acrimony. It was April 24, 1964, when Arthwell Hayton's wife, Elaine, died suddenly, and nothing good happened after that. Arthwell Hayton had taken his cruiser, *Captain's Lady*, over to Catalina that weekend; he called home at nine o'clock Friday night, but did not talk to his wife because Lucille Miller answered the telephone and said that Elaine was showering. The next morning the Haytons' daughter found her mother in bed, dead. The newspapers reported the death as accidental, perhaps the result of an allergy to hair spray. When Arthwell Hayton flew home from Catalina that weekend, Lucille Miller met him at the airport, but the finish had already been written.

It was in the breakup that the affair ceased to be in the conventional mode and began to resemble instead the novels of James M. Cain, the movies of the late 1930's, all the dreams in which violence and threats and blackmail are made to seem commonplaces of middle-class life. What was most startling about the case that the State of California was preparing against Lucille Miller was something that had nothing to do with law at all, something that never appeared in the eight-column afternoon headlines but was always there between them: the revelation that the dream was teaching the dreamers how to live. Here is Lucille Miller talking to her lover sometime in the early summer of 1964, after he had indicated that, on the advice of his minister, he did not intend to see her any more: 'First, I'm going to go to that dear pastor of yours and tell him a few things.... When I do tell him that, you won't be in the Redland's Church any more.... Look, Sonny Boy, if you think your reputation is going to be ruined, your life won't be worth two cents.' Here is Arthwell Hayton, to Lucille Miller: 'I'll go to Sheriff Frank Bland and tell him some things that I know about you until you'll wish you'd never heard of Arthwell Hayton.' For an affair between a Seventh-Day Adventist dentist's wife and a Seventh-Day Adventist personal-injury lawyer, it seems a curious kind of dialogue.

'Boy, I could get that little boy coming and going,' Lucille Miller later confided to Erwin Sprengle, a Riverside contractor who was a business partner of Arthwell Hayton's and a friend to both the lovers. (Friend or no, on this occasion he happened to have an induction coil attached to his telephone in order to tape Lucille Miller's call.) 'And he hasn't got one thing on me that he can prove. I mean, I've got concrete – he has nothing concrete.' In the same taped conversation with Erwin Sprengle, Lucille Miller mentioned a tape that she herself had surreptitiously made, months before, in Arthwell Hayton's car.

'I said to him, I said "Arthwell, I just feel like I'm being used." ... He started sucking his thumb and he said "I love you. ... This isn't something that happened yesterday. I'd marry you tomorrow if I could. I don't love Elaine." He'd love to hear that played back, wouldn't he?'

'Yeah,' drawled Sprengle's voice on the tape. 'That would be just a little incriminating, wouldn't it?'

'Just a *little* incriminating,' Lucille Miller agreed. 'It really *is*.'

Later on the tape, Sprengle asked where Cork Miller was.

'He took the children down to the church.'

'You didn't go?'

'No.'

'You're naughty.'

It was all, moreover, in the name of 'love'; everyone involved placed a magical faith in the efficacy of the very word. There was the significance that Lucille Miller saw in Arthwell's saying that he 'loved' her, and that he did not 'love' Elaine. There was Arthwell insisting, later, at the trial, that he had never said it, that he may have 'whispered sweet nothings in her ear' (as her defense hinted that he had whispered in many ears), but he did not remember bestowing upon her the special seal, saying the word, declaring 'love.' There was the summer evening when Lucille Miller and Sandy Slagle followed Arthwell Hayton down to his new boat in its mooring at Newport Beach and untied the lines with Arthwell aboard, Arthwell and a girl with whom he later testified he was drinking hot chocolate and watching television. 'I did that on purpose,' Lucille Miller told Erwin Sprengle later, 'to save myself from letting my head do something crazy.'

January 11, 1965, was a bright warm day in Southern California, the kind of day when Catalina floats on the Pacific horizon and the air smells of orange blossoms and it is a long way from the bleak and difficult East, a long way from the cold, a long way from the past. A woman in Hollywood staged an all-night sit-in on the hood of her car to prevent repossession by a finance company. A seventy-year-old pensioner drove his station wagon at five miles an hour past three Gardena poker parlors and emptied three pistols and a twelve-gauge shotgun through their windows, wounding twenty-nine people. 'Many young women become prostitutes just to have enough money to play cards,' he explained in a note. Mrs. Nick Adams said that she was 'not surprised' to hear her husband announce his divorce plans on the Les Crane Show, and farther north, a sixteen-year-old jumped off the Golden Gate Bridge and lived.

And, in the San Bernardino County Courthouse, the Miller trial opened. The crowds were so bad that the glass courtroom doors were shattered in the crush, and from then on identification disks were issued to the first forty-three spectators in line. The line began forming at 6 A.M., and college girls camped at the courthouse all night, with stores of graham crackers and No-Cal.

All they were doing was picking a jury, those first few days, but the sensational nature of the case had already suggested itself. Early in December there had been an abortive first trial, a trial at which no evidence was ever presented because on the day the jury was seated the San Bernardino *Sun-Telegram* ran an 'inside' story quoting Assistant District Attorney Don Turner, the prosecutor, as saying, 'We are looking into the circumstances of Mrs. Hayton's death. In view of the current trial concerning the death of Dr. Miller, I do not feel I should comment on Mrs. Hayton's death.' It seemed that there had been barbiturates in Elaine Hayton's blood, and there had seemed some irregularity about the way she was dressed on that morning when she was found under the covers, dead. Any doubts about the death at the time, however, had never gotten as far as the Sheriff's Office. 'I guess somebody didn't want to rock the boat,' Turner said later. 'These were prominent people.'

Although all of that had not been in the *Sun-Telegram*'s story, an immediate mistrial had been declared. Almost as immediately, there had been another development: Arthwell Hayton had asked newspapermen to an 11 A.M. Sunday morning press conference in his office. There had been television cameras, and flash bulbs popping. 'As you gentlemen may know,' Hayton had said, striking a note of stiff bonhomie, 'there are very often women who become amorous toward their doctor or lawyer. This does not mean on the physician's or lawyer's part that there is any romance toward the patient or client.'

'Would you deny that you were having an affair with Mrs. Miller?' a reporter had asked.

'I would deny that there was any romance on my part whatsoever.'

It was a distinction he would maintain through all the wearing weeks to come.

So they had come to see Arthwell, these crowds who now milled beneath the dusty palms outside the courthouse, and they had also come to see Lucille, who appeared as a slight, intermittently pretty woman, already pale from lack of sun, a woman who would turn thirty-five before the trial was over and whose tendency toward haggardness was beginning to show, a meticulous woman who insisted, against her lawyer's advice, on coming to court with her hair piled high and lacquered. 'I would've been happy if she'd come in with it hanging loose, but Lucille wouldn't do that,' her lawyer said. He was Edward P. Foley, a small, emotional Irish Catholic who several times wept in the courtroom. 'She has a great honesty, this woman,' he added, 'but this honesty about her appearance always worked against her.'

By the time the trial opened, Lucille Miller's appearance included maternity clothes, for an official examination on December 18 had revealed that she was then three and a half months pregnant, a fact which made picking a jury even more difficult than usual, for Turner was asking the death penalty. 'It's unfortunate but there it is,' he would say of the pregnancy to each juror in turn, and finally twelve were seated, seven of them women, the youngest forty-one, an assembly of the very peers — housewives, a machinist, a truck driver, a grocery-store manager, a filing clerk — above whom Lucille Miller had wanted so badly to rise.

That was the sin, more than the adultery, which tended to reinforce the one for which she was being tried. It was implicit in both the defense and the prosecution that Lucille Miller was an erring woman, a woman who perhaps wanted too much. But to the prosecution she was not merely a woman who would want a new house and want to go to parties and run up high telephone bills ($1,152 in ten months), but a woman who would go so far as to murder her husband for his $80,000 in insurance, making it appear an accident in order to collect another $40,000 in double indemnity and straight accident policies. To Turner she was a woman who did not want simply her freedom and a reasonable alimony (she could have had that, the defense contended, by going through with her divorce suit), but wanted everything, a woman motivated by 'love and greed.' She was a 'manipulator.' She was a 'user of people.'

To Edward Foley, on the other hand, she was an impulsive woman who 'couldn't control her foolish little heart.' Where Turner skirted the pregnancy, Foley dwelt upon it, even calling the dead man's mother down from Washington to testify that her son had told her they were going to have another baby because Lucille felt that it would 'do much to weld our home again in the pleasant relations that we used to have.' Where the prosecution saw a 'calculator,' the defense saw a 'blabbermouth,' and in fact Lucille Miller did emerge as an ingenuous conversationalist. Just as, before her husband's death, she had confided in her friends about her love affair, so she chatted about it after his death, with the arresting sergeant. 'Of course Cork lived with it for years, you know,' her voice was heard to tell Sergeant Paterson on a tape made the morning after her arrest. 'After Elaine died, he pushed the panic button one night and just asked me right out, and that, I think, was when he really — the first time he really faced it.' When the sergeant asked why she had agreed to talk to him, against the specific instructions of her lawyers, Lucille Miller said airily, 'Oh, I've always been basically quite an honest person. . . . I mean I can put a hat in the cupboard and say it cost ten dollars less, but basically I've always kind of just lived my life the way I wanted to, and if you don't like it you can take off.'

The prosecution hinted at men other than Arthwell, and even, over Foley's objections, managed to name one. The defense called Miller suicidal. The prosecution produced experts who said that the Volkswagen fire could not have been accidental. Foley produced witnesses who said that it could have been. Lucille's father, now a junior-high-school teacher in Oregon, quoted Isaiah to reporters: '*Every tongue that shall rise against thee in judgment thou shalt condemn.*' 'Lucille did wrong, her affair,' her mother said judiciously. 'With her it was love. But with some I guess it's just passion.' There was Debbie, the Millers' fourteen-year-old, testifying in a steady voice about how she and her mother had gone to a supermarket to buy the gasoline can the week before the accident. There was Sandy Slagle, in the courtroom every day, declaring that on at least one occasion Lucille Miller had prevented her husband not only from committing suicide but from committing suicide in such a way that it would appear an accident and ensure the double-indemnity payment. There was Wenche Berg, the pretty twenty-seven-year-old Norwegian governess to Arthwell Hayton's children, testifying that Arthwell had instructed her not to allow Lucille Miller to see or talk to the children.

Two months dragged by, and the headlines never stopped. Southern California's crime reporters were headquartered in San Bernardino for the duration: Howard Hertel from the *Times*, Jim Bennett and Eddy Jo Bernal from the *Herald–Examiner*. Two months in which the Miller trial was pushed off the *Examiner*'s front page only by the Academy Award nominations and Stan Laurel's death. And finally, on March 2, after Turner had reiterated that it was a case of 'love and greed,' and Foley had protested that his client was being tried for adultery, the case went to the jury.

They brought in the verdict, guilty of murder in the first degree, at 4:50 P.M. on March 5. 'She didn't do it,' Debbie Miller cried, jumping up from the spectators' section. 'She didn't *do* it.' Sandy Slagle collapsed in her seat and began to scream. 'Sandy, for God's sake please don't,' Lucille Miller said in a voice that carried across the courtroom, and Sandy Slagle was momentarily subdued. But as the jurors left the courtroom she screamed again: 'You're murderers. . . . Every last one of you is a *murderer*.' Sheriff's deputies moved in then, each wearing a string tie that read '1965 SHERIFF'S RODEO,' and Lucille Miller's father, that sad-faced junior-high-school teacher who believed in the world of Christ and the dangers of wanting to see the world, blew her a kiss off his fingertips.

The California Institution for Women at Frontera, where Lucille Miller is now, lies down where Euclid Avenue turns into country road, not too many miles from where she once lived and shopped and organized the Heart Fund Ball. Cattle graze across the road, and Rainbirds sprinkle the alfalfa. Frontera has a softball field and tennis courts, and looks as if it might be a California junior college, except that the trees are not yet high enough to conceal the concertina wire around the top of the Cyclone fence. On visitors' day there are big cars in the parking area, big Buicks and Pontiacs that belong to grandparents and sisters and fathers (not many of them belong to husbands), and some of them have bumper stickers that say 'SUPPORT YOUR LOCAL POLICE.'

A lot of California murderesses live here, a lot of girls who somehow misunderstood the promise. Don Turner put Sandra Garner here (and her husband in the gas chamber at San Quentin) after the 1959 desert killings known to crime reporters as 'the soda-pop murders.' Carol Tregoff is here, and has been ever since she was convicted of conspiring to murder Dr. Finch's wife in West Covina, which is not too far from San Bernardino. Carole Tregoff is in fact a nurse's aide in the prison hospital, and might have attended Lucille Miller had her baby been born at Frontera; Lucille Miller chose instead to have it outside, and paid for the guard who stood outside the delivery room in St. Bernardine's Hospital. Debbie Miller came to take the baby home from the hospital, in a white dress with pink ribbons, and Débbie was allowed to choose a name. She named the baby Kimi Kai. The children live with Harold and Joan Lance now, because Lucille Miller will probably spend ten years at Frontera. Don Turner waived his original request for the death penalty (it was generally agreed that he had demanded it only, in Edward Foley's words, 'to get anybody with the slightest trace of human kindness in their veins off the jury'), and settled for life imprisonment with the possibility of parole. Lucille Miller does not like it at Frontera, and has had trouble adjusting. 'She's going to have to learn humility,' Turner says. 'She's going to have to use her ability to charm, to manipulate.'

The new house is empty now, the house on the street with the sign that says

PRIVATE ROAD
BELLA VISTA
DEAD END

The Millers never did get it landscaped, and weeds grow up around the fieldstone siding. The television aerial has toppled on the roof, and a trash can is stuffed with the debris of family life: a cheap suitcase, a child's game called 'Lie Detector.' There is a sign on what would have been the lawn, and the sign reads 'ESTATE SALE.' Edward Foley is trying to get Lucille Miller's case appealed, but there have been delays. 'A trial always comes down to a matter of sympathy,' Foley says wearily now. 'I couldn't create sympathy for her.' Everyone is a little weary now, weary and resigned, everyone except Sandy Slagle, whose bitterness is still raw. She lives in an apartment near the medical school in Loma Linda, and studies reports of the case in *True Police Cases* and *Official Detective Stories*. 'I'd much rather we not talk about the Hayton business too much,' she tells visitors, and she keeps a tape recorder running. 'I'd rather talk about Lucille and what a wonderful person she is and how her rights were violated.' Harold Lance does not talk to visitors at all. 'We don't want to give away what we can sell,' he explains pleasantly; an attempt was made to sell Lucille Miller's personal story to *Life*, but *Life* did not want to buy it. In the district attorney's offices they are prosecuting other murders now, and do not see why the Miller trial attracted so much attention. 'It wasn't a very interesting murder as murders go,' Don Turner says laconically. Elaine Hayton's death is no longer under investigation. 'We know everything we want to know,' Turner says.

Arthwell Hayton's office is directly below Edward Foley's. Some people around San Bernardino say that Arthwell Hayton suffered; others say that he did not suffer at all. Perhaps he did not, for time past is not believed to have any bearing upon time present or future, out in the golden land where every day the world is born anew. In any case, on October 17, 1965, Arthwell Hayton married again, married his children's pretty governess, Wenche Berg, at a service in the Chapel of the Roses at a retirement village near Riverside. Later the newlyweds were feted at a reception for seventy-five in the dining room of Rose Garden

Village. The bridegroom was in black tie, with a white carnation in his buttonhole. The bride wore a long white *peau de soie* dress and carried a shower bouquet of sweetheart roses with stephanotis streamers. A coronet of seed pearls held her illusion veil.

## 'Adam Smith' from
# The money game

'Adam Smith''s articles on the money market are excellent examples of how the techniques of the New Journalism can be applied to technical subjects. Of all the major disciplines, economics has proved to be one of the dullest and most misleading to read about. 'Adam Smith''s work, first collected in The Money Game, was not merely readable, not merely a successful 'popularization' or even haute vulgarisation. It was recognized throughout the financial community as a book of great sophistication and considerable originality on the level of theory. Yet that only begins to explain the nature of its tremendous appeal in 1968 and 1969 at the height of the Sixties Boom. An investment analyst told me at the time: 'I took that book home and gave it to my wife and told her, "Read this. Now you'll know what I do all day."' What he was really saying was: 'She thinks I have a dull, repetitive job among a lot of boring men in dark suits. Now she'll know what a glamorous and exciting game I'm in!'

The fact is that The Money Game was the only book, in fiction or nonfiction, to capture both the economic reality and the emotional reality of the Boom on Wall Street. Through the use of scenes, dialogue, and details of status life, 'Adam Smith' was able to take the reader inside the central nervous systems of the gamblers themselves and at the same time make clear some of the most esoteric sides of finance, such as here, in the 'The Cocoa Game,' the matter of produce futures.

Why more technical writers do not use these techniques is a mystery to me. Perhaps it has something to do with the fact that academic professionals still look upon anything this readable and non-esoteric as necessarily frivolous. Certainly the psychologist Eric Berne discovered this to his considerable discomfort when he wrote Games People Play. The book's theory is a major contribution to psychology, but Berne chose to present it in terms of scenes or 'scenarios,' to use the going phrase, and rather amusing ones at that, with funny names. Games People Play was the most popular book in the United States for about *a year but — ergo — was generally scorned or ignored by academic psychologists.*

*'Adam Smith''s real name is George J. W. Goodman. Now forty-five, Goodman started out as a novelist, worked briefly as a screenwriter, then turned to playing the stock market. But his biggest score by far, both in literature and in finance, came with the publication of The Money Game. He picked up the techniques of the New Journalism by reading writers in Clay Felker's New York magazine and by working under Felker's tutelage. Most of The Money Game first appeared in article form in New York. T.W.*

## The cocoa game

The further we come along, the more apparent becomes the wisdom of the Master° in describing the market as a game of musical chairs. The most brilliant and perceptive analysis you can do may sit there until someone else believes it too, for the object of the game is not to own some stock, like a faithful dog, which you have chosen, but to get to the piece of paper ahead of the crowd. Value is not only inherent in the stock; to do you any good, it has to be value that is appreciated by others. (Analysts at White, Weld walk around repeating 'I have always preferred recognition to discovery' because that is an aphorism of one of the partners.)

It follows that some sort of sense of timing is necessary, and you either develop it or you don't. You could have a chapter on how to swim, but it wouldn't teach you a tenth as much as getting tossed into the water.

The best chapter written on this problem of timing was done by an unknown second-century author who wrote under the pen name of Koholeth, or the Preacher. What survives of Koholeth is not much, but it says all there is to say on the subject. (If you seem to hear a faint rock beat behind what follows, it is because Pete Seeger made a song, 'Turn, Turn, Turn,' out of this passage of Koholeth and the Byrds made a hit record of it.) In later versions of the Old Testament, Koholeth appears as Ecclesiastes, so you have the best chapter on timing right there on your shelf already.

To every thing there is a season,
And a time to every purpose under the heaven:
A time to be born, and a time to die;
A time to plant, and a time to pluck up that which is planted;

°John Maynard Keynes (Editor's note).

A time to break down, and a time to build up;
A time to mourn, and a time to dance;
A time to cast away stones, and a time to gather stones together;

A time to keep, and a time to cast away;
A time to rend, and a time to sew;
A time to keep silence, and a time to speak;

and so on.

There isn't anything else to say. There are some markets that want cyclical stocks; there are some that do a fugal counterpoint to interest rates; there are some that become as stricken for romance as the plain girl behind the counter at Woolworth's; there are some that become obsessed with the future of technology; and there are some that don't believe at all.

If you are in the right thing at the wrong time, you may be right but have a long wait; at least you are better off than coming late to the party. You don't want to be on the dance floor when the music stops.

If what you are doing doesn't seem to be working, the game may not be on even, though the brokers continue to mail our recommendations, and the pundits say things are getting fatter than ever, and the customers' men are busy with smooth reassurances.

It may be all very well to say: *When there's no game, don't play*, but the Propensity is very strong among those who have been playing. I once got involved in another game because the main game was not on, and the best I can say is that it kept me out of the main game at the right time. This particular cautionary tale is slightly afield, but since it contains international intrigue, lust, greed, piracy, power, valor, racism, witchcraft, and mass psychology, I am including it.

At that time the Dow-Jones average was pointing for 1,000, and all over Wall Street, the lads were so busy calling their customers with buy recommendations that their index fingers were beginning to bleed from all the dialing. I was sitting in the Great Winfield's seedy office, the same Great Winfield who hired the Kids. We were both watching the stock tape chug by, lazily, like two Alabama sheriffs in a rowboat watching the catfish on a hot spring day.

'They ain't movin' right,' said the Great Winfield, crossing one cowboy boot over the other. Years ago, as an earnest and sincere young man, I saw the Great Winfield wear suits from Paul Stuart and Tripler, back when he was trying to be a good boy on Wall Street. Then he made some money and bought a ranch and figured that if the Establishment didn't like him (and it didn't), why should he like the Establishment. So he gave away his Establishment clothes and came down to his office in corduroy coats and cowboy boots, his ranch identity, you see, coffee perkin' in an iron pot – as I said before, the whole Marlboro country commercial bit.

The Great Winfield does not bother with real facts. They only confuse things. He just watches the tape, and when he sees something moving, he hops aboard for a while, and when it stops moving, he gets off, just like a bus. This is good for about a million dollars a year.

Tape traders like the Great Winfield develop a feel for how these stock symbols 'act,' whether Polaroid is feeling bouncy or whether KLM wants to lie down and go to sleep for a while. The tape tells the story, they say, and they sniff and inhale the atmosphere and proceed on what their Indian-guide awareness tells them.

'No, sir, they ain't bitin', it's time to go home,' said the Great Winfield. Now, with hindsight this looks pretty acute, because there was the market near its all-time peak, so a lot of people were obviously buying, and there was the Great Winfield packing up, because the tape was telling him the game was not afoot any more.

'We should all go away for a year and come back fresh, just as everybody is fatigued from riding the market down and watching it rally,' said the Great Winfield. 'But we can't do nothing for a whole year, so I have us something that will give us ten times our money in six months.'

I began to tune in – $1,000 in January becomes $10,000 in July wins my attention any time.

'Cocoa,' said the Great Winfield. 'There isn't any cocoa. The world is just about out of it.'

Now all I know about cocoa is that it comes in little red cans in Gristede's, and as far as I could see there were a lot of little red cans on the shelves.

But the Great Winfield was warming up, in hypnotic tones. He does this with each little discovery, sort of hypnotizes himself. Then he can generate practically infinite enthusiasm for it.

'My boy,' said the Great Winfield, 'when the world is just about out of something that it wants, the price goes up. The Cocoa Exchange is unregulated. A three-cent rise in cocoa doubles your money. It's going to be wild. Come along for the party.'

What the price of cocoa is depends on how much cocoa there is. The main crop is picked from October to March, so along about February or

March every year, with the current crop in the bag, the speculation starts about the next year's crop. Now starts the political and international intrigue.

'My informants in Ghana tell me things are in a bad way,' said the Great Winfield, sounding like M giving 007 a new assignment. My informants in Ghana, he said. Usually his informant is one company treasurer, but now suddenly he is far-reaching and international.

'The Redeemer, Mr. Kwame Nkrumah, has built himself palaces and a socialist state. The socialist state is printing forms; bureaucrats are supposed to go out and count the cocoa and fill in the forms so the Ghana Marketing Board knows what it is doing. But under the Redeemer, the bureaucrats do not go out and count the cocoa because if they fill in the wrong numbers it throws the five-year plan out of kilter and they are executed. So they find out what the numbers are supposed to be and they fill in those numbers. Consequently, no one knows how much cocoa there is. And my informants tell me there isn't any.'

It is impossible to resist: international intrigue, the mockery of socialism, the chance to profit by the tides of history. 'Tell me the game,' I said.

'You buy a contract on the New York Cocoa Exchange,' said the Great Winfield. 'The seller promises to deliver to you, say next September, thirty thousand pounds of cocoa at the current price, twenty-three cents. Ten-percent margin, an unregulated market. One contract, one thousand dollars. Cocoa goes up three cents and you double your money. Cocoa goes up six cents, and you triple your money'.

'Cocoa goes *down* three cents, I lose *all* my money,' I said.

'How can cocoa go down?' said the great Winfield. 'Cocoa is going to forty cents. *Minimum*. Six times your money. With some luck, cocoa is going to fifty cents, nine times your money. In 1954 cocoa went to seventy cents.' Anyone can buy or sell cocoa in New York – just the way you can buy and sell flax, hides, silver, wheat, and just about any other commodity. Just bring money to your broker. These contracts for future delivery enable the producers and consumers to hedge their operations and they lubricate the flow of commerce.

Rapid calculation showed me a repeat of 1954 would bring $15,000 for every $1,000 contract. I went away, called a broker I knew who had never heard of the Great Winfield, just to get another pipeline open, and pretty soon for only $5,000 somebody was going to deliver me 150,000 pounds of cocoa in September.

Very heady stuff, being an international cocoa speculator. All of a sudden I was meeting guys I had never met before, fellow members of the International Cocoa Cabal. I met a tweedy consultant type whose business takes him to West Africa. We bought each other drinks.

'I do believe,' said the consultant, 'that our dark brothers have fabricated the figures. There is no cocoa.'

Two weeks later the Redeemer, Mr. Kwame Nkrumah, was paying a social call in Peking when the Opposition took the country away from him – all but the $25 million the Redeemer has stashed somewhere – and the afternoon papers had eight-column headlines, REVOLUTION IN GHANA. My phone rang. It was the Great Winfield's assistant.

'The Great Winfield,' he said, 'wanted you aboard in the cocoa game because you are a Communicator and you know people. So call up somebody in West Africa and find out who took over Ghana and what does it mean for cocoa.'

The Great Winfield had $3 million worth of cocoa, and by hypnotizing me into five contracts he had an intelligence service. But now I wanted to know myself, so there I was on the phone at midnight with a CBS correspondent I once met, his voice fading and burbling from Accra in distant Ghana. The situation was confused, he said. I wanted to know were the new fellows from a cocoa-producing tribe or not. The CBS man said he didn't know, but he thought some of the new cabinet was from the interior, where they produce the cocoa.

Now people I don't know were calling me out of the blue, saying, 'You don't know me, but what do you hear from Ghana? Is the new government pro-cocoa or not?'

Cocoa went to twenty-five cents. Now without putting up any more money I could buy two more contracts.

There was a dinner for the cocoa industry and a man from Hershey gave a speech and said there was plenty of cocoa for everybody. The next day, faced with this vast surplus, cocoa plummeted – cocoa is an unregulated market – so fast they had to shut up the trading. At the bottom the man from Hershey steps in and buys from the panickers. This confuses me. Why should he buy if there is going to be plenty later?

Now I suddenly realized there were three lions in the middle of this ring called Hershey, Nestle, and M&M, and we were all mice trying to cast them in a net. Hershey has only to lean on the market and the mice are mouse pâté. Hershey, Nestle, and M&M have to buy the real cocoa down the road somewhere, and meantime they were hedging themselves with millions of dollars, buying and selling cocoa contracts.

The object of the game is for the mice to keep the cocoa away from the lions so that the lions have to pay up for it when it comes time to make the chocolate bars. However, if the lions catch the mice, they skin them and take their cocoa contracts away, and then they can pay the going rate for cocoa. In their pockets they have the mice's contracts.

After the Hershey speech there was a mouse panic, cocoa dropped to twenty-two cents, and I got a margin call and several rolls of Tums. Happily, cocoa bounced to twenty-four cents immediately and I was saved.

The Great Winfield was on the phone, soothing. 'Hershey and M&M are trying to get cheap cocoa contracts, panicking the speculators,' he said. 'Well, we don't panic. *They* know there isn't any cocoa, that's why they're trying this. The farmers aren't spraying the trees. They're leaving the farms. This crop is already bad. If next year's crop is bad, we'll see cocoa at forty cents, at fifty cents, at sixty cents. The chocolate people will be screaming for cocoa, their backs to the wall.'

Cocoa went to twenty-five cents, and now I was beginning to get reports from brokers saying cocoa should be going up soon. That should have warned me, but it didn't. The phone rang. It was the Great Winfield's assistant.

'I am distressed to report violence in the cocoa-producing country of Nigeria,' he said, and the Great Winfield picked up the extension.

'Civil war!' he said happily. 'Civil war! The Hausas are murdering the Ibos! Tragedy! I don't see how they can get the crop in, do you?'

I didn't. Of course, a little research would have shown that the trouble between the Ibos and Hausas was in the East and North and the cocoa was in the West, where the Yorubas live, but there we were, a part of every headline. Now the bulletins came thick and fast.

'I am grieved to report,' said the Great Winfield's assistant, 'that General Ironsi, head of Nigeria, has been murdered. Civil war. No cocoa.'

Cocoa went up to twenty-seven cents.

'I am grieved to report,' said the Great Winfield's assistant, 'that the main rail line to the coast was blown up this morning. The Great Winfield had nothing to do with it, no matter what they are saying in London. We abhor violence. We love truth. Truth is that there is no cocoa, and that Hershey will be screaming for it at sixty cents.'

'Seventy cents!' cried the Great Winfield, on the extension. 'Not bad, making a couple of million when the stock market is falling apart, eh?'

Now I heard a rumor from another quarter that the Great Winfield was asking his friends in the drug industry if there was any way of injecting a tree so it would catch Black Pod, a dreaded cocoa disease.

'Wait a minute,' I said. 'You told me there wasn't any cocoa, the trees haven't been sprayed in five years, the farmers are leaving the farms, civil war, riot, chaos, no cocoa. Now all of a sudden there's cocoa out there and we need a plague so it won't grow and the price will go up.'

'Don't worry about it,' said the Great Winfield. 'The crop is going to be very bad. A little rain now, a little outbreak of Black Pod, and we've got 'em. You ever see cocoa trees with all their pods turning a horrible black? A terrible thing to behold, terrible. I think we'll get seventy cents for our cocoa.'

I heard another rumor: A doctor walked into the Philadelphia warehouse where the cocoa comes in and discovered rats. Rats! He was shocked. He embargoed the warehouse. The doctor was a friend of the Great Winfield's and had bought five contracts. Two hours later the Hershey doctor arrived at the warehouse and un-embargoed it, and the rats were all gone. I had no way of checking the story. I was building up my own set of anxieties: We needed rain, heavy rain, to encourage the Black Pod. If only torrential rains would burst from the heavens over Ghana, we had a chance for a Black Pod epidemic and sixty-cent cocoa. It was so much on my mind that I introduced myself to a Ghanaian diplomat at a cocktail party.

'Tell me, sir,' I said, 'is it raining in your country now?'

'It always rains in August,' he said.

'I know,' I said, 'but is it raining hard? Torrentially?'

The Ghanaian diplomat stared at me as if I were some kind of nut and walked away.

Meanwhile, to an old tape-trader, cocoa was not acting well. It had faltered at twenty-seven cents. The volume was huge. It was drifting down, and no one knew whether there was any cocoa or how big the crop would be. The Great Winfield decided we must send our man to West Africa to find out if it was raining and whether the Dreaded Black Pod Disease was spreading and whether indeed there was any cocoa crop at all. The Great Winfield picked Marvin from Brooklyn, a busted cocoa trader. Marvin usually bought a few cocoa contracts, pyramided them, made a lot of money, then got killed, went broke, and then hustled around for odd jobs trying to get a stake to get back in the game. At the time, Marvin was in the broke stage, so he could perform the mission. Marvin weighs 240 pounds, wears glasses, and had never been west of the Catskills or north of Hartford, and as far as I could tell, he didn't know a cocoa tree from an elderberry bush. To him cocoa was a piece of paper traded on Wall Street, but Marvin was Our Man in West Africa. I went up to Abercrombie & Fitch with him. The Great Winfield had $3 million worth of cocoa at stake, and he was paying Marvin $500 and expenses.

As Marvin got togged out in his safari suit I was beginning to get vague feelings this was no investment but a chapter from some early Waugh.

Marvin bought a hunting knife, a compass, a kit that kept the martinis cold, a waterproof cover for the cards. We spent a serious hour talking to a salesman about a Wesley Richards .475. That is an elephant gun.

'You're not going to run into any elephants, you're going to count cocoa,' I said.

'You never can tell what you need,' Marvin said, taking a careful bead on the elevator of Abercrombie & Fitch, the barrels wavering uncertainly.

Then we went to a drugstore where Marvin got pills for dysentery, jaundice, snake bite, yellow fever, ragweed allergy, poison ivy, and constipation. He also got 100 Meprobamate, a tranquilizer. Then we went to Kennedy, and Marvin hefted himself and his kits into a Pan American jet. He gave a gallant wave of his hand and was gone. Only twenty-four hours later we got our first intelligence.

RAINING OFF AND ON
MARVIN

Back to our man in Ghana went a cable:

GET PRODUCTION FORECAST BASED NUMBER TREES WHAT WEATHER HOW MANY TREES DISEASED WHAT PRICE TO FARMERS
WINFIELD

Back came a cable:

BRITISHER IN HOTEL SAYS SAME NUMBER OF TREES AS LAST YEAR AND CAPSID FLY UNDER CONTROL

'Capsid fly? Capsid fly?' I said.

'Eats cocoa trees,' said the Great Winfield's assistant.

'Dammit, I didn't send him there to sit in the hotel,' roared the Great Winfield. 'Tell him to get out and check the cocoa warehouses, the major plantations, find out about the crop. I got three million bucks in this and cocoa is down to twenty-six cents.'

'Maybe he doesn't feel safe without that elephant gun,' I said. Cocoa was down to 25.5 cents. Somebody knew something we didn't know, or perhaps the lions were frightening the mice again, no way to tell. The next cable was not much help.

BRITISHER HERE SAYS SOME BLACK POD IN ASHANTI REGION LEAVING FOR ASHANTI REGION TOMORROW STOP IT HAS STOPPED RAINING MARVIN

In the next two days, cocoa dropped to 24.5 cents. I got a margin call and they sold two of my contracts. The Great Winfield scowled and wondered where the hell Marvin was. I visualized Marvin, in his inimitable way, going up to a Ghanaian outside a warehouse, asking, 'Say, boy, any cocoa in there?' And the Ghanaian saying, 'Nosuh, boss, no cocoa in deah.' And then, as Marvin trudges off, the Ghanaian, who had been to the London School of Economics, goes back in the warehouse, chock-full of cocoa, puts his Savile Row suit back on, gets on the phone to the next warehouse, and says in crisp British tones, 'Marvin heading north by northwest.'

That was the last we heard from Marvin for some time. Apparently it happened this way: Marvin rents a car and a driver. The road turns into a mud track and the mud track becomes impassable, so the driver goes ahead to get some help. The driver doesn't return and Marvin sets forth by himself, gets lost, finds himself stumbling through the dark humid jungle, gnats and flies buzzing around his head, the laughter of howling monkeys overhead. Leeches six inches long fasten themselves to his legs. His safari suit is soaked through.

Hours later, frantic and nearly out of his mind, Marvin stumbles to a clearing, to find himself surrounded by grinning citizens pointing spears at him. The grinning citizens seize him and strip him of his clothes. Marvin lets out a great scream.

Meanwhile on the other side of the world cocoa has plummeted another hundred points and the Great Winfield sent another cable:

NO NEWS EXYOU LONDON REPORTS CROP AT LEAST FAIR CABLE AT ONCE WINFIELD

The grinning citizens have now laid down their spears and are hoisting Marvin into a big vat of oil heated by a fire. Marvin is bellowing like a steer on the way to the steak house.

In New York, the panicked speculators were unloading their cocoa and the price plummeted to twenty cents. At that price the gentlemen from Hershey and M&M were at the Cocoa Exchange buying. Cocoa had gone down three cents from the original twenty-three cents and M&M got all my cocoa contracts. The Great Winfield was unavailable. Brooding, said his assistant.

It turns out the grinning citizens with the spears are friendly. They know when a visitor comes through the jungle with leeches, a bath of warm oil soothes the hurt. So they are doing Marvin a favor by stripping him and plunking him in the warm oil, and as a matter of fact, after a few more bellows Marvin stops screaming when he finds out the oil is not boiling. He is a rather delectable morsel at 240 pounds, but the citizens dry him off and feed him and trot him along to a police outpost, and eventually to a government cocoa station, where his own driver is waiting to be paid.

There were revolutions in Nigeria and Ghana and outbreaks of Black Pod, and railroads blown up, but apparently something like this happens almost every year and there is still a cocoa crop.

So there was a cocoa crop. Not big. Not small. Medium.

But the cocoa crop was less than consumption, so going into next year's crop there will be very small supplies.

I was busted and the Great Winfield's assistant was busted. The Great Winfield himself lost about half his contracts and kept half. 'If you can't make it one way, you make it another,' he said cavalierly, and went off to chase the shorts in KLM and Solitron Devices, and made his cocoa loss back in the chase.

Marvin has been back a while now. The warm oil really did heal his leech bites, and he is willing to go back to Ghana or Nigeria any time anyone will send him. Just give him a stake to get back in the game and he will have his safari suit packed.

Every once in a while, I glance at cocoa quotations. Nigeria has broken up into real civil war. Ghana has devalued its currency. Black Pod is everywhere. A bad crop and cocoa could be at fifty cents. Every year the world uses up more cocoa than is produced, and yet the price of cocoa seems to stay in the same range. It doesn't make sense, so I have to assume that in this game the lions are too far ahead of the mice. I know which side I am on, and the next time someone says there is nothing going on in the stock market, but an interesting situation has come up on commodities, I am going off to some mouse beach and wait in the sun until it all blows over.

# Robert Christgau
# Beth Ann and macrobioticism

*This was Robert Christgau's first magazine article. It teaches a valuable lesson in reporting: namely, it is often much easier for a reporter to penetrate a delicate situation than he or anyone else has any reason to believe. At the time (1965) Christgau was a twenty-three-year-old reporter for the Dorf Feature Service in Newark, an outfit somewhat like the old Chicago City News Bureau, providing local news stories for newspapers. Christgau was the only reporter on duty one night when the call came in from the New York Herald Tribune for a story on the death of Beth Ann Simon, a girl who had apparently starved to death from a fanatical adherence to Zen Macrobiotic diet No. 7. Christgau's immediate task was to call up her father and see what he had to say about it.*

*'This really freaked me out,' says Christgau, 'because I really hated that kind of stuff where you call up the dead girl's father and so on. It's ghoulish. But I finally got up my guts and called him, and to my amazement he talked to me for forty minutes. I think it was the fact that I knew the word macrobiotic.'*

*He had a harder time with Beth Ann's husband, Charlie, but Charlie finally opened up even more fully than her father. 'Charlie said he could feel me circling around him like a moth,' said Christgau. Both parties – Charlie and the father – ended up wanting the story to be told in full rather than simply left as the sensational 'Zen Diet Case,' as it was known in most newspapers.*

*'Beth Ann and Macrobioticism' seemed to be written so effortlessly that one is likely to overlook the tightness of its structure, which has a classic American short-story quality. It is as if Christgau took dead aim on the final image in the story – the dribble of carrot juice – and discarded every detail that did not sharpen the focus on it. The one thing the story lacks is dialogue – a shortcoming that, as I say, is built into almost all stories where the reporter has had to reconstruct the scenes rather than view them himself. T.W.*

One afternoon last February, Charlie Simon and his wife, Beth Ann, were walking in Washington Square Park. The Simons did not get out often, but when they did, people noticed them. Charlie, lean and dark, wore a bushy beard and shoulder-length hair, striking even in the Village. Beth Ann, small in the bust and full in the hip, with shimmering black hair and a wide-eyed olive-skinned face, was more than striking – she was beautiful.

Beth Ann and Charlie were feeling high. They were high on the weather which was clear and mild. They were also high on marijuana, which was nothing new. They had been high on marijuana very often ever since returning from Mexico at the end of 1963. During that time they had also been high on hashish, cocaine, heroin, amphetamine, LSD and DMT (Di-Methyl-Tryptamine) not to mention sex, food, art and the infinite reaches of the human spirit.

Unfortunately, they had also been wretched on precisely the same things, and the wretchedness seemed to be taking over. The sexual freedom of their marriage was turning a little scary. They were thinking of becoming vegetarians without knowing exactly why. They produced art objects in a compulsive stream, though they suspected that art was only an ego defense, a fortification erected by the self against the self's larger possibilities. And yet it was these larger possibilities, illuminated by drugs, which made them most wretched of all, for they had discovered that the religious experience induced by hallucinogens had its diabolic side, and the Devil had been taking them on trips they didn't really want to make.

The Simons were in deep, and they knew it could get deeper. Physical addiction was not the problem; the addiction was psychological and social. Kicking drugs would mean kicking a whole way of life. Yet, though it seemed impossible, they were trying. They managed to give up coffee and cigarettes and dreamed of moving to the country and having the baby they had almost had two years before, when Beth Ann miscarried. It is likely that as they tasted a bit of Nature in the park, with the sun beaming down among the bare trees, they were dreaming just that dream – the two of them off on a farm, away from all the ugliness and complexity of the urban drug scene, with time to meditate, to work, to grow. The dream must have seemed almost palpable in the freshening air. Then Nature turned around and kicked Charlie in the head.

For the wretchedness wasn't just spiritual – it manifested itself physically. Beth Ann suffered from intermittent leg pains, Charlie from migraine headaches. The migraines had struck almost daily for years, as often as four or five times a day. A two-hour headache was not uncommon, and one siege had lasted two days. Doctors could do nothing; psychoanalysts were helpless. Once in a while there was a respite — LSD had provided relief for almost a month — but they always came back. And so, inevitably, on that lovely day in Washington Square, a bolt of pain seared through Charlie Simon's head.

The Simons lived at 246 Grand Street, between Chrystie and the Bowery, where they rented the two floors over a luncheonette for $100. But Charlie, Fiorinal and Cafergot pills in his pocket, decided to seek relief at the home of a friend on Bedford Street in the West Village, and when he got there, the friend had something new for him to try.

His wife had been fooling around with the macrobiotic diet, a largely vegetarian regime based on organically grown whole grain and the avoidance of sugar, which is expounded in a book called *Zen Macrobiotics* by self-described philosopher–scientist Georges Ohsawa. The book contains a lengthy section in which cures for virtually every human ailment from dandruff to leprosy are prescried, as: 'MIGRAINE: Diet No. 7 with a little gomasio. You will be cured in a few days.'

Charlie was skeptical. He had eaten at the macrobiotic restaurant, the Paradox, about six months before, and had not been impressed with food or clientele. But he consented to a spoonful of gomasio, a mixture of sea salt and sesame seeds, which is the staple condiment of the macrobiotic diet. He swallowed. The headache vanished. It was the end of the old life for Charlie. For Beth Ann, it was the end of a lot more.

Charlie and Beth Ann — friends invariably speak of them as a unit — were something special on the scene. Both 23, they lived largely on the weekly check from Charlie's father, a prosperous but by no means opulent Clifton, N.J., dentist. Although the run-of-the-mill coffee-house gabbler might pine for such an arrangement, it is rarely considered cool among working artists to live off your parents. Yet the working artists in the Simons' circle never asked questions. The mystical tenor of the Simons' involvement with drugs was also unusual. For most of their older friends, marijuana was a giggle, not a way of life, and the other stuff was to be handled with extreme caution.

But Charlie and Beth Ann were not cautious people, and it was that, more than their considerable artistic and intellectual gifts, which made them charismatically attractive to a good number of serious and moderately successful young artists. Charlie and Beth Ann were the enthusiasts, the extremists, the evangelists. If there was something to be tried – be it jazz or Morgan automobiles or psychedelics (consciousness-expanding drugs) or a new recipe for meat loaf – they would try it to the limit. Their involvement was always complete. And they always came back to spread the word.

Suddenly, macrobiotics was the new gospel, as the Simons completely transformed their lives in a few weeks. They cut off drugs, and politely but firmly informed the itinerant hopheads who were in the habit of dropping around that they would have to turn on somewhere else. They gave up sex, not permanently, they told themselves, but until they could readjust to the new life. Beth Ann stopped taking birth-control pills. Charlie shaved his beard and cut his hair. They sold books, records and hi-fi equipment to make a little extra money and they stopped painting. Their new-found time was spent studying, discussing and contemplating the philosophy of macrobiotics.

Macrobiotics has almost nothing to do with Zen. Its central concept, yin and yang, is borrowed from Taoism. Ohsawa contends that all of the physical and spiritual diseases of modern man result from his consuming too much yin (basically, potassium, although there are dozens of parallels) or too much yang (sodium) – usually too much yin. Grain is the basic food because it contains the same five-to-one potassium-sodium balance which is found in healthy blood. Dieters increase their intake of (yang) salt and drink as little (yin) liquid as possible.

Most fruits (too yin) and all red meat (too yang) are shunned, as are chemicals (additives and drugs, almost all yin, as well as 'unnatural') and Western medicine. According to Ohsawa, the diet is not merely a sure means to perfect physical health. Adhered to in religious faiths and humility, it is also the path to spiritual health and enlightenment. And significantly for the Simons, whose psychedelic journeys had turned into nightmares, the source of health is placed not in the depths of the self, but in 'the absolute justice and infinite wisdom of the Order of the Universe.'

Most nutritionists regard the diet as dangerously unsound. Even in its most liberal form it provides virtually no calcium or Vitamin C, and the version which the Simons followed, Diet No. 7, was anything but liberal, consisting entirely of grain and tea. The reason they chose No.

7, of course, was that it *wasn't* liberal; Ohsawa proclaims it as the most extreme, most direct way to health. As usual, Charlie jumped on first, but Beth Ann, after some initial skepticism, soon overtook him in enthusiasm.

Enthusiasm was necessary, for Diet No. 7 was difficult. The worst trial was Charlie's third day, when he went through a period of 'sugar withdrawal,' which he claims was every bit as violent as a previous withdrawal from heroin. After that it was just a little rigorous for a while, and then it became a way of life. Although Ohsawa places no limit on quantity, the Simons ate relatively little – it's hard to gorge yourself when you're required to chew every mouthful 50 times – and each lost 20 pounds in a month, with Beth Ann's weight settling at about 110 and Charlie's at 120. But the loss didn't bother them; in fact, they took it as a sign of health.

And why not? They felt better than they ever had in their lives. Not only were the migraines and leg pains gone, but all of the minor fatigues and aches, the physical annoyances that everyone lives with, seemed to have disappeared. They slept less than six hours a night. They even felt high on the diet, with spontaneous flashes that seemed purer and more enlightening than anything they had felt on drugs. Always domestic, Beth Ann became an excellent macrobiotic cook. She and Charlie spent most of their time outdoors, together, although they were seeing their old friends occasionally and converting many of them to modified versions of the diet. One joyous day, they threw out every useless palliative in the medicine cabinet and then transformed their empty refrigerator – a beautiful $250 Gibson Double-Door Deluxe – into a piece of pop sculpture, with sea shells in the egg compartments and art supplies and various pieces of whimsy lining the shelves.

But at least one person was totally unimpressed – Sess Wiener, Beth Ann's father. A vigorous pragmatist who had fought off both poverty and tuberculosis in his youth to become a prominent Paterson lawyer, all Sess knew was that his beautiful daughter was much too skinny. Unlike the drugs, which had been more or less out of his ken, the diet ran directly contrary to his own experience, and he opposed it vehemently. It was one more false step on the road to nowhere which his daughter had been traveling ever since she had insisted on marrying one of the most conspicuous young bums in the state of New Jersey four years before. The salubrious effects of the diet he regarded as a combination of self-hypnosis and folk medicine. He certainly didn't think they had anything to do with the absolute justice and infinite wisdom of the Order of the Universe.

Charlie himself experienced similar suspicions occasionally, but Beth Ann's faith in the diet was always strong. Her only doubts were about herself. She felt she was dangerously *sanpaku*, which is to say (in Japanese) that the whites of her eyes showed underneath the iris, which is to say (in Macrobiotic) that she was gravely ill and destined for a tragic end. She was ashamed of the yang-ness of her upper legs, which were still muscular (strength is male, yang) and covered with downy hair. ('If a Japanese man discovers hair on the legs of a woman,' Ohsawa writes, 'it makes his flesh crawl.') The yang troubles in her legs she attributed to meat, a food she had always eaten but never relished, and she assumed the complete cure for both herself and her husband would be a long, long process because of the poisonous drugs their systems had accumulated. Their sin had been deep. She did not feel ready to start sex again.

But after a few months, the Simons did feel ready for art. Before the diet, they had balanced their pastoral impulse with a pop sensibility which delighted in the trivia of an affluent culture. That sensibility slowly atrophied. Beth Ann's work, in which the romantic mood had always been tempered by a hard-edge quality, became softer and vaguer. But she was happy with it — all of its 'diabolic aspects,' she said, had disappeared.

In the ensuing months, the Simons studied Oriental philosophy, theories of reincarnation, hara, breathing exercises, astrology, alchemy, spiritualism and hermeticism, and became more and more impatient with Western thought. They went for rides in the country, or swimming with Irma Paule, head of the Ohsawa Foundation on Second Avenue, where most macrobiotic people in New York buy their food. At Irma's request they provided lodging for a Zen monk named Oki. Beth Ann suspected he was a fraud — in a month they saw him consume nothing but tea and beer, and he laughed at macrobiotics. Early in August, they took Oki to visit Paradox Lost, a macrobiotic camp in New Jersey. The Wiener summer home was near by, so the Simons decided to drop in. It was a mistake.

Sess Wiener had not seen his daughter in three weeks, and what he saw now appalled him. She had begun to lose weight again. There were red spots on her skin. She was complaining of pains in her hips and back and having some difficulty walking. Charlie was troubled with what he said were kidney stones, and sometimes his kidney attacks were accompanied by migraine. The Simons took a quick swim, then looked at each other. The vibrations from Sess were very bad. They left.

But Beth Ann was sick, and she kept on getting sicker. Her legs began to swell, and when she took the macrobiotic specific for swelling, a third of a pint of radish drink for three successive days, nothing happened. (Later, when Charlie's legs began to swell, he followed his instincts instead of the book and took a full pint of the drink every day, a most unmacrobiotic quantity. He got better.) Irma Paule, who claims to have been cured of paralytic arthritis on macrobiotics five years ago, told Beth Ann she had been through a similar period. She could have told Beth Ann some other things. She could have told her about Monty Scheier, who had died at her side in Union City on April 18, 1961. Or she could have told the story of Rose Cohen, who died in Knickerbocker hospital early in October, 1961, of salt poisoning and malnutrition, after having gone on macrobiotics a few months before. Or she might have told Beth Ann she was showing all the symptoms of scurvy. Instead, she told Beth Ann to vary Diet No. 7 with some raw vegetables.

As far as it went, this was good advice. In his books in English, Ohsawa's endorsement of No. 7 is somewhat ambiguous – while he prescribes it for almost every ill, he also implies that it is not a lifetime regimen. Beth Ann's sister Wendy and her brother-in-law Paul Klein, both on a more liberal macrobiotic diet, tried to tell her this, and so did Charlie. But Beth Ann was unmoved.* Irma, she said, a little self-righteously, was a coward – afraid to 'encounter the deep change' which continued adherence to Diet No. 7 entailed. Instead of widening her diet, she fasted altogether – four times for a total of about fourteen days in September. During each fast she would seem to improve, then tail off when it was over. The same thing would happen in the aftermath of any especially painful period of suffering. By the end of September she was bedridden, and Charlie was doing all the cooking and housework. He never really tried to convince Beth Ann that she should get off the diet, or even that she should see a doctor, although he did broach the subject a few times. Sometimes his will to stick with it was even stronger than hers. He was not feeling too well either. Sex had ceased to be a possibility.

* She may very well have been suffering from *anorexia neurosa*, a compulsive inability to eat.

On the evening of October 13, Sess and Min Wiener came to visit their daughter in New York. When Sess glimpsed her lying on a mattress in a corner, he gasped and visibly turned color. Beth Ann was a living skeleton. Her legs were no longer yang, they were skin and bones. Her eyes, still *sanpaku*, were sunken in their sockets. She could barely sit up. She could not have weighed more than 80 pounds.

'Beth Ann,' Sess said, 'You are going to die. Do you want to die?'

Slowly, Beth Ann explained it once again. 'Daddy, I am not going to die. I am going to get well, and when I get rid of all these poisons in my body I will be well for the rest of my life.'

For the next two hours, Sess Wiener used every iota of his hortatory power to get Beth Ann to see a doctor, but it was useless. For Beth Ann, this was just another version of the argument she and her father had been having ever since her marriage, and before. Now she could show him once and for all that it was possible to do things differently and still be right. She had never understood her father's values, grounded in the everyday world he had overcome with such difficulty. The everyday world had never been a problem for her, and now she felt herself on the verge of conquering a much greater world, the world within. She had arrived at the perfect antithesis. What better way to set yourself against materialism than to destroy the very substance of your own body? As her father's vehemence grew, she became more and more immovable. It was very bad, and before it was over Min Wiener had threatened to kill Charlie if he let her daughter die, and Charlie had threatened to call the police because Min threatened to kill him, and Sess had dared Charlie to do just that, and Beth Ann had decided she never wanted to see her parents again. The vibrations were just too much.

But Sess Wiener could not desert his daughter. The next day he enlisted the aid of Paul Klein, who together with Charlie, convinced Beth Ann to move in with Charlie's parents in Clifton. She had two conditions: that under no circumstances would a doctor be summoned, and that under no circumstances would her parents be permitted to see her.

Charlie was relieved. He had felt for a long time that it would do Beth Ann good to get away from the city, and especially Grand Street, which had so many bad connotations for both of them. And although Beth Ann carped and complained for the entire ambulance ride to Clifton, she cheered up when she got there, and did some watercolors – from a prone position, for she could no longer sit up – of the garden outside her window. Her parents tried to see her after she arrived, but the Simons stuck to their promise.

Beth Ann was still on Diet No. 7, with extra salt to counteract what she now believed was an excess of yin. She had written to Ohsawa describing her case and asking his advice. A few days after she got to Clifton she got her reply: You are a brave girl; stay on No. 7. Charlie, meanwhile, made an alarming discovery: in one of Ohsawa's innumerable books in French, he warns specifically that no one is to stay on Diet No. 7 for more than two months except under his personal care.

But Beth Ann stayed on No. 7. She got no better. She spoke to one of her parents on the phone almost every day, but she claimed their negative waves were making it harder for her to get well. And she could feel negative waves from Dorothy Simon all the way across the house. She wrote Ohsawa again.

About two weeks after the move to Clifton, Charlie got a telegram from Oki asking for a lift from Kennedy Airport. As he drove out, Charlie had a sudden premonition that Beth Ann wasn't going to make it. He had never felt that way before, but at the airport he asked Oki, who was famous as a healer, to come and take a look at Beth Ann. Oki said he'd try to find the time. He didn't.

Two days later, Beth Ann sat up – not by herself, but with the aid of Dorothy Simon. Charlie, too weak to assist, watched as she agonized. It was awful. There had always been something people couldn't quite get hold of in Beth Ann, and as she had advanced on the diet this ethereal side had become more prominent. Even Charlie no longer felt in complete touch. But now he looked into his wife's face and was sure of what he saw: horror, horror at the extent of her own weakness and at the outpouring of will it would take to overcome it. Then the horror changed to resignation, and Charlie's premonition returned. For the next five days his temperature ranged between 102 and 104 degrees.

On the morning of November 9, he woke at six in a high fever. Across the room, Dr. and Mrs. Simon were sitting with Beth Ann. He could not understand what was wrong and drifted off. When he got up again, his parents were gone, but Beth Ann told him what she believed was wrong – she had poisoned herself with too much salt.

Despite Irma Paule's reluctance to discuss such matters, almost every macrobiotic person has heard the story of the 24-year-old macrobiotic in Boston who died with carrot juice being poured down his throat after an overdose of salt. Charlie called Paul Klein, then set about fixing his wife some carrots. Paul arrived. They decided Irma must be summoned. Paul went back to New York for Irma.

Charlie sat at the head of his wife's bed. In the mail that morning there had been another letter from Ohsawa, telling Beth Ann she had misunderstood the diet completely and advising her to start all over again. He advised her especially to avoid salt. But all Charlie could do now was to give her carrots. He lifted her head and fed her a spoonful. An orange dribble remained on her mouth.

'That's good,' she said. Then her head rolled back in his hands, her eyes became very *sanpaku*, and she died. Charlie was still giving mouth-to-mouth resuscitation when the police arrived half an hour later.

# Hunter S. Thompson from
# The Hell's Angels,
# a strange and terrible saga

*One of the strengths of* The Hell's Angels *is the skill with which Thompson depicts the milieu not only of the Angels themselves but also of the people whose lives they invade. Many stories were written about the Angels' weekend at Bass Lake in 1965, but only Thompson caught such overtones as the counterterror of the country boys with the ax handles who were just dying to lay waste the Hell's Angels right down to the last bone splinter, and the fever of the tourists who, far from fleeing the Angels, came to Bass Lake to watch them. I particularly like the exchange between Sheriff Tiny Baxter and Sonny Barger, maximum leader of the Hell's Angels, that ends with Barger saying, 'Come off it, Sheriff. You know we're all fuck-ups or we wouldn't be here.'*

*Thompson's use of the first person – i.e., his use of himself, the reporter, as a character in the story – is quite different from the way he uses the first person later in his Gonzo Journalism. Here he uses himself solely to bring out the character of the Angels and the locals. T.W.*

Everyone knows our horsemen are invincible.
They fight because they're hungry.
Our empire is surrounded by enemies.
Our history is written in blood, not wine.
Wine is what we drink to toast our victories.

Anthony Quinn as Attila in the film
*Attila the Hun*

Bass Lake is not really a town, but a resort area – a string of small settlements around a narrow, picture-postcard lake that is seven miles long and less than a mile wide at any point. The post office is on the north side of the lake in a cluster of stores and buildings all owned by a man named Williams. This was the Angels' rendezvous point ... but the local sheriff, a giant of a man named Tiny Baxter, had decided to keep them out of this area by means of a second roadblock about a half mile from the center of downtown. It was Baxter's decision and he backed it with his three-man force and a half dozen local forest rangers.

By the time I got there the outlaws were stopped along both sides of the highway, and Barger was striding forth to meet Baxter. The sheriff explained to the Angel chieftain and his Praetorian Guard that a spacious campsite had been carefully reserved for them up on the mountain above town, where they wouldn't 'be bothered.' Baxter is six-foot-six and built like a defensive end for the Baltimore Colts. Barger is barely six feet, but not one of his followers had the slightest doubt that he would swing on the sheriff if things suddenly came down to the hard nub. I don't think the sheriff doubted it either, and certainly I didn't. There is a steely, thoughtful quality about Barger, an instinctive restraint that leads outsiders to feel they can reason with him. But there is also a quiet menace, an egocentric fanaticism tempered by eight years at the helm of a legion of outcasts who, on that sweaty afternoon, were measuring the sheriff purely by his size, his weapon and the handful of young rangers who backed him up. There was no question about who would win the initial encounter, but it was up to Barger to decide just what that victory would be worth.

He decided to go up the mountain, and his legion followed without question of bitterness. The ranger who pointed out the route made it sound like a ten-minute drive up a nearby dirt road. I watched the outlaw horde boom off in that direction, then talked for a while with two of the rangers who stayed to man the roadblock. They seemed a little tense but smiled when I asked if they were afraid the Hell's Angels might take over the town. They had shotguns in the cab of their truck, but during the confrontation the guns had remained out of sight. Both were in their early twenties, and they seemed very cool, considering the much-publicized threat they had just met and side-tracked. I chalked it up later to the influence of Tiny Baxter, the only cop I've ever seen put Sonny Barger on the defensive.

It was about 3:30 P.M. when I started up the dirt road to the designated Angel campground. Thirty minutes later I was still following motorcycle tracks up a fresh bulldozer cut that looked like something hacked out of a Philippine jungle. The angle was low gear all the way, it zigzagged like a deer trail and the campsite itself was so high that when I finally arrived it seemed that only a heavy ground fog lay between us and a clear view of Manhattan Island, at the other end of the continent. There was no trace of water, and by this time the Angels had worked up a serious thirst. They had been shunted off to a parched meadow nine or ten thousand feet up in the Sierras and it was obviously a bum trip. They hadn't minded the climb, but now they felt deceived and they wanted to retaliate. The prevailing ugly mood was shared by Barger, who felt the sheriff had duped him. The campsite was fit only for camels and mountain goats. The view was excellent, but a camp without water on a California Fourth of July is as useless as an empty beer can.

I listened to the war talk and shouting for a while, then hustled down the mountain to call a Washington newspaper I was writing for at the time, to say I was ready to send one of the great riot stories of the decade. On the way down the road I passed outlaw bikes coming the other way. They'd been stopped at the Bass Lake roadblock and pointed up to the campsite. The Frisco swastika truck came by in first gear, with two bikes in the back and a third trailing twenty feet behind at the end of a long rope in a cloud of dust. Its rider was hanging on grimly behind green goggles and a handkerchief tied over his nose and mouth. Following the truck was a red Plymouth that erupted with shouts and horn blasts as I passed. I stopped, not recognizing the car, and backed up. It was Larry, Pete and Puff, the new president of the Frisco chapter. I hadn't seen them since the night of the meeting at the DePau. Pete, the drag racer, was working as a messenger in the city, and Larry was carving totem poles out of tree stumps in other Angels' front yards. They had broken down on the freeway near Modesto and been picked up by three pretty young girls who stopped to offer help. This was the Plymouth, and now the girls were part of the act. One was sitting on Pete's lap in the back seat, half undressed and smiling distractedly, while I explained the problem of the campsite. They decided to push on, and I said I'd see them later in town ... or somewhere, and at that point I thought it would probably be in jail. A very bad scene was building up. Soon the Angels would be coming down the mountain en masse and in no mood for reasonable talk.

In the Carolinas they say 'hill people' are different from 'flatlands people,' and as a native Kentuckian with more mountain than flatlands blood, I'm inclined to agree. This was one of the theories I'd been nursing all the way from San Francisco. Unlike Porterville or Hollister, Bass Lake was a mountain community ... and if the old Appalachian pattern held, the people would be much slower to anger or panic, but absolutely without reason or mercy once the fat was in the fire. Like the Angels, they would tend to fall back in an emergency on their own native sense of justice — which bears only a primitive resemblance to anything written in law books. I thought the mountain types would be far more tolerant of the Angels' noisy showboating, but – compared to their flatlands cousins – much quicker to retaliate in kind at the first evidence of physical insult or abuse.

On the way down the mountain I heard another Monitor newscast, saying the Hell's Angels were heading for Bass Lake and big trouble. There was also mention of a Los Angeles detective who had shot one of the suspects rounded up for question about the rape of his daughter the day before. The sight of the suspect being led through the hall of the police station was too much for the detective, who suddenly lost control and began firing point blank. The victim was said to be a Hell's Angel, and newspapers on sale in Bass Lake that afternoon were headlined: HELL'S ANGEL SHOT IN RAPE CASE. (The suspect, who survived, was a twenty-one-year-old drifter. He was later absolved of any connection with either the Angels or the rape of the detective's daughter ... who had been selling cookbooks, door to door, when she was lured into a house known to be frequented by dragsters and hot-rod types. The detective admitted losing his head and shooting the wrong man; he later pleaded temporary insanity and was acquitted of all charges by a Los Angeles grand jury.) It took several days, however, for the press to separate the rape-shooting from the Hell's Angels, and in the meantime the headlines added fuel to the fire. On top of the Laconia stories, including the one in *Life*, the radio bulletins and all the frightening predictions in the daily press – now this, a Hell's Angels rape in Los Angeles, and just in time for the July 3 papers.

Given all these fiery ingredients, I didn't feel a trace of alarmist guilt when I finally got a Bass Lake–Washington connection and began outlining what was about to happen. I was standing in a glass phone booth in downtown Bass Lake – which consists of a small post office, a big grocery, a bar and cocktail lounge, and several other picturesque redwood establishments that look very combustible. While I was talking, Don Mohr pulled up on his bike – having breached the roadblock with his press credentials – and indicated that he was in a hurry to call the *Tribune*. My editor in Washington was telling me how and when to file, but I was not to do so until the riot was running under its own power, with significant hurt to both flesh and property ... and then I was to send no more than an arty variation of the standard wire-service news blurb: Who, What, When, Where and Why.

I was still on the phone when I saw a big burr-haired lad with a pistol on his belt walk over to Mohr and tell him to get out of town. I couldn't hear much of what was going on, but I saw Mohr produce a packet of credentials, stringing them out like a card shark with a funny deck. I could see that he needed the phone, so I agreed with my man in Washington that first things would always come first, and hung up. Mohr immediately occupied the booth, leaving me to deal with the crowd that had gathered.

Luckily, my garb was too bastard for definition. I was wearing Levis, Wellington boots from L. L. Bean in Maine, and a Montana sheep-herder's jacket over a white tennis shirt. The burr-haired honcho asked me who I was. I gave him my card and asked why he had that big pistol on his belt. 'You know why,' he said. 'The first one of these sonsof-bitches that gives me any lip I'm gonna shoot right in the belly. That's the only language they understand.' He nodded toward Mohr in the phone booth, and there was nothing in his tone to make me think I was exempted. I could see that his pistol was a short-barreled Smith & Wesson .357 Magnum – powerful enough to blow holes in Mohr's BSA cylinder head, if necessary – but at arm's length it hardly mattered. The gun was a killer at any range up to a hundred yards, and far beyond that in the hands of a man who worked at it. He was wearing it in a police-type holster on the belt that held up his khaki pants, high on his right hip and in an awkward position for getting at it quickly. But he was very conscious of having the gun and I knew he was capable of raising bloody hell if he started waving it around.

I asked him if he was a deputy sheriff.

'No I'm workin for Mr. Williams,' he said, still studying my card. Then he looked up. 'What are you doin with this motorcycle crowd?'

I explained that I was only a journalist trying to do an honest day's work. He nodded, still fondling my card. I said he could keep it, which seemed to please him. He dropped it in the pocket of his khaki shirt, then tucked his thumbs in his belt and asked me what I wanted to know. The tone of the question implied that I had about sixty seconds to get the story.

I shrugged. 'Oh, I don't know. I just thought I'd look around a bit, maybe write a few things.'

He chuckled knowingly. 'Yeah? Well, you can write that we're ready for em. We'll give em all they want.'

The dusty street was so crowded with tourists that I hadn't noticed the singular nature of the group that surrounded us. They weren't tourists at all; I was standing in the midst of about a hundred vigilantes. There were five or six others wearing khaki shirts and pistols.

At a glance they looked like any bunch of country boys at any rustic hamlet in the Sierras. But as I looked around I saw that many carried wooden clubs and others had hunting knives on their belts. They didn't seem mean, but they were obviously keyed up and ready to bust some heads.

The merchant Williams had hired a few private gunmen to protect his lakefront investment; the rest were volunteer toughs who'd been waiting all day for a fight with a bunch of hairy city boys who wore chains for belts and stank of human grease. I remembered the mood of the Angels up on the mountain and I expected at any moment to hear the first of the bikes coming down the hill into town. The scene had all the makings of a king-hell brawl, and except for the pistols it looked pretty even.

Just then the door of the phone booth opened behind me, and Mohr stepped out. He looked curiously at the mob, then raised his camera and took a picture of them. He did it as casually as any press photographer covering an American Legion picnic. Then he straddled his bike, kicked it to life and roared up the hill toward the roadblock.

Burr-head seemed confused and I took the opportunity to stroll off toward my car. Nobody said anything and I didn't look back, but at any instant I expected to be whacked on the kidneys with a big stick. Despite the press credentials, both Mohr and I had been firmly identified with the outlaws. We were city boys, intruders, and under these circumstances the only neutrals were the tourists, who were easily identifiable. On my way out of town I wondered if anybody in Bass Lake might take one of my aspen-leaf checks for a fluorescent Hawaiian beach suit and some stylish sandals.

The scene at the roadblock was surprisingly peaceful. The bikes were again parked along both sides of the highway, and Barger was talking to the sheriff. With them was the chief forest ranger for the area, who was explaining cheerfully that another campsite had been set aside for the Angels . . . Willow Cove, about two miles down the main road and right on the edge of the lake. It sounded too good to be true, but Barger signaled his people to follow the rangers' jeep and check it out. The strange procession moved slowly down the highway, then veered into the pines on a narrow jeep trail that led to the campsite.

There were no complaints this time. Willow Cove lacked only a free-beer machine to make it perfect. A dozen of the Angels leaped off their bikes and rushed into the lake fully clothed. I parked under a tree and got out to look around. We were on a small peninsula jutting into Bass Lake and cut off from the highway by a half mile of pine forest. It was an idyllic kind of setting and a very unlikely place to be put aside for an orgy. But it was, and the outlaws set about occupying it like a victorious army. Sheriff Baxter and the head ranger explained to Barger that there were only two conditions on their use of the site: (1) that they would leave it as clean and unlittered as they found it and (2) that they would keep to themselves and not menace the campgrounds on the other side of the lake, which were full of tourists. Sonny agreed, and the weekend's first crisis was over. The outlaw clan, which now numbered about two hundred, was agreeably settled in a private kingdom, with nothing of substance to bitch about. Beyond that, the Maximum Angel was committed to the task of keeping his people under control. It was an unnatural situation for Barger to find himself in. Instead of spending the weekend rallying his boozy legion from one piece of unfriendly turf to another, beset at all times by a cruel authority wearing guns and badges, he now found his people in a pleasant cul-de-sac ... a state of rare equality with the rest of humanity, which they could only disturb by committing some deliberate outrage – by violating an agreement that the Prez had honored with his word.

The transaction had been carried out in Hollywood Indian style. There was a childlike simplicity in the dialogue between Barger and the lawmen:

'If you play straight with us, Sonny, we'll play straight with you. We don't want any trouble and we know you guys have as much right to camp on this lake as anybody else. But the minute you cause trouble for us or anyone else, we're gonna come down on you hard, it's gonna be powder valley for your whole gang.'

Barger nods, seeming to understand. 'We didn't come here for trouble, Sheriff. The way we heard it, you had trouble waitin for us.'

'Well, what did you expect? We heard you were coming in for a rumble, to tear things up.' Baxter forces a smile. 'But there's no reason why you can't enjoy yourselves here like everybody else. You guys know what you're doing. There's nothing wrong with you. We know that.'

Then Barger smiles, very faintly, but he smiles so seldom that even a grimace means he thinks something is very funny. 'Come off it, Sheriff. You know we're all fuck-ups or we wouldn't be here.'

The sheriff shrugged and walked back to his car, but one of the deputies picked up the conversation and soon found himself telling five or six grinning Angels what basically decent fellows they were. Barger

went off to get a beer kitty going. He stood in the middle of the big
clearing and called for donations. We had been there about half an
hour and by this time I'd suffered a fatal run on my own stock. Puff
had spotted the cooler in my car. I hadn't planned to roll into camp
and instantly dispose of my beer supply for the weekend, but under the
circumstances I had little choice. There was no hint of intimidation,
but neither was there any question in anyone's mind that I'd brought
the beer for any other purpose than to share it at this crucial, bone-dry
time. As it happened, I had barely enough money for gas back to San
Francisco. Once my two cases were gone I couldn't buy a single can all
weekend without cashing a check, and that was out of the question.
Beyond that, I was – and might still be – the only journalist the Angels
had ever seen who didn't have an expense account, so I was a little
worried at their reaction when I'd be forced to plead poverty and start
drinking out of the kitty. My own taste for the hops is very powerful,
and I had no intention of spending a beerless weekend in the withering
sun.

In retrospect this seems like a small point, but it didn't at the time.
It was an ill-chosen moment to cast my bread on the waters ... the
suck-tide was running. Somewhere in the cacophony of foaming and
hissing that followed the discovery of my cache, I recall saying, to
nobody in particular: 'All right, goddamnit, this thing had better work
both ways.' But there was no reason to believe it would. At that stage
of their infamy the Angels equated all reporters with *Time* and *News-
week*. Only a few of them knew me, and the others were not going to
be happy when I began lurking around the beer supply, draining one
can after another in a feverish effort to even the score.

Many hours later, after the beer crisis had passed, I felt a little
foolish for having worried. The outlaws gave it no thought. To them it
was just as natural for me to have their beer as for them to have mine.
By the end of the weekend I'd consumed three or four times as much
as I'd brought with me ... and even now, looking back on nearly a year
of drinking with the Angels, I think I came out ahead. But that isn't the
way they balance their books. Despite their swastika fetish, the fiscal
relationship between Angels is close to pure communism: 'from each
according to his abilities and to each according to his needs.' The
timing and the spirit of the exchange are just as important as the
volume. Much as they claim to admire the free enterprise system, they
can't afford it among themselves. Their working ethic is more on the
order of 'He who has, shares.' There is nothing verbal or dogmatic

about it; they just couldn't make it any other way.

But none of this was apparent that afternoon in Bass Lake as I watched my stock disappear while Barger called for funds. Although Sheriff Baxter had left, six deputies had attached themselves to the camp on what appeared to be a permanent basis. I was talking to one of them when Barger joined us with a handful of money. 'The sheriff said that place by the post office will sell us all the beer we want,' he said. 'How about using your car? There's likely to be trouble if we take one of the trucks.'

I didn't mind and the deputy said it was a socko idea, so we counted out the money on the hood of the car. It came to $120 in bills and roughly $15 in change. Then, to my astonishment, Sonny handed me the whole bundle and wished me well. 'Try to hustle,' he said. 'Everybody's pretty thirsty.'

I insisted that somebody come with me to help load the beer in the car ... but my reason for not wanting to go alone had nothing to do with loading problems. I knew all the outlaws lived in cities, where the price of a six-pack ranges from $.79 to $1.25. But we were nowhere near a city, and I also knew, from long experience, that small stores in remote areas sometimes get their pricing policy from *The Gouger's Handbook*.

Once, near the Utah-Nevada border, I had to pay $3.00 for a six-pack, and if that was going to be the case at Bass Lake, I wanted a reliable witness — like Barger himself. At normal city prices, $135 would fetch about thirty cases of beer, but up in the Sierras it would only cover twenty, or maybe fifteen if the merchants were putting up a solid front. The Angels were in no position to do any comparison shopping, and if they were about to be taught a harsh lesson in socioeconomics, I figured they'd be more receptive to the bad news if it came from one of their own people. There was also the fact that sending a penniless writer to get $135 worth of beer was — as Khrushchev said of Nixon — 'like sending a goat to tend the cabbage.'

I mentioned this on the way to town, after Sonny and Pete had agreed to come with me. 'You'd of come back with it,' Sonny said. 'A person would have to be awful stupid to run off with our beer money.' Pete laughed. 'Hell, we even know where you live. And Frenchy says you got a boss-lookin old lady, too.' He said it jokingly, but I noted that raping my wife was the first form of retaliation that came to his mind.

Barger, like the politician he is, hastened to change the subject. 'I read that article you wrote about us,' he said. 'It was okay.'

The article had appeared a month or so earlier, and I remembered a
night in my apartment when one of the Frisco Angels had said, with a
beery smile, that if they didn't like what I wrote they'd come over
some night to kick down my door, throw gasoline in the hall and then
put a match to it. We were all in good spirits at the time, and I recall
pointing to the loaded double-barreled shotgun on my wall and reply-
ing, with a smile, that I would croak at least two of them before they
got away. But none of this violence had come to pass, so I assumed
they either hadn't read the article or had managed to live with what it
said. Nonetheless, I was leery of having it mentioned, and especially by
Barger, whose opinions automatically became the Hell's Angels' official
line. I had written the piece with the idea that I would never again have
any contact with motorcycle outlaws, whom I'd referred to as 'losers,'
'ignorant thugs' and 'mean hoodlums.' None of these were terms I
looked forward to explaining while surrounded at a remote Sierra
campsite by two hundred boozing outlaws.

'What are you doin now?' Barger asked. 'Are you writin somethin
else?'

'Yeah,' I said. 'A book.'

He shrugged. 'Well, we don't ask for nothin but the truth.* Like I
say, there's not much good you can write about us, but I don't see
where that gives people the right to just make up stuff ... all this
bullshit, hell, ain't the truth bad enough for em?'

We were almost to Williams' store, and suddenly remembered my
burr-haired inquisitor with his high-powered language barrier. We
made the turn at the bottom of the hill and I parked the car as incon-
spicuously as possible about thirty yards from the store. According to
the deputy at the campsite, the sale was already arranged. All we had
to do was pay, load the beer and leave. Sonny had the cash, and as far
as I was concerned, I was just the chauffeur.

It took about fifteen seconds to understand that something had bog-
gled the plan. As we stepped out of the car the vigilantes began moving
toward us. It was very hot and quiet, and I could taste the dust that
hung over the parking area. A Madera County paddy wagon was parked
at the other end of the shopping center, with two cops in the front
seat. The mob stopped short of the car and formed a bristling human

---

*Several months later they decided that truth was not enough. There would have
to be money too. This created tension, which blossomed into resentment and
finally violence.

wall on the boardwalk outside the store. Apparently they hadn't been informed of the pending transaction. I opened the trunk of my car, thinking that Sonny and Pete would go in for the beer. If things got serious I could jump into the trunk and lock it behind me, then kick out the back seat and drive away when it was all over.

Neither Angel made a move toward the store. Traffic had stopped and the tourists were standing off at a safe distance, watching. The scene reeked of Hollywood: the showdown, *High Noon*, *Rio Bravo*. But without cameras or background music it didn't seem quite the same. After a long moment of silence the burr-haired fellow took a few steps forward and shouted, 'You better get your asses out of here. You don't have a chance.'

I walked over to talk with him, thinking to explain the beer agreement. I wasn't particularly opposed to the idea of a riot, but I didn't want it to happen right then, with my car in the middle and me a participant. It would have been ugly: two Hell's Angels and a writer against a hundred country toughs on a dusty street in the Sierras. Burr-head listened to my reasoning, then shook his head. 'Mr. Williams changed his mind,' he said. And then I heard Sonny's voice right behind me: 'Well, fuck that! We can change our minds too.' He and Pete had walked out to join the argument, and now the vigilantes moved forward to support Burr-head, who didn't look at all worried.

Well, I thought, here we go. The two cops in the paddy wagon hadn't moved: they were in no hurry to break the thing up. Getting beaten by a mob is a very frightening experience ... like being caught in a bad surf: there is not much you can do except try to survive. It has happened to me twice, in New York and San Juan, and it came within seconds of happening again at Bass Lake. All that prevented it was the suspiciously timely arrival of Tiny Baxter. The crowd parted to make room for his big car with the flashing red light on top. 'I thought I told you to stay out of town,' he snapped.

'We came for the beer,' Sonny replied.

Baxter shook his head. 'No, Williams says he's running low. You gotta go over to the market on the other side of the lake. They have plenty.'

We left instantly. Like the first campsite, the first beer contact had all the signs of a calculated botch. Baxter may or may not have known what he was doing, but if he did he deserves credit for coming up with a subtle and ingenious strategy. He made a limited number of appearances during that weekend, but each one came at a critical moment and he always arrived with a solution. After the fixing of the beer crisis the Angels began to view him as a secret sympathizer, and by midnight of the first day Barger had been made to feel almost personally responsible for the welfare of everybody in Bass Lake. Each time Baxter fixed something he put the Angels more in his debt. The strange burden eventually ruined Barger's holiday. The vagaries of the restraining order and the numerous agreements he'd made with the sheriff caused him to worry constantly. One of his few pleasures was the knowledge that Baxter wasn't getting any sleep either.

On the way around the lake we speculated about what sort of mob might be waiting at the next store. 'Those bastards were gonna stomp us,' said Pete.

'Yeah, and that would have been it,' Sonny muttered. 'That sheriff don't know how close he was to havin a war on his hands.'

I didn't take his remark very seriously, but by the time the weekend was over I knew he hadn't been kidding. If Barger had been stomped by a mob of locals, nothing short of a company of armed militia could have kept the main body of outlaws from swarming into town for vengeance. An attack on the Prez would have been bad enough, but under those circumstances – a police-planned beer run – it would have been evid nce of the foulest treachery, a double cross, and the Angels would have done exactly what they all came to Bass Lake expecting to do. Most would have finished the weekend in jail or the hospital, but they were expecting that too. It would have been a good riot, but looking back, I no longer think the initial clash would have been evenly matched. Many of the vigilantes would have lost their taste for the fight the moment they realized that their opponents meant to inflict serious injury on anybody they could reach. Big Frank from Frisco,* for instance, is a black belt in karate who goes into any fight with the idea of jerking people's eyeballs out of their sockets. It is a traditional karate move and not difficult for anyone who knows what he's doing ... although it is not taught in 'self-defense' classes for housewives, businessmen and hot-tempered clerks who can't tolerate bullies kicking sand in their faces. The intent is to demoralize your opponent, not blind him. 'You don't really jerk out the eyeball,' Big Frank explained. 'You just sorta *spring* it, so it pops outta the socket. It hurts so much that most guys just faint.'

Red-blooded American boys don't normally fight this way. Nor do they swing heavy chains on people whose backs are turned ... and when they find themselves in a brawl where things like this are happen-

*Or Frank Number Two – not legendary Frank, ex-outlaw and president.

ing, they have good reason to feel at a disadvantage. It is one thing to get punched in the nose, and quite another to have your eyeball sprung or your teeth shattered with a wrench.

So if there had been a full-strength fight that afternoon, the locals would probably have been routed after the first clash. But it would have taken a while for the police to muster enough strength to prevail, and in the meantime the outlaws would have wreaked all manner of destruction on the merchant Williams' property — breaking windows, looting beer coolers and probably rifling some cash registers. A few would have been shot by Burr-head and his crew, but most would have tried to flee at the first sign of serious police action. This would have led to wild chases and skirmishing, but Bass Lake is a long way from Angel turf and not many of them could have made it all the way home without being captured at roadblocks.

Barger knew this and he didn't want it to happen. But he also knew that it was not a sense of hospitality or concern for social justice that had got them a campsite. Tiny Baxter had a bomb on his hands, and he had to tread carefully to keep it from going off. This was Barger's leverage — the certainty that his people would behave like wild beasts if they were pushed too far. But it would last only as long as things stayed quiet. John Foster Dulles might have called it a 'balance of terror,' a volatile standoff which neither side wanted to upset. Whether this was a just or desirable situation for a woodsy American community to find itself in is, again, pretty much beside the point. As weird and unreal as the Bass Lake confrontation might have sounded to radio listeners in New York or Chicago, nobody on the scene had any doubt about what they were seeing. Right or wrong, it was happening, and by the time the Angels were settled at Willow Cove, even the locally made restraining order was irrelevant. The outlaws simply had to be dealt with in terms of moment-to-moment reality.

I hadn't planned to get physically involved, but after the narrow escape at Williams' store I was so firmly identified with the Angels that I saw no point in trying to edge back to neutrality. Barger and Pete seemed to take me for granted. As we drove around the lake they tried earnestly to explain the importance of the colors. Pete seemed puzzled that the question had ever come up. 'Hell,' he said, 'That's what it's all about.'

The other market was in the center of the main tourist area, and when we got there the crowd was so dense that the only place to park was between the gas pump and the side door. If trouble broke out we'd be hopelessly penned in. At a glance the scene looked even worse than the one we'd just been rescued from.

But this was a different crowd. They'd apparently been waiting for hours to see the Angels in action, and now, as the two stepped out of the car, a murmur of gratification went up. These were not locals, but tourists — city people, from the valley and the coast. The store was full of newspapers featuring the Hell's Angels rape in Los Angeles, but nobody looked frightened. A curious crowd gathered as the outlaws bargained with the owner, a short moon-faced man who kept saying, 'Sure thing, boys — I'll take care of you.' He was aggressively friendly, even to the point of putting his arm around Pete's grimy shoulders as they made their way to the beer vault.

I bought a paper and went to the bar and lunch counter at the far end of the store. While I was reading the rape story I heard a little girl behind me ask, 'Where are they, Mommy? You said we were going to see them.' I turned to look at the child, a bandy-legged pixie just getting her permanent teeth, and felt thankful again that my only issue is male. I glanced at the mother and wondered what strange grooves her mind had been fitted to in these wonderfully prosperous times. She was a downbeat thirty-five, with short blond hair and a sleeveless blouse only half tucked into her tight bermuda shorts. It was a vivid Pepsi Generation tableau ... on a hot California afternoon a sag-bellied woman wearing St. Tropez sunglasses is hanging around a resort-area market, trailing her grade-school daughter and waiting in the midst of an eager crowd for the arrival of The Hoodlum Circus, as advertised in *Life*.

I remembered the previous spring, when I was driving one night from San Francisco to Big Sur and heard a radio bulletin about a tidal wave due to strike the California coast around midnight. Shortly before eleven I got to Hot Springs Lodge — which sits on a cliff just above the ocean — and rushed inside to sound the alarm. It was a slow night, and the only people still awake were a half dozen locals sitting around a redwood table with some bottles of wine. They had already heard the warnings and were waiting for the thing to hit. A tidal wave was a sight worth waiting for. That same night, according to anguished police reports, more than ten thousand people flocked to Ocean Beach in San Francisco, creating a night-long traffic jam on the Coast Highway. They too were curious, and if the wave had come up on schedule most of them would have been killed. Luckily it petered out somewhere between Honolulu and the West Coast ...

A crowd of about fifty people gathered to watch us load the beer. Several teen-agers got up the nerve to help. A man wearing madras shorts and black business socks kept asking Pete and Sonny to pose while he backed off for panoramic sequences with his home-movie camera. Another man, also wearing bermudas, sidled up to me and asked quietly, 'Say, are you guys really Nazis?'

'Not me,' I said. 'I'm Kiwanis.'

He nodded wisely, as if he had known all along. 'Then what's all this stuff you read?' he asked. 'You know, this stuff about swastikas.'

I called to Sonny, who was showing our helpers how to stack the cases in the back seat. 'Hey, this man wants to know if you're a Nazi.' I expected him to laugh, but he didn't. He made the usual disclaimers regarding the swastikas and Iron Crosses ('That don't mean nothin, we buy that stuff in dime stores'), but just about the time the man seemed satisfied that it was all a rude put-on, Barger unloaded one of those jarring ad libs that have made him a favorite among Bay area newsmen. 'But there's a lot about that country we admire,' he said, referring to prewar Germany. 'They had discipline. There was nothing chickenshit about em. They might not of had all the right ideas, but at least they respected their leaders and they could depend on each other.'

The audience seemed to want to mull this over, and in the meantime I suggested we get back to Willow Cove. At any moment I expected somebody to start yelling about Dachau and then to see some furious Jew lay Barger out with a campstool. But there was no sign of anything like that. The atmosphere was so congenial that we soon found ourselves back inside the store, eating hamburgers and sipping draft beer. I was beginning to feel almost relaxed when we heard motorcycles outside and saw the crowd surge toward the door. Seconds later, Skip from Richmond appeared, saying he'd waited as long as he could for the beer and had finally decided to seek it on his own. Several more Angels arrived, for the same reason, and the owner scurried around behind the bar, serving up the mugs with a nice enthusiasm: 'Drink up, boys and take it easy – I bet you're thirsty as hell after that long ride, eh?'

The man's attitude was very odd. As we left he stood by the car and told us to come back real soon, 'with the other fellas.' Considering the circumstances, I listened closely for a telltale lilt of craziness in his voice. Maybe he's not even the owner, I thought ... Maybe the owner had fled with his family to Nevada, leaving the village loony to mind the store and deal with the savages in his own way. Whoever he was,

the eager little person had just sold eighty-eight six-packs of beer at
$1.50 each and guaranteed himself a booming trade for the rest of the
weekend ... Without spending a penny, he'd landed the West Coast's
top animal act, a sure-fire crowd-pleaser that would put the traditional
lakeside fireworks display in deep shade. All he had to worry about was
the possibility that the act might go haywire at any moment, destroy-
ing both the profits and the customers in a brutal eruption which the
next day's newspapers would describe as:

THE RAPE OF BASS LAKE: FIRE AND PANIC IN MOUNTAIN RESORT; COPS
BATTLE HELL'S ANGELS AS RESIDENTS FLEE

The locals seemed resigned to it, and it was no surprise to find them
armed and surly. Nor was it strange to find the police unusually tense.
This was the first major rally since Monterey, and the vast publicity
surrounding it was a factor that neither the outlaws nor the police had
ever had to contend with. Things like roadblocks and restraining orders
were new problems for both sides. The idea of a carefully reserved
campsite had been tried before, but it had never been effective except
late at night, when the outlaws were not likely to move around anyway. The real shocker, however, was the beer situation. The Angels
have always prided themselves on the one contribution they inevitably
make to any community they visit. In spite of the terror they inspire,
they leave many dollars in local taverns. Because of this, they found it
unthinkable that anyone would refuse to sell them beer – and especially without fair warning, which would have caused them to bring a
whole truck load from the city.

But Bass Lake was a different scene. The locals had had nearly a
week to work themselves into a swivet, and by Saturday morning they
were braced for the worst. Among the safety measures they were
counting on was the knowledge that the hoodlums would be much less
dangerous if denied large quantities of drink. This was evident to
everyone concerned – even the beer-sellers – and besides, it was going
to be a bad money weekend anyway, since the rotten publicity would
cause large numbers of vacationers to go elsewhere. What manner of
man would bring his family to camp on a battleground, a place almost
certain to be invaded by an army of vicious rabble?

The question still pertains, but it doesn't alter the fact that people
came from all over California that weekend to enjoy the rustic pleasures of Bass Lake. When they were turned away from motels or regular
campsites they slept in roadside turn-outs and dirty ravines. By Mon-

day morning the lakefront looked like the White House lawn after Andrew Jackson's inaugural ball. The crowd was abnormal even for a big summer holiday.

Californians are known to be enthusiastic outdoorsmen; in 1964, near Los Angeles, thousands of weekend campers had to be restrained by barriers from moving into an area that had just been gutted by a forest fire. When it was under control and the barriers were opened, the blackened campsite quickly filled to capacity. A reporter on the scene said the campers were 'pitching their tents among smoking stumps.' One man who had brought his family explained that there was 'no place else to go, and we only have two days.'

As a pathetic comment, it made a pathetic kind of sense. But nothing that simple and tangible could explain the capacity crowd at Bass Lake. Anybody who really wanted no part of the outlaws had plenty of time to find a safer vacation spot. Police reports of possible 'Hell's Angels strikes' had Bass Lake near the top of every list.

So it must have been a giddy revelation for the Bass Lake Chamber of Commerce to discover that the Hell's Angels' presence — far from being a plague — was in fact a great boon to the tourist trade. It is eerie to consider the meaning of it. If the Hell's Angels draw standing room only, any half-hip chamber-of-commerce entertainment chairman should see the logical follow-up; next year, bring in two fighting gangs from Watts and pit them against each other on one of the main beaches ... with fireworks overhead while the local high school band plays *Bolero* and 'They Call the Wind Maria.'

# Garry Wills
# Martin Luther King is
# *still on the case*

*Here is an example of the casualness the New Journalism still enjoys in terms of form. Wills starts off by sketching the scene at Martin Luther King's funeral – in the 'novelistic' fashion – but breaks off into a dissertation on Southern Negro preacher rhetoric as soon as he feels like it. Novelists didn't hesitate to do this sort of thing in the early and mid-nineteenth centuries before the Jamesian notion of point of view began to seem like an imperative. Wills is a student of classical rhetoric, incidentally. He was a Greek scholar, on the faculty of Western Maryland University, author of many scholarly monographs, when he wrote the first of several pieces for* Esquire *in tandem with Ovid Demaris, one of them being the highly regarded 'You All Know Me – I'm Jack Ruby!' T.W.*

Of course, Mailer had an instinct for missing good speeches—
at the Civil Rights March in Washington in 1963 he had gone
for a stroll just a little while before Martin Luther King began,
'I have a dream,' so Mailer – trusting no one else in these matters,
certainly not the columnists and the commentators – would never know
whether the Reverend King had given a great speech that day,
or revealed an inch of his hambone.
Norman Mailer *The Armies of the Night*

'Nigger territory, eh?' He was a cabdriver, speculative; eyed the pistol incongruous beside him on the seat, this quiet spring night; studied me, my two small bags, my raincoat. The downtown streets were empty, but spectrally alive. Every light in every store was on (the better to silhouette looters). Even the Muzak in an arcade between stores reassured itself, at the top of its voice, with jaunty rhythms played to no audience. Jittery neon arrows, meant to beckon people in, now tried to scare them off. The curfew had swept pedestrians off the street, though some cars with white men in them still cruised unchallenged.
    'Well, get in.' He snapped down every lock with four quick slaps of his palm; then rolled up his window; we had begun our safari into

darkest Memphis. It *was* intimidating. Nothing stirred in the crumbling blocks; until, almost noiseless – one's windows are always up on safari – an armored personnel carrier went nibbling by on its rubber treads, ten long guns bristling from it (longer because not measured against human forms, the men who bore them were crouched behind the armored walls); only mushroom helmets showed, leaning out from each other as from a single stalk, and, under each, bits of elfin face disembodied.

At last we came to lights again: not the hot insistence of downtown; a lukewarm dinginess of light between two buildings. One was modern and well-lit; a custodian sat behind the locked glass door. This is the headquarters of a new activism in Memphis, the Minimum Salary Building (designed as national headquarters for raising the pay of ministers in the African Methodist Episcopal Church and now encompassing other groups). Its director, Reverend H. Ralph Jackson, was a moderate's moderate until, in a march for the striking sanitation workers, he was Maced by police. Since then his building has been a hive of union officials, Southern Christian Leadership Conference staff, and members of various human-rights organizations.

Next to it is the Clayborn Temple, a church from which marchers have issued almost daily for the past two months. Marchers fell back to this point in their retreat from the scuffle that marred Dr. King's first attempt to help the strikers. Some say tear gas was deliberately fired into the church; others that it drifted in. But the place *was* wreathed with gas, and a feeling of violated sanctuary remains. Churches have been the Negro's one bit of undisputed terrain in the South, so long as they were socially irrelevant; but this church rang, in recent weeks, with thunderous sermons on the godliness of union dues.

I pay the cabdriver, who resolutely ignores a well-dressed young couple signaling him from the corner, and make my way, with bags and coat, into the shadow of the church porch. In the vestibule, soft bass voices warn me. I stop to let my eyes, initiated into darkness, find the speakers and steer me through their scattered chairs. They are not really conversing; their meditative scraps of speech do not meet each other, but drift off, centipetally, over each one's separate horizon of darkness. This uncommunicative, almost musical, slow rain of words goes on while I navigate my way into the lighted dim interior of the church.

About a hundred people are there, disposed in every combination: family groups; clots of men, or of women; the lean of old people toward each other, the jostle outward of teen-agers from some center (the church piano, a pretty dress on a hanger); or individuals rigid in their pews as if asleep or dead. The whole gathering is muted – some young people try to pick out a hymn on the piano, but halfheartedly. There are boxes of food, and Sunday clothes draped over the backs of pews. The place has the air of a rather lugubrious picnic – broken up by rain, perhaps, with these few survivors waiting their chance to dash out through the showers to their homes. Yet there is a quiet sense of purpose, dimly focused but, finally, undiscourageable. These are garbage collectors, and they are going to King's funeral in Atlanta. It is ten p.m.; in twelve hours the funeral will begin, 398 miles away.

They have been told different things, yesterday and today, by different leaders (some from the union, some from S.C.L.C.). They have served as marshals in the memorial march that very afternoon, and preparations for that overshadowed any planning for this trip. Some have been told to gather at ten o'clock; some at eleven. They believe there will be two buses, or three; that they will leave at eleven, or at twelve; that only the workers can go, or only they and their wives, or they and their immediate families. Yesterday, when they gathered for marshals' school, a brusque young Negro shouted at them to arrive sharply at ten: 'We're not going by C.P. Time – Colored People's Time. And if you don't listen now, you won't find out how to get to Atlanta at all, 'cause *we'll* be on the *plane* tomorrow night.' The speaker seemed to agree with much of white Memphis that 'you have to know how to talk to these people.'

And so they wait. Some came before dark, afraid to risk even a short walk or drive after curfew. Some do not realize the wait will be so long; they simply know the time they were asked to arrive. Most will have waited three hours before we start; some, four or five. I try to imagine the mutters and restlessness of a white group stranded so long. These people are the world's least likely revolutionaries. They are, in fact, the precisely *wrong* people – as the Russian fieldworker was the wrong man to accomplish Marx's revolt of the industrial proletariat.

People such as these were the first 'Memphians' I had met in any number. That was four days ago. And my first impression was the same as that which nagged at me all night in the church: these Tennessee Negroes are not unlikely, they are impossible. They are anachronisms. Their leaders had objected for some time to J. P. Alley's 'Hambone' cartoon in the local paper; they say, rightly, that it offers an outdated depiction of the Negro. Nonetheless, these men are Hambones. History has passed them by.

I saw them by the hundred, that first morning, streaming past the open casket in a hugger-mugger wake conducted between the completion of the embalmer's task and the body's journey out to the Memphis airport. I had arrived in Memphis several hours after King's death; touched base at the hotel, at the police station, at the site of the murder – dawn was just disturbing the sky; flashbulbs around and under the balcony still blinked repeatedly against the room number – 306 – like summer lightning. As the light strengthened, I sought out the funeral home police had mentioned – R. S. Lewis and Sons.

Clarence Lewis is one of the sons, he has been up all night answering the phone, but he is still polite; professionally sepulchral, calm under stress. 'They brought Dr. King here because we have been connected with the Movement for a long time. We drove him in our limousines when he was here last week [for the ill-fated march]. They brought the body to us from the morgue at ten-thirty last night, and my brother has been working on it ever since. There's so much to do: this side [he pulls spread fingers down over his right cheek and neck] was all shot away, and the jawbone was just dangling. They have to reset it and then build all that up with plaster.' I went through the fine old home (abandoned to trade when the white people moved from this area) into a new addition – the chapel, all cheap religious sentiment, an orange cross in fake stained glass. There are two people already there, both journalists, listening to the sounds from the next room (Clarence calls it, with a mortician's customary euphemism, 'the Operating Room'), where a radio crackles excerpts from Dr. King's oratory, and men mutter their appreciation of the live voice while they work on the dead body. We comment on the ghoulishness of their task – knowing ours is no less ghoulish. We would be in there, if we could, with lights and cameras; but we must wait – wait through an extra hour of desperate cosmetic work. We do it far less patiently than Memphis garbage men wait in their church. 'Hell of a place for Dr. King to end up, isn't it?' the photographer says. 'And one hell of a cause – a little garbage strike.'

When, at eight o'clock, the body is brought out, bright TV lights appear and pick out a glint of plaster under the cheek's powder. Several hundred people file past; they have sought the body out, in their sorrow, and will not let it leave town without some tribute. But not one white person from the town goes through that line.

Those who do come are a microscosm of the old Southern Negro community. Young boys doff their hats and their nylon hair caps — their 'do rags' — as they go by. A Negro principal threatened to expel any child from a local high school who came to class with an 'Afro' hairdo. Possessive matrons take up seats in the back, adjust their furs, cluck sympathetically to other women of their station, and keep the neighborhood record straight with bouts of teary gossip. They each make several passes at the coffin; sob uncontrollably, whip out their Polaroid cameras, and try an angle different from that shot on their last pass. One woman kisses the right cheek. Clarence Lewis was afraid of that: 'It will spoil the makeup job. We normally put a veil over the coffin opening in cases of this sort; but we knew people would just tear that off with Dr. King. They want to see him. Why, we had one case where the people lifted a body up in the coffin to see where the bullet had gone into a man's back.'

Outside, people mill around, making conversation, mixing with stunned friendliness, readjusting constantly their air of sad respect. Again, the scene looked like a disconsolate picnic. Some activists had called him 'De Lawd.' He always had to be given either his title ('Doctor King,' even the 'Reverend Doctor King') or his full historic name ('Luther Martin King' one prim lady mourner called him in the funeral home, understandably stumbling over the big mouthful). Even that title 'Doctor' — never omitted, punctiliously stressed when whites referred to him, included even in King's third-person references to himself — had become almost comical. He was not only 'De Lawd,' but 'De Lawd High God Almighty,' and his Movement was stiff with the preacher-dignities of the South; full of Reverends This and Bishops That and Doctors The-Other. No wonder the militants laughed at it all. And now, damned if he hadn't ended up at a Marc Connelly fish fry of a wake — right out of The Green Pastures.

Connelly learned to read by poring over the pages of the Memphis Commercial Appeal and he learned his lesson well: he was able to create a hambone God: 'Dey's gonter to be a deluge, Noah, an' dey's goin' to be a flood. De Levees is gonter bust an' everything dat's fastened down is comin' loose.' These are unlikely people, I thought at that sad fish fry, to ride out the deluge whose signs had already thundered from several directions on the night King died. But then, so was Noah an unlikely candidate. Or Isaac, who asked: 'Does you want de brainiest or the holiest, Lawd?' 'I want the holiest. I'll make him brainy.' And there was one note, at King's makeshift wake, not heard anywhere in

Connelly's play. As one of the mammy types waddled out the front door, she said with matter-of-fact bitterness to everyone standing nearby: 'I wish it was Henry Loeb lying there' — handsome lovable Henry Loeb, the city's Major, who would later tell me, in his office, how well he liked his Negroes; unaware, even now, that they are not his. Connelly's 'darkies' do not hate white people: 'the white folk' simply do not exist in his play, which was meant to fortify the Southern conviction that 'they have their lives and we have ours,' an arrangement convenient to the white and (so whites tell themselves) pleasant for all. The whites get servants, and the blacks get fish fries. That whole elaborate fiction was shattered by the simple words, 'I wish it was Henry Loeb.' Massah's not in the cold, cold ground. She wishes he were. These people may be Hambones, but not J. P. Alley's kind. They are a paradox, a portent white Memphis still must come to grips with — hambone militants, 'good darkies' on the march. When even the stones rise up and cry out, the end has come for Henry Loeb's South.

The signs of it are everywhere — at the Lorraine Motel, where King died; it is an extension of the old Lorraine Hotel, once a white whorehouse. Then, when the neighborhood began to go black, it was thrown to a Negro buyer as, in the South, old clothes are given to 'the help.' A man named William Bailey bought it, and laboriously restored it to respectability. King stayed there often on his visits to Memphis. It is now a headquarters for the S.C.L.C.'s Project Memphis, a program designed — as its assistant director says — 'to make Memphis pay for the death of Dr. King.' Yet the Lorraine is run by a man who could pose for 'Uncle Ben' rice ads — an ex-Pullman porter who is still the captain of porters at a Holiday Inn. He works for the white man, and does it happily, while he owns and runs a black motel where activists plot their campaigns. 'I'm very proud to be part of the Holiday Inn family,' he told me. 'Why, the owners of the whole chain call me Bill Bailey.' That's the Negro Henry Loeb has always known. It is the other side of him — the owner of the Lorraine, the friend of Dr. King — that is the mystery.

King made the mistake of staying, on his penultimate visit to Memphis, at one of the posher new Holiday Inns — in the kind of place where Bill Bailey works, not in the motel he owns. The Memphis paper gleefully pointed out that King *could* stay in the Inn because it had been integrated — 'without demonstrations.' But the Lorraine is not integrated (except in theory). Neither was the white flophouse in which the sniper lurked. It is good that King came back to the real world, the de-facto segregated world, to die. He was in the right place, after all. Memphis indeed, had taught him to 'stay in his place' – a thing it will come to regret. For 'his place' is now a command post, a point where marches are planned, and boycotts, and Negro-history classes.

These garbage men are that new thing, Hambones in rebellion – and they have strange new fish to fry. The people who filed past King's body had said no to the whole city of Memphis; said it courteously, almost deferentially (which only made it more resounding); they had marched every day under their employers' eyes; boycotted the downtown; took on, just for good measure, firms like Coca-Cola and Wonder Bread and Sealtest Milk; and were ready, when the time came, to join with King in taking on Washington. Patience radiates from them like a reproach. Perhaps that is why the white community does not like to see them in a mass – only in the single dimension, the structured encounter that brings them singly into the home or the store for eight hours of work. These Negroes seem almost too patient – wrong people for rebels. Yet their like has already made a rebellion. A tired woman in Birmingham was the wrong sort to begin all the modern civil-rights activism; but Rosa Parks did it. King was drawn into that first set of marches almost by accident – as he was involved, finally, in the garbage men's strike: 'Dat's always de trouble wid miracles. When you pass one you always gotta r'ar back an' pass another.'

The buses were late. They were supposed to arrive at eleven-thirty for loading baggage (each man had been told to bring toothbrush, change of underwear, change of outer clothes if he wanted it, and most wanted it). Besides, there had been talk of a bus for teen-agers, who were now giggling and flirting in the dark vestibule (surrendered to them by their elders). Jerry Fanion, an officer of the Southern Regional Conference, scurried around town looking for an extra bus; like all Negroes, he was stopped everywhere he went. Police recognized him, and they had been alerted about the men who would be leaving their homes for the funeral; but they made him get out of the car anyway, and laboriously explain himself. He never did get the bus. Later in the week, the teen-agers made a pilgrimage to King's grave.

Meanwhile, the wives in the Clayborn Temple still did not know whether they could go with their husbands. About eleven-thirty, T. O. Jones showed up, with P. J. Ciampa. Jones is the spheroid president of the sanitation local – a man too large in some ways and too small in others for any standard size of shirt, coat, pants. He is content with floppy big pants and a windbreaker that manages to get around him, but only by being too long in the sleeves and too wide in the shoulders. He is a quiet man in his early forties, determined but vague, who began the strike by going to the office of the Director of Public Works and — when the Director told him there was an injunction against any strike by city employees — changing into his 'prison clothes' on the spot.

Ciampa is the fiery Italian organizer who came into town for the union and amused people with televised arguments against Mayor Loeb (who insisted that all negotiations be carried on in public). Jones and Ciampa have lost the list of men signed up for the buses; they don't know how many buses are coming, how many can ride on each. They try to take two counts — of workers alone, and workers with their wives; but it's difficult to keep track of those who wander in and out of shadows, doors, anterooms.

After an hour of disorder, it becomes clear that everyone can fit into the three buses if folding chairs are put down in the aisles. T.O. had told me to save a seat for him, but the chairs in the aisle barricade us from each other. I sit, instead, with a sleepy young man who describes the route we *have* to take, and then finds confirmation of his theory, with a kind of surprised triumph, all along the way. The route one travels through Mississippi and Alabama is a thing carefully studied by Southern Negroes. After giving T.O. a check for the bus drivers, Ciampa went back to the hotel, T.O. swung onto the lead bus, and we pulled out.

In the seat behind me, a woman is worried over the teen-agers still standing by the church, hoping they will get a bus. 'How they gonna get home?' she asks. 'Walk, woman,' her husband growls. 'But what of the curfew?' 'What of it?' 'I don't trust those police. If I hadn't got on the bus with you, I'd have stayed all night in the church.' As the bus rolls through downtown Memphis, on its way South, the woman sees cars moving. 'What are they doing out during the curfew? Why aren't *they* stopped?' She knows, of course. Her husband does not bother to answer her.

In our bus, all the animation comes from one voice in the back. A tall laughing man I had watched, in the church, as he moved from one cluster to another, mixing easily, asked to sit beside me while I was still saving a seat for T.O. I was sorry later I had not said yes. As the riders shouldered sleepily into their chair backs, he joked more softly, but showed no signs of fatigue himself — though he had been a marshal all the long afternoon of marching. And as fewer and fewer responded to him, he moved naturally from banter and affectionate insults to serious

things: 'That Dr. King was for us.' The response is a sigh of yesses. 'He
didn't have to come here.' A chorusing of noes. As he mused on, the
crowd breathed with him in easy agreement, as if he were thinking for
them. This 'audience participation' is what makes the Southern
preacher's sermon such an art form. I had been given a dazzling sample
of it three days before in the garbage men's meeting at the United
Rubber Workers Union Hall. That was the day after King's death, and a
formidable lineup of preachers was there to lament it. They all shared
a common language, soaked in Biblical symbol: Pharaoh was Mayor
Loeb, and Moses was Dr. King, and Jesus was the Vindicator who
would get them their dues checkoff. But styles were different, and
response had to be earned. The whole hall was made up of accompanists for the improvising soloist up front. When he had a theme that
moved them, they cheered him on: 'Stay there!' 'Fix it.' 'Fix it up.'
'Call the roll.' 'Talk to me!' 'Talk and a half.' The better the preacher,
the surer his sense of the right time to tarry, the exact moment to
move on; when to let the crowd determine his pace, when to push
against them; the lingering, as at the very edge of orgasm, prolonging,
prolonging; then the final emotional breakthrough when the whole
audience 'comes' together.

Memphis is not really the birthplace of the blues, any more than
Handy was the father of them; but these are the same people who
created the form – the triple repeated sighing lines, with a deep breathing space between each, space filled in with the accompanists' 'break'
or 'jazz.' That is the basic pattern for the climactic repetitions, subtle
variations, and refrains of the preacher's art. That kind of sermon is
essentially a musical form; and the garbage men are connoisseurs.
When a white pastor from Boston got up, he gave them slogans and
emotion; but without a response from the audience – he didn't know
the melody.

Nor did all the black preachers succeed, or win equal acceptance.
The surprise of the afternoon, at least for me, came when an S.C.L.C.
delegation reached the hall, and the Reverend James Bevel got up to
preach. He and his associates looked almost out of place there amid
the 'do rags' and scarred ebony skulls; they were immaculately
dressed, with educated diction, wearing just the proper kind of 'natural' and a beard.

Bevel was the fourteenth, and last, speaker of the afternoon. It
seemed that earlier emotional talks would have drained these men of
all response left them after the shock of the preceding night. But Jim

Bevel slowly built them up, from quiet beginnings to an understanding of what it means to be 'on the case.' (This is a phrase he invented a year ago to describe musicians who are perfectly interacting; it is now an S.C.L.C. phrase of wide applicability.) 'Dr King died on the case. Anyone who does not help forward the sanitation workers' strike is not on the case. You getting me?' (They're getting him.) 'There's a false rumor around that our leader is dead. Our leader is not dead.' ('No!' They know King's spirit lives on – half the speeches have said that already.) 'That's a false rumor!' ('Yes!' 'False.' 'Sho' nuff.' 'Tell it!') 'Martin Luther King is not—' (yes, they know, not dead; this is a form in which expectations are usually satisfied, the crowd arrives at each point with the speaker; he outruns them at peril of losing the intimate ties that slacken and go taut between each person in the room; but the real artist takes chances, creates suspense, breaks the rhythm deliberately; a snag that makes the resumed onward flow more satisfying) —'Martin Luther King is not our leader!' ('No!' The form makes them say it, but with hesitancy. They will trust him some distance; but what does he mean? The 'Sho' nuff' is not declamatory now; not fully interrogatory, either; circumflexed.) 'Our leader – ('Yes?') – is the man – ('What man?' 'Who?' 'Who?' Reverend Abernathy? Is he already trying to supplant King? The trust is almost fading) – who led Moses out of Israel.' ('Thass the man!' Resolution; all doubt dispelled; the bridge has been negotiated, left them stunned with Bevel's virtuosity.) 'Our leader is the man who went with Daniel into the lions' den.' ('Same man!' 'Talk some.') 'Our leader is the man who walked out of the grave on Easter morning.' ('Thass the leader!' They have not heard, here in hamboneland, that God is dead.) 'Our leader never sleeps nor slumbers. He cannot be put in jail. He has never lost a war yet. Our leader is still on the case.' ('That's it!' 'On the case!') 'Our leader is not dead. One of his prophets died. We will not stop because of that. Our staff is not a funeral staff. We have friends who are undertakers. We do business. We stay on the case, where our leader is.'

It is the most eloquent speech I have ever heard. I was looking forward, a day later, to hearing Bevel again, before a huge audience in the Mason Temple. He was good – and gave an entirely different speech. But the magic of his talk to the sanitation workers was gone. It was not merely the size of the crowd (though that is important – the difference between an intimate combo and some big jazz band only partially rehearsed). The makeup of the crowd was also different. Those in the Union Hall were predominantly male. Men accompany;

women compete – they talk over the preacher's rhythms. Their own form is not the jazz combo, but the small group of gospel singers, where each sister fights for possession of the song by claiming a larger share of the Spirit. In a large place like the Mason Temple, women set up nuclei around the hall and sang their own variations on the sermon coming out of the loudspeakers.

But that night on the bus, there was no fighting the jolly voice that mused on 'Dr. King's death.' Responses came, mingled but regular, like sleepy respirations, as if the bus's sides were breathing regularly in and out. This is the subsoil of King's great oratory, of the subtly varied refrains: 'I have a *dream* ... I have a dream today.' He must have been a great preacher in his own church; he could use the style out in the open, before immense crowds. He made the transition more skillfully than Bevel had – and far better than Abernathy does. That very day, the Monday before King's funeral, Abernathy had paused long on the wrong phrases: 'I do not *know* ... I do not *know*.' He had let the crowd fool him by their sympathy; he took indulgence for a *demand* to linger. He did not have King's sure sense of when to move.

I suppose I heard thirty or forty preachers on that long weekend of religious eloquence; but not one of them reached King's own level of skill in handling a crowd. That was the mystery of King. He was the Nobel Prize winner and a Southern Baptist preacher; and, at places like the Washington Mall in 1963, the two did not conflict but worked together. As the man in the bus kept saying, 'He was for *us*.' ('Unh-*hmmm*!') 'He was *one* with us.' ('That he was.' 'That he was.')

But King's rapport with his people was not the natural thing it seems now. He had to learn it, or relearn it. The man's voice rose behind us in the bus: 'You know what Dr. King said?' ('What?') 'He said not to mention his Nobel Prize when he died.' ('Thass what he *said*.') 'He said, "That don't mean nothing." ' ('Sho' nuff.') 'What matters is that *he* helped *us*.' ('Thass the truth.' 'That *is* the Truth.' '*That* is.')

In several ways, King was very bright, a quick study. He skipped two grades to finish high school at the age of fifteen. He was ordained at eighteen; graduated from college at nineteen. It was a fast start, for a career that is one long quick record of youthful accomplishment. He got his theology degree at the age of twenty-two. While a pastor (from the age of twenty-five), he got his Ph.D. from Boston University at twenty-six. And he went direct from graduate school to a position of national leadership. His major achievements were already behind him when he became the youngest man (thirty-five) to receive the Nobel Prize. He was dead before he reached the age of forty; and there are constant little surprises in remembering how young he was – as when Harry Belafonte, speaking in Memphis, referred to King as his junior by a year. Was 'De Lawd' really younger than that baby-faced singer? And why did we never think of him as young?

He had the strained gravity of the boy who has moved up fast among his elders. That unnatural dignity is in his writing, too, which labors so for gravity that it stretches grammar: 'President Kennedy was a strongly contrasted personality ... trying to sense the direction his leadership could travel.' His acceptance speech will not rank with the great Nobel speeches: 'transform this *pending* cosmic elegy into a creative psalm ... unfolding events which surround ... spiral down a militaristic stairway ... blood-flowing streets....'

The young King wanted to study medicine. He majored in sociology at Morehouse College. He thought preachers not quite intellectually respectable, though his father and grandfather and great-grandfather had all been preachers. Even when he accepted ordination, he thought he should become a theologian-minister, perhaps a professor, rather than a mere preacher. He took his first parish – in Montgomery – to get 'pastoring background' before accepting a teaching post. To the end of his life he talked of turning to an academic career.

But he was never convincing as a scholar. An account of his own intellectual development reads as if it were lifted from a college catalog: 'My intellectual journey carried me through new and sometimes complex doctrinal lands, but the pilgrimage was always stimulating, gave me a new appreciation for objective appraisal and critical analysis, and knocked me out of my dogmatic slumber.' He was not even a very perceptive commentator on the men who created his doctrine of civil disobedience – Thoreau and Gandhi. When he began the Montgomery boycott, he liked to refer vaguely to Hegel as the prophet of 'creative tensions.' It was not till someone suggested more likely patrons of nonviolent rebellion that he began referring to Gandhi and Gandhi's American forerunner – *referring* to them – as saints. He never really discusses their philosophy. And his most ambitious defense of civil disobedience – the Letter from a Birmingham Jail, written eight years after the Montgomery boycott – does not even *refer* to Gandhi or Thoreau. Instead, King uses tags from Augustine and Aquinas (hardly anti-authoritarians). Nor does the Letter deserve high marks for logic. It offers as the model of civil disobedience, not Ghandi, but Socrates, the stock platonic figure suborned for all noble causes, but something of an embarrassment in this context, since Plato makes him preach history's most rigorous sermon against civil disobedience in the *Crito*. The Letter gives three qualifications for a valid act of civil disobedience: 1) that it be open, 2) that it be loving (nonviolent), and 3) that those engaged in it accept their punishment willingly. Then he gives as a historical example of this the Boston Tea Party, whose perpetrators: 1) were clandestine (they disguised themselves as Indians), 2) were armed for violence (they forced wharf guards away and were ready to repel any interruption), and 3) evaded all punishment (Sam Adams and his Committee of Correspondence *dared* England to attempt punishment). Indeed, none of the historical examples of civil disobedience given in King's Letter meets the three requirements he had just set up.

Like Moses, he was not 'de brainiest.' He only knew one book well— the Bible. It was enough. All the other tags and quotes are meant to give respectability to those citations that count – the phrases sludged up in his head from earliest days like a rich alluvial soil. He could not use these with the kind of dignity he aspired to unless he were more than 'just a preacher.' Yet the effect of that *more* was to give him authority *as* a preacher. By trying to run away from his destiny, he equipped himself for it. He became a preacher better educated than any white sheriff; more traveled, experienced, poised. He was a Hambone who could say 'no' and make it sound like a cannon shot.

It is interesting to contrast him with another preacher's son – James Baldwin. Baldwin became a boy preacher himself as a way of getting out into the secular world. King became a student as a way of getting into a larger world of *religion*, where the term 'preacher' would not be a reproach. He needed a weightiness in his work which only that 'Doctor' could give him. He needed it for personal reasons – yes, he had all along aspired to be 'De Lawd' – and in order to make Southern religion relevant. That is why King was at the center of it all: he was after *dignity*, which is the whole point of the Negro rebellion. His talent, his abilities as a 'quick study,' his versatility, his years studying philosophy and theology (for which he had no real natural bent) were means of achieving power. His books and degrees were all tools, all weapons. He had to put that 'Doctor' before his name in order to win a 'Mister' for every Southern Negro. They understood that. They rejoiced in his dignities as theirs. The Nobel Prize *didn't* matter except as it helped them. As T.O. Jones put it, 'There can never be another leader we'll have the feeling for that we had for him.'

Our three buses had a long ride ahead of them – ten hours, an all-night run, through parts of Mississippi, Alabama, and Georgia. They were not luxury buses, with plenty of room; the Greyhound Company had run out of vehicles and leased these from a local firm. One could not even stretch one's legs in the aisle; the folding chairs prevented that. Ten hours there. Ten hours back.

Minutes after our departure, the man behind me said, 'We're in Mississippi now.' 'Oh no!' his wife groaned. It is well to be reminded that our citizens are afraid to entertain certain states. The man most frightened was T.O. Jones. He knows what risks an 'uppity' Negro takes in the South. He does not give out his address or phone number. The phone is changed automatically every six months to avoid harassment. He has lived in a hotel room ever since the beginning of his union's strike, so his wife and two girls will not be endangered by his presence in the house. 'This is risky country,' he told me. 'And it gets more dangerous as you go down that road. That Mississippi!' We were going down the road.

The lead bus had no toilet, and the chairs in the aisle effectively barricaded it from anyone's use in the other buses. The technique for 'rest stops' was for all three buses to pull off into a darkened parking lot: the chairs were folded; then people lined up at the two toilets (one bus for men, one for women). At our first stop, some men began to wander off into the trees, but T.O., sweating in the cool night, churning all around the buses to keep his flock together, warned them back. 'Better not leave the bus.' I asked him if he expected trouble. 'Well, we're in Mississippi, and folks tend to get flustered at—' He let it hang. He meant at the sight of a hundred and forty Negroes pouring out of buses in the middle of the night. 'You didn't see that man over there, did you – in the house by the gas station. There was a man at the door.' Some had tried to go near the dark station, to get Cokes from an outdoor vending machine. T.O. pulled them back to the buses. He carries his responsibility very self-consciously.

Back in the bus, there was a spasm of talk and wakefulness after our stop. The deep rumbling voice from the rear got chuckles and approval as he mused on the chances of a strike settlement. 'We got Henry Loeb on the run now.' ('Yeah!' 'Sure do!') 'He don't know what hit him.' Fear is not surprising in the South. This new confidence is the surprising thing. I had talked to a watery little man, back in the church, who seemed to swim in his loose secondhand clothes — a part-time preacher who had been collecting Memphis' garbage for many years. What did he think of the Mayor? 'Mr. Loeb doesn't seem to do much thinking. He just doesn't *understand*. Maybe he can't. The poor man is just, y'know — kinda — *sick*.' It is King's word for our society, a word one hears everywhere among the garbage men; a word of great power in the Negro community — perhaps the key word of our decade. It is no longer a question of courage or fear, men tell each other; of facing superior white power or brains or resources. It is just a matter of understanding, of pity. One must be patient with the sick.

Henry Loeb does not look sick. He is vigorous, athletic, bushy-browed, handsome in the scowling-cowboy mold of William S. Hart and Randolph Scott. And he has a cowboy way of framing everything as part of his personal code: '*I* don't make deals.... *I* don't believe in reprisals.... *I* like to conduct business in the open.' There is an implicit contrast, in that repeatedly emphasized pronoun, with all the other shifty characters in this here saloon. He even has a cowboy's fondness for his 'mount' — the P.T. boat he rode during the war, a loving if unskilled portrait of which hangs behind his desk. (His office biography makes the inevitable reference to John F. Kennedy.)

Loeb is an odd mixture of the local and the cosmopolitan. He comes from a family of Memphis millionaires; he married the Cotton Carnival Queen. Yet as a Jew he could not belong to the Memphis Country Club (he has become an Episcopalian since his election as Mayor); and he went East for his education. A newsman who knows him made a bet with me: 'When he hears you are from a national magazine he will not let five minutes go by without a reference to Andover or Brown.' When I went into his office, he asked for my credentials before talking to me (he would later boast that he talks to anyone who wants to come see him). Then he asked where I live. Baltimore. 'Oh, do you know so-and-so?' No. Why? 'He was in my class at Andover, and came from Baltimore.' That newsman could clean up if he made his bets for money.

Loeb did not mention Brown. But he did not need to. As I waited for him in his office, his secretary took the Dictaphone plug out of her ear and began flipping through her dictionary, and confided to me, as she did so, 'The Mayor was an English major at Brown University, and he uses words so big I can't even find them.' Later, his executive assistant found occasion to let me know that his boss was 'an English major at Brown University.'

But the Mayor also plays the role of local boy protecting his citizens from carpetbaggers out of the North. He has the disconcerting habit of leaving his telephone amplifier on, so that visitors can hear both ends of a conversation; and when a newspaperman with a pronounced Eastern accent called him for some information, he amused local journalists, who happened to be in his office, by mimicking the foreigner in his responses. When a group of white suburban wives went to his office to protest his treatment of the garbage strikers, he listened to them, then slyly asked the five who had done most of the talking where they were from; and his ear had not betrayed him – not one was a native 'Memphian.' He has a good ear for classes, accent, background. He wanted to know where I had gone to college. The South is very big on 'society.'

But Loeb has no ear at all for one accent – the thick, slow drawl of men like T.O. Jones. He knows they haven't been to college. I asked him whether he thought he could restore good relations with the Negro community after the sanitation workers settlement. 'There is good understanding now. I have Negroes come to me to firm up communications – I won't say to reestablish them, because they had not lapsed.' I told him I attended a mass rally at Mason Temple, where more than five thousand Negroes cheered as preacher after preacher attacked him. 'Well, you just heard from a segment of the community whose personal interests were involved. Why, I have open house every Thursday, and just yesterday I had many Negroes come in to see me about different things.' Imagine! And Massah even talked to them! And they came right in the front door, too! It is the conviction of all Henry Loebs that the great secret of the South, carefully hidden but bound to surface in the long run, is the Negro's profound devotion to Henry Loeb. After all, look at everything he has done for them. '*I* took the responsibility of spending fifteen thousand dollars of city money – multiplied many times over by federal food stamps – to feed the strikers.' *Noblesse oblige.*

The odd thing is that white Memphis really *does* think that – as citizen after citizen tells you – 'race relations are good.' Its spokesman cannot stop saying, 'How much we have done for the Negro' (the Southern bigot is nothing but the Northern liberal caricatured – we have *all* done so much for the Negro). A journalist on the *Press-Scimitar*, the supposedly 'liberal' paper in town, says, 'We have been giving Negroes the courtesy title' (that is, calling Mr. and Mrs. Jones *Mr.* and *Mrs.* Jones) 'ever since the Korean War.' (It embarrassed even the

South to call the parents of a boy killed in action *John* and *Jane* Jones.)
But the executive secretary of the local N.A.A.C.P. was considered a
troublemaker when, arrested in a demonstration supporting the strikers, she held up the booking process time after time by refusing to
answer the officer's call for 'Maxine' instead of Mrs. Smith. ('Why, *isn't*
your name Maxine?' one honestly befuddled cop asked her.)

Mrs. Smith is one of the many Negroes who protested the morning
paper's use of the 'Hambone' cartoon. But she ran up against the typical, infuriating response: 'Hambone' was actually the white man's way
of saying how much he *loves* the Negro. It was begun in 1916 by J.P.
Alley, who – this is meant to settle the question once for all – won a
Pulitzer Prize for attacking the Klan. It was kept up by the Alley family
(one of whom is married to the morning paper's editor), and Memphis
felt it would lose a precious 'tradition' if their favorite darkie disappeared from their favorite newspaper – as, at last, a month after
King's death, he did; with this final salute from the paper: 'Hambone's
nobility conferred a nobility upon all who knew him.'

Nowhere is the South's sad talk of 'tradition' more pitiful than in
Memphis. The city was founded as part of a land deal that brought
Andrew Jackson a fortune for getting Indians to give up their claims to
the site. The city's great Civil War hero – to whom Forrest Park is
dedicated – could not belong to the antebellum equivalent of the Memphis Country Club because he was not a 'gentleman' – that is, he was
not a slave *owner* but a slave *trader*. After the war, however, he took
command of the Ku Klux Klan, which made him 'society.' The Memphis
Klan no doubt boasted of all the things it did for the Negro, since it
*was* more selective and restrained than the Irish police force, which
slaughtered forty-six Negroes in as many hours during 1866. Later in
the century, yellow fever drove the cotton traders out of town; and
Irish riffraff took over; the municipality went broke, surrendered its
charter, and ceased to exist as a city for a dozen years. Then, just as
Memphis regained its right of self-government, a small-town boy from
Mississippi, Ed Crump, came up the pike and founded the longest-
lasting city 'machine' of this century. The main social event for the
town's 'aristocracy' – the Cotton Carnival – goes back only as far as
1931, when it was begun as a gesture of defiance to the Depression:
the city is built on a bluff, and run on the same principle.

When Dr. King's planned second march took place, four days after
his death, men built the speaker's platform inconveniently high up, so
Mrs. King would be standing before the city emblem, above the doors

of City Hall, when she spoke. It was meant, of course, as a rebuke to the city. But her standing there, with that background, is henceforth the only tradition Memphis has worth saving.

Yet the city keeps telling itself that 'relations are good.' If that is so, why was Henry Loeb guarded by special detectives during and after the strike? (One sat in during my session with him; they stash their shotguns under his desk.) Why did some white ministers who supported the strike lose their jobs? Why are black preachers called Communists in anonymous circulars? But the daily papers will continue to blink innocently and boast on the editorial page: 'Negro football and basketball players figure prominently in all-star high-school teams selected by our Sports Department.' What *more* do they want?

When dawn came, our buses had reached Georgia, the red clay, the sparse vegetation. By the time we entered Atlanta, it was hot: the funeral service had already begun at Ebenezer Church. The bus emptied its cramped, sleepy load of passengers onto a sidewalk opposite the courthouse (Lester Maddox is hiding in there behind *his* bodyguard, conducting the affairs of office on a desk propped up, symbolically, with shotguns). The garbage men who brought their good clothes have no opportunity to change. The women are especially disappointed; the trip has left everyone rumpled. Men begin to wander off. T.O. does not know what to do. He ends up staying where the bus stopped, to keep track of his flock. Some men get the union's wreath over to the church. Others walk to Morehouse College. But for most, the long ride simply puts them in the crowd that watches, at the Capitol, while celebrities march by.

It was a long ride for this; and the ride back will seem longer. The buses leave Atlanta at eight-thirty on the night of King's burial, and do not reach Memphis until six the next morning. But no one regretted the arduous trip. T.O. told me he *had* to go: 'We were very concerned about Dr. King's coming to help us. I talked with the men, and we knew he would be in danger in Memphis. It was such a saddening thing. He was in Memphis for only one reason – the Public Works Department's work stoppage. This is something I lay down with, something I wake up with. I know it will never wear away.'

A week after the funeral, Mayor Loeb finally caved in to massive pressures from the White House. The strike was settled, victoriously. At the announcement, T.O. blubbered without shame before the cameras. It was the culmination of long years – almost ten of them – he had poured into an apparently hopeless task, beginning back in 1959 when he was fired by the city for trying to organize the Public Works Department. After the victory I went with him to an N.A.A.C.P. meeting where he was introduced, to wild applause, by Jesse Turner, head of the local chapter: 'Our city fathers tell us the union has been foisted on us by moneygrubbing outsiders. Well, here's the outsider who did it all, Carpetbagger Jones.' The applause almost brought him to tears again: 'I was born in Memphis, and went to school here. I haven't been out of the state more than three days in the last ten years. Is that what they mean by an outsider?' A man got up in the audience and said, 'When my wife saw you on television, she said "I feel sorry for that fat little man crying in public." But I told her, "Don't feel sorry for him. I've seen him for years trying to get something going here, and getting nowhere. *He* just *won*." '

When the strike was still on, Henry Loeb, if asked anything about it, liked to whip out his wallet and produce the first telegram he got from the union's national office, listing nine demands. He would tick off what he could and couldn't do under each heading, giving them all equal weight, trying to bury in technicalities the two real issues – union recognition and dues checkoff. When I went to see him after the settlement, he brought out the tired old telegram, now spider-webbed with his arguments and distinctions. Then he searched the grievance-process agreement for one clause that says the final court of appeal is the Mayor (still built on a bluff.) He assured me that, no matter how things look, *he* does not make deals. They really settled on *his* terms. But isn't there a dues checkoff? No. The city does not subtract union dues before pay reaches the men; their credit union does (a device the union had suggested from the outset). What about recognition of the union; wasn't that guaranteed? No, it was not. There is no contract, only a memorandum signed by the City Council. Well, is that not a binding agreement – i.e., a contract? 'No, it is a *memorandum*' (see how useful it is to be an English major?) – 'but we have a way of honoring our commitments.' The code. Well, then, didn't the union get a larger raise than the Mayor said it would? Not from the city. Until July 1, when all city employees were scheduled for a raise, the extra demands of the union will be met by a contribution of local business-men. *Noblesse oblige* – see what we have done for our Negroes. Will the Mayor handle promised union agitation by the hospital and school employees in a new way, after the experience of the garbage strike? 'No. Nothing has changed.'

Wrong again, Henry. Everything has changed. The union is here to stay, it will spread: Jesse Epps and P.J. Ciampa and T.O. Jones will see to that. The S.C.L.C. is here to stay: Jim Bevel is in charge of Project Memphis. The city is his case now, and he is on it. A coalition of local preachers that backed the strikers has made itself a permanent organization, Community on the Move for Equality; preachers like James Lawson, better educated than some Brown graduates, are convinced that the God of Justice is not dead, not even in Memphis. Most important, Memphis is now the place where Dr. King delivered one of his great speeches – those speeches that will outlive his labored essays.

The excerpt most often published from that last speech told how King had been to the mountaintop. But those who were there at the Mason Temple to hear him, the night before he died, remember another line most vividly.

He almost did not come to that meeting. He was tired; the weather was bad, he hoped not many would show up (his first march had been delayed by late spring *snows* in Tennessee); he sent Ralph Abernathy in his stead. But the same remarkable people who rode twenty hours in a bus to stand on the curb at his funeral came through storm to hear him speak on April 4. Abernathy called the Lorraine and told King he could not disappoint such a crowd. King agreed. He was on his way.

Abernathy filled in the time till he arrived with a long introduction on King's life and career. He spoke for half an hour – and set the mood for King's own reflection on the dangers he had faced. It was a long speech – almost an hour – and his followers had never heard him dwell so long on the previous assassination attempt, when a woman stabbed him near the heart. The papers quoted a doctor as saying that King would have died if he had sneezed. 'If I had sneezed,' he said, he would not have been in Birmingham for the marches. 'If I had sneezed—' ('Tell it!' He was calling the roll now, talking 'and a half,' tolling the old cadences.) He could never, had he sneezed, have gone to Selma; to Washington for the great March of 1963; to Oslo. Or to Memphis.

For the trip to Memphis was an important one. He did not so much climb to the mountaintop there as go back down into the valley of his birth. Some instinct made him return to the South, breathing in strength for his assault on Washington, which he called the very last hope for nonviolence. He was learning, relearning, what had made him great – learning what motels to stay at; what style to use; what were his roots. He was learning, from that first disastrous march, that he could not come in and touch a place with one day's fervor; that he had to *work with* a community to make it respond nonviolently as Montgomery had, and Birmingham, and Selma.

It is ironic that the trouble on that first march broke out on Beale Street, where another man learned what his roots were. W.C. Handy did not come from Memphis, like Bessie Smith; he did not grow up singing the blues. He learned to play the trumpet in Alabama from a traveling bandmaster, a real Professor Harold Hill. Then he went North, to tootle transcribed Beethoven on 'classical cornet' afternoons in Chicago. It was only when he came back South, and saw that the native songs *worked* better with audiences, that he began to write down some of those songs and get them published.

King, after largely ineffectual days in Chicago, returned to Memphis, the deracinated Negro coming home. Home to die. His very oratory regained majesty as he moved South. He had to find out all over what his own movement was about — as Marc Connelly's 'Lawd' learns from his own creation: 'Dey cain't lick you, kin dey Hezdrel?' Bevel said the leader was not Martin King. That was true, too, in several ways. In one sense, Rosa Parks was the true leader. And T.O. Jones. All the unlickable Hezdrels. King did not sing the civil-rights blues from his youth. Like Handy, he got them published. He knew what *worked* — and despite all the charges of the militants, no other leader had his record of success. He was a leader who, when he looked around, had armies behind him.

This does not mean he was not authentic as a leader. On the contrary. His genius lay in his ability to articulate what Rosa Parks and T.O. feel. Mailer asks whether he was great or was hamboning; but King's unique note was precisely his *ham* greatness. That is why men ask, now, whether *his* kind of greatness is obsolete. Even in his short life, King seemed to have outlived his era. He went North again — not to school this time, but to carry his movement out of Baptist-preacher territory — and he failed. The civil-rights movement, when it left the South, turned to militancy and urban riots. Men don't sing the old songs in a new land.

Yet it may be too soon to say that the South's contribution has been made. After all, the first two riots in 1968 were in South Carolina and Tennessee. The garbage strike opens a whole new possibility of labor-racial coalition in those jobs consigned exclusively to Negroes throughout the South. And, more important, the Northern Negro, who has always had a love–hate memory for the South, begins to yearn for his old identity. The name for it is 'soul.'

The militant activists insist on tradition (Africa) and religion (Muslimism, black Messianism, etc.) and community (the brothers). Like the young King, many Negroes feel the old Baptist preachers were not dignified. Better exotic headdress and long gowns from Africa than the frock coat of 'De Lawd.' But the gowns and headgear *are* exotic foreign things that men wear stiffly, a public facade. There are more familiar Negro traditions and religion and community. Black graduate students have earned the right to go back to hominy and chitlins and mock anyone who laughs. The growth of 'soul' is a spiritual return to the South -- but a return with new weapons of dignity and resistance. Religion, the family, the past can be reclaimed now without their demeaning overtones. In this respect, the modern Negro is simply repeating, two decades later, King's brilliant maneuver of escape and reentry. He got the best of both worlds -- the dignity that could only be won 'outside,' and the more familiar things which that dignity can transform. King was there before them all.

He remained, always, the one convincing preacher. Other civil-rights pioneers were mostly lawyers, teachers, authors. They learned the white man's language almost too well. King learned it, too; but it was always stiff. He belonged in the pulpit, not at the lectern. Bayard Rustin, with his high dry professional voice and trilled r's, cannot wear the S.C.L.C.'s marching coveralls with any credibility. The same is true, in varying measure, of most first-generation 'respectable' leaders. Some of them would clearly get indigestion from the thinnest possible slice of watermelon. Adam Powell, of course, can ham it with the best; but his is a raffish rogue-charm, distinguished by its whiff of mischief. King, by contrast, was an Uncle Ben with a degree, a Bill Bailey who came home -- and turned the home upside down. That is why he infuriated Southerners more than all the Stokelys and Raps put together. In him, they saw *their* niggers turning a calm new face of power on them.

King had the self-contained dignity of the South without its passivity. His day is not past. It is just coming. He was on his way, when he died, to a feast of 'soul food' -- a current fad in Negro circles. But King was there before them. He had always loved what his biographer calls, rather nervously, 'ethnic delicacies.' He never lost his 'soul.' He was never ashamed. His career said many things. That the South cannot be counted out of the struggle yet. That the Negro does not have to go elsewhere to find an identity -- he can make his stand on American soil. That even the Baptist preacher's God need not yield, yet, to Allah. God is not dead -- though 'De Lawd' has died. One of His prophets died.

# Tom Wolfe from
# Radical chic & mau-mauing the flak catchers

*I have placed these two selections from* Radical Chic & Mau-Mauing the Flak Catchers *together to try to illustrate the use of a device I have categorized as 'the downstage narrator.' In the first selection, from 'Radical Chic,' the milieu is Park Avenue in the classic Social sense, and in the telling of the story itself I tried to capture the precious tones that still prevail, however unconsciously, in that world. In the second selection, from 'Mau-Mauing the Flak Catchers,' the milieu is the opposite end of the social scale, slum life in San Francisco, and here I have purposely narrated the story in the street tones of the black militant. To make this work, I found I had to avoid certain obvious slang expression such as cat, meaning* man *or* person, *because they made the mimicry too arch.*

*In both stories I also depended heavily on details of status life to try to draw the reader inside the emotional life of the characters. I enjoyed the contrast created by drawing these details largely from the top of the social scale in 'Radical Chic' and from the bottom in 'Mau-Mauing the Flak Catchers.' There was little opportunity to use the point of view in the conventional sense in either story except at the very opening of 'Radical Chic.' Some critics apparently thought that I fabricated Leonard Bernstein's insomniac version. In fact, every detail of his 'Negro by the piano' fantasy, including the Negro's remarks, comes from Bernstein's own words as recorded in a book called* The Private World of Leonard Bernstein *by his friend John Gruen.*

*One final note: I was also accused of sneaking a tape recorder into Bernstein's home in order to get the dialogue with which 'Radical Chic' is filled (to the bursting point, perhaps). I took this as a great left-handed compliment to my accuracy, which I achieved in the oldest and most orthodox manner possible: I came to the Bernsteins' party for no other reason than to write about it, arrived with a notebook and ball-point pen in plain view and took notes in the center of the living room throughout the action described. In fact, I doubt that anyone could have recorded the dialogue as accurately with a conventional tape re-*

*corder, because on tapes it is so hard to identify voices in crowd scenes. (I understand there is a marvelous new machine that sorts out the voices for you through some sort of voice-print mechanism.) T.W.*

## From 'Radical Chic'

At 2 or 3 or 4 a.m., somewhere along in there, on August 25, 1966, his forty-eighth birthday, in fact, Leonard Bernstein woke up in the dark in a state of wild alarm. That had happened before. It was one of the forms his insomnia took. So he did the usual. He got up and walked around a bit. He felt groggy. Suddenly he had a vision, an inspiration. He could see himself, Leonard Bernstein, the *egregio maestro*, walking out on stage in white tie and tails in front of a full orchestra. On one side of the conductor's podium is a piano. On the other is a chair with a guitar leaning against it. He sits in the chair and picks up the guitar. A guitar! One of those half-witted instruments, like the accordion, that are made for the Learn-To-Play-in-Eight-Days E-Z-Diagram 110-IQ fourteen-year-olds of Levittown! But there's a reason. He has an anti-war message to deliver to the great starched white-throated audience in the symphony hall. He announces to them: 'I love.' Just that. The effect is mortifying. All at once a Negro rises up from out of the curve of the grand piano and starts saying things like, 'The audience is curi-ously embarrassed.' Lenny tries to start again, plays some quick num-bers on the piano, says, 'I love. *Amo ergo sum.*' The Negro rises again and says, 'The audience thinks he ought to get up and walk out. The audience thinks, "I am ashamed even to nudge my neighbor." ' Finally, Lenny gets off a heartfelt anti-war speech and exits.

For a moment, sitting there alone in his home in the small hours of the morning, Lenny thought it might just work and he jotted the idea down. Think of the headlines: BERNSTEIN ELECTRIFIES CONCERT AUDI-ENCE WITH ANTI-WAR APPEAL. But then his enthusiasm collapsed. He lost heart. Who the hell was this Negro rising up from the piano and informing the world what an ass Leonard Bernstein was making of himself? It didn't make sense, this superego Negro by the concert grand.

Mmmmmmmmmmmmmmmmm. These are nice. Little Roquefort cheese morsels rolled in crushed nuts. Very tasty. Very subtle. It's the way the dry sackiness of the nuts tiptoes up against the dour savor of the cheese that is so nice, so subtle. Wonder what the Black Panthers eat here on the hors d'oeuvre trail? Do the Panthers like little Roquefort

cheese morsels rolled in crushed nuts this way, and asparagus tips in
mayonnaise dabs, and *meatballs petites au Coq Hardi*, all of which are
at this very moment being offered to them on gadrooned silver platters
by maids in black uniforms with handironed white aprons ... The
butler will bring them their drinks ... Deny it if you wish to, but such
are the *pensées métaphysiques* that rush through one's head on these
Radical Chic evenings just now in New York. For example, does that
huge Black Panther there in the hallway, the one shaking hands with
Felicia Bernstein herself, the one with the black leather coat and the
dark glasses and the absolutely unbelievable Afro, Fuzzy-Wuzzy-scale,
in fact – is he, a Black Panther, going on to pick up a Roquefort cheese
morsel rolled in crushed nuts from off the tray, from a maid in uniform, and just pop it down the gullet without so much as missing a
beat of Felicia's perfect Mary Astor voice ...

Felicia is remarkable. She is beautiful, with that rare burnished
beauty that lasts through the years. Her hair is pale blond and set just
so. She has a voice that is 'theatrical,' to use a term from her youth.
She greets the Black Panthers with the same bend of the wrist, the
same tilt of the head, the same perfect Mary Astor voice with which
she greets people like Jason, John and D.D., Adolph, Betty, Gian-Carlo,
Schuyler, and Goddard, during those *après*-concert suppers she and
Lenny are so famous for. What evenings! She lights the candles over
the dining-room table, and in the Gotham gloaming the little tremulous
tips of flame are reflected in the mirrored surface of the table, a
bottomless blackness with a thousand stars, and it is that moment that
Lenny loves. There seem to be a thousand stars above and a thousand
stars below, a room full of stars, a penthouse duplex full of stars, a
Manhattan tower full of stars, with marvelous people drifting through
the heavens, Jason Robards, John and D.D. Ryan, Gian-Carlo Menotti,
Schuyler Chapin, Goddard Lieberson, Mike Nichols, Lillian Hellman,
Larry Rivers, Aaron Copland, Richard Avedon, Milton and Amy Greene,
Lukas Foss, Jennie Tourel, Samuel Barber, Jerome Robbins, Steve
Sondheim, Adolph and Phyllis Green, Betty Comden, and the Patrick
O'Neals ...

... and now, in the season of Radical Chic, the Black Panthers. That
huge Panther there, the one Felicia is smiling her tango smile at, is
Robert Bay, who just forty-one hours ago was arrested in an alterca-
tion with the police, supposedly over a .38-caliber revolver that someone had, in a parked car in Queens at Northern Boulevard and 104th
Street or some such unbelievable place, and taken to jail on a most

Radical chic & mau-mauing the flak catchers   415

unusual charge called 'criminal facilitation.' And now he is out on bail and walking into Leonard and Felicia Bernstein's thirteen-room penthouse duplex on Park Avenue. Harassment & Hassles, Guns & Pigs, Jail & Bail – they're *real*, these Black Panthers. The very idea of them, these real revolutionaries, who actually put their lives on the line, runs through Lenny's duplex like a rogue hormone. Everyone casts a glance, or stares, or tries a smile, and then sizes up the house for the somehow delicious counterpoint ... Deny it if you want to! but one *does* end up making such sweet furtive comparisons in this season of Radical Chic ... There's Otto Preminger in the library and Jean vanden Heuvel in the hall, and Peter and Cheray Duchin in the living room, and Frank and Domna Stanton, Gail Lumet, Sheldon Harnick, Cynthia Phipps, Burton Lane, Mrs. August Heckscher, Roger Wilkins, Barbara Walters, Bob Silvers, Mrs. Richard Avedon, Mrs. Arthur Penn, Julie Belafonte, Harold Taylor, and scores more, including Charlotte Curtis, women's news editor of *The New York Times*, America's foremost chronicler of Society, a lean woman in black, with her notebook out, standing near Felicia and big Robert Bay, and talking to Cheray Duchin.

Cheray tells her: 'I've never met a Panther – this is a first for me!' ... never dreaming that within forty-eight hours her words will be on the desk of the President of the United States ...

*This is a first for me.* But she is not alone in her thrill as the Black Panthers coming trucking on in, into Lenny's house, Robert Bay, Don Cox the Panthers' Field Marshal from Oakland, Henry Miller the Harlem Panther defense captain, the Panther women – Christ, if the Panthers don't know how to get it all together, as they say, the tight pants, the tight black turtlenecks, the leather coats, Cuban shades, Afros. But real Afros, not the ones that have been shaped and trimmed like a topiary hedge and sprayed until they have a sheen like acrylic wall-to-wall – but like funky, natural, scraggly ... wild ...

*These are no civil-rights Negroes wearing gray suits three sizes too big—*

– no more interminable Urban League banquets in hotel ballrooms where they try to alternate the blacks and whites around the tables as if they were stringing Arapaho beads—

– *these are* real men!

Shoot-outs, revolutions, pictures in *Life* magazine of policemen grabbing Black Panthers like they were Vietcong – somehow it all runs together in the head with the whole thing of how *beautiful* they are. *Sharp as a blade.* The Panther women – there are three or four of them on hand, wives of the Panther 21 defendants, and they are so lean, *so lithe*, as they say, with tight pants and Yoruba-style headdresses, almost like turbans, as if they'd stepped out of the pages of *Vogue*, although no doubt *Vogue* got it from them. All at once every woman in the room knows exactly what Amanda Burden meant when she said she was now anti-fashion because 'the sophistication of the baby blacks made me rethink my attitudes.' God knows the Panther women don't spend thirty minutes in front of the mirror in the morning shoring up their eye holes with contact lenses, eyeliner, eye shadow, eyebrow pencil, occipital rim brush, false eyelashes, mascara, Shadow-Ban for undereye and Eterna Creme for the corners ... And here they are, right in front of you, trucking on into the Bernsteins' Chinese yellow duplex, amid the sconces, silver bowls full of white and lavender anemones, and uniformed servants serving drinks and roquefort cheese morsels rolled in crushed nuts—

But it's all right. They're *white* servants, not Claude and Maude, but white South Americans. Lenny and Felicia are geniuses. After a while, it all comes down to servants. They are the cutting edge in Radical Chic. Obviously, if you are giving a party for the Black Panthers, as Lenny and Felicia are this evening, or as Sidney and Gail Lumet did last week, or as John Simon of Random House and Richard Baron, the publisher, did before that; or for the Chicago Eight, such as the party Jean vanden Heuvel gave; or for the grape workers or Bernadette Devlin, such as the parties Andrew Stein gave; or for the Young Lords, such as the party Ellie Guggenheimer is giving next week in *her* Park Avenue duplex; or for the Indians or the SDS or the G.I. coffee shops or even for the Friends of the Earth – well, then, obviously you can't have a Negro butler and maid, Claude and Maude, in uniform, circulating through the living room, the library, and the main hall serving drinks and canapés. Plenty of people have tried to think it out. They try to picture the Panthers or whoever walking in bristling with electric hair and Cuban shades and leather pieces and the rest of it, and they try to picture Claude and Maude with the black uniforms coming up and saying, 'Would you care for a drink, sir?' They close their eyes and try to picture it *some way*, but there *is* no way. One simply cannot see that moment. So the current wave of Radical Chic has touched off the most desperate search for white servants. Carter and Amanda Burden have white servants. Sidney Lumet and his wife Gail, who is Lena Horne's daughter, have three white servants, including a Scottish nurse. Everybody has white servants. And Lenny and Felicia – they had it worked out before Radical Chic even started. Felicia grew up in Chile. Her father, Roy Elwood Cohn, an engineer from San Francisco, worked for the American Smelting and Refining Co. in Santiago. As Felicia Monte-alegre (her mother's maiden name), she became an actress in New York and won the *Motion Picture Daily* critics' award as the best new television actress of 1949. Anyway, they have a house staff of three white South American servants, including a Chilean cook, plus Lenny's English chauffeur and dresser, who is also white, of course. Can one comprehend how perfect that is, given . . . the times? Well, many of their friends can, and they ring up the Bernsteins and ask them to get South American servants for them, and the Bernsteins are so gen-erous about it, so obliging, that people refer to them, good-naturedly and gratefully, as 'the Spic and Span Employment Agency,' with an easygoing ethnic humor, of course.

The only other thing to do is what Ellie Guggenheimer is doing next week with her party for the Young Lords in her duplex on Park Avenue at 89th Street, just ten blocks up from Lenny and Felicia. She is giving her party on a Sunday, which is the day off for the maid and the clean-ing woman. 'Two friends of mine' -- she confides on the telephone -- 'two friends of mine who happen to be . . . not white -- that's what I hate about the times we live in, the *terms* -- well, they've agreed to be butler and maid . . . and I'm going to be a maid myself!'

Just at this point some well-meaning soul is going to say, Why not do without servants altogether if the matter creates such unbearable tension and one truly believes in equality? Well, even to raise the question is to reveal the most fundamental ignorance of life in the great co-ops and townhouses of the East Side in the age of Radical Chic. Why, my God! servants are not a mere convenience, they're an absolute psychological necessity. Once one is into that life, truly into it, with the morning workout on the velvet swings at Kounovsky's and the late mornings on the telephone, and lunch at the Running Footman, which is now regarded as really better than La Grenouille, Lutèce, Lafayette, La Caravelle, and the rest of the general Frog Pond, less ostentatious, more of the David Hicks feeling, less of the Parish-Hadley look, and then -- well, then, the idea of not having servants is unthinkable. But even that does not say it all. It makes it sound like a matter of convenience, when actually it is a sheer and fundamental matter of -- *having servants*. Does one comprehend?

God, what a flood of taboo thoughts run through one's head at these Radical Chic events . . . But it's delicious. It is as if one's nerve endings were on red alert to the most intimate nuances of status. Deny it if you want to! Nevertheless, it runs through every soul here. It is the matter of the marvelous contradictions on all sides. It is like the delicious shudder you get when you try to force the prongs of two horseshoe magnets together ... *them* and *us* ...

For example, one's own servants, although white, are generally no problem. A discreet, euphemistic word about what sort of party it is going to be, and they will generally be models of correctness. The euphemisms are not always an easy matter, however. When talking to one's white servants, one doesn't really know whether to refer to blacks as *blacks*, *Negroes*, or *colored people*. When talking to other ... well, *cultivated* persons, one says *blacks*, of course. It is the only word, currently, that implicitly shows one's awareness of the dignity of the black race. But somehow when you start to say the word to your own white servants, you hesitate. You can't get it out of your throat. Why? *Counter-guilt!* You realize that you are about to utter one of those touchstone words that divide the cultivated from the uncultivated, the attuned from the unattuned, the *hip* from the dreary. As soon as the word comes out of your mouth – you know it before the first vocable pops on your lips – your own servant is going to size you up as one of those *limousine liberals*, or whatever epithet they use, who are busy pouring white soul all over the black movement, and would you do as much for the white lower class, for the domestics of the East Side, for example, fat chance, sahib. Deny it if you want to! but such are the delicious little agonies of Radical Chic. So one settles for *Negro*, with the hope that the great god Culturatus has laid the ledger aside for the moment... In any case, if one is able to make that small compromise, one's own servants are no real problem. But the elevator man and the doorman – the death rays they begin projecting, the curt responses, as soon as they see it is going to be one of *those* parties! Of course, they're all from Queens, and so forth, and one has to allow for that. For some reason the elevator men tend to be worse about it than the doormen, even; less of *politesse*, perhaps.

Or – what does one wear to these parties for the Panthers or the Young Lords or the grape workers? What does a woman wear? Obviously one does not want to wear something frivolously and pompously expensive, such as a Gerard Pipart party dress. On the other hand one does not want to arrive 'poor-mouthing it' in some outrageous turtle-neck and West Eighth Street bell-jean combination, as if one is 'funky' and of 'the people.' Frankly, Jean vanden Heuvel – that's Jean there in

the hallway giving everyone her famous smile, in which her eyes narrow down to f/16 – frankly, Jean tends too much toward the funky
fallacy. Jean, who is the daughter of Jules Stein, one of the wealthiest
men in the country, is wearing some sort of rust-red snap-around
suede skirt, the sort that English working girls pick up on Saturday
afternoons in those absolutely *berserk* London boutiques like Bus
Stop or Biba, where everything looks chic and yet skimpy and raw
and vital. Felicia Bernstein seems to understand the whole thing
better. Look at Felicia. She is wearing the simplest little black frock
imaginable, with absolutely no ornamentation save for a plain gold
necklace. It is perfect. It has dignity without any overt class symbolism.

Lenny? Lenny himself has been in the living room all this time,
talking to old friends like the Duchins and the Stantons and the Lanes.
Lenny is wearing a black turtleneck, navy blazer, Black Watch plaid
trousers and a necklace with a pendant hanging down to his sternum.
His tailor comes here to the apartment to take the measurements and
do the fittings. Lenny is a short, trim man, and yet he always seems
tall. It is his head. He has a noble head, with a face that is at once
sensitive and rugged, and a full stand of iron-gray hair, with sideburns,
all set off nicely by the Chinese yellow of the room. His success radiates from his eyes and his smile with a charm that illustrates Lord
Jersey's adage that 'contrary to what the Methodists tell us, money and
success are good for the soul.' Lenny may be fifty-one, but he is still
the *Wunderkind* of American music. Everyone says so. He is not only
one of the world's outstanding conductors, but a more than competent
composer and pianist as well. He is the man who more than any other
has broken down the wall between elite music and popular tastes, with
*West Side Story* and his children's concerts on television. How natural
that he should stand here in his own home radiating the charm and
grace that make him an easy host for leaders of the oppressed. How
ironic that the next hour should prove so shattering for this *egregio
maestro!* How curious that the Negro by the piano should emerge
tonight!

A bell rang, a dinner-table bell, by the sound of it, the sort one sum-
mons the maid out of the kitchen with, and the party shifted from out
of the hall and into the living room. Felicia led the way, Felicia and a
small gray man, with gray hair, a gray face, a gray suit, and a pair of
Groovy but gray sideburns. A little gray man, in short, who would be

popping up at key moments ... to keep the freight train of history on
the track, as it were ...

Felicia was down at the far end of the living room trying to coax
everybody in.

'Lenny!' she said. 'Tell the fringes to come on in!' Lenny was still in
the back of the living room, near the hall. 'Fringes' said Lenny. 'Come
on in!'

In the living room most of the furniture, the couches, easy chairs,
side tables, side chairs, and so on, had been pushed toward the walls,
and thirty or forty folding chairs were set up in the middle of the floor.
It was a big, wide room with Chinese yellow walls and white moldings,
sconces, pier-glass mirrors, a portrait of Felicia reclining on a summer
chaise, and at the far end, where Felicia was standing, a pair of grand
pianos. A pair of them; the two pianos were standing back to back,
with the tops down and their bellies swooping out. On top of both
pianos was a regular flotilla of family photographs in silver frames, the
kind of pictures that stand straight up thanks to little velvet- or moiré-
covered buttresses in the back, the kind that decorators in New York
recommend to give a living room a homelike lived-in touch. 'The
million-dollar *chatchka* look,' they call it. In a way it was perfect for
Radical Chic. The nice part was that with Lenny it was instinctive; with
Felicia, too. The whole place looked as if the inspiration had been to
spend a couple of hundred thousand on the interior without looking
pretentious, although that is no great sum for a thirteen-room co-op,
of course ... Imagine explaining all that to the Black Panthers. It was
another delicious thought ... The sofas, for example, were covered in
the fashionable splashy prints on a white background covering deep
downy cushions, in the Billy Baldwin or Margaret Owen tradition –
without it looking like Billy or Margaret had been in there fussing
about with teapoys and japanned chairs. *Gemütlich* ... Old Vienna
when Grandpa was alive ... That was the ticket ...

Once Lenny got 'the fringes' moving in, the room filled up rapidly. It
was jammed, in fact. People were sitting on sofas and easy chairs along
the sides, as well as on the folding chairs, and were standing in the
back, where Lenny was. Otto Preminger was sitting on a sofa down by
the pianos, where the speakers were going to stand. The Panther wives
were sitting in the first two rows with their Yoruba headdresses on,
along with Henry Mitchell and Julie Belafonte, Harry Belafonte's wife.
Julie is white, but they all greeted her warmly as 'Sister.' Behind her
was sitting Barbara Walters, hostess of the *Today Show* on television,

wearing a checked pants suit with a great fluffy fur collar on the coat. Harold Taylor, the former 'Boy President' of Sarah Lawrence, now fifty-five and silver-haired, but still youthful-looking, came walking down toward the front and gave a hug and a big social kiss to Gail Lumet. Robert Bay settled down in the middle of the folding chairs. Jean vanden Heuvel stood in the back and sought to focus ... f/16 ... on the pianos ... Charlotte Curtis stood beside the door, taking notes.

And then Felicia stood up beside the pianos and said: 'I want to thank you all very, very much for coming. I'm very, very glad to see so many of you here.' Everything was fine. Her voice was rich as a wood-wind. She introduced a man named Leon Quat, a lawyer involved in raising funds for the Panther 21, twenty-one Black Panthers who had been arrested on a charge of conspiring to blow up five New York department stores, New Haven Railroad facilities, a police station, and the Bronx Botanical Gardens.

Leon Quat, oddly enough, had the general look of those fifty-two-year-old men who run a combination law office, real estate, and insurance operation on the second floor of a two-story taxpayer out on Queens Boulevard. And yet that wasn't the kind of man Leon Quat really was. He had the sideburns. Quite a pair. They didn't come down just to the intertragic notch, which is that little notch in the lower rim of the ear, and which so many tentative Swingers aim their sideburns toward. No, on top of this complete Queens Boulevard insurance-agent look, he had real sideburns, to the bottom of the lobe, virtual mutton-chops, which somehow have become the mark of the Movement.

Leon Quat rose up smiling: 'We are very grateful to Mrs. Bernstein' – only he pronounced it 'steen.'

'STEIN!' – a great smoke-cured voice booming out from the rear of the room! It's Lenny! Leon Quat and the Black Panthers will have a chance to hear from Lenny. That much is sure. He is on the case. Leon Quat must be the only man in the room who does not know about Lenny and the Mental Jotto at 3 a.m. For years, twenty at the least, Lenny has insisted on -stein not -steen, as if to say, I am not one of those 1921 Jews who try to tone down their Jewishness by watering their names down with a bad soft English pronunciation. Lenny has made such a point of -stein not -steen, in fact, that some people in this room think at once of the story of how someone approached Larry Rivers, the artist, and said, 'What's this I hear about you and Leonard Bernstein' – steen, he pronounced it – 'not speaking to each other any more?' – to which Rivers said, 'Stein!'

'We are very grateful ... for her marvelous hospitality,' says Quat, apparently not wanting to try the name again right away.

Then he beams toward the crowd: 'I assume we are all just an effete clique of snobs and intellectuals in this room ... I am referring to the words of Vice-President Agnew, of course, who can't be with us today because he is in the South Pacific explaining the Nixon doctrine to the Australians. All vice-presidents suffer from the Avis complex — they're second best, so they try harder, like General Ky or Hubert Humphrey ...' He keeps waiting for the grins and chuckles after each of these mots, but all the celebrities and culturati are nonplussed. They give him a kind of dumb attention. They came here for the Panthers and Radical Chic, and here is Old Queens Boulevard Real Estate Man with sideburns on telling them Agnew jokes. But Quat is too deep into his weird hole to get out. 'Whatever respect I have had for Lester Maddox, I lost it when I saw Humphrey put his arm around his shoulder ...' and somehow Quat begins disappearing down a hole bunging Hubert Humphrey with lumps of old Shelley Berman material. Slowly he climbs back out. He starts telling about the oppression of the Panther 21. They have been in jail since February 2, 1969, awaiting trial on ludicrous charges such as conspiring to blow up the Bronx Botanical Gardens. Their bail has been a preposterous $100,000 per person, which has in effect denied them the right to bail. They have been kept split up and moved from jail to jail. For all intents and purposes they have been denied the right to confer with their lawyers to prepare a defense. They have been subjected to inhuman treatment in jail — such as the case of Lee Berry, an epileptic, who was snatched out of a hospital bed and thrown in jail and kept in solitary confinement with a light bulb burning over his head night and day. The Panthers who have not been thrown in jail or killed, like Fred Hampton, are being stalked and harassed everywhere they go. 'One of the few higher officials who is still ... in the clear' — Quat smiles — 'is here today. Don Cox, Field Marshal of the Black Panther Party.'

'Right on,' a voice says to Leon Quat, rather softly. And a tall black man rises from behind one of Lenny's grand pianos ... *The Negro by the piano* ...

## From 'Mau-Mauing the Flak Catchers'

Every now and then, after the poverty scene got going, and the confrontations became a regular thing, whites would run into an ethnic group they drew a total blank on, like the Indians or the Samoans.

Well, with the Samoans they didn't draw a blank for long, not once they actually came up against them. The Samoans on the poverty scene favored the direct approach. They did not fool around. They were like the original unknown terrors. In fact, they were unknown terrors and a half.

Why so few people in San Francisco know about the Samoans is a mystery. All you have to do is see a couple of those Polynesian studs walking through the Mission, minding their own business, and you won't forget it soon. Have you ever by any chance seen professional football players in person, like on the street? The thing you notice is not just that they're big but that they are *so* big, it's weird. Everything about them is gigantic, even their heads. They'll have a skull the size of a watermelon, with a couple of little squinty eyes and a little mouth and a couple of nose holes stuck in, and no neck at all. From the ears down, the big yoyos are just one solid welded hulk, the size of an oil burner. You get the feeling that football players come from a whole other species of human, they're so big. Well, that will give you some idea of the Samoans, because they're bigger. The average Samoan makes Bubba Smith of the Colts look like a shrimp. They start out at about 300 pounds and from there they just get *wider*. They are big huge giants. Everything about them is wide and smooth. They have big wide faces and smooth features. They're a dark brown, with a smooth cast.

Anyway, the word got around among the groups in the Mission that the poverty program was going to cut down on summer jobs, and the Mission was going to be on the short end. So a bunch of the groups in the Mission got together and decided to go downtown to the poverty office and do some mau-mauing in behalf of the Mission before the bureaucrats made up their minds. There were blacks, Chicanos, Filipinos, and about ten Samoans.

The poverty office was on the first floor and had a big anteroom; only it's almost bare, nothing in it but a lot of wooden chairs. It looks like a union hall minus the spittoons, or one of those lobbies where they swear in new citizens. It's like they want to impress the poor that they don't have leather-top desks ... All our money goes to you ...

So the young aces from the Mission come trooping in, and they want to see the head man. The word comes out that the No. 1 man is out of town, but the No. 2 man is coming out to talk to the people.

This man comes out, and he has that sloppy Irish look like Ed McMahon on TV, only with a longer nose. In case you'd like the local

viewpoint, whites really have the noses ... enormous, you might say
... a whole bag full ... long and pointed like carrots, goobered up like
green peppers, hooked like a squash, hanging off the face like cucum-
bers ... This man has a nose that is just on the verge of hooking over,
but it doesn't quite make it.

'Have a seat, gentlemen,' he says, and he motions toward the
wooden chairs.

But he doesn't have to open his mouth. All you have to do is look at
him and you get the picture. The man's a lifer. He's stone civil service.
He has it all down from the wheatcolor Hush Puppies to the wash'n'
dry semi-tab-collar shortsleeves white shirt. Those wheatcolor Hush
Puppies must be like some kind of fraternal garb among the civil-service
employees, because they all wear them. They cost about $4.99, and the
second time you move your toes, the seams split and the tops come
away from the soles. But they all wear them. The man's shirt looks like
he bought it at the August end-of-summer sale at the White Front. It is
one of those shirts with pockets on both sides. Sticking out of the
pockets and running across his chest he has a lineup of ball-point pens,
felt nibs, lead pencils, wax markers, such as you wouldn't believe,
Papermates, Pentels, Scriptos, Eberhard Faber Mongol 482's. Dri-
Marks, Bic PM-29's, everything. They are lined up across his chest
like campaign ribbons.

He pulls up one of the wooden chairs and sits down on it. Only he
sits down on it backwards, straddling the seat and hooking his arms
and his chin over the back of the chair, like the head foreman in the
bunkhouse. It's like saying, 'We don't stand on ceremony around here.
This is a shirtsleeve operation.'

'I'm sorry that Mr. Johnson isn't here today,' he says, 'but he's not
in the city. He's back in Washington meeting some important project
deadlines. He's very concerned, and he would want to meet with you
people if he were here, but right now I know you'll understand that the
most important thing he can do for you is to push these projects
through in Washington.'

The man keeps his arms and head hung over the back of his chair,
but he swings his hands up in the air from time to time to emphasize a
point, first one hand and then the other. It looks like he's giving wig-
wag signals to the typing pool. The way he hangs himself over the back
of the chair – that keeps up the funky shirtsleeve-operation number.
And throwing his hands around – that's *dynamic* ... It says, 'We're
hacking our way through the red tape just as fast as we can.'

'Now I'm here to try to answer any questions I can,' he says, 'but you have to understand that I'm only speaking as an individual, and so naturally none of my comments are binding, but I'll answer any questions I can, and if I can't answer them, I'll do what I can to get the answers for you.'

And then it dawns on you, and you wonder why it took so long for you to realize it. This man is the flak catcher. His job is to catch the flak for the No.1 man. He's like the professional mourners you can hire in Chinatown. They have certified wailers, professional mourners, in Chinatown, and when your loved one dies, you can hire the professional mourners to wail at the funeral and show what a great loss to the community the departed is. In the same way this lifer is ready to catch whatever flak you're sending up. It doesn't matter what bureau they put him in. It's all the same. Poverty, Japanese imports, valley fever, tomato-crop parity, partial disability, home loans, second-probate accounting, the Interstate 90 detour change order, lockouts, secondary boycotts, G.I. alimony, the Pakistani quota, cinch mites, Tularemic Loa loa, veterans' dental benefits, workmen's compensation, suspended excise rebates – whatever you're angry about, it doesn't matter, he's there to catch the flak. He's a lifer.

Everybody knows the scene is a shuck, but you can't just walk out and leave. You can't get it on and bring thirty-five people walking all the way from the Mission to 100 McAllister and then just turn around and go back. So . . . might as well get into the number . . .

One of the Chicanos starts it off by asking the straight question, which is about how many summer jobs the Mission groups are going to get. This is the opening phase, the straight-face phase, in the art of mau-mauing.

'Well,' says the Flak Catcher – and he gives it a twist of the head and a fling of the hand and the ingratiating smile – 'It's hard for me to answer that the way I'd like to answer it, and the way I know you'd like for me to answer it, because that's precisely what we're working on back in Washington. But I can tell you this. At this point I see no reason why our project allocation should be any less, if all we're looking at is the urban-factor numbers for this area, because that should remain the same. Of course, if there's been any substantial pre-funding, in Washington, for the fixed-asset part of our program, like Head Start or the community health centers, that could alter the picture. But we're very hopeful, and as soon as we have the figures, I can tell you that you people will be the first to know.'

It goes on like this for a while. He keeps saying things like, 'I don't know the answer to that right now, but I'll do everything I can to find out.' The way he says it, you can tell he thinks you're going to be impressed with how honest he is about what he doesn't know. Or he says, 'I wish we could give *everybody* jobs. Believe me, I would like nothing better, both personally and as a representative of this Office.'

So one of the bloods says, 'Man, why do you sit there shining us with this bureaucratic rhetoric, when you said yourself that ain't nothing you say that means a goddam thing?'

*Ba-ram-ba-ram-ba-ram-ba-ram* — a hunch of the aces start banging on the floor in unison. It sounds like they have sledge hammers.

'Ha-unnnnh,' says the Flak Catcher. It was one of those laughs that starts out as a laugh but ends up like he got hit in the stomach halfway through. It's the first assault on his dignity. So he breaks into his shit-eating grin, which is always phase two. Why do so many bureaucrats, deans, preachers, college presidents, try to smile when the mau-mauing starts? It's fatal, this smiling. When some bad dude is challenging your manhood, your smile just proves that he is right and you are chicken-shit — unless you are a bad man yourself with so much heart that you can make that smile say, 'Just keep on talking, sucker, because I'm gonna count to ten and then *squash* you.'

'Well,' says the Flak Catcher, 'I can't promise you jobs if the jobs aren't available yet' — and then he looks up as if for the first time he is really focusing on the thirty-five ghetto hot dogs he is now facing, by the way of sizing up the threat, now that the shit has started. The blacks and the Chicanos he has no doubt seen before, or people just like them, but then he takes in the Filipinos. There are about eight of them, and they are all wearing the Day-Glo yellow and hot-green sweaters and lemon-colored pants and Italian-style socks. But it's the headgear that does the trick. They've all got on Rap Brown shades and Russian Cossack hats made of frosted-gray Dynel. They look *bad*. Then the man takes in the Samoans, and they look worse. There's about ten of them, but they fill up half the room. They've got on Island shirts with designs in streaks and blooms of red, only it's a really raw shade of red, like that red they paint the floor with in the tool and dye works. They're glaring at him out of those big dark wide brown faces. The monsters have tight curly hair, but it grows in long strands, and they comb it back flat, in long curly strands, with a Duke pomade job. They've got huge feet, and they're wearing sandals. The straps on the sandals look like they were made from the reins on the Budweiser draft horses. But what really gets the Flak Catcher, besides the sheer size of the brutes, is their Tiki canes. These are like Polynesian scepters. They're the size of sawed-off pool cues, only they're carved all over in Polynesian Tiki Village designs. When they wrap their fists around these sticks, every knuckle on their hands pops out the size of a walnut. Anything they hear that they like, like the part about the 'bureaucratic rhetoric,' they bang on the floor in unison with the ends of the Tiki sticks — ba-ram-ba-ram-ba-ram-ba-ram — although some of them press one end of the stick onto the sole of their sandal between their first two toes and raise their foot up and down with the stick to cushion the blow on the floor. They don't want to scuff up the Tiki cane.

The Flak Catcher is still staring at them, and his shit-eating grin is getting worse. It's like he *knows* the worst is yet to come . . . Goddamn . . . that one in front there . . . that Pineapple Brute . . .

'Hey, Brudda,' the main man says. He has a really heavy accent. 'Hey, Brudda, how much you make?'

'Me?' says the Flak Catcher. 'How much do I make?'

'Yeah, Brudda, you. How much money you make?'

Now the man is trying to think in eight directions at once. He tries out a new smile. He tries it out on the bloods, the Chicanos, and the Filipinos, as if to say, 'As one intelligent creature to another, what do you do with dumb people like this?' But all he gets is the glares, and his mouth shimmies back into the terrible sickening grin, and then you can see that there are a whole lot of little muscles all around the human mouth, and his are beginning to squirm and tremble . . . He's fighting for control of himself . . . It's a lost cause . . .

'How much, Brudda?'

*Ba-ram-ba-ram-ba-ram-ba-ram* — they keep beating on the floor.

'Well,' says the Flak Catcher, 'I make $1,100 a month.'

'How come you make so much?'

'Wellllll' — the grin, the last bid for clemency . . . and now the poor man's eyes are freezing into little round iceballs, and his mouth is getting dry—

*Ba-ram-ba-ram-ba-ram-ba-ram*

'How come you make so much? My fadda and mudda both work and they only make six hundred and fifty.'

Oh shit, the cat kind of blew it there. That's way over the poverty line, about double, in fact. It's even above the guideline for a family of twelve. You can see that fact register with the Flak Catcher, and he's trying to work up the nerve to make the devastating comeback. But he's not about to talk back to these giants.

'Listen, Brudda. Why don't you give up your paycheck for summer jobs? You ain't doing shit.'

'Wellll' – the Flak Catcher grins, he sweats, he hangs over the back of the chair—

*Ba-ram-ba-ram-ba-ram-ba-ram* – 'Yeah, Brudda! Give us your paycheck!'

There it is ... the ultimate horror ... He can see it now, he can hear it ... Fifteen tons of it ... It's horrible ... it's possible ... It's so obscene, it just might happen ... Huge Polynesian monsters marching down to his office every payday ... Hand it over, Brudda ... ripping it out of his very fingers ... eternally ... He wrings his hands ... the little muscles around his mouth are going haywire. He tries to recapture his grin, but those little amok muscles pull his lips up into an O, like they were drawstrings.

'I'd gladly give up my salary,' says the Flak Catcher. 'I'd *gladly* do it, if it would do any good. But can't you see, gentlemen, it would be just a drop in the bucket ... just a *drop in the bucket!*' This phrase *a drop in the bucket* seems to give him heart ... it's something to hang onto ... an answer ... a reprieve ... 'Just consider what we have to do in this city alone, gentlemen! All of us! It's just a *drop in the bucket!*'

The Samoans can't come up with any answer to this, so the Flak Catcher keeps going.

'Look, gentlemen,' he says, 'you tell me what to do and I'll do it. Of *course* you want more summer jobs, and we want you to have them. That's what we're here for. I wish I could give everybody a job. You tell me how to get more jobs, and we'll get them. We're doing all we can. If we can do more, you tell me how, and I'll gladly do it.'

One of the bloods says, 'Man, if you don't *know how*, then we don't *need* you.'

'Dat's right, Brudda! Whadda we need you for!' You can tell the Samoans wish they had thought of that shoot-down line themselves – *Ba-ram-ba-ram-ba-ram-ba-ram* – they clobber the hell out of the floor.

'Man,' says the blood, 'you just taking up space and killing time and drawing pay!'

'Dat's right, Brudda! You just drawing pay!' *Ba-ram-ba-ram-ba-ram-ba-ram*

'Man,' says the blood, 'if you don't know nothing and you can't do nothing and you can't say nothing, why don't you tell your boss what we want!'

'Dat's right, Brudda! Tell the man!' *Ba-ram-ba-ram-ba-ram-ba-ram*

'As I've already told you, he's in Washington trying to meet the deadlines for *your* projects!'

'You talk to the man, don't you? He'll let you talk to him, won't he?'

'Yes...'

'Send him a telegram, man!'

'Well, all right—'

'Shit, pick up the telephone, man!'

'Dat's right, Brudda! Pick up the telephone!' *Ba-ram-ba-ram-ba-ram-ba-ram*

'Please, gentlemen! That's pointless! It's already after six o'clock in Washington. The office is closed!'

'Then call him in the morning, man,' says the blood. 'We coming back here in the morning and we gonna *watch* you call the man! We gonna stand right on *top* of you so you won't forget to make that call!'

'Dat's right, Brudda! On *top* of you!' *ba-ram-ba-ram-ba-ram-ba-ram*

'All right, gentlemen ... all right,' says the Flak Catcher. He slaps his hands against his thighs and gets up off the chair. 'I'll tell you what...' The way he says it, you can tell the man is trying to get back a little corner of his manhood. He tries to take a tone that says, 'You haven't really been in here for the past fifteen minutes intimidating me and burying my nuts in the sand and humiliating me ... We've really been having a discussion about the proper procedure, and I am willing to grant that you have a point.'

'If that's what you want,' he says, 'I'm certainly willing to put in a telephone call.'

' If we *want!* If you *willing!* Ain't no want or willing *about* it, man! You *gonna* make that call! We gonna be here and *see* you make it!'

'Dat's right, Brudda! We be seeing you' — *Ba-ram-ba-ram-ba-ram* — 'We coming *back!*'

And the Flak Catcher is standing there with his mouth playing bad tricks on him again, and the Samoans hoist their Tiki sticks, and the aces all leave, and they're thinking ... We've done it again. We've mau-maued the goddamn white man, scared him until he's singing a duet with his sphincter, and the people sure do have power. Did you see the look on his face? Did you see the sucker trembling? Did you see the sucker trying to lick his lips? He was *scared*, man! That's the last time that sucker is gonna try to *urban-factor* and *pre-fund* and *fix-asset* with us! He's gonna go home to his house in Diamond Heights and he's gonna say, 'Honey, fix me a drink! Those mother-fuckers were ready to kill me!' That sucker was some kind of *petrified* ... He could see eight kinds of Tiki sticks up side his head ...

Of course, the next day nobody shows up at the poverty office to make sure the sucker makes the telephone call. Somehow it always seems to happen that way. Nobody ever follows it up. You can get everything together once, for the demonstration, for the confrontation, to go downtown and mau-mau, for the fun, for the big show, for the beano, for the main event, to see the people bury some gray cat's nuts and make him crawl and whine and sink in his own terrible grin. But nobody ever follows it up. You just sleep it off until somebody tells you there's going to be another big show.

And then later on you think about it and you say, 'What really happened that day? Well, another flak catcher lost his manhood, that's what happened.' Hmmmmmm ... like maybe the bureaucracy isn't so dumb after all ... All they did was sacrifice one flak catcher, and they've got hundreds, thousands ... They've got replaceable parts. They threw this sacrifice to you, and you went away pleased with yourself. And even the Flak Catcher himself wasn't losing much. He wasn't losing his manhood. He gave that up a long time ago, the day he became a lifer ... Just who is fucking over who ... You did your number and he did his number, and they didn't even have to stop the music ... The band played on ... *Still* – you did see the *look* on his face? That sucker—